THE LOST ELEMENTARY SCHOOLS OF VICTORIAN ENGLAND

The People's Education

PHIL GARDNER

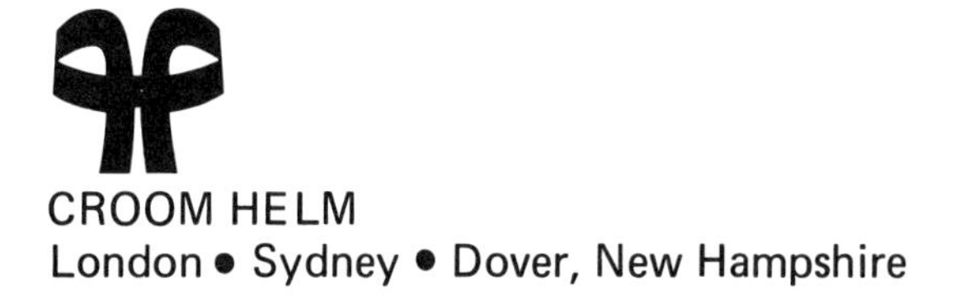

CROOM HELM
London • Sydney • Dover, New Hampshire

Croom Helm Ltd, Provident House, Burrell Row,
Beckenham, Kent BR3 1AT
Croom Helm Australia Pty Ltd, First Floor,
139 King Street, Sydney, NSW 2001, Australia

British Library Cataloguing in Publication Data

Gardner, Phil
The Lost Elementary Schools of Victorian England.
1. Labor and laboring classes — Education —
Great Britain — History — 19th century
I. Title
371.96′7 LC5056.G7

ISBN 0-7099-1156-4

Croom Helm, 51 Washington Street,
Dover, New Hampshire 03820, USA

Library of Congress Cataloging in Publication Data

Gardner, Phil 1951–
The lost elementary schools of Victorian England.

Bibliography p.
Includes index.
1. Labor and laboring classes — Education (Elementary) —
England — History — 19th century. 2. Private
schools — England — History — 19th century.
I. Title.
LC5056.G7G37 1984 372.942 84-9503

ISBN 0-7099-1156-4

Photoset in Times by
Patrick and Anne Murphy Typesetters
Highcliffe, Dorset

Printed and bound in Great Britain by
Biddles Ltd, Guildford and King's Lynn

CONTENTS

TABLES

FIGURES

For my Father

PREFACE

Writing history is not easy. One of its most inescapable and demoralising features must always be the sense of inadequacy with the finished product. This is inevitable for, to be true to his or her subject, the historian is always aware of more research which might have been done; of points in the argument where amplification or wider development were called for; of things which might have been done better.

This feeling has to be balanced against the need to stop somewhere, and to present something which makes a coherent, if incomplete, contribution to the history of elementary education in the nineteenth century.

Whilst all historians are aware of the weaknesses in the work they produce, there is in this case a particularly welcome consolation. Whatever the substantive failings or flaws of this book, it does at least draw attention to a part of our educational history which has been poorly served in the past, and which is worthy of more serious attention in the future. If the book contributes to this, then it will have fulfilled its purpose.

I have received much generous help and support in the making of this book, and whilst I am alone answerable for it, it is in part the product of all those whom I am pleased to acknowledge here. Thanks especially to my family and friends for their support; to Anne, for her care, her interest and her patience; to John Harrison for so much of his time, unfailing consideration and invaluable advice; to Stephen and Eileen Yeo for their conversation, their hospitality, and for always being on hand when help was needed; to Colin Lacey who helped me to see many things in a new light; to Asa Briggs and Carol Dyhouse for their helpful comments on the doctoral thesis on which the book is based; to all those kind people who have corresponded with me and permitted me to interview them; to the staffs of Libraries and Record Offices, particularly in Bristol, London and Walsall, for their assistance and co-operation; to my friend Steve Humphries, special thanks for his immeasurable contribution; above all, to my sister, Sue Hewitt, for her unflagging and calm support over the last few years, for her skilled secretarial assistance, and for efficient typing of the manuscript — thanks.

Finally, I would like to register my thanks and my respect to the central subjects of this book — to the teachers of the people and their supporters — partially because they deserve it, and partially because they have been cruelly and unfairly abused in the past. I feel that I have come close to some of them over the last four years, and it has been a privilege to try to tell some of their side of the story.

INTRODUCTION

The history of elementary education in the nineteenth century remains one of the most desolate areas of contemporary scholarship. Its relative poverty derives not solely from the familiar theoretical weaknesses of liberal historiography, but also from a particular narrowness of approach, method and empirical investigation. The result of these shortcomings has been the maintenance of an orientation which looks overwhelmingly to the study of institutions and of official policy. The central focus continues to be the progressive expansion and refinement of formal educational provision *for* the working class, *through* the combined — and generally laudable — efforts of Church and State. In this perspective, the concept of 'education' is narrowed to a known and agreed facility, to a neutral process that is simply 'done' to people, both for their individual benefit and for the good of society as a whole. In so far as the notions of power and conflict impinge on this view at all, they are restricted to accounts of the competition between rival institutional suppliers of an essentially similar and straightforward product. And what of the working class themselves? Their contribution to 'the growth of education' has been a minimal one. Indeed, they have frequently been characterised as a major obstacle to educational progress, or, at best, as the passive and indifferent recipients of 'education' ladled out in successively larger scoops by benevolent middle-class agencies. The limitations of this perspective are severe, and have been quite extensively analysed in theoretical terms in recent years.[1]

Fundamentally, our perspectives on 'education and the working class' need to be broadened and refined. We cannot continue to be content with versions of history which simply catalogue the intentions of legislative activity and institutional innovation and then smuggle in the idea that these magically translated themselves in a pure form into the real world of the classroom, which, after all, ought to stand at the centre of any study of educational endeavour. Such a broadening of perspective should aim to develop our understanding on at least four fronts.

First, and at the most general level, we should seek to investigate the complex mutual relationship between educational formations and wider social and political structures. In particular, there is a need to pressurise the view that education somehow develops and operates in a social and political vacuum.

Secondly, there has to be an attempt to understand more clearly the gap between legislative and administrative intent and practical reality. In other words, how the officially prescribed patterns and practices of education presented themselves in the classroom, and how the educational process was experienced by those for whom it was intended.

Thirdly, the nature of working-class *response* to what was provided needs careful study. An especially important focus here is the way in which encounters with formal popular schooling reacted with other areas of working-class cultural experience.

Finally, leading on from the previous point, working-class culture itself needs to be probed for evidence of a distinctive, independently generated educative element which can claim to have offered a genuine alternative to the species of education officially prescribed.

Whilst the need for this kind of broadening of approach and analysis has frequently been discussed at a general or theoretical level, comparatively little has been achieved in terms of detailed historical investigation. It is primarily in this area that the present study therefore seeks to make its contribution. In so doing, it will concentrate chiefly on the last of the aims described above, though it will in places contribute to the other three. The guiding ambition of the work is to restore something of the working-class voice — so massively and centrally absent — to the familiar chorus of educational history. The recovery of this voice will, it is hoped, contribute to the characterisation of elementary education in the nineteenth century, not simply as a fount of civilisation and progress, but as an important site of class-cultural conflict. In this task, two principal approaches present themselves.

The first is to concentrate on charting the pattern of working-class responses to the provision of publicly provided education. In particular, this would involve a re-examination of well-established beliefs about the nature and extent of alleged working-class 'apathy' towards education. At the same time, large areas of working-class behaviour would need to be assessed and possibly recast as expressions of purposeful, class-based resistance to that which was provided. As has been recently demonstrated, this approach can yield valuable and exciting results.[2] There are dangers, however, in conceiving working-class educational behaviour purely as a response to the facilities which were institutionally provided. Ultimately, this may lead us to offer explanations conceived simply as negatives of middle-class sponsored provision.

The second possible approach therefore pushes beyond this, seeking to concentrate on positive traditions of independent working-class educational activity, and to see these traditions as providing part of the cultural bedrock on which resistance to provided institutions was based. This is the approach which the present study will principally adopt. It can be summed up in the following series of basic propositions.

The shape and pace of educational development as a whole in the nineteenth century were directly and critically influenced by deep conflicts of cultural value, meaning and experience between the providers of publicly sponsored elementary schooling and its putative beneficiaries. That this was so was largely because there was a powerful identifiable working-class educational culture — both a cause and and a consequence of broader class conflicts — with its own characteristic values, goals and practices, which was quite distinct from those officially prescribed. Resistance to formal, institutionalised schooling was fed by the currents of this alternative culture which, more positively, also supported its own networks of independent practical educational activity. Until these were destroyed, the dominance of a provided system of elementary schooling 'for' the working class could not be fully or finally completed. The depth and resilience of this alternative educational culture is demonstrated by its sustained popularity over time, and by its failure to die the natural death universally predicted for it.

Where was this alternative educational culture to be found? Not merely in organised movements like Owenism or Chartism, but less dramatically, though certainly more significantly, in the tradition of working-class private schooling.[3] Such schooling was, as we shall see, unorganised, amorphous and inwardly oriented. It produced little independent documentary evidence of its own existence and has habitually been passed over in favour of more glamorous, more dramatic, more accessible — though far less numerically impressive — connections between 'education' and the 'working class'. Working-class private schooling, as we shall go on to define it, is in fact best understood as a residual rather than an emergent cultural form.[4] As such, it did not make the explicit link between educational activity and political activity which organised working-class movements could make. Nevertheless, it represented a genuine, class-based alternative in the learning of basic skills which strongly 'refused the equation "education equals school"', and which operated automatically on the assumption 'that education should permeate day-to-day living'.[5] In its curriculum, in its pedagogy and in the control and direction of educational resources, the working-class private school presents an implicit rejection of the emerging varieties of publicly regulated schooling. As such, it cannot go on being ignored.

It is not as though the schools in this tradition are a new historical discovery, suddenly unearthed. They have been under the nose of historical scholarship all the time. There is no unknown vein of secret working-class schools. Working-class private schooling has long been known of, after a fashion, though it has not been recognised or studied quite as such. It has been ignored, passed over time and again by historians of all political colours. Why has this been so?

In part, our ignorance has had a lot to do with methodological inadequacy. Quite simply, the schools have been too difficult to get at. Adequate sources and methodological tools have not been available, and this has been allowed to serve as a tacit confirmation that the schools were unimportant in their day.

But beyond this, the difficulty has been due to the approach and orientation of educational historians. They have not *expected* to find and evidence of large-scale, positive, working-class educational activity in the nineteenth century. After all, educational development worked its way downwards, from above, *in spite* of the working class and certainly not *because* of them. In the absence of any proper analysis, our understanding has been inherited directly from the blanket condemnation of nineteenth-century educationists who had a particular interest in promoting the demise of working-class private schooling.[6] Where the schools have been discussed, the pejorative terminology of the nineteenth century remains in use; they remain as 'dames' schools', 'inferior schools', 'common day schools' and 'adventure schools'. They are denied the generic title of the independent schools of a distinct class — 'the people's schools'. Under such labels, the schools make only fleeting appearances — if at all — in the pages of the standard histories, to be passed over with a few well-worn phrases, for the study of 'real' or 'genuine' educational institutions.

With some notable exceptions, it could be fairly charged that contemporary scholarship has done little to alter the view of working-class private schools from that which was originally developed in the main body of nineteenth-century educational reporting.[7] It is of course possible that this might be because such reports have in fact represented the schools fairly and exhaustively to the historian's critical perception. The more likely explanation is that working-class private schooling has simply not been thought of as a subject worthy of serious consideration. We have been content to pass it off in the terms originally created by the education experts of the nineteenth century. It is precisely these judgements which have closed the working-class private school as a potential site for worthwhile historical research. The schools in this tradition inhabit a blind alley leading off the well-signposted historical highway which has carried a steady stream of liberal accounts celebrating the benevolent provision of educational facilities 'for' the people.

Despite their impressive volume and authoritative mien, Richard Johnson has well observed that, 'the most obvious fact [about the educational reports of the nineteenth century] is that they are full of middle class people . . . puzzling about the schooling of the children of the working class'.[8] To the extent to which these same reports, uncritically received, are the bedrock of contemporary historical understanding, this quality of puzzlement remains, though now latent and unacknowledged. It remains as the same cultural barrier effectively segregating independent working-class educational activity from scholarly gaze. Indeed, the barrier is yet greater because such independent activity has long since ceased to exist in this particular form. Unknown now, it is a presence with which historians are unfamiliar, and which they do not seek in the past. This is why the available secondary sources are such barren ground for the working-class private school. It is only when the formative primary sources are examined closely that the pervasive quality of puzzlement is once more fully released.

One of the clearest ways in which this quality presents itself is through the inconsistency and internal contradiction which, in spite of the prevailing hostile bias, trickle through most of them. Unless these are actively chased out, it is easy to overlook them in favour of the surfeit of general condemnation in which they are buried. In terms of broad evaluation and prescription, the reports are rarely equivocal and the tone of their condemnation can be traced unmistakeably through successive academic generations in the shape of direct quotation, plagiarism, summary and restatement.[9] This tone can be set with any number of quotations plucked from the original sources themselves.

> To enumerate any other [than public day and Sunday] schools as giving *instruction* to the children of the poor is a grave error, or a grievous perversion of terms.[10]

> The numbers of children of the different schools in Sheffield, comprising every description of school, was made the subject of minute and accurate inquiry . . . I do not reckon the dame-schools, as they are merely loose boxes for turning the young children into to be out of harm's way.[11]

> . . . nurseries of innacuracy and superficiality . . .[12]

> . . . worthless. I do not know whether I was most astonished at the badness of the premises or the poverty of the instruction . . .[13]

> . . . misnamed a school . . .[14]

> . . . monstrous that the efforts of your Lordships to educate the masses of the people should be frustrated . . . by reason of the persistent opposition of these miserable adventure schools.[15]

> . . . impossible to exaggerate the dullness . . . intellectual stagnation . . . badness of the methods . . . waste of time . . . utter lack of noble purpose which characterise these schools as a class.[16]

On foundations such as these came later influential judgements, from which we may select a representative handful; Philpott in 1904: '. . . these wretched private schools [were] unworthy of the name school'[17]; Adamson in 1930: these 'so-called schools . . . had no valid right to the name'[18]; more recently, Simon: dames' schools 'taught little or nothing'[19]; Sutherland: '. . . it is clear that many of them were no more than child-minders'[20]; Hurt: 'the omission of some dame and common day schools is of little importance. Such institutions were not "schools".'[21] Even the most sympathetic of modern treatments, despite its revisionist intent, is unwilling, 'to defend the many thousands of dame schools which undoubtedly were travesties of schools even by general nineteenth-century standards . . .'[22] Significantly, working-class private schooling has in fact been best comprehended not by specialist educational histories, but in a more incidental fashion, by recent compilations of nineteenth-century working-class autobiographies.[23] That is, by work drawing not on the familiar body of official reports, but on the direct experience of individual working people.

For this study, it will perhaps be less fruitful to pursue the question of history's failure to engage working-class private schooling, than to anticipate the likely objections which the conventional interpretations might raise against a revision in favour of the working-class private school. Objections made, in other words, by those who are reasonably satisfied with the existing historical picture of educational development; who see this picture as perhaps needing refinement or nuance of minor or local kinds, but not any fundamental revision.

Potential objections are numerous, but most would fall under two main headings. The first would question the very existence of something which might legitimately be labelled as 'working-class private schooling' at all; and the second, supposing that there might have been such a thing, denies it to have possessed any recognisable educational value or sometimes, even, intent. Both objections therefore refuse to recognise that a study directed at 'working-class private schooling' can have any useful contribution to make our understanding of nineteenth-century education. It is worth examining such objections a little further, for it is in challenging them that the shape of this study has been largely determined. No serious historian of education will question the proposition that, as a proportion of the total available provision of schooling in the nineteenth century, the private sector contribution was enormous.[24] But most would further argue that education of this type was, as today, primarily the preserve of the middle and upper classes. Some will concede that 'the wealthier members of the working class' or 'the better-off artisan' might have had some experience of private schools, though not on an extensive or particularly significant scale. But where this was the case, it is seen to represent a particular expression of the desire for enhanced social status or spurious refinement.

This, however, is to apply a particularly modern understanding of what 'private education' represents today, to a different historical period in which the designation 'private' carried a different and less specific emphasis. This study will in fact argue that, for most of the nineteenth century, a large, enduring and distinctive part of the private sector was operated by, and on behalf of, the working class in general. Further, that this part was distinguished by a unity of character and purpose which makes it analytically separable from other contemporary species of private schooling as well as from modern versions, in all but the manner of its financial support.

Many historians who might feel able to accommodate the view that this was perhaps broadly so, continue to see such a phenomenon as without serious significance for the history of education. In this perspective, working-class private schools were not schools at all, but 'mere baby-minding establishments' kept by 'illiterate old women'; or they were 'mock schools' under the charge of otherwise unemployable cripples and moral and intellectual incompetents. Products of an earlier and unenlightened age, such places possessed little or no educative value and were doomed to natural extinction as more advanced and efficient forms of 'mass' education were developed. It is the latter which properly belong under the microscope of the educational historian, whilst serious study of the former can contribute only to a dangerous romanticisation of the social conditions and cultural quality of working-class life in the nineteenth century. Such a warning has something to recommend it — especially if those who give it are ready to apply a similar circumspection to the Whiggish studies of public elementary education and its achievements which dominate the field. Regrettably, this has seldom been the case. Nevertheless, for this study, the charge of 'romanticisation' seems to involve principally the inflation of the extent and particularly the effectiveness of working-class private schooling. This study will attempt to build its claims for the numerical extent of working-class private schooling on a sound empirical footing. And it will not counter accusations of educational dereliction in the working-class private schools with vague, unsubstantiated or extravagant claims about their educative value, but will argue that within the scope of their modest educational aims, they were viable and largely successful.

An enduring problem in a work such as this, is the nature and availability of source materials. A few words on this, and on the organisation of the work, need to be said.

There is very little worthwhile secondary material on the subject of working-class private schooling, and for the most part, the present study is based on primary material in the form of contemporary journals and newspapers, Parliamentary Papers and the files of local archives and the Public Record Office. The difficulty with the overwhelming majority of evidence from these sources is that it emanates from middle-class sources, which were almost entirely hostile. Nevertheless, this material has to be greatly valued, for it constitutes virtually the entire available stock of documentary evidence. Moreover, when thoroughly analysed, as much for its omissions and inconsistencies as its stated findings and opinions, it has considerably more to tell us than has previously been allowed. But we are still in the position of having no corresponding material which derives more closely from working-class sources. In short, existing documentary evidence is not enough; there needs to be some alternative measure against which it can be set. Where is this to be found?

An obvious starting point was with working-class autobiography, which often produces telling — though tantalisingly brief — insights into the daily world of the working-class private school. But such anecdotal evidence needed more extensive support. Oral testimony seemed a possibility, though a rather remote one, for the main body of nineteenth-century working-class private schools now lies just beyond the reach of old age. However, as will be seen, an extensive search for evidence was made and has produced some valuable and detailed returns.

A second method has been to exploit the relatively neutral columns of the books of the Population Census enumerators. This too, has produced a surprising amount of new material relating to the schools, expressed, if not in the direct voice of its working-class users, then in something very close to it. To have any real explanatory use, however, sample material needed to be extensive, coherent and complete. The most effective way of achieving this was to mount an exhaustive local survey of a relatively large area. The area chosen was the city of Bristol, each individual entry being scrutinised for the three decennial censuses from 1851 to 1871. The principal product of this exercise was a register of 2,602 names and related details being the record of every individual connected with school teaching in the city over a thirty-year period.[25] The methods used in this endeavour are set out in Appendix A.

Both the search for oral recollection and the study of the

Population Census have generated new sources of evidence which have thrown fresh light on the working-class private school. The material produced by oral testimony has, by and large, been concentrated within a single chapter, whilst that derived from the Population Census Study is dispersed throughout remaining chapters, and in Appendix B. In this way, findings and hypotheses based on the Population Census work are throughout set alongside the contemporary official documentary records which they sometimes clearly challenge. The material generated by oral interview is kept separate because it has an internal unity of its own, and because it necessarily relates to a slightly later period. Also, its substantive descriptive content can stand clearly and comparatively alongside documentary descriptions from an earlier period to which oral history cannot extend. In this way, it is hoped that readers may be able to judge for themselves how similar or different were the schools described on the one hand by the spoken word, and on the other by official document.

The study does therefore have evidence originating with the working class to offer. This will allow us to begin to develop new perspectives on the working-class private school, and offer alternative perceptions to those of the nineteenth-century education 'expert'. Such evidence remains, however, comparatively sparse. Each piece has to be won or teased out rather than simply consulted. Because of this, the material builds up into a picture that is general rather than local. Though intensive local investigations were undertaken, the nature of the evidence produced was inevitably sometimes patchy and incomplete, making the construction of a coherent and complete local study impossible. Instead, all the material to hand — all the pieces of the jigsaw — were assembled to make a composite picture. This seems legitimate. It is apparent from nineteenth-century written sources — both official and literary — that the working-class private school was a ubiquitous presence, both in town and country, at least up to the 1870s. Regional variations existed, though these would have been more evident in the number and locations of schools than in any substantial differences of organisation or procedure. These seemed to have conformed to a remarkably stable pattern. Both the scope and intent of the work are then, general. Though illustrative material will be drawn from a range of local sources, it is hoped that the resulting observations and judgements will command a broader validity.

The overall organisation of the work is straightforward. Seven chapters will follow, each closely linked though thematically distinct, with a particular focus on various aspects of the working-class private school. Except in one of the chapters — the penultimate — a chronological approach is inappropriate. As a subsequent chapter will demonstrate, the scale of working-class private schooling over time cannot be determined with any great precision. More than this, the history of the working-class private school is a cultural history; there are no key dates, no 1833 or 1846; no great names, no Kay-Shuttleworth or Forster; there is no traceable institutional foundation.[26] There are only people and their schools. The only point at which we can usefully employ a chronological perspective is in the early 1870s, when the schools came under intense pressure from central and local educational authorities. This, in effect, is the chronology of the disappearance of the working-class private school and its origin lies not in the schools themselves, but in a concerted official campaign against them.

The first chapter will concern itself with the terminology of the working-class private school as it evolved in the nineteenth century, and will argue that the labels that have been used to signify such schools are in themselves important constituents of the ways in which they have been understood and explained.

The second chapter will try to make some sense of the jumble of available educational statistics and will attempt to give some idea of the probable scale of working-class private schooling.

In the third chapter, there will be a discussion of the broader cultural context in which working-class private schooling operated, and an assessment of the relationship of the cultures of home and school. The study does not wish to confine itself solely to an investigation of the educative importance of the working-class private school, but will seek to relate this to the wider culture of which it was both a determined and determining element.

The teachers of the schools — who remain, for the most part a very elusive and shadowy group — form the subject of Chapter 4.

Chapter 5 will offer description and analysis of the characteristic organisation and activity of the schools themselves.

Chapter 6 tells the story of the final confrontation of the tradition of independent working-class schooling by its official, publicly sanctioned rival, and of the unsurprising outcome.

In the final chapter is concentrated the material which was

produced by oral interview and recollection; surely the last echoes of a once strong tradition.

So far, the term 'working-class private school' has been used freely. A detailed definition and justification of the phrase will follow in the next chapter. But in purely descriptive terms, to what type of school does it relate? It will be as well, at this early point, to sketch a rough picture of the sort of school with which we are dealing, particularly as it has commonly featured so indistinctly in the standard histories.

Such a school was 'private' through the absence of any financial aid or institutional regulation beyond those of the parents who sent their children to it.[27] And it was working class by the distinctive background and character of its pupils and their parents, and the majority of its teachers. But the most convenient and objective method of distinguishing a working-class private school from other private schools, and that which was formally employed by the Education Department, was the calculation of average individual weekly fees. These were set at a maximum of 9d per week but were commonly considerably lower. Such schools possessed universal defining characteristics which marked them off from the alternative publicly provided or sanctioned institutions. The main points of difference were these. As well as being self-financing, working-class private schools were completely beyond the reach or control of the Inspectorate. They responded naturally to demand from below and not the dictates of supply. The teachers — predominantly female — of such schools were generally without any kind of formal training or certification, and were, as far as their teaching went, wholly self-employed. Usually such teachers worked alone, though sometimes with an element of informal or occasional help, usually coming from within the same family or household. The schools were very rarely held in a building designed for the purpose, the majority being kept in the home of the teacher. This automatically determined that the average weekly attendance was far smaller than at public schools, usually working out at between 10 and 30. Segregation or formal grouping of the children on the basis of age, sex or ability was unusual, and teaching and learning took place on an individual and informal basis.

Notes

1. See R. Dale and G. Esland, 'Mass Schooling', Open University E202, *Schooling and Society*, Units 2–3; ibid., Stuart Hall, 'Review of the Course', Unit 32. Also *Unpopular Education*, Education Group, Centre for Contemporary Social Studies (1981). Dan Finn *et al.*, 'Social Democracy, Education and the Crisis', in *On Ideology*, CCCS (1977), pp. 144–95; Michael Katz, *Class Bureaucracy and Schools* (New York, 1975), Ch. 1; M. Sarup, *Marxism and Education* (1978), esp. Part One. Also Raymond Williams, *The Long Revolution* (1961), esp. pp. 145–76. Also R. Johnson, 'Notes on the Schooling of the English Working Class 1780–1850', in R. Dale *et al.*, *Schooling and Capitalism* (1976), pp. 44–54.
2. See, for example, S. Humphries, *Hooligans or Rebels*? (1981).
3. R. Johnson, 'Education and Popular Politics', in Open University E353, *Education and the State*, Unit 1, *The State and the Politics of Education*. p. 28. Also Johnson, 'Really Useful Knowledge: Radical Education and Working Class Culture' (1979), pp. 75–102. *See too,* J. F. C. Harrison, *Learning and Living 1790–1960* (1961); P. Hollis, *The Pauper Press* (1970), Ch. 1; H. Silver, *English Education and the Radicals 1780–1850* (1975); E. P. Thompson, *The Making of the English Working Class* (1968), Ch. 16; B. Simon, *Studies in the History of Education 1780–1870* (1960); *Education and the Labour Movement 1870–1920* (1965).
4. See R. Williams, *Marxism and Literature* (1977), pp. 121–7. Also E. P. Thompson, 'Time, Work Discipline and Industrial Capitalism', *Past and Present*, no. 38 (1967), pp. 56–97.
5. R. Johnson, 'Education and Popular Politics', Open University E353, *Education and the State*, Unit 1, p. 29.
6. On the subject of educational reporting in the nineteenth century, see R. Johnson, 'Elementary Education: The Education of the Poorer Classes', in G. Sutherland *et al.*, *Education in Britain* (1977), pp. 5–37. A particularly helpful background survey is the same author's 'Educating the Educators: "Experts" and the State 1833–9', in A. Donajgrodzki, *Social Control in Nineteenth Century Britain* (1977), pp. 77–107; also see his 'Educational Policy and Social Control in Early Victorian England', *Past and Present*, no. 49 (1970), pp. 96–119. Also valuable is M. Cullen, *The Statistical Movement in Early Victorian Britain* (1975). Useful material on Her Majesty's Inspectorate can be found in G. Sutherland, *Policy Making in Elementary Education 1870–1895* (1973), Ch. 3.
7. See the works cited in the bibliography by Johnson, Laquer, West, Field and Wardle. Also P. McCann, 'Popular Education, Socialization and Social Control: Spitalfields 1812–1824', in P. McCann, *Popular Education and Socialization in the Nineteenth Century* (1977), pp. 1–40; S. Frith, 'Socialization and Rational Schooling: Elementary Education in Leeds before 1870', ibid., pp. 67–92; D. Leinster-Mackay, 'A Question of Ephemerality: Indices for Longevity of 19th-Century Private Schools', *J.E.A.H.*, vol. X (1978), pp. 1–7; Leinster-Mackay, 'Dame Schools: A Need for Review', *B.J.E.S.*, vol. xxiv (1976), pp. 33–48; A. F. B. Roberts, 'A New View of the Infant School Movement', *B.J.E.S.*, vol. xxii (1974), pp. 166–81.
8. R. Johnson, 'Elementary Education', in Sutherland *et al.*, *Education in Britain*, p. 8.
9. For instance, Assistant Commissioner Hodgson's denunciation of the teachers of popular private schools (see Chapter 4) can be found, among others, in M. Sadler and J. Edwards, *Special Reports . . .* (1898), p. 466; H. B. Philpott, *London at School . . .* (1904), p. 11; G. Bartley, *The Schools of the People* (1871), p. 404; F. Smith, *A History of English Elementary Education* (1931), p. 247; S. J. Curtis and

M. Boultwood, *History of English Education Since 1800* (1960), p. 301. For the much quoted verse of Shenstone and Crabbe relating to private schools, see V. Neuburg, *Popular Education in Eighteenth Century England* (1971), pp. 18–21.

10. 'Education in the Mining and Manufacturing District of South Staffordshire . . . being a Report to . . . the Statistical Society of London', *J.S.S.*, (1847), p. 237.

11. P.P. 1843 [431] xiv, *C.E.C. Appendix to Second Report (Trades and Manufactures). Pt. I*, p. E20.

12. HMI Duport, *C.C.E.*, 1872–3, p. 74.

13. HMI Oakley, *C.C.E.*, 1873–4, p. 141.

14. Jenkins, 1861 [2794] xxi, *Royal Commission on the State of Popular Education in England* (Newcastle), vol. 2, p. 529.

15. HMI Smith, *C.C.E.*, 1876–7, p. 565.

16. J. G. Fitch, 1870 (91) liv, *Schools for the Poorer Classes in Birmingham, Leeds, Liverpool and Manchester. Special Reports*, p.102.

17. H. B. Philpott, *London at School* (1904), p. 11.

18. J. W. Adamson, *English Education 1789–1902* (1930), p. 207.

19. B. Simon, *Studies in the History of Education 1780–1870* (1960), p. 184.

20. G. Sutherland, *Elementary Education in the Nineteenth Century* (1971), p. 12.

21. J. Hurt, 'Professor West on Education', *Economic History Review*, vol. xxiv (1971), p. 632. See also J. Tizard *et al.*, *All Our Children: Pre-School Services in a Changing Society* (1976), pp. 50–1.

22. D. Leinster-Mackay, 'The English Private School, 1830–1914 . . .', Unpublished PhD thesis, Durham University, 1972.

23. See particularly D. Vincent, *Bread, Knowledge and Freedom* (1981), pp. 94–105, and J. Burnett, *Destiny Obscure* (1982), pp. 144–6.

24. See, for example, D. Wardle, *Education and Society in Nineteenth Century Nottingham* (Cambridge, 1971), p. 148.

25. This register is available for inspection.

26. See T. Laquer, 'Working-Class Demand and the Growth of English Elementary Education, 1750–1850', in L. Stone (ed.) *Schooling and Society* (1976), pp. 192–205, esp. p. 192. Also V. Neuburg, *Popular Education in Eighteenth Century England* (1971), esp. Ch. 1, Ch. 4.

27. This is the sense in which the 1851 Education Census understood the term 'private'. *Education Census*, pp. xliv–xlv. By 1870, however, it was accorded a rather different definition; see Chapter 1 below. The worthwhile elements in E. G. West's right-wing revisionism are considerably weakened by confusion over the meaning of 'private'. West follows a definition which includes any school not directly controlled by the state. In his discussion of the Education Census, for example, he argues that '. . . the term "public school" was a technical one. It referred to all those private (voluntary) schools that received any philanthropic or government aid whatever — however small', *Education and the Industrial Revolution in England and Wales* (1975), p. 78, also p. 185. The nineteenth-century working class certainly did not see the distinction between 'public' and 'private' schools as 'technical'. It in fact involved fundamental issues of control, access, method and product. Similarly, for the contemporary education expert, the two categories represented clearly differing varieties. The development of the language of 'public elementary schooling' is in itself significant, implying a classless, caring and simply popular provision expanding into a cultural desert with no serious pre-existing working-class educational presence.

1 NAMES

Any attempt to come to terms with the reality of the working-class private school in the nineteenth century has to begin with the question of how such schools were described and evaluated. Description and evaluation were not, however, simply produced and expressed through the use of a neutral, standardised or agreed nomenclature. The labels used by contemporaries in the study of the working-class private school possessed a strongly determining character. Their use was informed by no simple or direct reflection of an external reality, but by a set of partial and specific images of that reality. A classic example is the powerful label, 'dame's school', which conveys to the modern understanding, as it did to many nineteenth-century writers, an automatic catalogue of substantive associations — a handful of babies and infants; 'mere child-minding'; domestic squalor; ignorance; educational and pedagogic uselessness — all of which have only a partial or distorted validity.

This chapter examines some of the labels which were used to refer to the 'working-class private school' — itself a label, but conceived in this study as the one which carries the greatest descriptive accuracy and analytical utility. We will ask who used the labels and when; how the labels evolved over time; and how they shaped and coloured the understanding that they were supposed merely to express.

Childhood experience of schooling in the nineteenth century was endlessly varied in terms of form, quality and duration. Individual educational biographies display little of the homogeneous regularity which marks our modern experience of organised learning. Instead, knowledge and skills were picked up during brief favourable periods through an enormously diverse network of educational agencies. These can however be broadly simplified into two groups, public and private. The former subsumes all those institutions which received public financial support of some kind, or which were subject to some degree of formal and external administrative control. This includes the schools operated by the two great Societies, by the denominations, by School Boards, by endowed schools (though some of these catered for small numbers of private pupils in addition to foundation scholars), workhouse schools and some factory and colliery schools, though the degree of external control in these latter was often minimal. The extensive private sector, which Horace Mann found to comprise nearly one-third of the total, was made up of schools which were entirely supported by the payments of scholars and in which there was no element of administrative authority independent of the teacher and proprietor.[1] Excepting these universal defining characteristics, the private sector was internally differentiated to the degree that its several distinct parts responded to the specific educational demands of particular class groupings.

The earliest systematic attempts to develop a comprehensive classification of private schooling are to be found in the important series of local surveys undertaken particularly by the Manchester Statistical Society and the Statistical Society of London in the late 1830s and early 1840s. These reports began by estabishing a simple tripartite division based on the social class of the clients of any given school. At the top were the prestigious 'superior schools', both day and boarding. These catered for 'the children of professional men and private gentlemen', and were therefore felt to lie outside the legitimate and proper scope of enquiries of which the object 'was principally to ascertain the condition of the working classes with respect to education'.[2] As a general consequence, 'little more [was] attempted in reference to superior schools, than obtaining a correct numerical account of the scholars, teachers, and subjects of instruction . . .'.[3] Next in order of descending status came the 'middling day schools', which in Westminster, for example, were found to serve 'almost entirely . . . tradespeople and persons employed in offices of various descriptions, such as lawyers' clerks, messengers in the public offices, inferior officers of the House of Commons, etc., with a few mechanics of a superior class'.[4] Finally, there were the 'Private Schools for the Education of the Poor', or, as they were later labelled by the 1851 Education Census, 'Inferior Schools', upon which the reports principally focused.[5] This category was invariably divided into two subgroups; these were 'dames' schools', and 'common day schools'. This division needs to be handled with great care and will be examined in detail.

First, however, it is important to look briefly at the terminology of the working-class private school as it existed in the earlier years of the nineteenth century. Before the systematising work of the

Statistical Societies, the nomenclatures were confused indeed. The returns of the 1833 Education Enquiry — the statistically unreliable Kerry Returns — surprisingly made no use of the terms 'dames' school' or 'common day school'.[6] The returns were gathered under just three heads — Infant Schools, Daily Schools and Sunday Schools. Those which the Statistical Societies were shortly to classify as 'dame' and 'common day' were scattered, indistinguishable from other classes of private school beneath the first two of the three headings, which themselves could not 'be accurately discriminated', although Infant Schools were nominally defined as those in which the upper age limit was seven.[7] It is worth noting that such schools — that is, those which had an upper age limit of seven — comprised just 8 per cent of the total of all private schools.[8] And it is certainly ironic that schools which would shortly be castigated by the experts as 'mere dames' schools', were classed by the Kerry Returns as 'Infant Schools' — the very category which was celebrated a few years later as forming 'a striking contrast to the dame and common day schools'.[9]

The simple omnibus classifications of the 1833 returns did little then to highlight the enormously complex and variegated educational reality which they are supposed to represent. They had been preceded some 15 years earlier by another national enquiry, undertaken by the 1818 Select Committee on the Education of the Poor.[10] The tabular summaries produced by this body, like Kerry, offer two categories of private school, and again, the division apparently rests nominally upon the ages of pupils, though these are very rarely given. The 1818 survey, however, favours the designations 'Dames' Schools' and 'Ordinary Schools'. This is a particularly interesting classification, since it clearly comes very near to the later 'dame'/'common day' formula. It would be easy to conclude that the similarity occurred because both terminologies corresponded to an existing educational reality; to a reality that was indeed legitimately reducible to just such distinct school types. The picture, however, changes quite dramatically if the tabular summaries are set aside, and the individual parochial declarations (made by the local minister of religion) are examined. The uniform impression of the simple bipartite classification is immediately replaced by an array of local designations so varied and imprecise as to make an accurate summary classification into two categories impossible — an admission which the later Kerry Return was forced to make directly. The point can be demonstrated with any selection from the 1818 returns. In the tiny parish of Osmaston in Derbyshire, for example, there was: 'A day school kept by a mistress containing 9 boys and 7 girls', whilst at Mickleover in the same county were recorded: 'A dame's school in which about 30 children are educated. At Littleover (chapelry) there is a school taught by a dame.'[11] But what were the criteria, other than those of subjective judgement, by which one clergyman referred to a 'day school' and another to a 'dame's school'? On this feeble evidence, the former would ultimately be classed as an 'ordinary' school and the latter as a 'dame's school', whilst in reality, they were likely to have been very similar. But this is only the start of the problem. Other Derbyshire returns refer variously to 'several preparatory schools', 'four petty schools', 'six schools of different descriptions', 'three small schools for children kept by women', 'one large school and one dame's school', 'two or three small day schools kept by females in which from 44 to 52 children are altogether instructed', 'three schools taught by masters and six or seven small schools by mistresses, containing together 240 children', 'a day school in which 9 or 10 children are taught by a poor woman', 'one common day school', 'one school kept by an elderly woman'. And examples drawn from other countries include 'two or three common reading schools', 'some day schools for poor children', 'two or three inconsiderable schools', 'an old woman's school for little children', 'many schools', 'a woman's school', 'a private school for writing and arithmetic', 'a day school of the better sort', 'one school kept by an old woman at 3d. a week for each child, containing about 9', 'a school containing 10 infants, the parents paying 4d. per week for their education'.[12] What these examples speak of is an educational patchwork of enormous local variety and flexibility which the terms cannot help but reflect. The comparison between this jumbled list and the homogenised summary tables into which they were somehow packed, stands as a metaphor for all subsequent official investigations into popular education. Throughout the century, inadequacy of nomenclature and subjective carelessness of classification were as much a feature of such investigations as were their routine bias and distortion. It has to be recognised that a history which works uncritically with the labels which were then applied — 'dame', 'common', 'ordinary' or whatever — remains as ignorant of working-class educational culture as were their original users.

It will be recalled that the terms favoured in the important series of reports produced by the Statistical Societies were 'dame' and 'common day'. Coming back now to these reports in detail, and with the educational patchwork illustrated by the 1818 returns in mind, we have to ask what picture the use of these two terms produced — what educational characteristics did it indicate? What, in other words, can the two terms be taken to mean, and more importantly, what validity might they claim? It is initially tempting to visualise the distinction between 'dame' and 'common day' as an essentially sequential one, attendance at the former leading on automatically to the latter as it did in the case of the public infant and elementary schools.[13] Whilst such transfers of school certainly did occur, the nature of the distinction between the two types cannot be reduced merely to this; indeed, this particular point was seldom, if ever, made in the reports. Nor does the sex of an individual teacher offer any sure distinction between 'dame' and 'common day'. Many of the teachers of the common day schools were women and despite the apparent lack of ambiguity about the label, it was not unknown for men to keep dame schools.[14]

It might also be argued that the central distinguishing criterion between dame and common day schools was, as in the case of the superior and middling schools, a matter of comparatively higher or lower ascribed status. But though the maximum fees of common day schools were, in general, greater than those of dames' schools, this differential was unconnected with status, and in no way offers a definitive distinction which captures the reality within which these schools operated. Indeed, the reports are at pains to establish the essential unity between the two types of school in terms of status. This is a very general feature. The report dealing with Liverpool, for example, declares that 'Although those two classes of school have been separated in the tables, in their general condition they represent so few points of real difference, that the committee has thought it advisable in their report to consider them as constituting one large class.'[15]

The authentic differences between the dame school and the common day school were in fact determined by the nature of working-class educational demands. These fluctuated considerably with time, place and economic circumstance, highlighting the need for the responsiveness and flexibility of educational provision which the two types of school provided. So the leading distinction between them — by which all other subsidiary differences were determined — lay in the varying practical benefits which they offered. It lay, in other words, in what they taught; in their curriculum. By this criterion, the dame school's *raison d'être* was to teach reading above all else. This fundamental characteristic was initially acknowledged by the Statistical Societies. In 1839 Richard Edmonds, an amateur statistician from Penzance, wrote a contribution for the *Journal of the Statistical Society*. In his area, he had sought to classsify private schools on the basis of pupil age, but had found that 'the dame schools could not be distinguished from the common daily schools . . . inasmuch as children of all ages from 3 to 16 years are generally found in each school'. Edmonds was upbraided in a very clear editorial footnote: 'The distinction adopted by the Statistical Societies of Manchester and London with regard to dame-schools [is] to consider as belonging to that class the schools in which nothing but reading and a little sewing are taught.'[16] And in many of their earlier enquiries, the two Societies appear to adhere quite closely to this guideline. In their survey of 50 dame schools in the county of Rutland for example, they recorded all 50 as teaching reading, to which 39 added sewing and 43 also included knitting.[17] The enquiry into Westminster conveys a similar impression, though it does suggest that here a few of the schools were capable of broadening their range if necessary. Of the 63 schools listed, all taught reading and 52 needlework. But in addition, 8 offered writing, 5 arithmetic, 13 grammar, 5 geography and 3 history.[18]

Dames' schools which attempted this kind of expanded curriculum probably existed in most localities, but they were likely to have been a minority of the total. In teaching subjects beyond basic reading — probably only to a handful of pupils — they were encroaching on the curricular province of the common day school.[19] But the distinction was by no means a hard and fast one. The common day school taught basic reading skills like the dame school, but once these were mastered, there was scope to move on to other subjects under the same roof. Writing was the most highly prized of these additional skills, but to the mystification of middle-class observers, it was scarcely ever tackled concurrently with reading; '. . . in the national schools, reading, writing and arithmetic go hand in hand; but in the private schools a boy is not put to writing and accounts until he has been taught to read; consequently, it not unfrequently happens that a boy coming from one of these schools is fit for one of our higher classes in reading, but in writing and accounts only fit for the lowest classes'.[20]

The professed range of the curriculum of the common day school against that of the dame school can be gauged by returning to the two examples given earlier, Rutland and Westminster. In the former, of 25 common day schools, all taught reading and writing, 18 taught arithmetic, 22 sewing, 16 knitting, 9 grammar, 7 geography and 4 history; in the latter, of a total of 41 schools, all offered reading, writing and arithmetic, 33 needlework, 38 grammar, 32 geography, 28 history, with a few offering additional skills such as mensuration or drawing.[21] The Birmingham Statistical Society summed up the contribution of the common day school as follows: 'Taken as a whole, the utmost amount of benefit which accrues to the public from this class of schools will include facility in reading and writing and some knowledge of arithmetic; to which must be added, in the girls' schools, needlework, with occasionally an acquaintance with the rudiments of grammar, history, or geography.'[22]

But once this broadening of the curriculum has been acknowledged in the reports, they revert to their familiar general theme — the two types of school being portrayed in all other respects as sharing the same characteristics. The London Statistical Society described the common day schools as 'in fact little else than superior Dame schools'.[23] Henry Althans, the British Society's inspector in London, echoed this assessment in the evidence he gave before the 1837 Select Committee on the Education of the Poorer Classes; 'Some of [the private day schools] are very little better than dame schools.'[24] In fact, they shared the same localities and physical conditions, the same methods, and were generally operated by teachers of similar backgrounds. Most importantly, they both drew their pupils from the same sections of society. When further asked by the Select Committee, 'Do you know, at all, what class of people send their children to these schools?', Henry Althans replied, 'I should say, chiefly, the working class.'[25] And the London Statistical Society, forbearing to enquire deeply into the educational behaviour of the middle and upper classes, confined its investigations primarily to 'poor families (. . . families who have not a street-door of their own, and whom a person would visit without first seeking permission . . .) assuming, for the sake of argument that these persons send their children to the Charity, Infant, Common Day and Dame schools'.[26] The Society further indicated the working-class character of such schools through their geographical distribution; 'It is impossible to help being struck with the small proportion of private schools for the poor which exist in the west of London, and the gradual increase of them as we proceed eastward; Westminster having only one scholar for every 48.6 inhabitants and Wapping one for every 18.2.'[27]

In general, dames' schools and the majority of common day schools with fees of less than 9d can fairly be said to have catered for an essentially working-class demand, and to have exhibited the same general class characteristics. Such differences as did exist between them stemmed either directly from the declared extent of the curriculum or from secondary features determined by variations in the the curriculum.[28] The most noticeable of these secondary features concern the level of fees and the age of pupils. But it has to be noted that both features offer only a limited use as independent indicators for the classification of schools, though some reports sometimes do come close to elevating them in this way. As regards fees, the financial problems — and sacrifices — of prolonged attendance at a common day school were in some circumstances likely to have been considerably greater than at a dame school and must have put the former beyond the range of some working-class families. But it is extremely important not to overstate this point, for there was a very large area of overlap between the two types, making it quite possible for a dame school to charge almost as much, for a similar course of teaching, as its common day counterpart.[29] This was because each type of school offered a basic instruction for a fixed sum, adding a few pence for any additional subjects taught, as demanded.[30] Taking the city of Birmingham in 1838 as an example, the average fees for a specified level of instruction in the 267 dame schools and the 99 common day schools with maximum fees of 9d were as follows. The average weekly cost for reading, sewing and knitting at a dame school was 3½d; and for reading, writing, arithmetic and, frequently, sewing and knitting at a common day school, the average weekly charge was about 7d.[31] In Rutland, with 50 dames' schools and 21 common day schools at 9d per week or less, the respective figures were 3¼d, and just over 6d.[32] But again, it needs to be underlined that this financial differential between dame and common day was a nominal one, based on the fees for a maximised given curriculum. There is no reason to suppose that the majority of children at common day schools followed such a curriculum in its entirety, and there is evidence that most did not.

> It has been seen that in the Dame Schools, to teach the children to read is the whole of what is professed. In the Common Day Schools, much more than this is professed, but little more is actually done. The pupils are in very few cases obliged to go through any course of instruction prescribed by the master. They may learn as little as they, or their parents, please. A separate charge is made for each subject, and consequently the fewer the subjects a child is instructed in, the smaller is the cost of his schooling. It was found that in thirty-six schools, taken promiscuously, (note: In the remaining schools belonging to this class, the agent failed in his attempt to obtain this information with a sufficient degree of accuracy to give any valuable result), having 1,563 scholars,
> 1,016 were receiving instruction in reading only
> 299 were receiving instruction in reading and writing.
> 238 were receiving instruction in reading, writing and arithmetic.
> 10 were receiving instruction in reading, writing, arithmetic and some other subject.[33]

In this case — Liverpool in 1836 — 65 per cent of the pupils at common day schools were in fact following a dame school curriculum, and were probably paying a comparable amount for it. The advantage of the common day school was that additional subjects were conveniently on hand in the event of familial educational demand — and almost certainly, domestic income — periodically increasing.

As with the question of fees, an examination of the relative ages of pupils attending the two types of school points to a distinction of a kind, but again, it is neither fixed nor deep. The evidence in the Statistical Societies' reports on this subject is not always as detailed as might be hoped, but, as one report points out, this was in part determined by the comparative lack of significance which some responding teachers placed on pupil age; '. . . it may be right here to make the general remark, that there is a great uncertainty in these calculations as to ages. The teachers seldom know more of their scholars' ages than the visitor who enquires respecting them; they are therefore distinguished, in a great measure, by guess . . . .'[34]

Most reports content themselves with a classification into three age groups — those under 5, those from 5 to 15, and those above

15. The lack of differentiation in the second group is disappointing, for it does not permit any precision or much value in comparative analysis. The under-five group does however shed some light on the almost universally accepted proposition that the dames' schools were 'mere baby-minding establishments'. If this were the case, then a broad difference could be expected on this ground from the situation in the common day schools, which have never been castigated on this particular issue. But from the tabular returns of all the reports, it appears that the common day schools also had a proportion — though much smaller — of under-fives, whilst the number of those from 5 to 15 in dames' schools was frequently larger than official sources might imply. In Rutland, for example, 36.8 per cent of children in dames' schools were indeed under five, but so were 14.2 per cent of those at common day schools. And if only those common day schools run by women are included, then the proportion rises to 19 per cent.[35] In the case of Birmingham, the respective figures were 44.2 per cent, 14 per cent and 20.5 per cent.[36] This evidence points to a degree of similarity between the dames' schools and the common day schools kept by women which was not shared to the same extent with those kept by men.

The Birmingham report is especially significant because it alone makes some attempt to differentiate the 5 to 15 age group at dames' schools by giving the numbers of over-sevens as well as over-fives. 'Out of 3,900 children attending dame schools in Birmingham, 1,726, or 44.2%, are under 5 years of age, 1,216, or 31.2%, are above 5 but under 7 years of age, 958, or 24.6%, are above 7 years of age.'[37] And in Westminster, where the bald tabular details record 296 under-fives and 425 from 5 to 15 attending dame schools, the text of the report supplies the following nuance: 'Although a large number of these children are of an age varying from 2 to 5 years, the schools appear to be attended by others far more advanced in years, varying from 5 to 14 years.'[38] J. R. Wood, the agent who carried out those enquiries initiated by the Manchester Statistical Society, felt that the general leaving age at a dame's school was about seven; but to this he added, 'many get no day-school instruction at all but what they receive at these dame schools'.[39] And Joseph Fletcher's report on the Coventry hand-loom weavers indicated that of 1,629 children 'at Private Schools', the ages of 1,043 (64 per cent) were 'not distinguished' by their teachers. Of the remainder, 40 per cent were given as being above seven years old.[40]

Other contemporary sources further demonstate how uncertain is the classification of schools by pupil age alone. Jellinger Symons, whose special interest in the question of popular education makes his reports to the Children's Employment Commission particularly valuable, used the same three age-group divisions in his study of Sheffield on behalf of that body. He identified 46 dames' schools with a total of 1,037 scholars. Of these, 96 pupils were in a handful of schools catering exclusively for under-fives. In the remaining schools, 31 per cent of scholars came into this category, with 67.8 per cent being aged from 5 to 15. In the common day schools, the under-five presence was very markedly lower at 7.5 per cent, the remaining 92.5 per cent being entirely within the 5 to 15 category. However, the only scholars over 15 were in fact recorded in the dames' schools where they comprised 1.2 per cent of the total.[41]

In sum then, the available evidence suggests that the internal classification of working-class private schools on the basis only of fee or pupil-age is substantially invalid, and presents an oversimplified and distorted picture.

By the late 1840s, what limited value the 'dame and common day' paradigm had possessed was fast draining away into a more confused and undefined terminology. Even at the point of its most careful usage, however, the paradigm was never so useful a way of approaching the educational reality of this period, than a continuum of working-class private schooling within which the determining variable involved the teaching of reading. Whilst schools which concentrated solely upon this skill naturally attracted a preponderance of very young children and were correspondingly cheaper on paper than those which offered additional skills, these were not independent distinctions. Variations in fees and in ages were very wide and are seldom satisfactorily comprehended by the label 'dame's school'. If any additional distinction is to be made, it has to be one which the working-class users of the schools themselves made and recognised, namely, the distinction between schools kept by women, and those kept by men — a distinction which corresponded only partially with the dame/common day divide.

The terms 'dame's school' and 'common day school' therefore only have analytical or descriptive value to the extent that they are employed in very closely defined contexts and their tendency towards oversimple and sometimes erroneous classification is recognised.

Turning away now from the reports of the education 'experts', there exist other, more scattered terminological references to be considered. Perhaps the most important and certainly the most interesting of these concern the colloquial names by which working people themselves referred to their schools. Though working-class autobiographies often refer to attendance at 'a dame's school', or, more rarely, 'a common day school', it seems that these were labels retrospectively applied. They were, in other words, the terms formally known to educational experts which were subsequently learned by working-class authors and then associated with their early experience of schooling.[42] But there is little evidence to suggest that the working-class users of such schools knew them habitually as 'dame' or 'common day', or that they ever referred to them as such in everyday speech. Wherever independent working-class testimonies have been recorded, reference is very often simply to 'school' without qualification or development. Good examples come from the reports of the Children's Employment Commission which include numerous individual interviews, sometimes quoted verbatim and sometimes in reported speech. For instance, Martha Francis of Truro, recorded in 1841, 'is 50 years old; is a widow; has 5 children, all miners . . . all of them went to school, but "poor people cannot do all they would"'.[43] And Michael Finley, a pit-boy at Killingworth colliery at the same period; 'Aged about 15. Has been down 6 years . . . reads well. Writes his name . . . was some time at school once.'[44]

In this kind of case, there is no way of knowing what kind of school was involved. Where a particular school is specified by its category, it is generally some form of publicly sponsored provision. This is not surprising, for the formal titles by which public schools knew themselves must have registered strongly among their clients. Thus references to 'Infant School', 'Church School', 'British School', and so on are fairly common. Sometimes though, to the obvious disgust of investigators, such official designations were completely misunderstood; there is more than one instance of 'National School' being rendered in common parlance as 'natural school'.[45] This is an example of an externally applied label — not unlike the educational experience to which it referred — having no meaning or significance to working-class experience. But in cases where private schools are identified, the labels grow more naturally outwards from the defining characteristics of particular schools. Sometimes this simply took the form of a conscious recognition of a school's distinctively private character. Thus Margaret Henderson, a 12-year-old server to a hair-seating weaver in Sheffield: 'I think I was nine years old when I first went to work. I was two years at a private day-school before I went to work; and now I go to St. Paul's Sunday-school, and to Queen-street evening-school twice-a-week. (Reads very well in the 12th chapter of St. Mark . . . Writes well also)'.[46] This account also demonstrates the virtually universal practice of distinguishing schools by the period of their opening — day, Sunday or evening. Evening schools were nearly always kept by the teachers of (common) day schools, but once again, it is not always easy to differentiate private from public where the broad term 'day school' was used. Sometimes this is possible where the fee paid is also given, as for instance in the case of Samuel Elliott, a Derbyshire pit-boy; 'Eleven years old . . . went to a day school before he went in the pit; paid 6d. a-week; learned to read and write.'[47] A fee of this size was certainly more than might be expected in a public school in the early 1840s. More normally, private schools can be identified from the simple but highly specific terms used. Often, the age, and more importantly, the sex of the teacher are indicated. Eliza Pandleton, an 11-year-old lace-worker from Chesterfield describing her education: 'Can read, can't write. Goes to Sunday-school. Went a year to a day-school kept by an old woman; was taught to read the Testament.'[48] Agnes Perryman, a Honiton lace-worker, 'age 7 . . . Learned reading at an old lady's school, but nothing else.'[49] And Edward Rowe, a nail-maker in Birmingham, aged 15: 'Can read and write; has been at Sunday-school 8 or 9 years; went when he was little to a day school kept by a young woman.'[50] Frequently the teacher's sex was used adjectivally to make the shorter but telling label, as used by John Barker from Newcastle; 'Aged nearly 11 . . . works with Robert Burn, the saucer-maker. Cannot read or write at all; has no clothes to go to Sunday-school . . .; went to a woman's school when he was very young; could read the spelling-book then, but has forgotten all now.'[51] Thomas Lashley who worked at Willington Colliery and who was nine years old, 'has been at [the pit] these 2 or 3 years. Was at a woman's school for a year before he went down.'[52] And Emmanuel Lovekin, a mining butty from Tunstall recorded that when he was young — in the 1820s — 'there was but very few schools. I never knew but one with a man teacher. There was a few old women's schools.'[53]

'Woman's school' — the phrase would have had a universal

currency throughout working-class districts and would have been instantly understood and appreciated where 'dame's school' might not. And similarly, the 'man's school'; John Robson, employed in Cookson's Glass Works in South Shields in 1842 attended such school; 'Aged 11½ years old . . . His father is a joiner . . . can read an easy book, write his name. Goes to a Sunday school only . . . Went to a man's school when he was three years old; stopped there 2 years.'[54] John Robson's evidence further reveals a familiar pattern of movement from school to school, and also introduces the most common method of all to describe a private school.

After his two years at the 'man's school', John 'then went to Errington's school and stopped two years. Then went to Lawson's school and stopped two years. Then went to Burnam's school and stopped there a year . . . Learnt at that school reading, writing and ciphering.' Working-class private schools were most commonly talked of by their users in just this way — by the name of the teacher. This is not surprising. Such schools followed no externally designed and regulated system of teaching which could be conveniently designated by official labels like 'National' or 'British'. Moreover, the private teachers were usually well-known local people, the friends and neighbours of their customers. They were familiar and accessible in a way that trained public teachers frequently were not; their schools were nothing other than the reflection of their own qualities or weaknesses, and for their schools to be popularly comprehended and referred to by their individual names was not only natural but precisely accurate. Whatever an individual private school offered depended only on the particular teacher who operated it. The last surviving working-class private school traced in this study was locally known, after the teacher, as 'Miss Beetlestone's', or just 'Beetlestone's'.

Schools named in this way must have been very familiar to working-class children in the mid-nineteenth century. Sarah Wilford, for example, a Nottinghamshire lace-worker of eleven; 'Can read and write a little. Went to a day-school as soon as she could walk and stayed till a year and a half ago; went to Mrs. Newbold's, Mrs. Henderson's and Miss Wyatt; was taught to read and write.'[55] And Joseph Kenworthy, a twelve-year-old Birmingham screw factory worker; 'Can read and write a little. Went to Mr. Raysbeck's day school, Holloway Road for 12 months; for last two months has gone 4 nights a-week to Mr. Raysbeck's night-school. Is taught to read, write, spell and sum.

Thinks he gets on pretty well . . .'[56] Sometimes the school was referred to by the full name of its teacher. Such a school was attended by John Marsden who worked in a pit in the West Riding; he was 8½; '. . . when I was a 'little 'un', I went varry near 'holf' a year to Benjamin Firth's day-school and learn a, b, abs; I never went to Sunday-school.'[57] Also Joseph Taylor from Heaton Colliery; 'Going on 10 . . . Goes to the Methodist school on the Sunday. Went to a day-school before he came to work for about a year or two. Learnt the Bible and ciphering. Peter James taught him. Can read (pretty well). Cannot write at all.'[58]

Name and sex, then, were indications of primary importance in the construction of working-class educational terminology. There were however others of an almost equal significance. These too originated from the internal characteristics of the schools themselves. In some districts, for example, the domestic tone and organisation of private schools was acknowledged in such labels as 'cottage school', 'home school' and 'house school'. An example of this type of application — particularly interesting also for its subsidiary detail — was given by twelve-year-old pottery worker, James Hulme: 'I am a mould runner . . . I went to day school eight years at *Natural* School, and learnt Testament and Bible; I can [spell] a bit, and write a little bit; I could do both very well till I went to the Natural. I used to go to a house school before . . . [At the National School] they used to put boys over me that could na read better than *meesel*; I did na like that . . . I told my father then, and I came away and came to work.'[59]

Distinction of schools by curriculum — a distinction which we earlier saw was present but blurred in the official reports — was also very common within the popular terminologies. Indeed it is perhaps in this connection that independently generated working-class labels come closest to the imposed 'dame' and 'common day' paradigm. In the working-class perspective, the distinction between a 'reading school' and a 'writing school' was often clearly drawn. Thus, for example, Sarah Jane Perry of Branscombe; 'Went to a reading school. Spells easy words.'[60] Quite possibly her teacher was Mrs Mary Ann Gay, from the same town, who declared in the same report that she 'keeps a school of little readers'.[61] Sarah Platt, a lace-maker from Stony Stratford, 'always attended Sunday schools, and every evening, except Saturday, attended a writing school . . .'.[62] It is important to note once again that these labels were nothing more than practical and straightforward productions of the particular nature of working-class educational demand. They bear no hidden or coded significance and token an attitude towards education which was exclusively oriented towards the gaining of knowledge and skills. The designations 'reading' and 'writing' did not mean that each type taught nothing other than this. What it did signify to a parent though, given the inevitable and pressing constraints of little available time and money, was a degree of declared specialisation in the rapid teaching of a particular required skill, with little diversion or unwanted complication.

Very similar examples of such descriptive labelling can be seen in the case of the little 'schools of industry', popularly known as 'lace schools', 'straw plait schools', 'seaming schools', according to the particular skill taught. Most of these schools were also, on a limited scale, reading schools. In lace-making districts for example, 'It is considered . . . in many places to be the duty of the mistress to teach reading as well as lace making, and though but a few minutes in the day are devoted to this, when it is practised its good effects appear traceable in a power of reading . . .'[63] Such reading was done at convenient spare moments. At Mrs Woodleigh's in Newton Poppleford, 'All the children read when they come in the morning and when they leave in the evening, the big girls out of a chapter, the younger out of a little book.'[64] And at Mrs Westcott's, near Otterton, 'All the bigger girls read to her together for half-an-hour at dinner time from the Testament, and the two little girls, age 6 and 8, from the Psalter.'[65] At Leicestershire seaming schools, 'A mistress takes perhaps from 1 to 4 girls, and teaches a little reading once in the morning and once in the afternoon. The children pay nothing and give their work for their teaching.'[66]

The working reality of the popular private school was then the subject of two nomenclatures. The first was developed by professional investigators of education in the 1830s, for whom working-class private education represented a largely unknown and unexplained cultural territory. They were conscious of the pioneering character of their work. 'It is to the *private schools for the education of the poor* that the attention of your Committee has been especially directed; because whilst the charity and Sunday schools are sufficiently known to the public . . . the census of private schools has never yet been taken, or a description of them attempted.'[67] Largely as a result of their own preconceptions about the nature of worthwhile education, such researchers sought to divine some fixed *system* in operation in the world of the private school. The labels used to describe this system, together with the notion that such a system actually existed and functioned in an idealised form, quickly passed — together with their subsidiary associations — into a common currency among educational experts, and from them to modern historians.

But it is clear from the second, alternative nomenclature — as well as from much of the empirical findings of the Statistical Societies themselves — that the officially favoured terminology as it developed is seriously misleading. In their enquiries into the teaching methods of the private schools, investigators repeatedly bemoaned the lack of any recognised system. If they had cared to examine more closely the labels by which the schools were popularly known, they would perhaps have noted a parallel absence of terminological order and precision. The distinctively working-class nomenclature is important precisely because of that similarity. The names were formed by, and reflect the exigencies of, daily life for a particular disadvantaged social group in a particular society. The classificatory terminology of the experts catches only a fraction of this reality. On the one hand it frequently fails to comprehend the conditions of an essential cultural unity which made all varieties of the working-class private school part of a single form. But on the other, it also fails to understand the capacity of this form to respond to the fluctuating and unpredictable patterns of popular demand with such a nuanced, varied and overlapping range of educational options as to elude the comprehension of a simple formal classification. As we have seen, there are some elements of truth in the picture which the 'dame and common day' paradigm seeks to draw; but these are mostly no more than partial truths, and they have been established only by ignoring or obscuring others. If we are to approach the reality of the working-class private school, then we must be prepared to operate with greater care and flexibility than the 'dame and common day' paradigm allows. If we do not, then we are left with the worst of both worlds — a terminology with neither the breadth nor the precision needed to comprehend a complex cultural phenomenon. To the extent that we continue to rely exclusively on the terminologies used by middle-class investigators, we understand not the schools themselves, but only a particular way of looking at them.

The failure of the simple dame/common day formula to correspond adequately to the reality of the working-class private school may in part account for the changes in official terminology which began to occur around the middle of the century. From this point on, descriptive categories became considerably less stable though the schools which they sought to classify remained much the same as they had been in the 1830s and 1840s.[68]

The most dramatic change was the disappearance of the term 'common day' altogether. A signpost of this development is the Education Census of 1851. In this document, the 'common day school' does not figure anywhere, though an American-influenced and altogether different version of the formulation does appear; 'the system of "common schools" in which the children of different classes of society are educated all together, is not likely to succeed in England, where the tone of social feeling is decisively opposed to such a democratic admixture'.[69] Instead, the author of the Census Report, Horace Mann, offers a single broadly-based category — the 'inferior private school'. This is certainly a term which offers more scope for dealing with the range of working-class private schooling as it existed than the earlier bipartite division. But Mann's simple and unified label did not stand without qualification; it carried the additional definition — 'Principally *dame* schools; only reading and writing taught, the latter not always.'[70] So, while 'inferior private school' did acknowledge a distinctive cultural and educational unity, it was immediately linked to the lowly half of the old division. It is important to note that in this definition the Statistical Societies' determining variable of classification — the teaching of reading alone or together with the other basic skills — has been ignored. No new principles for differentiating dames' schools from other inferior private schools are given. It might be inferred from this that more 'dames' schools' were teaching a broader curriculum — including writing — than had been the case in the 1830s and 1840s. In fact, as the later evidence of the Newcastle Commission demonstrated, the emphasis on reading in the working-class private school remained paramount.[71] It is also worth pointing out that whilst the category which Horace Mann understood as 'dames' schools' are noticed by him as being the numerically dominant type of working-class private school, this is the reverse of earlier interpretations. The returns of 1818 show 'ordinary schools' outnumbering 'dames' schools' by 3.3:1 and Kerry's private 'daily schools' dwarfing the 'Infant' category by a massive 11.4:1.[72] This certainly suggests that the 1851 census classified as 'dames' schools' many examples which the Statistical Societies would probably have recognised as 'common day' schools.

Whilst terminological compression and confusion of this kind was to continue for the next 25 years, it was a trend that had had precedents in some types of educational reporting outside the Statistical Societies in the 1830s and 1840s. The best examples can be found in the reports of the Factory Inspectors, whose credentials as guardians of popular education derived from the provisions for part-time schooling laid down by the Factory Act. They were considerably troubled by the number of parents who opted to make use of private rather than public schools to comply with attendance regulations. Their reports, composed in the same period as those of the Statistical Societies, though without much of their detail, habitually operated with a minimum of terminological differentiation, rarely distinguishing different types of working-class private shool. The majority refer simply to 'private schools' — usually prefaced by an uncomplimentary adjective — or to the conflated expression 'private or dame school' — usually thought to be sufficiently damaging as it stood. R. J. Saunders's report of 1843 illustrates the way in which all working-class schools could be confidently comprehended by these broad labels. 'Under the term *private or dame schools*, I place all the schools kept by a master or mistress for their own profit, and not under the control of any other person whatsoever.'[73] Such terminological contraction is also evident in other contemporary reports whose concern with popular education is incidental. Thus, to take another example, the 1848 report of Assistant Commissioner Fletcher on hand-loom weavers in the Midlands, concentrates all working-class private schools (or 'pay schools'), 'under the general head of "day and dame schools"'.[74]

The official reports of the second half of the nineteenth century, marked by an absence of precision, either of clear definition or classification, also belong, like the 1851 Education Census, in this tradition of reporting. The enduring label, 'dame's school' continues to be widely used — in contexts of broader and increasingly pejorative character — with still less consistency of meaning. This is evident in the reports of the Assistant Commissioners to the Newcastle Commission. The very instructions to the Assistant Commissioners set the tone for this vagueness and lack of classificatory precision; they refer to 'private schools generally, and to those commonly called dames' school . . .'.[75] Each Assistant Commissioner's understanding of what constituted a dame's school appears, not surprisingly, to have varied. Sometimes it applies to any working-class private school taught by a woman, sometimes to a school with few pupils, sometimes to any school felt to be deficient in curriculum, teaching or physical condition, and frequently the term is used to approximate to the public infant school.[76] The precise nature of this approximation is not made clear, but in practice it seems to relate more to the basic and introductory level of curriculum rather than to the age of pupils. The private schools which Mr Wilkinson, for example, lists as dames' schools have an average upper pupil age of nearly nine and a half years, which was not far from the average elementary school-leaving age in many working-class districts.[77]

Whilst the idea of the 'mere dame school' was increasingly employed as a synonym for, or symbol of, the worthlessness of working-class private schooling as a whole, it was clear that the entire species could not be collapsed realistically into this term. And it is in this context that some of the Assistant Commissioners began to make use of a new label that started to appear in the late 1850s — the 'private adventure school'. Initially, the new term was used to fill part of the gap left by the disappearance of the old 'common day' and which, in the interim, had been comprehended by the unspecific 'private day' school and by the expansion of the 'dame school' label. Part of the appeal of the new term seems to have been — as with 'dame's school' — in its pejorative impact which drew attention not so much to the schools as a class, as to the character and motivations of their teachers.[78] Emphasis was shifted away from the positive features of the ways in which schools were actually operated and controlled, towards a suggestion that the school keepers were fraudulently exploiting their ignorant and gullible customers.

However, the new label did not re-establish the classificatory pretension of the dame/common day paradigm as developed in the 1830s and 1840s. Though it was used throughout the Assistant Commissioners' reports to differentiate between working-class schools — for example: 'I may here say a word concerning the . . . dames' and other private adventure schools'[79] — it was also used in a much wider sense to apply to all working-class private schools, for example: 'The low private adventure schools are, for the most part, in a deplorable state.'[80]

It was the latter, wider sense that had become the dominant one by the early 1870s. This is illustrated by the returns of educational provision required under the Act of 1870. The Education Department designated three classes of school for this return. The first of these was 'Public Schools', defined as schools 'held in premises secured by Deed for Education, with Managers acting under that Deed, who appoint and control the Teacher'. The second group, which would formerly have been comprehended under the first heading, was relegated to the status of 'Private Schools', being defined as 'governed by Private Managers, or a Committee, not acting under any Deed'. This dramatic act of reclassification broke entirely with the meaning of 'private' popular schooling as it had been understood by the Statistical Societies, the 1851 Census and the Newcastle Commission. The entire sector of working-class private schooling was now subsumed under a single generic title — 'Adventure Schools'. These were described as being 'conducted by the Teacher at his (or her) own risk, and on his (or her) own responsibility'.[81] Under this title, for the first time, all working-class private schools were recognised officially as comprising an educational unity. The process of terminological contraction and unification, which had been under way since the 1850s, and which had been immanent in the original reports of the Statistical Societies, was completed. From this point on, as the period of the legislative offensive against working-class private schooling approached, the pre-existing categories of 'inferior private school' and 'dame's school' did not disappear, but were collapsed into the new term to be used synonymously with it. It is in the annual reports of Her Majesty's Inspectorate that this final stage is best seen, as all pretence of serious differentiation and classification is submerged beneath the weight of pejorative insult and condemnation. Thus, 'Of the private adventure schools which it has been our duty to visit . . . few have proved themselves efficient . . . it is impossible not to feel sympathy for the poor old dames . . .';[82] 'there is still . . . a considerable number of private adventure schools . . . the dames earn from their schools a precarious livelihood'.[83] And the most striking example spoke of,

> what are called private adventure schools; most of these are dame schools, only a very few being taught by men . . . The teacher of the adventure school has a personal following. She is probably related to half of her neighbours . . . A private school is, for some occult reason, held to be more respectable . . . [improvement] can never be carried out . . . so long as children

> are allowed to attend dame schools . . . Nor do I think we should [worry about] depriving the *adventurers* of the means of subsistence.[84]

In the end, accurate classification was, as it had ever been, impossible because working-class private schooling had never conformed to the neatness and regularity of pattern which professional educationists sought to impose.

The literary confusion of nomenclature — as in the examples given above — can, for the first and only time in the nineteenth century, be measured, for the year of 1870, against comprehensive descriptive lists of *individual* private schools. This is a facility which not even the most painstaking of the Statistical Societies' reports can offer, and it is provided by the surviving returns of the national Education Enquiry of 1870. When these results are set out in tabular form, they strongly suggest, once more, that the uncertainties and inconsistencies of nineteenth-century official nomenclatures were in fact occasioned by the real diversity of an informal and uncontrolled popular educational tradition; a diversity which, as was suggested at the beginning of this chapter, was just as strongly apparent in the Kerry Returns, some 50 years earlier.

The returns of 1870 show that the Southwark Division of the London School Board, with nearly 22 per cent of its scholars at private adventure schools, bore the greatest proportional weight of such schools in the metropolis (closely followed by Hackney and Greenwich, with about 21 per cent each).[85] Southwark's full total of 230 recorded private adventure schools are too many to offer as an exemplary list, therefore one of the district's parishes, St James, Bermondsey, has been chosen.[86] This parish is credited with 63 such schools, the individual details of which are set out in Table 1.1.

Table 1.1: Private Schools in St James, Bermondsey, in 1871

	Number of: (+ age range) Boys	Girls	Fees	Length of teaching experience	Duration of this school	Age
1.	4 (3–6)	9 (3–7)	2d–4d	3 m	3 m	
2.	11 (3–6)	14 (5–8)	2d–6d		2 y	20
3.	4 (3–8)	7 (3–7)	2d–6d	6 y	This year	
4.	4 (6–10)	2 (10–11)	4d–6d	2 y	This year	
5.	7 (3–12)	13 (5–13)	2d–4d		1 y	
6.	'"Establishment for young Ladies". Refused inspection.'					
7.	10 (3–13)	22 (3–13)	4d–9d	3 y	3 y	

TABLE 1.1 — continued

	Number of: (+ age range) Boys	Girls	Fees	Length of teaching experience	Duration of this school	Age
8.	30 (3–12)	18 (3–10)	2d–9d	25 y	9 y	
9.	9 (6)	9 (3–12)	4d–9d +	1y	1y	
10.	'"Young ladies' School". Not examined.'					
		35 (3–13)	4d–9d +	14 y	7y	31
11.	3	25 (3–13)	6d–9d +	15 y		
12.	13 (3–6)	10 (3–9)	4d–6d	25 y	12 y	
13.	5 (3–11)	9 (3–13)	2d–4d	1 y	1 y	
14.	17 (3–7)	8 (3–6)	2d–4d	2 m	2 m	
15.	37 (3–13)	43 (3–13)	3d	4 y	4 y	39
16.	7 (3–7)	3 (5–7)	2d–4d	5 y	4 y	
17.	6 (5–7)	14 (6–10)	4d–9d	7 y		23
18.	16 (3–9)	15 (3–10)	2d–4d	4 y	2 y	18
19.	13 (3–9)	8 (3–8)	2d–4d	1 y	1 y	
20.	9 (3–10)	12 (3–10)	4d–6d	2 y	2 y	
21.	7 (3–10)	5 (6–10)	4d–6d	2 y	This year	
22.	'This school has only opened this week, other scholars are shortly expected.'					
	1		6d–9d			
23.	4 (3–7)	6 (3–8)	2d–4d		This year	
24.	7 (3–8)	15 (3–9)	2d–4d	4 y	3 y	18
25.	10 (3–9)	12 (3–9)	4d–6d	15 y	3 y	
26.	6 (3–8)	10 (3–10)	2d–4d	3 y	3 y	
27.	16 (3–11)	11 (3–11)	2d–4d	3 y	3 y	
28.		5 (5–11)	9d	1 y	1 y	
29.	16 (3–8)	19 (3–13)	2d–9d		2 y	34
30.	4 (3–6)	9 (3–7)	4d–6d	3 y	3 y	
31.	2 (5–6)	11 (3–8)	2d–4d	8 y	8 y	
32.	10 (3–9)	9 (3–9)	4d–6d	20 y		
33.	15 (3–7)	21 (3–9)	4d–6d	30 y	3 y	
34.	9 (5–12)	9 (6–13)	4d–9d	30 y	13 y	63
35.	7 (3–8)	23 (3–13)	4d–9d	3 y	3 y	18
36.	'Ladies' School'.					
	7 (3–9)	4 (3–6)	6d–9d	3 y	1 y	
37.	2 (5–6)	8 (3–9)	4d–9d	1 y	1 y	
38.	'Ladies' School'.					
	12 (3–9)	16 (3–12)	4d–9d	3 y	3 y	19
39.	13 (3–9)	13 (3–9)	4d–6d	4 y	4 y	
40.	11 (5–10)	16 (5–11)	2d–9d	4 y	4 y	52
41.	10 (3–7)	15 (3–9)	2d–4d	10 y	10 y	
42.	2 (5–6)	18 (5–9)	4d–9d	5 y	3 y	34
43.	8 (3–6)	12 (3–6)	1d–2d		This year	
44.	7 (3–8)	16 (3–13)	4d–9d +	14 y	2 y	
45.	8 (3–8)	10 (3–8)	4d–6d)	6 y	6 y	
46.	7 (3–6)	11 (3–6)	2d–6d	3 y		30
47.	8 (3–8)	6 (3–6)	2d–4d	3 y	This year	

TABLE 1.1 — continued

	Number of: (+ age range) Boys	Girls	Fees	Length of teaching experience	Duration of this school	Age
48.	14 (3–8)	7 (3–8)	2d–9d	12 y	2 y	
49.	6 (3–7)	8 (3–7)	4d–9d	2 y	1 y	
50.		9 (3–7)	4d–9d	5 y	This year	
51.	8 (3–6)	6 (3–6)	2d–9d	2 m	2 m	
52.	10 (3–13)	32 (3–13)	6d–9d	15 y	4 y	
53.	13 (3–9)	14 (3–9)	2d–4d	28 y	26 y	
54.	7 (3–9)	23 (3–9)	2d–4d	6 y	3 y	
55.	10 (3–10)	12 (3–11)	2d–4d	3 y	3 y	
56.	3 (3–13)	8 (5–13)	6d–9d	1 y	1 y	
57.	7 (3–8)	6 (3–7)	2d–4d	1 y	1 y	
58.	25 (3–13)		4d–9d +	5 y	2 y	27 (male)
59.		19 (3–13)	4d–6d	12 y	1 y	29
60.	38 (3–12)	25 (3–13)	2d–9d	14 y	3 y	
61.	47 (3–13)		4d–9d	35 y	3 y	59 (male)
62.	47 (3–13)	24 (5–13)	4d–9d	10 y	2 y	
63.	16 (7–13)	32 (7–13)	4d–9d	7 y	7 y	

A list such as that shown in Table 1.1 speaks for itself. It defies straightforward categorisation. Its demonstration of significant variety within a characteristic unity indicates that the broad term, 'working-class private schools', is the most legitimate and accurate which the historian can use. Its strength is in recognising all such schools as elements within a single educational and cultural tradition — but a tradition whose primary characteristic was a flexibility and closeness of response to local working-class demand; a tradition whose schools were therefore endlessly varied in detail though similar in character. Other terms — especially those emanating from working-class usage — are by no means valueless. But the validity of the terminologies employed by middle-class investigators is much diluted by the carelessness of their application, their built-in tendency towards pejorative bias, and above all, their classificatory clumsiness; their compulsion to draw easy demarcation lines over a reality of enormous variety.

Notes

1. Comparing its findings with those of the Education Census, the Newcastle Commissioners gave the proportion of private scholars to the total number of

scholars as follows (*Newcastle*, vol. 1, p. 95):

Region	Percentage of private scholars 1851	1859
E. Agricultural	37.4	32.6
W. Agricultural	29.7	28.4
Metropolitan	33.7	35.0
Metropolitan Southern	24.4	32.7
Bradford and Rochdale	37.8	40.0
Staffordshire	39.7	42.1
Wales	18.8	15.1
Durham and Cumberland*	30.9	24.3
Bristol and Plymouth	35.9	38.0
Hull, Yarmouth and Ipswich	46.7	42.9

* The Durham Union was not included in these figures.

2. 'Second Report of a Committee of the Statistical Society of London, appointed to enquire into the State of Education in Westminster', *J.S.S.*, vol. 2 (1839), p. 199.
3. 'Report on the State of Education in Birmingham', *J.S.S.*, vol. 3 (1840), p. 35.
4. 'Second Report . . . Westminster', *J.S.S.* (1839), p. 67. See also, 'On the Condition of the Working Classes in the Inner Ward of St. George's Parish, Hanover Square', *J.S.S.*, vol. 6 (1843), p. 152; 'Third Report of a Committee of the Statistical Society of London appointed to enquire into the State of Education in Westminster', *J.S.S.*, vol. 1 (1839), p. 455.
5. 'Fifth Report and Summary of the Education Committee of the Statistical Society of London', *J.S.S.*, vol. 6 (1843), p. 212.
6. P.P. 1835 (62) xliii. *Education Enquiry, Abstract of the Answers and Returns made pursuant to an Address to the House of Commons dated 24th May, 1833* (Kerry), p. 1330. For a debate which bears on the reliability of the returns, see J. Hunt, 'Professor West on Early Nineteenth-Century Education', in *Economic History Review*, vol. 24 (1971), pp. 624–32; E. G. West, 'The Interpretation of Early Nineteenth-Century Education Statistics', ibid., pp. 633–42. Also West, *Education and the Industrial Revolution* (1975), Ch. 2.
7. *Kerry*, p. 1331.
8. Ibid., p. 1330.
9. 1837–8 (589) vii *Select Committee on the Education of the Poorer Classes*, p. 108.
10. P.P. 1819 (224) ix, Parts 1–2. *Digest of Returns to a Circular letter from the Select Committee on the Education of the Poor Etc. (1818)*. Also P.P. 1820 (151) xii. *A General Table showing the State of Education in England*.
11. '*Digest*', Part 1, pp. 140–1.
12. Ibid., pp. 137; 135; 135; 138; 139; 144; 181; 361; 351; 392; 396; 299; 307; 392; 391.
13. See for instance, Bartley, *The Schools for the People*, p. 404.
14. See, 'Report of the Education Committee of the Statistical Society of London on the Borough of Finsbury', *J.S.S.* (February 1843), p. 30; *Select Committee*, p. 105.
15. *Select Committee*, p. 102.
16. 'A Statistical Account of the Parish of Madron, containing the Borough of Penzance, in Cornwall', *J.S.S.*, vol. 2 (1839), p. 224. See also 'Analysis of the

Reports of the Committee of the Manchester Statistical Society on the State of Education in the Boroughs of Manchester, Liverpool, Salford and Bury', *C.S.E. First Publication* (1837), p. 295; 'Dame schools — under this head are included all those schools in which reading and a little sewing are taught.'

17. 'Report of a Committee of the Manchester Statistical Society on the State of Education in the County of Rutland in the year 1838', *J.S.S.*, vol. 2 (1839), p. 310. It was quite common for boys as well as girls to be taught the skills of sewing and knitting. 'In 22 of these schools the boys are taught to knit.' Also see Joseph Gutteridge in Valerie Chancellor (ed.), *Master and Artisan in Victorian England* (1969), p. 84, '. . . the old lady . . . not only taught us her limited stock of general knowledge, but instructed us — boys and girls alike — in the art of sewing and knitting and many others of a peculiarly feminine character'.

18. 'Second Report . . . Westminster', *J.S.S.* (1839), p. 207.

19. See for example, 'Third Report . . . Westminster', *J.S.S.* (1839), p. 462.

20. P.P. 1843 [431] xiv. *C.E.C. Appendix to Second Report of the Commissioners. Trades and Manufactures. Part One*, p. e2.

21. 'Rutland . . .', *J.S.S.* (1839), p. 310; also 'Second Report . . . Westminster', *J.S.S.* (1839), p. 207.

22. Birmingham . . .', *J.S.S.*, vol. 3 (1840), p. 35.

23. 'Third Report . . . Westminster', *J.S.S.* (1839), p. 452.

24. *Select Committee*, p. 137.

25. Ibid., p. 136. They were not though, according to Althans, 'the poorest working class'. The implications of the label 'common' day school is revealing — a school for the 'common people'. For some indications of the historical shift towards derogation in the term, see Raymond Williams's discussion in *Keywords* (1976), pp. 61–2. But in contemporary classification, the term 'common day school' was often stretched a good deal. For instance, see 'Finsbury . . .', *J.S.S.* (1843), p. 37, where fees for such schools are given as ranging from 3d a week to two guineas a quarter.

26. Third Report . . . Westminster', *J.S.S.* (1839), p. 450.

27. 'Fifth Report . . .', *J.S.S.* (1843), p. 12. For a similar distribution pattern in Bristol, see Chapter 2, Fig. 2.1.

28. Many of the reports of the Statistical Societies have tabular breakdowns of the subjects professed to be taught in various kinds of school.

29. See 'Rutland . . .', *J.S.S.* (1839), p. 308; 'Finsbury . . .', *J.S.S.* (1843), p. 37; 'Second Report . . . Westminster', *J.S.S.* (1839), p. 206.

30. See for example P.P. 1842 [381] xvi. *C.E.C. Appendix to First Report (Mines)*, Part 1, p. 594; 'Second Report . . . Westminster', *J.S.S.* (1839), p. 195. Also see Table 1.1.

31. Birmingham . . .', *J.S.S.* (1840), p. 43.

32. 'Rutland . . .', *J.S.S.* (1839), p. 308. Nationally, the Newcastle Commission found that 'in 68.95% of the [private] schools, containing 66.77% of the scholars, the highest charge is from 2d. to 6d., that in 16.57% of the schools, containing 17.73% of the scholars, the highest fee ranges from 7d. to 1s., and that in 13.82% of the schools, containing 14.72% of the scholars, the highest charge is upwards of 1s. a week', *Newcastle*, vol. 1, p. 75. For a detailed tabular breakdown, ibid., p. 590. But see note 33 below; also pp. 00–00.

33. 'Report on the State of Education in the Borough of Liverpool in 1835–36', *M.S.S.* (1836), p. 16. Also 'Report on the State of Education in the Borough of Bury in July, 1835', *M.S.S.* (1835), p. 6. Also *Select Committee*, p. 120. Also 'West Bromwich', *J.S.S.* (1839), p. 377.

34. Third Report . . . Westminster', *J.S.S.* (1839), p. 451; also p. 452. For modern assumptions of an inflexible pupil-age differential between 'dames' and 'common day' schools, see D. Wardle, *Education and Society in Nineteenth Century Nottingham*, p. 167, 'The dame school catered almost entirely for very

young children and was usually no more than a baby-minding establishment, while the common day school took some rather older pupils and perhaps added writing and even a little arithmetic to its curriculum.' Also P. McCann, 'Popular Education, Socialization and Social Control: Spitalfield 1812–1824' in P. McCann, *Popular Education and Socialization in the Nineteenth Century* (1977), pp. 1–40; 'Dame schools for children under six years and common day schools for older children . . .', p. 30.

35. 'Rutland . . .', *J.S.S.* (1839), p. 309.

36. 'Birmingham . . .', *J.S.S.* (1840), p. 41.

37. Ibid., p. 30.

38. 'Second Report . . . Westminster', *J.S.S.* (1839), p. 196.

39. *Select, Committee*, p. 117. These remarks were made in connection with the Birmingham survey. It is noteworthy that Wood should have here offered seven as a general leaving age when his enquiry showed that in fact 25 per cent of dames' scholars were over this age. See note 37.

40. P.P. 1840 [220] xxiv. *Reports from Commissioners: Hand Loom Weavers*, p. 95. This source is cited by D. P. Leinster-Mackay, 'The English Private School 1830–1914, with special reference to the private preparatory school', unpublished PhD, Durham, 1972, vol. 1, p. 217, p. 655, p. 658.

41. P.P. 1843 [431] xiv, *C.E.C.*, p. E19. The Newcastle Commission, though it too did not effectively distinguish dames' from 'common day' schools, did offer an interesting national comparison between private schools and public schools on the basis of pupil age. The results show that each species contained a preponderance of younger children, though this was substantially more marked in the private schools. See *Newcastle*, vol. 1, p. 656, also see p. 653.

Ages	Centesimal proportion of scholars in public schools	Centesimal proportion of scholars in private schools
Under 3 years	3.0	5.4
3–6 years	19.8	34.7
6–7 years	11.3	13.4
7–8 years	12.3	11.0
8–9 years	12.4	9.0
9–10 years	11.6	7.4
10–11 years	10.3	5.8
11–12 years	7.9	4.8
12–13 years	6.0	3.9
13–14 years	3.1	2.3
14–15 years	1.3	1.3
over 15 years	1.0	1.0

See also note 77 below

42. See for example the autobiography of Joseph Gutteridge (1816–99) 'At five I was sent to a dame school kept by a Quakeress . . .', V. Chancellor, *Master and Artisan*, p. 84.

43. P.P. 1842 [381] xvi, *C.E.C.*, p.831.

44. Ibid., p. 591.

45. See for instance, P.P. 1843 [431] xiv, *C.E.C.*, p. C57.

46. Ibid., p. e30.

47. P.P. 1842 [382] xvii, *C.E.C. Appendix to First Report (Mines)*, Part 2, p. 281.
48. P.P. 1843 [431] xiv, *C.E.C.*, p. f78.
49. P.P. 1843 [3170] xviii, *C.E.C. Reports of the Commissioners on the Employment of Children and Young Persons in Trades and Manufactures not already regulated by Law*, First Report, p. 255.
50. Ibid., p. f167.
51. P.P. 1843 [432] xv, *C.E.C. Appendix to Second Report of Commissioners (Trades and Manufactures)*, Part 2, p. 123. But see Cumin, *Newcastle*, vol. 3, p. 83, 'It is quite true that there are some excellent dames' or women's schools.' Here, the breadth of the working-class term is compressed into a middle-class pejorative label.
52. P.P. 1842 [381] xvi, *C.E.C.*, p.570.
53. J. Burnett (ed.), *The Annals of Labour* (1974), p. 290. Lovekin writes of his own experience, 'When quite young, I was sent to an Old Lady's School, whose name I know they called Tilly Wilson.'
54. P.P. 1843 [432] xv, *C.E.C.*, p. 18.
55. P.P. 1843 [431] xiv, *C.E.C.*, p. f41.
56. Ibid., p. f156.
57. P.P. 1842 [382]xviii, *C.E.C.*, p. 113.
58. P.P. 1842 [381] xvi, *C.E.C.*, p. 571. The most famous examples of named private schools are probably those attended by Thomas Cooper — 'Old Gatty's' and 'Dame Brown's'.
59. P.P. 1843 [431] xiv, *C.E.C.*, p. c57. See also Coode, *Newcastle*, vol. 2, p. 296. For working-class distaste for the monitorial system, see Chapter 5.
60. P.P. 1863 [3170] xviii, *C.E.C.*, p. 251. Also, P.P. 1864 [3414] xxii, *C.E.C.*, Second Report, p.xl.
61. P.P. 1863 [3170] xviii, *C.E.C.*, p. 251.
62. P.P. 1843 [431] xiv, *C.E.C.*, p. a50. Also, 'Schools for the Industrious Classes', *C.S.E. Second Publication* (1838), p. 392, p. 395. See too, D. Wardle, *Education and Society in Nineteenth Century Nottingham*, pp. 165–6.
63. P.P. 1863 [3170] xviii, *C.E.C.*, p. 185. But see Horn, 'Victorian Villages from Census Returns', *The Local Historian*, vol. 15 (February 1982), pp. 25–32. 'Most of these youngsters attended a lace "school" . . . In such institutions academic instruction was neglected; the cultivation of manual dexterity was all that was sought', p. 27.
64. P.P. 1863 [3170] xviii, *C.E.C.*, p. 254.
65. Ibid., p. 255.
66. Ibid., p. 288.
67. 'Fifth Report . . . London', *J.S.S.* (1843), pp. 212, 218.
68. The same process, though viewed from an altogether different perspective, is noted by J. Hurt, 'West . . .', *Economic History Review* (1971). 'By the late 1850's, the semantic ambiguities of the word "school" had been resolved. "Dame schools" were seen for what they really were, that is nurseries, and the "schooldames" were seen as child-minders', pp. 628–9.
69. *Education Census*, p. xlv.
70. Ibid., p. xxxiii.
71. See *Newcastle*, vol. 1, pp. 660, 665.

Percentage of scholars learning		Subject
Public	Private	
93.3	71.7	Religious
95.1	93.5	Reading
78.1	43.2	Writing
69.3	33.8	Arithmetic
75.8	73.8	Needlework
3.8	3.4	Other industrial work

72. P.P. 1820 (151) xii, *General Table* . . ., p. 341; *Kerry*, p. 1330.

73. P.P. 1844 [524]xxviii, *Reports by Factory Inspectors*, p. 21. Also P.P. 1847 [779] xv, *Reports*, p. 23; P.P. 1851 [1396] xxiii, *Reports*, p. 8, p. 12.

74. P.P. 1840 [220] xxiv, p. 84.

75. See 'Instructions to Assistant Commissioners', *Newcastle*, vol. 2, p. 8.

76. See also, Bartley, *Schools for the People*, p. 400. But note this interesting and specific conflation to describe a London school with scholars from two years old to six. 'An Infant dame school . . . in a back parlour.' P.R.O. Ed. 3/11.

77. Wilkinson, *Newcastle*, vol. 3, p. 378. See also P.P. 1863 [3170] xviii, *C.E.C.*, p. 287. At Hinckley National School, 'There are about 280 names on the books . . . and of these about 100 boys and as many girls attend. The average age of the boys is not more than 9 or 10, and that of the girls not more than 8 or 9.' Also ibid., p. 24; 'little more than 3% of the children [at public schools in the Potteries] are over 12 years of age, about 12% are over 10 years of age'. See also J. Hurt, *Elementary Education* (1979), p. 27. Also G. Sutherland, *Elementary Education* (1971): 'in 1895, only fourteen per cent of the children on the registers of inspected elementary schools . . . were aged twelve and over', p. 44. In spite of Assistant Commissioner Fraser's famous remark — 'with a view to the real interests of the peasant boy . . . We must make up our minds to see the last of him, as far as the day school is concerned, at 10 or 11' (*Newcastle*, vol. 1, p. 243) — premature withdrawal of scholars and endemic irregularity of attendance presented nineteenth-century educationists with a persistent problem. See for example, A. Hill, *Essays upon Educational Subjects*, p.v., 'That the main defect in the present state of popular education is this country is not so much the lack of schools, as the insufficient attendance of the children of the working-class (many never coming at all, and most others being withdrawn before they have had time to derive much benefit), is a truth which has for some years past been impressing itself more and more upon those who are best informed on the subject.' In Birmingham, the figures of attendance 'allow to each child between the ages of 5 and 15 . . .an average period of 3.3 years' attendance at a day-school . . .', 'Birmingham', *J.S.S.* (1840), p. 26. For other comments on attendance patterns, 'Second Report . . . Westminster', *J.S.S.* (1839), p. 195; 'Hull'. *J.S.S.* (1841), p. 158, p. 160; 'Rutland', *J.S.S.* (1839), pp. 305–6; particularly see 'Pendleton', *J.S.S.* (1839), pp. 69–73. Also *Select Committee*, pp. 14, 27, 107–8. For complaints from the Childrens' Employment Commission on the subject of early leaving, see P.P. 1842 [381] xvi, *C.E.C.*, p. 803; P.P. 1842 [383] xvii, *C.E.C.*, p. 240; P.P. 1843 [431] xiv, *C.E.C.*, pp. F36–7, p. f111; P.P. 1843 [432] xv, *C.E.C.*, p. Q17. For individual examples of ragged attendance patterns from the same source, P.P. 1842 [381] xvi, *C.E.C.*, pp. 83, 252, 268, 571–2, 591, 633, 823, 852, 853; P.P. 1842 [382] xvii, *C.E.C.*, pp. 111, 140, 275, 298. A further useful collection of individual profiles is in *C.S.E. Second Publication* (1838), 'Schools for the Industrious Classes', *C.S.E. Second Publication* (1838), pp. 388–97.

78. Patterns of pejorative use were complicated by the fact that both 'dame' and, more frequently, 'private adventure' were labels also applied to middle-class schools. See for example, A. Waugh, 'A Victorian Dame School', *Fortnightly Review*, vol. 133 (1930), pp. 41–56. Also Leinster-Mackay, (PhD Thesis), pp. 25–9. For a rejection of the label 'private adventure' by a teacher of a middle-class private school, see R. W. Hiley, *Sundry Attacks on Private Schools and Strictures Thereon* (1884), esp. Ch. 5.

79. Howson, *Newcastle*, vol. 4, p. 378.

80. Foster, *Newcastle*, vol. 2, p. 336.

81. See for example, P.P. 1871 (201) lv, *Return: Elementary Education (Civil Parishes)*.

82. H.M.I. Smith, *C.C.E.*, 1872–3, p. 134.

83. H.M.I. Faber, *C.C.E.*, 1881–2, p. 271.

84. H.M.I. Smith, *C.C.E.*, 1876–7, p. 565. This kind of terminological confusion has remained endemic. For a more modern example, see F. Smith, *A History of English Education*, p. 40, p. 359.

85. *School Board for London. Tables of the Elementary Schools within the District of the Metropolis*, August 1871. G.L.C. Record Office, SBL 1518. The full list of proportions of private scholars to the total, by district, is as follows: Southwark, 21.8%; Hackney, 21.3%; Greenwich, 20.8%; Lambeth, 16.2%; Tower Hamlets, 15.8%; Finsbury, 11.3%; Chelsea 9.8%; Westminster, 5.8%; City of London, 5.4%; Marylebone, 5.2%; pp. 213–14; 115–16; 87–8; 161–2; 249–50; 63–4; 29–30; 261–2; 11–12; 189–90.

86. P.R.O. Ed. 3/20.

2 NUMBERS

How many working-class private schools were there in 1850, in 1860, or in 1870? How many children attended them? The questions are quite simple, but the answers — assuming that satisfactory answers exist — are extraordinarily complex. We are faced from the outset with two major problems. The first is primarily a technical one, concerning the range of difficulties which confront any enquiry into the extent of schools and scholarship in the nineteenth century. By no means all such difficulties apply only to the study of private schools; indeed, the more important impinge upon private and public schools alike. The second problem, particularly affecting private schooling, centres upon the manner in which the official statistics, upon which we rely so heavily, were originally produced. The substance of these two problems can be briefly elucidated before they are confronted in detail.

Much has been written on the subject of the total numerical extent of elementary schooling in the nineteenth century, but the collective result of such work has been disappointing.[1] There are several reasons for this, but the more important have to do with the weaknesses of the positivist approach in general, and with particular difficulties in the interpretation of data. Research has commonly operated under the influence of a set of guiding assumptions, the most basic of which supposes that definitive statistical answers actually exist and only await final discovery through the application of this or that methodological refinement; a kind of 'hunt the number' game that is difficult but capable of final resolution. But the trouble with such solutions is that they are achieved at the expense of elevating important non-statistical variables into constants; of smuggling judgement and value into conclusions which are ostensibly purely numerical, and of dispensing with any interpretive perspective on the production of statistics. Not surprisingly, the further we get from the primary sources — that is, to contemporary histories — the less clear this becomes. Statistics are commonly presented in a form wherein they are drained of the imperfections and uncertainties which attended their original production. This is a measure of our failure to challenge the original sources sufficiently strongly. And this is, in turn, principally due to our reluctance to devalue what are, in effect, our only statistical sources. Without them, we are stranded and without alternative. It is understandable then that historians of education have not been willing to bite the hand that has fed them. Nevertheless, it remains the case that posterity has not given the educational statisticians of the nineteenth century the rougher ride that their work deserves.

Consider some of the principal technical weaknesses upon which rests our knowledge of the extent of elementary schooling in the nineteenth century. Take for example such fundamental and apparently unambiguous terms as 'scholar' and 'school' itself. Clearly, it is impossible to count accurately if we do not know what it is that we are supposed to be counting. Definition of concepts is therefore critical. What is a 'scholar'? And what is a 'school'? As will become apparent in the following pages, neither term had an agreed currency in the nineteenth century.

In the case of 'scholarship', the defining characteristics of this condition were not agreed among the educational 'experts' themselves. More significantly, those various definitions which were offered were idealised and regularised to the extent that they failed to comprehend the reality of working-class experience which characteristically produced a more erratic and untidy conception of 'scholarship', less rigidly tied to age-range or period of study. By the arbitrary application of such frames of reference upon actual patterns of working-class education activity, it was not very hard for nineteenth-century reporters to produce claims of massive educational 'deficiency'.[2] Of course, such writers were not blind to the implications of such a flaw, but most were happy enough to ignore it out of a combination of class-cultural elitism and the demand for statistical precision and tidiness. Nevertheless, some agencies, such as the Statistical Society of Bristol in 1841, did give uneasy voice to the problem: 'we must consider that very few children indeed are scholars for a *continuous* period of ten or even five years, and that out of the number appearing at any given time to be "without instruction", because then not actually *at school*, there may be a large proportion who *have had* more or less instruction, but have been called from school . . .'.[3] Called from school perhaps temporarily, to be returned when conditions improved? Such a pattern of intermittent scholarship is a recurring one throughout working-class autobiographies. And a small though graphic illustration comes from the columns of the 1851 Census returns from the city of Bristol. The census called for an unequivocal categorisation of children; either they were scholars or they were not. Probably the majority of casual scholars were returned as being without education. But Isaac May, a Bristol 'Haulier of Coals' sought to express the reality of his children's situation by offering a singular and technically inadmissable designation. They — James, aged nine and Elizabeth, aged seven — were returned as 'Schollor [*sic*] occasionally'.[4]

In truth, what most statisticians were recording in the nineteenth century was not the number of children who were not, or who never had been, scholars, but the number who did not conform to the requirements of an idealised definition of the term which took little account of the material hardships which obstructed the winning of an education. The practical difficulty of effectively estimating the number of working-class children who were being educated under such constraints will be considered from a more empirical perspective towards the end of this chapter.

What can be argued at this point is that as far as the history of elementary education in the nineteenth century is concerned, the statistical 'facts' relating to 'scholars' emphatically do not speak for themselves. Any attempt to approach the educational impact of schooling on the working class, rather than trying to homogenise sets of flawed statistics, should accord to such statistics only a partial or provisional credence and must look to other sources and approaches for confirmation or contradiction, and for nuance.

Thus far, we have concentrated on technical weaknesses of a general kind, but for this study, there is another difficulty which affects statistics of working-class private schooling exclusively. Leaving aside the *quality* of the statistics, there is also a serious dearth in the *quantity* of figures relating to private schooling. Original sources and modern histories alike have tended to concentrate overwhelmingly on officially regulated varieties of schooling, which were easily accessible and for which an abundance of statistical material was generated. Private schooling, on the other hand, has simply been ignored. The implications of this have been profound. Of itself, the very paucity of material concerning private schooling has frequently persuaded researchers that this alternative variety was of correspondingly minimal importance in its day; where there are no statistics, there could have been no schools.

There is perhaps a way out of this impasse, and that is to try to generate new sources of statistical information, and to use these alongside with the few official figures which are available to us. We will turn to just such an exercise shortly. But let us first return briefly to the concept of the 'school'.

It is on the enumeration of schools, rather than the more problematical issue of scholars, that this chapter will principally concentrate, for the base of statistical variation is considerably lower. Nevertheless, the concept of the school too, has suffered from a chronic lack of clear definition. We saw this in some detail in the last chapter. But from a statistical point of view, such confusion has a ramification of special importance. In Chapter 1, variations in the labelling of a known phenomenon — working-class private schools — were considered as a substantive issue. What now has to be recognised is that, for the purposes of enumeration, many nineteenth-century investigators saw such schools — whatever the label — as inadmissable. They could not be counted for they were not, according to middle-class understanding, schools at all. Their existence was instead explained in terms of domestic or social convenience, strengthened by traditional working-class idiosyncrasies.[5] Without an educative element acceptable to the enumerator, such places were often simply not counted. At its most extreme, this could entail the disqualification of any 'school' — and, by implication, its 'scholars' — not under some kind of official supervision. Particularly liable to exclusion was any example which could be labelled a 'dame's school'. Thus for example could the Report of the 1837 Select Committee explain that,

> in much of the Evidence adduced before Your Committee, the worthless nature of the Education supposed to be given in the common Day and Dame Schools has been dwelt upon; so that in many places it may be left almost out of account.
>
> If these be entirely omitted, then the amount of instruction given in public schools will stand thus. . .[6]

An officer of the Children's Employment Commission working in the Potteries in the early 1840s could confidently assert that 'The small private schools are very bad and not worthy of investigation.'[7] And one of his colleagues based in Lancashire could similarly argue — in a footnote — that having drawn up a complete table of the available schools in his district, 'In addition to the above there are four or five (perhaps more) private schools for the poor, where reading and sewing are taught.'[8]

Leaving aside for a moment the question of potential technical flaws in the original statistics, let us now consider the issue of how such figures were achieved in the first place. Their value to us will be considerably enhanced if we remember that they were essentially cultural productions and not factual reflections. The notion that they can legitimately be presented as accurate images of reality produced by objective methodologies is an unreasonable one. This does not mean that the statistics as they stand are valueless, but it does mean that their use to the historian has to be augmented by probing the relations as well as the means of their production. If they are not historically relocated in this way, then we allow them to assume the authority of an objective Court of Final Historical Appeal.

At the same time as presenting those statistics which remain to us, along with an assessment of their technical weaknesses, this chapter will therefore also have to offer a consideration of the cultural arena within which they were produced. What essentially needs to be recovered here is some understanding of the interactions and subjective meanings at the back of statistical production; that physical point at which the middle-class investigator, together with his methodological equipment, presented himself — in whatever form and through whichever agency — to working-class respondents and sought to recover cultural information to digest into tables of statistical 'fact'. It cannot be assumed that this process was ever straightforward, uncontested or attended only by difficulties of a technical kind. It can never be further assumed that the working-class objects of middle-class social investigation passively revealed that which was demanded, or that they should have had any interest whatever in the accuracy of the information returned.

With these points in mind, we can now turn to an empirical consideration of the statistics of working-class private schooling which are to hand. Throughout the following discussion, the themes of technical and cultural weakness inherent in the production of the figures will be developed.

So, against the broader background of the total resources of nineteenth-century elementary schooling, what was the numerical extent, according to the official figures, of the private sector? Was it perhaps a rare and unrepresentive variety; an unimportant handful of untidy assemblages scattered without pattern over the educational landscape? Or might it be conceived on a wider scale, though still as a marginal, transient and essentially worthless presence which simply evaporated whenever and wherever facilities for public elementary education were made available? And what evidence is there for the alternative view to be argued throughout these pages — that working-class private schooling was a numerically strong, ubiquitous and resilient feature of an independent working-class culture?

At a national level, statistics of working-class private schooling are few and far between. The first survey to distinguish clearly public and private schools was the Education Census of 1851 which identified a minimum of 13,879 private schools designed for working-class use, with a total of 225,000 scholars. This latter number was exceeded by that of public scholars in the ratio of approximately 1:5.3.[9] This unique enquiry was not repeated as part of the next decennial census principally because of the detailed investigations which were at that time being undertaken by the agents of the Newcastle Commission.[10] The various reports produced by the Commissioners and Assistant Commissioners of that body contained statistical breakdowns of ten specimen districts and national projections based upon them. The Commissioners more than doubled the 1851 attendance figures, reckoning that working-class private schools were attended by 573,576 children. Comparison with the numbers in public schools was in the ratio of approximately 1:2.8. The number of working-class private schools can be estimated at about 26,000.[11] A third, and as far as can be established, a final national statistic for the extent of working-class private schooling was given by Lord Sandon, Vice President of the Committee of Council in a parliamentary speech in November 1875. His calculation, given without source, assessed the number of pupils at such schools at 130,571.[12]

Taken at face value, these figures present a number of puzzling features. These however are difficult to address very usefully, given such broadly-based and sparse statistics. If we are to find evidence of the sort of statistical weaknesses indicated earlier, then we will need to leave the desert landscape of these few national figures — which are after all simply conflations or projections of thousands of local investigations — and plunge into the tangled thickets of local statistical production.

Local statistics exist in the form of surveys made by local Statistical Societies or private individuals; in the detailed tabular breakdowns of the 1851 Census; in the Newcastle Commission's reports;

in the local enquiries into elementary education provision required under the 1870 Act; and in the responses to a national survey carried out in 1875 and limited specifically to working-class private schools.[13] By careful selection of this or that local statistic, it is not difficult to provide supporting evidence for a whole range of conflicting hypotheses. Such figures can be casually adduced in any game of statistical push and pull depending on the particular aims or interests of the protagonists. They can however be made to yield more valid information when they are not used in isolation, but are kept within the tighter confines of an intensive local study.

Such a study forms a part of the present work. It was designed to answer two aims. First, to assess the numerical extent of working-class private schooling in a single locality over a period of some 30 years using every available statistical source. Secondly, and more importantly, to seek out patterns and trends which might have a more general historical application. This certainly did not mean the extrapolation of national statistics from a local study. Rather, it was hoped to isolate and highlight areas of weakness in official statistical technique and method and to suggest practical ways in which they might have occurred. If sustained inaccuracies and flaws of this kind could be established and supported in the evidence then this *would* be a finding that might legitimately be held to apply beyond the circumstances of the local study, as long as the substantive elements of any such finding could be tested by duplicating the appropriate procedures in other localities. The area selected for this local study was the city of Bristol.

Before embarking on the study, the range and extent of available statistical information needs to be assembled. An obvious starting point was with the figures of local educational provision provided in the extensive tabular analyses of the Education Census of 1851.[14] In addition, there exist the results of a local statistical survey conducted in 1841 principally by C. B. Fripp on behalf of the Statistical Society of Bristol.[15] Furthermore, Bristol formed a part of one of the ten specimen districts selected for special investigation by the Newcastle Commission and was therefore the subject of a detailed statistical and descriptive report by Assistant Commissioner Patrick Cumin, in later years to become Secretary to the Committee of Council on Education.[16] The returns relating to elementary education required under the 1870 Act have, in common with those from all cities excepting London, been destroyed. Happily, a list supplying crucial though brief details was published in the local press and is easily available.[17] Finally, the published results of the 1875 investigation into working-class private schools are similarly accessible.[18]

In combination, these sources are useful, but they all present in one degree or another a common feature which threatens to prevent us from using them as a basis to develop a statistical critique. Quite simply, these sources, like virtually all those upon which we rely for our understanding of nineteenth-century elementary education, were written by the practitioners or prophets of a developing system of public education. They were the products of the educational 'expert', and carry all the preconceived prejudices and value judgements of that kind. They exhibit a particular and uniform cultural construction of the notion of 'school', of learning, of teaching — of education. And we have already suggested that such an orientation was likely to produce particular statistical repercussions. Whilst historians can make themselves aware of this as a part of the general one-sidedness of these documents, and can voice their doubts about them, there are simply no other substantive sources available to redress the balance and to confirm or dispel misgivings. Without these, the unchallenged dominance of the official record remains, at best, as a citadel everlastingly besieged but never in danger of defeat.

If the stranglehold of the official statisticians of education will not be broken from sources emanating from within their own walls, then enquiry must look beyond them for evidence which, whilst still the product of reputable official agencies, was unconcerned with promoting any incidental educational information which it might have carried, in any particular way. If such a source existed, and if the period of its production paralleled that of the narrowly educational sources, it might afford an opportunity of grounding unsubstantiated doubts on a firmer comparative base. And indeed, there is such a source, though at first sight, the very considerable time and difficulty in using it systematically and the comparative paucity of the empirical return, make it appear unattractive. This source is the decennial Population Census.

The strength of the census for this study has three central elements. In the first place, the educational evidence which it yields is a by-product of a larger project unconnected with a purely educational goal. Though such evidence has to be teased out from a mass of irrelevant detail, it has the merit of not being produced under the constraint of an education establishment. Secondly, the Population

Censuses of 1851, 1861, and 1871 coincided either exactly or very closely with the periods at which the major educational surveys — 1851 Education Census, Newcastle Commission, 1870 Education Enquiry — took place. This permits analysis from three approaches: an examination of the educational sources over time; an examination of the non-educational sources over the same period; a comparative examination of three separate sets of concurrent educational and non-educational sources at three different periods. Thirdly, and unlike much of the strictly educational material, the Population Census goes right to the point at which the statistics were actually produced — the moment of contact between enumerator and respondent and all the confusion, misunderstanding and variety of response which it produced. The richness and suggestiveness of this detail is entirely masked in the published Census Abstracts which tell us only that in 1871, for example, there were in Bristol 1,035 men and women in teaching occupations of some description.[19] The real potential of the census returns is only released when these undifferentiated figures are followed back to their source and reclassified on the basis of likely social class, thereby giving some indication of the possible extent of working-class private schooling in Bristol at a given point. The key information in the Population Census was the returns of occupation. Every entry relating to teaching for each of the three censuses was listed, evaluated and categorised.[20] Those related to middle-class schools and public elementary schools were deleted, leaving a residue of potential working-class private teachers and therefore of schools. The number of schools was in fact lower than that of the teachers, for households with more than one teacher were counted only as a single school.

A long process of careful analysis, cross checking and grading for each of the three censuses eventually produced three maximum figures of potential working-class private schools. Though generated from familiar nineteenth-century documents, such figures represented a wholly new source, and, for the first time, a valid and effective measure for existing educational statistics. Distilled as they were from a mountain of raw material, the final figures presented a remarkable degree of consistency and uniformity over time. In short, they suggested that there were in the city of Bristol in the year 1851, a maximum of 218 potential working-class private schools; in 1861, 200 such; and in 1871, 191.

With these figures in mind, the question of the extent of

working-class private schooling in Bristol in the second half of the nineteenth century can now be tackled more fully and comparatively.

The most convenient starting point is with the easily accessible statistics provided by the 1851 Education Census. These however require careful and critical examination. The value of the Education Census to the particular issue of working-class private schooling rests solely on our acceptance that the elegantly constructed techniques and procedures formally set out in Horace Mann's Explanatory Notes coincide exactly with what actually happened in the real world. It is possible that such close coincidence did indeed occur, and that the formal methods provided by the Education Census therefore succeeded as intended in capturing every single existing private school. But need this necessarily be taken for granted? The monumental detail and the confident tone of the census lowers our guard; it convinces us that the Census Report and accompanying tables constitute a genuine statistical production and that this in itself is somehow validation enough. How, after all, can research get further back than this — a genuine fount of 'primary' evidence? The point is, of course, that this is not primary evidence in the true sense. It is one step removed from the real point of production.[21] Those who composed and collated the final document were not those who produced the data. This is an obvious point but one that is seldom faced largely because of the historian's need to have *some* unimpeachable reference points. After all, if a document with the internal rigour and enormous labour input of the Education Census is impugned, then where is there left to go to establish *any* statistical accuracy?

This study in fact takes the view that accurate statistical assessments of the extent of a phenomenon like working-class private schooling are not in the end possible and it is unhelpful to suppose that they are. Furthermore, the evidence suggests, as we shall see, that those assessments which have been made are likely to have a built-in bias towards under-estimation.

Nevertheless, the local study of Bristol seemed to offer the possibility of nudging a step closer to the truth. It will be recalled that analysis of the 1851 Population Census produced a figure of 218 potential working-class private schools. This has to be set against an estimated total of 126 recorded by the parallel Education Census of the same year. How can this very large discrepancy be explained? Our answer needs to focus particularly on the authentic moment at which statistics were produced — that is, the interaction of enumerator and working-class respondent. Little is known about these tens of millions of cultural encounters which ought to form the bedrock of our historical understanding. Imagination, speculation and a few scraps of empirical information are certainly poor tools to quarry this particular historical mine, but they are all that are available to us if we wish to escape from pit-head refinement to the coal-face.

The Education Census of 1851 recorded a total of 346 schools within the municipal boundary; these were subdivided into 77 public day schools and 269 private day schools. This latter number was not broken down further. However, Horace Mann did provide in his Report, 'a rough attempt to classify [private schools] according to efficiency' which offered the following general conclusions: superior private schools were assessed at 16.8 per cent of the total; middling schools at 24.1 per cent; inferior — 'principally *dame* schools' — at 47.2 per cent; and undescribed schools at 11.9 per cent.[22] If these proportional divisions are applied to the total of Bristol's private schools, a figure of 126 inferior schools is produced. This number is nearly 100 short of that produced by analysis of the corresponding Population Census, which was taken at precisely the same time. Even if the entire 'undescribed' category is taken as part of the 'inferior' total, and even if Mann's estimates of the size of the middle-class share of the private school total be questioned as being too high, the discrepancy remains large.[23]

How else then could this occur? An apologist for the integrity of the Education Census would point out that official error was virtually impossible since the enquiry took place at *exactly* the same moment as the parallel Population Census and was conducted by the same enumerator. Mann's Explanatory Notes explain how this was done. During the week ending 31 March 1851, enumerators delivered Population Census 'Householder's Schedules' to each household. In the course of this visit, 'the enumerator was instructed . . . to inquire if a school of any sort was carried on there: if there was, a form was to be left to be filled up ready for his visit on the Monday following' — that is, on the Monday on which all schedules were to be collected.[24] On that Monday, then, how could an individual declare himself or herself on the Householder's Schedule of the Population Census to be a private school keeper and yet avoid completing an Education Census schedule?

This question needs to be considered in some depth. First of all, it is clear that the official statistics depend entirely on the quality of the local enumerators.[25] Any assumption of an automatic and necessary relationship between the processed official figures and educational reality turns on this critical point. Yet it is apparent from the enormous variety in the quality of the Enumeration Books produced in the Population Census that the reliability of the enumerators was far from consistent. Whilst many were conscientious and thorough, others were careless, hurried and inaccurate. Leaving aside genuine errors — by no means uncommon — it seems that some enumerators failed more generally to comply fully with their instructions in making entries. This is particularly so in the case of occupational returns, which are frequently incomplete or ambiguous. However, where particularly diligent enumerators have tried to make the returns as complete as possible, some intriguing findings have come to light. For example, the enumerator operating in the central parish of Temple in 1851, made an occupational entry for every individual, recording 'None' if none were stated.[26] He initially entered such a designation against labourer's wife, Mary Ann Sloney, of Melsom's Buildings. But subsequently, 'None' was deleted and replaced by 'Keeps a school'. What might this single incident represent? Was this no more than a straightforward error, subsequently corrected, or was this a case of a teacher initially seeking to conceal her school's existence, only to be confounded by the enumerator's thoroughness? To take a similar example, what are we to make of the entry relating to Mary Horne, a 40-year old widow living in a poor district of St Augustine's?[27] In this instance, the enumerator has initially recorded her occupation simply as 'Dressmaker' but has subsequently added the words 'and mistress school'. Again, it may have been that the lady made a spurious, partial or indeed unwitting declaration, only to have her school-keeping exposed in some unknown way. Moreover, it is likely that a less conscientious enumerator would not have bothered to amend his entry, leaving Mrs Horne to go down in history as nothing more than a dressmaker and consigning her school to historical oblivion.

It is not difficult to conceive many reasons why working-class school-keepers might seek to avoid detection — probably fear, suspicion, confusion, embarrassment and the avoidance of a detailed and quite intimidating three-page document to be completed — all these played a part.[28] An interesting further point which bears directly on the relationship between enumerator and respondent is that many of the former were the masters of publicly supported schools, temporarily recruited for census duty. The implications of this may well have been considerable. To give an example: Enumeration District One of the in-parish of Saint Philip and Jacob was in 1871 the charge of William Mapowder, master of a public day school but a few hundred yards away in the neighbouring parish of Castle Precincts.[29] It does not seem particularly likely that such an investigator would be the most sympathetic to working-class private schools which were commonly maligned by educational experts, and it is not very surprising that Mapowder's returns indicate no working-class private schools in his area.

Isolated cases like these may begin to allow us some purchase — however tenuous — on the meeting of enumerator and respondent. They begin to hint at the ease, given the less zealous approach of many enumerators, with which working-class private school keepers, whether by conscious design or not, could escape official detection. As a working hypothesis, we might therefore suggest that some school-keepers — especially if they were not heads of households, in whom enumerators seem to have been principally interested — remained unknown to the officials of the Population Census.

This likelihood however does nothing to satisfy the anomaly in the numbers of working-class private schools suggested by the 1851 Education Census and that which emerges from the 1851 Population Census. The simultaneous operation of the two censuses appears to render it axiomatic that any teacher keeping a private school and occupationally declared as such, would be required to complete an Education Census return.

But this need not have been the case. And it is not difficult to envisage circumstances under which this might have occurred. How, for instance, might an enumerator working under considerable pressure to collect householders' returns on Monday, 31 March 1851, have reacted to the following circumstances? Suppose on his first visit to a household, he had enquired as to the existence of a school at the address, and suppose no such school had been declared. In this case, no Education Census form would have been left. But on returning to the household on the Monday of the collection, suppose further that the enumerator discovered one member to be returned on the householders schedule as a school teacher of some sort. He might simply accept this declaration without comment, assuming that it related to employment in a publicly supported school or as an assistant at a school held at a different address. If, however, the enumerator was diligent and had time in hand, he might query the entry; and if this led to an admission that a school *was* held at the address, it would place him, and not the respondent, in an awkward position. He would be obliged to issue an Education Census form — supposing that he had had the foresight to bring copies with him — explain how the document was to be completed and possibly supervise its completion. This would certainly have been a most unwelcome interruption on a day which was devoted simply to the collection of completed schedules. But the inconvenience would not have ended there. After having distributed schedules in the week before Monday 31 March, each enumerator was required 'to make a *list* of all the schools within his district stating the names of the parties to whom the forms had been delivered. The list was at once deposited with the next superior officer, the Registrar . . . who would use it as a check upon the number of returns to be received from that enumerator.'[30] The discovery of a previously undeclared school on Monday 31 March, would therefore require the enumerator to amend the list already submitted to his superior. Again, this prospect cannot have been a welcome one. The enumerator could avoid this last-minute work and potential unpleasantness by simply overlooking the declaration, for there was no provision for cross-checking the information derived from the two separate censuses. A private school keeper night thus be returned in the Population Census as 'School Mistress' whilst remaining entirely unknown to the Education Census.

Evidence of a similar kind, demonstrating the lack of consonance between the two censuses where agreement *should* have been virtually exact, comes from the number of individuals returned by each as 'scholars'. The total so returned by the Education Census nationally falls 135,893 short of that declared in the Population Census.[31] There could, of course, be several explanations for this disagreement, but it does clearly illustrate the essentially separate operation of the two enquiries as well as offering circumstantial support to the view that a large number of private schools were not revealed to the Education Census.

But let us return again to the central issue of the interaction of enumerator and respondent and the resultant production of statistics. It would not be hard to extend discussion of the areas of potential error in enumeration into a catalogue of possibilities.

How, for example, did individual enumerators define and comprehend the term 'school'? And how certain was it that they all took care to enquire as to the existence of a school at *every* household they called on during their first visit? Our present knowledge substantially depends on the fact that this requirement was *always* complied with. Indeed, this knowledge rests on a series of such assumptions which can be collectively expressed in a single proposition — that the provisions of the Education Census were coherent, unambiguous and scrupulously adhered to by the local enumerators though they were manifestly not always followed in the case of the Population Census; and that keepers of working-class private schools could automatically be relied upon to co-operate with the operation of such provisions. In other words, that the taking of such censuses was simply a matter of accurately apprehending unproblematical social facts through the use of carefully refined methods of counting, rather than an enormously complex and varied process of cultural encounter.

Yet perhaps the possibility of error at the point of contact between official and respondent need not rest solely on ungrounded speculation. Such conjecture can be directly linked to areas of potential confusion which actually exist in the stated procedures which the enquiry followed. A good example of this can be found in the Explanatory Notes which accompany the Education Census Report. Here it is made clear that when 'delivering the [Education Census] forms, the Enumerator notified to those receiving them that they were not *compellable* to furnish information: it was left entirely to their option'.[32] This passage does not make it clear whether a private school keeper who declined to co-operate would necessarily be issued with, or indeed accept, an Education Census form. It must be considered as a possibility that those who made it clear that they would not co-operate with the census would not have been issued with forms at the enumerator's first visit and therefore would not have been included on the list to be forwarded to the Registrar and which was intended as a check to ensure that all schools were included. This possibility may explain why, once the forms had been issued, 'a refusal [to complete the form] was of rare occurrence' — a result which seems at first sight surprising.[33]

Nevertheless, all such hypotheses cannot escape a speculative element. In the end, the moment of statistical production can never be recovered as it actually occurred. Conjectures about that moment, whatever the strength of circumstantial supporting evidence, remain as conjectures and cannot be pushed much further. On this point, the objectives of this study are limited. It does not set out a proof, but a challenge to an orthodoxy which has not been made to defend its pretensions. It does not argue that 'things necessarily happened' in this way or that, but that it seems possible, and indeed likely, that they could have done so. This is sufficient to challenge the careless notion that 'the way things really were', is necessarily identical with that which the official published record implies. On its own strength alone, the Education Census Report cannot demonstrate that — in the confrontation between enumerator and respondent — things positively happened one way or another. The conjectures given above aim not just to add support to the main propositions of this study, but to put the ball, as it were, in an unaccustomed court — in the court of the 1851 Education Census. That document is by no means beyond contention, and it is not enough to stand by it as if it were, in some way, its own guarantor. The hypotheses offered here are not easy to demonstrate from the evidence; they are still harder to disprove.

Finally, it has to be said that there are, in fact, some positive indications within the Education Census Report itself which add substance to the sort of speculations which have been made. Most notable among these is Horace Mann's own admission that some private schools had slipped through the net. This important remark was not made in the body of the Report, but was consigned to a brief and unamplified footnote. Referring to the final totals of schools enumerated in the census, it declared that the figures offered represent 'the state of things as shown by the information which has reached the Census Office through the instrumentality of the enumerators. It is unquestionably an understatement of the existing means of education; since no doubt a certain number of schools were not enumerated by these officers . . .'[34] Mann went on to expand the acknowledged extent of schooling to account for this under-enumeration, though only by a tiny 2.6 per cent.[35] How this proportion was arrived at is not stated, though this is clearly an issue of cardinal importance. It seems probable that it could have been no more than an informed guess since, by definition of their given instructions, enumerators could hardly have been the agents to supply information as to the extent of their own failure to enumerate all schools. It is only in this single brief reference that the author of the census vacated the highly plausible and extensively detailed territory of an abstracted methodological exposition for the uncertainties of the actual relations which partially determined the production of statistics. Mann's own telling phrase, 'the instrumentality of the enumerators', needs to be dragged from the peripheral obscurity of its footnote and reinstated as a central focus.

To sum up thus far: it has been argued that the real point of statistical production for the 1851 Education Census lies further back than the collation and compiling of the completed printed document itself. Furthermore, the construction of this source can be seen as the site of considerable cultural confusion and possibly conflict. It has been argued that some schools — whether by design or not — probably escaped enumeration and that the figure given by the 1851 Education Census is accordingly too low.

Bristol's next major encounter with the educational statisticians took place eight years after the Education Census. This took the form of Patrick Cumin's statistical investigation of 1859, undertaken as evidence for the deliberations of the Newcastle Commission. His report was marked with the same self-confidence of that earlier official enquiry. His statistical analysis, Cumin wrote, 'required the greatest care. In order to render [the statistics] as accurate as possible, I sought the aid of the poor rate collectors . . . I . . . summoned these officers, and told them that I required a complete list of every place of education — from the first-class school down to the dame's school — and that this must be done by a house-to-house visitation.' This considerable enterprise was, 'within a short time . . . completed . . . I must add that the lists of schools furnished by the rate collectors were extremely accurate, and indeed, I feel statisfied that I obtained a perfectly accurate list of the schools of every sect in my district'.[36]

In the absence of the more detailed notes of procedure and method which exist for the Education Census, it is difficult to offer a serious critique of Cumin's results. Though employing the services of a different collecting agency, there is no reason to suppose that the potential sources of error which have been mentioned in connection with the Education Census should have been any the less. The conditions of statistical contact remained in essence the same, as did the possibilities of confusion, ambiguity, carelessness or deliberate evasion. There is no reason therefore to suppose that the findings of 1859 recommended themselves as any more reliable than those of 1851.

It is not easy to compare the results of the two surveys, for the former offers figures only for the Registration Districts of Bristol and Bedminster, and not for the city itself, which comprised the Bristol District, about half of the Bedminster District and, in addition, virtually the entire Clifton District. To make an acceptable comparison, it is first necessary to total the numbers of private schools in each of the three districts in their entirety. The 1851 figures are easily available from the Education Census, giving 139, 63 and 135 for Bristol, Bedminster and Clifton respectively. This gives a grand total of 337, of which an ascertained 269 were within the city of Bristol itself. When Horace Mann's proportional calculations are applied, it appears that at least 126 of these would have been of a working-class character. For 1859, Cumin provides totals for Bristol and Bedminster; a fall for Bristol to 128, and a massive and unexplained rise in Bedminster to 117.[37] The Clifton total can, for the purposes of this study, be estimated by assuming a decline in numbers equivalent to that in the Bristol District — that is, 8.6 per cent — though the Clifton District, like its Bedminster neighbour, would have been more likely to have seen expansion in this period. However, an 8.6 per cent decline in Clifton's 1851 figure of 135 would indicate a number of about 123 in 1859. This gives a grand total for the three districts of 368. Again applying the proportional divisions as calculated in 1851, this would suggest a presence of about 294 private schools within the city limits, of which about 139 would have been used by the working class. By comparison, the number of working-class private schools suggested by analysis of the Population Census of 1861 was 200.

Setting other issues to one side, the clearest point to emerge from these comparisons is the relative degree of internal consonance in the two sets of figures, official (Mann and Cumin) and unofficial (returns of occupation). This degree of consistency indeed points to the large and enduring statistical variation *between* the two sources. In short, they tell different stories. The Population Censuses suggest a possible total of 218 working-class private schools in 1851, falling to 200 in 1861; the Education Census and the Newcastle Commission indicate 126 and 139 respectively. Where might we turn in the hope of corroboration for one source or the other? One likely possibility is the Bristol Statistical Society's investigation of 1841. How do the statistical findings of this enquiry accord with later ones?

In the New Year of 1841 — ten years before the Education Census — the Statistical Society of Bristol appointed a committee to investigate 'the state of the local population in respect to education'. The mode of this enquiry was set out only in outline; it was 'conducted by means of the same agent who had been engaged in the [earlier] investigation into the condition of the working classes in Bristol, and the facts obtained are all derived from his personal visits and examination of the schools, and from the testimony of the several teachers'.[38] But what is particularly interesting were the provisos which this enquiry set upon its own findings. 'Without pretending that the returns now presented are altogether free from inaccuracies, and as perfect as might be wished, the Committee feel convinced that no pains have been spared on the part of the agent to render them in every way complete, and that no general results of this kind can so justly merit public confidence as those which have been obtained — as in this case — by the *personal* inquiry of a disinterested and impartial agent'. Whilst this recognition of the practical difficulties of accurate enumeration of schools is in itself valuable, more significant still is its cautious general tone which distances it from ringing self-confidence of the official reports.

The findings of the 1851 Education Census were based entirely on two short visits to each household over the course of a single week; the Statistical Society's enquiry 'occupied altogether nearly six months'. Moreover, though the agency of enumeration is not made clear, it is apparent that its entire energies, and indeed the sole reason and justification for the undertaking, were concentrated upon an analysis of local facilities for education, and upon nothing else. Yet more important is the reference made in the Society's report to the difficulty in collecting all the relevant detail immediately and to the existence of a popular suspicion of officialdom which the major state-sponsored enquiries did not acknowledge. The Society's report points out that

> with respect to the great majority of the schools, the information desired was obtained without much difficulty, though it not unfrequently required repeated visits to obviate objections, and supply deficiencies in the first returns. In some cases, suspicion was entertained that the enquiry had a reference to Government proceedings, and though the agent's instructions were to assure the teachers that the only object of the Society was the investigation of the truth . . . it was found impossible in some cases to get over the unwillingness of the masters to give information.[39]

If the sheer numerical extent of the private schools noticed by the Society is any guide, then this particular enquiry penetrated the veil of suspicion with some degree of success. In respect of purely private schools, the Society's report listed an astonishing total of 446, broken down into 217 dame schools, 177 common day schools, 38 superior private and boarding schools and 14 evening schools.[40]

It is in the first two categories, totalling 394 schools, that those belonging to the working class would be found, though the report does not seek to differentiate further the schools on the basis of social class. Fortunately, however, the numbers *were* divided according to the average weekly fee paid by pupils. This exercise yielded the following result:

212	dame schools	with an average weekly payment of 3⅔d
53	common day schools under 9d per week	with an average weekly payment of 7d
112	common day schools	with an average quarterly payment of 18s 5½d
13	evening schools	with an average weekly payment of 7⅓d
18	schools with unascertained fees.[41]	

This division shows particularly clearly the distinction within the total number of private schools between those of working-class and lower middle-class types. The 112 common day schools charging quarterly fees (working out at an average of about 1s 6d a week) were doubtless aimed at a different sector of the market than were the dame schools and most of the remaining 53 common day schools.[42] When the numerical strengths of the latter two groups are aggregated, a maximum figure of 265 working-class private schools in the city in 1841 is produced. This appears to correspond quite well with the figures which analysis of the later Population Censuses indicated, fitting into a pattern of slow decline up to the inception of the Act of 1870. But the 1841 figure does not accord at all well with the official figures of 1851 and 1859. These indicate a catastrophic collapse in working-class private schooling in the 1840s — a period which Horace Mann himself thought of as one of general expansion for private education.[43]

This then is the comparative picture which emerges from a study of the likely number of working-class schools in Bristol as suggested by the official enquiries of 1851 and 1859 and the far larger number of schools indicated by analysis of the Population Censuses.

There are then reasonable grounds for supposing the figures of the educational statisticians to have been substantial under-estimations. However, the extent of such under-estimation may have been yet greater. Still more unrecorded working-class private schools existed, though at still murkier and virtually inaccessible historical depths. These were the schools which in 1851 revealed themselves to neither the Education Census, nor the Population Census, and which therefore, in terms of historical evidence, have no existence. Such schools — and their counterparts in 1861 — can be traced in no way, though a footnoted reference in an article in the *Journal of the Statistical Society* for 1843 referred to their existence at the time of the 1841 Census. The note alleged that,

> The little estimation in which the proprietors, and more especially the mistresses, of schools hold their profession, is shown by the circumstance, that whenever they had any other trade or calling, they entered that other trade by preference at the census of 1841. Thus a woman who took in needlework would be almost certain to describe herself as 'dressmaker', not as 'school mistress'. When the census of 1841 is published, it will probably be found that the figures under the head of 'Schoolmasters, etc.' will bear a very small proportion to the real number.[44]

This important passage might incidentally help to explain the case of Mary Horne which was referred to earlier. It might be remembered that in the 1851 Census, she too was initially designated simply as 'Dressmaker' only to have her school-keeping activity added later. And there is more evidence — this time for a later period — to show that school-keepers were still failing to declare themselves as such in the Population Census of 1871, thereby strongly suggesting that this practice was also followed in 1851 and 1861.

It will be recalled that the Education Act of 1870 provided for a national enquiry into the numerical extent of elementary school provision. We will now turn to a consideration of our last set of statistics, those produced in the 1870s. The results of the 1870

Education Enquiry undertaken and supervised by the Town Clerk in Bristol appear in the *Bristol Times and Mirror* of 24 December 1870. The particular value of this investigation is that it supplies for the first time the names and addresses of the known keepers of 'inferior' private schools in the city — that is, of schools where the weekly fee did not exceed 9d per week. This is a rare opportunity in the course of a study where the closest encounters with this type of school are generally made with aggregated, undifferentiated and unidentifiable statistical totals. This local survey brings us, in a way that is unique, to the edge of a real knowledge not of working-class private schools as a general category, but of genuine and identified individual examples. As a result, analysis can take a step from the more speculative level at which it was obliged to operate for the earlier periods and move towards a more stable empirical base.

The local survey in Bristol, as it was published, recorded 61 individually identified private adventure schools operating in the city.[45] This figure falls massively short of the 191 potential working-class private schools which analysis of the 1871 Population Census produced — though the higher figure incidentally fits well with these produced for 1851 (218) and 1861 (200).The scale of the discrepancy suggests — as might be expected — that the 1870 survey, which was less grandiose in its operation than those of 1851 and 1859, had rather less success in tracing the majority of the schools. However, the Town Clerk did report that 'the number of schools (of all types, public and private), that refused or omitted to fill up the forms was 37'. If *all* these recalcitrant schools were private adventure schools, as most indeed probably were, then the total identified number would still only be about one half of those suggested by the Population Census analysis — broadly similar to the comparative results for 1851 and 1861.

What additional light, if any, might the availability for the first time of evidence positively identifying individual private schools — in effect, a control group — shed on this persistent imbalance?

The refusal of co-operation by a number of private schools in Bristol further supports the view that there were *some* schools which would have been likely to appear only in the occupational returns of the Population Census, and not in the results of a specifically educational survey. But more than this, the sample powerfully demonstrates the existence of the trend working in reverse. Thirteen of the keepers of the schools positively identified by the survey of 1870 failed to declare themselves as such in the census a few months later. It seems unlikely that all these schools should cease to operate in this short space of time, and this could mean only that they were not declared to the Population Census, just as the Statistical Society's *Journal* had indicated for the census of 1841. This finding has two implications. First, it suggests that the secretion of a working-class private school in the face of *any* official enquiry — whether the Population Census or a survey of educational provision — was a common practice, again indicating the dangers of assuming *necessary* working-class compliance. Secondly, it could mean that the figures which have so far been given for potential working-class schools, figures which are based solely on the failure of educational enquiries to discover schools which *were* declared to the Population Census, are still yet too small. Evasion was taking place in the other direction too, though probably at a smaller rate. Even where a school had been tracked down by an official education enquiry, the proprietor might still fail to disclose her occupation later, and some schools must have remained totally unknown to *any* official agency. The numbers of the keepers of such schools — represented in the occupational returns of the census as perhaps 'Laundress', 'Dressmaker', or simply as a blank space — must remain forever unknown.

The overall conclusion to all this must be that the keepers of working-class private schools were content to continue their work away from the gaze of officialdom, which could only have appeared as a potential source of irritation or harassment and possible loss of livelihood. If official investigations of any kind could be avoided at low risk, then it appears that they were.

Using the 1870 enquiry's list of known schools together with the Population Census returns of 1871, it is possible to look more closely at those individuals who failed to declare their occupations and thereby succeeded in concealing their schools. Before turning to this, however, some important internal distinctions need to be applied to the group of 61 known schools. They will be examined from a more descriptive and qualitative viewpoint elsewhere, but it needs to be pointed out here that the group appears to be divided into the two distinct categories noticed in the 1841 investigation — schools which were clearly of a working-class character, and those which can more accurately be seen as catering for the lower middle class. This was also apparent from the assigned grades which were given to all potential working-class school-keepers as they were detected in the columns of the Population Census. The results of this grading, as they relate to the control group of 61, are as follows.

In the first place, nine of the teachers listed could not be traced in the census. This is not in itself surprising, for many of the names and addresses given proved to be inaccurate or imprecise in some degree, making detection extremely difficult. It is of course possible that any or all of these nine individuals might have moved within or away from the city in the few months between the two investigations. If they continued to keep school at a new address in the city, and if they failed to declare their occupation in the census, then they will remain impossible to trace. In any event, there remain 52 schools which have been positively traced in the census returns. These can be divided according to two separate criteria; by declaration or non-declaration of occupation as school teacher, and by assigned grade or social class. By the first criterion, 37 individuals declared themselves to be school teachers whilst 15 did not. Of the 37 declarations, 30 can be classed as working class (4 grade 'A', 9 'A/B', 10 'B', 5 'B/C', 2 'C') and 7 as lower middle class (grade 'C/D'); of the non-declarations, 13 were working class (6 grade 'A', 2 'A/B', 2 'B', 1 'B/C', 2 'C') whilst 2 were lower middle class (grade 'C/D'). If the 52 schools are taken together, then 44 of them (85 per cent) were of a working-class character. The 'inferior' private adventure school was, then, of two types, comprising the entire working-class complement, together with the humbler echelons of a lower middle-class species of school which straddled the ninepenny distinction, and which shaded upwards into the varieties of the middle-class private school proper, in which fees would commonly be settled on a quarterly basis.

What the 1870 survey seems to have done in Bristol is to capture probably the most accessible or easily identifiable examples of working-class private school, together with the modest tail section of a more elevated and qualitatively different body of schools. Far from enumerating every inferior private school in the city, the enquiry had simply produced an incomplete *mélange*; an indication, and no more, of what was actually happening in this diverse educational and cultural landscape.

Those 13 known working-class schools where no occupational declaration was made in the census need now to be looked at more closely. And a pattern is immediately apparent. Ten of those concerned were married women at home — a category from whom an occupational declaration was not generally required. In most cases the occupation column was simply left blank, as for instance in the case of Mrs Catherine Taylor from Bedminster whose husband was returned as 'Labourer in spirit warehouse', or Mrs Sarah Stiff from St Mary Redcliffe whose husband was a sawyer.[46] In some instances, the individual concerned has been entered as 'Wife' or as in the case of Mrs Eliza Davis who kept a school of 30 children in the Redcliff area, as 'Wife of the above — Philip Davis, a joiner'.[47]

The overwhelming preponderance of wives with employed husbands among the non-declarers is a finding of considerable interest. It points to a specific working-class grouping of school-keepers whose activities would have been wholly unknown to investigators. Moreover, it illustrates the mechanism by which their occupations could be hidden. They simply allowed themselves to be categorised as housewives and nothing more; they sheltered behind their husband's declaration, which would have been all that an enumerator would have commonly required. If there were ten such women keeping schools out of an incomplete sample of 61 (over 16 per cent), then it cannot be unlikely that there were many more, though on what scale it is impossible to say.

Probably the most difficulty in disguising a school from the census enumerators would have been experienced by those who were themselves heads of households. Such individuals would have been obliged to declare an occupation of some sort, and it does not seem unreasonable to suppose that the census apprehended most school-keepers of this description. There is however at least one exception that has come to light. This is a particularly interesting case which illustrates some of the difficulties of working with such slight evidence as we have available. The 1870 Education Enquiry records a school for 16 children kept by a Miss Ravenhill at Little Paradise, Bedminster. This checks against the 1871 Census, in which a Louisa Ravenhill is listed at number 42, Little Paradise, as head of household; she was unmarried and is recorded as the mother of a child, Walter Harding.[48] But, in the manner which the *Journal of the Statistical Society* claimed was common at the 1841 census, Louisa had returned herself as 'Milliner and dressmaker'. It is possible that she had just turned to this employment after having ceased to keep school, but the evidence of the earlier census of 1861 makes this seem unlikely. For in 1861, the Ravenhill family was bigger; they were listed as living at number 40, Little Paradise, and Louisa's father, John, a widower, was still alive.[49] Louisa, then aged 24, also had a sister, Selina, who was eight years her senior. Louisa's occupation is given, as in 1871, as 'Dress Maker and Milliner', but Selina, who had died or moved away by 1871, is returned as 'School Mistress'. It is likely that Louisa initially helped her sister with the school, and eventually took it over. Examples of a school passing on through members of the same family like this are not uncommon.[50] Louisa clearly kept the school in addition to continuing her dressmaking — again this was by no means an unusual arrangement — and preferred to offer the latter occupation to the census official. Once again, it is not possible to say how widespread this practice was, though another of the remaining two non-declarers — an unmarried daughter of a laundress — also falls into this category. She is returned as an envelope maker.[51] The final non-declarer was also a young unmarried daughter from St Philip's, though in this particular instance — following the practice of the married school-keepers — she declared no occupation at all.[52]

Was the practice of failing to declare the occupation of school-keeper peculiar to Bristol? Where the details of surveys made in other areas survive, this can be checked by using the same comparative method. Such a check was made, though on a smaller scale, using a sample of 16 known private adventure schools listed in the 1870 Education Enquiry returns for the parish of Poplar in East London.[53] Of this sample, three cases were found to be non-declarers, and two of these were married women, the wives of a stevedore and a carpenter. The London survey in fact furnishes considerably more detail than that which survives for Bristol. Drawing on this, a suprisingly full profile can be developed for some individual schools. The remaining non-declarer, Maria Mackay, can serve as an example. She was a 66-year-old unmarried woman — though the 1870 survey refers to her as 'Mrs' Mackay — with lodgings in Phoebe St, Poplar. There was possibly some equivocation about her occupational status, for the enumerator has not left the column blank, but has inserted a couple of ambivalent dashes. However, he clearly did not record her as the teacher of a private school. But the 1870 enquiry states that this had been her occupation for the previous 22 years. At the time of the survey, her school comprised ten boys and ten girls ranging in age from under three to eight. They paid a weekly fee varying from 1d to 4d.[54]

To close our local study of Bristol's working-class private schools, there is yet one more important statistic that is available, and which permits analysis to be extended well into the School Board era. Bristol was one of a large number of boards which complained in the course of 1875 to the Education Department that their work was being impeded by the continued existence of working-class private schools.[55] The Department responded with a request for each board to continue to undertake a local investigation which was unique in that it was confined to this type of school alone; it was not part of a wider educational survey. Moreover, in the person of the board's attendance officer, such an investigation could be undertaken by an agent with an extensive local knowledge of, and vested interest in, the state of elementary education in the city. Whilst this would not entirely obviate the weaknesses of earlier surveys, it must promote the relative reliability of this particular investigation. The results of the enquiry indicated the existence of 160 private adventure schools — 'a large and fluctuating number . . . which are not considered . . . as affording efficient instruction to the large number of children attending them . . .'[56] There can only be two explanations for this very large number. Either there had been a mushrooming of such schools since the 1870 Act, or the enquiry was simply more thorough and successful than its counterpart of 1870.[57] It is however worth noting that the 1875 figure does fit quite well into the overall pattern of potential working-class private schools produced from the analysis of the Population Censuses (see Figure 2.1).

In so far as we can conclude anything from our examination of the statistics of Bristol's working-class private schools, it is this. We do not know how many such schools there were in Bristol in the period from 1851 to 1871; and neither did the educational statisticians of the nineteenth century. The figures they offered with such certainty — and which have commonly been accepted in the same spirit — cannot be seen as reliable. The methods by which they arrived at these figures, however unimpeachable they may seem in the abstract, cannot be seen as the working out of a straightforward exercise in the collection of easily recoverable data, but as the product of a series of encounters between two distinctive, class-based educational cultures. The exact numbers of working-class private schools can never be finally known. Characteristically, they did not lend themselves to precise quantification and it is unrealistic to suppose that they did, or indeed that they should have done. Whenever it was possible, many working-class school-keepers seemed to have avoided official detection if it could be achieved

Figure 2.1: Working-class Private Schools in Bristol, 1841–75

Key:

= Official figures
= Estimates based on Population Census analysis
1 = 1841 Statistical Society Enquiry
2 = 1851 Education Census
3 = 1859–61 Newcastle Commission
4 = 1870 Education Enquiry
5 = 1875 Private Adventure School Survey
6 = 1851 Population Census
7 = 1861 Population Census
8 = 1871 Population Census

without difficulty or great risk. This should not surprise us. Private teachers of this type knew that they had nothing to gain from the activities of the official agencies, and possibly everything to lose.[58] It is therefore a reasonable assertion that all official statistics are under-representations of the true picture, and that the scale of such under-representation might well be of a considerable order. The more important figures which have been discussed so far can be summarised in the form of a simple graph (see Figure 2.1).

It can be seen that the findings derived from the Population

Censuses (points 6, 7 and 8), accord well with the surveys of 1841 and 1875, revealing a picture of gradual and steady numerical decline, rather than the violently fluctuating impression which is gained if we substitute the official national enquiries (points 2, 3 and 4).

It is also worth pointing out that the symmetry and constancy of the picture of Bristol's working-class private schools which emerges from the analysis of the Population Censuses were not solely temporal characteristics. Results produced for each parish in quite separate analyses maintain the same overall distribution pattern. Particularly notable is the consistently high concentration of schools in the large, predominantly working-class parishes of Bedminster in the south and St Philip and Jacob in the east (see Appendix B).

If it is excessively difficult to assess accurately the number of working-class private schools in Bristol at any given point, then it is quite impossible to calculate the number of children attending them or to say what proportion they represented of the total of all scholars. At a national level, the existing figures have to be treated with the greatest care. Their inaccuracies spring not just from the formlessness and irregularity of the schools in practice, but also from the difficulties we noted in defining the term 'scholar'. Without registers of admittance or attendance, without compulsion, and given the high geographical mobility and financial precariousness of urban working-class life, the numbers attending each school saw considerable variation from week to week and from day to day.

Once again, this can best be demonstrated by moving from bland national statistics to the confusion of local experience. Take for example the London returns of the 1870 Education Enquiry, where discrepancies in the number of scholars declared by school-keepers and those given by inspectors who visited the schools a few months later, are often substantial. The return made by Miss Bloomfield of Russell Street, Wandsworth, for example, listed the school as containing 20 boys and no girls; the inspector's report indicated that there were 11 boys and 21 girls. And to take another example from hundreds — Eleanor Hill's school in Tonsley Road, Wandsworth, contained, on her initial admission, just 4 girls. When it was inspected shortly after, there were 16 girls as well as 11 boys.[59] In any event, it is clearly misleading to base our understanding of the real impact of the schools in the local community upon idealised prescriptive notions of 'correct' length or regularity of scholarship.

However, if analysis based upon 'what ought to be' is replaced by analysis which roots itself in the reality of working-class life as it was experienced by its individual members, then different interpretations open up. Such interpretations must start with a reality in which a central place was occupied by the desire to obtain prized basic skills as rapidly as possible, and upon which the constraints of scarce resources — time and money — were key factors. Educational achievement in nineteenth-century working-class culture was of necessity contemplated in an intensely practical and instrumental manner. The culture was essentially unconcerned with the vision — to become a dominant one in the decades following the Act of 1870 — of 'education' defined as the operation of a single rational form. Defined, in other words, not simply as the mastery of particular skills, however achieved, but also as the sustained and regular experience of a special form of learning. Over the last three or four generations, our thinking about learning and about the legitimate forms of knowledge have been principally defined and directed by the notion of 'correct' or 'natural' processes of schooling. But for the greater part of the nineteenth century such processes were, for large portions of the working class, neither correct nor natural. Their right to be so considered was not automatically conceded as bringing a benefit of instantly recognisable worth; the concession was won only after considerable cultural struggle. And a vital part in the winning of this concession was the discrediting and eventual elimination of pre-existing, alternative and independent forms of working-class educational activity.

If the issue of how the working class 'ought' to have been behaving is set on one side in favour of a consideration of what they were actually *doing*, the picture which emerges is of patterns of school attendance which were characteristically shorter, less consistent and more fractured than those officially prescribed. The image of a small proportion of working-class children obtaining a 'proper' education has to be replaced with that of a much larger proportion receiving a much shorter and unapproved version. This would mean that the typical private school teacher would see a rapid turnover of pupils, keeping comparatively few for long periods, but handling a great many more individuals over time than the small weekly total at any single point would suggest. Rather in the way that figures of newspaper sales do not indicate the scale of the true readership, the impact of an individual private school upon the culture of the local community would have spread far beyond the limits conveyed by attendance figures at a given moment. Commenting on the total figure of 2,046,848 'ascertained scholars', in 1851, Horace Mann himself suggests that,

> if we have recourse to the opinions and experience of able writers and instructors on this point, the inference seems to be, that, while among the middle and upper classes the average time expended on their children's school-education is about six years, and average time amongst the labouring classes cannot much exceed four years. If this be so, the inference appears inevitable, that very few children are *completely* uninstructed; nearly all, at some time or another of their childhood, see the inside of a schoolroom . . .[60]

In Bristol, the existing statistics as they relate to attendance at private schools are as follows. The 1841 enquiry returned a total of 2,934 scholars at 212 dame schools (an average of nearly 14 pupils per school), and 1,127 at the 53 cheapest common day schools (an average of just over 21).[61] Together, these figures suggest that the minimum known attendance of working-class children at private schools in the city would not have been lower than 3,500. In 1851, using Horace Mann's assumption of an average attendance of 15, this total slumps to an estimated 1,890. The 1870 enquiry gives a total of 1,415 pupils in the 61 identified domestic adventure schools; an average of about 23 for each school, though the range — 61 in the largest school and 6 in the smallest — is large. Five years later, the investigations of the School Board produced a figure of 4,280 children at 160 schools; an average of nearly 27.

This information reinforces the fluctuating results which different official agencies tended to produce, but it does positively offer some indication of the size of most working-class private schools — something between 10 and 30 weekly pupils. But with no standard 'school life' with which to work, it is impossible to say just how many children received their education, or part of their education, at such places. Nor indeed can any firm comparison be made between the relative proportions of working-class children in private and publicly-aided or sponsored schools, for the possible sources of error and variation over time and place are infinite. The broadest indication which seems to accord least badly with the picture which emerges locally is that produced by the Newcastle

Commission in 1861. This indicated a ratio of attendance between the public and private sectors of about 2.8:1.[62]

In general, it seems that the extent of real decline in the tradition of working-class private schooling in the period from 1850 to 1875 was not dramatic. Indeed, in Bristol in 1875 — five years after the celebrated turning point of 1870 — the 4,280 pupils at private adventure schools in the city remained a full 24 per cent of the number attending elementary schools. However, attendance figures of various kinds can be adduced in a variety of ways to demonstrate this or that proposition. On the whole, they offer a considerably less satisfactory avenue of approach to the question of the scale of working-class private schooling than do the less problematical statistics of *schools* on which this chapter has concentrated principally. But throughout, the research has had to cope with a paradox. Historical enquiry, in just the same manner as the various statistical investigations of the nineteenth century, has to address the issues of scale and relative proportion. But the subject of enquiry declines, in its nature, to co-operate with a counting of heads designed essentially to enumerate very particular educational forms which were officially sponsored, operated and regulated. In a sense, the statistical positivism of the nineteenth century and the institution of public elementary schooling shared their origins in the same moral culture. But the working-class private school was a product of a different culture and its operation could not be simply statistically apprehended in this way. To suppose that it could makes scarcely more sense than to imagine that such schools should have generated their own statistical surveys of themselves. They belonged to a quite different tradition. And the statistics which exist, and which from necessity we have to work with, were produced only by violating or ignoring this fact.

Notes

1. But see P. McCann, 'Elementary Education in England and Wales on the Eve of the 1870 Education Act', *J.E.A.H.*, vol. II (1969), pp. 20–9; W. B. Stephens, *Regional Variations in Educational during the Industrial Revolution 1780–1870* (Leeds, 1973); N. Ball, 'Elementary School Attendance and Voluntary Effort before 1870', *History of Education*, vol. 2 (1973), pp. 19–34; W. R. Hamilton, 'Popular Education in England and Wales before and after the Elementary Education Act of 1870', *J.S.S.*, vol. 46 (1883), pp. 283–340; M. E. Sadler and J. W. Edwards, 'Some Statistics of Elementary Education in 1833', in *Special Reports on Education Subjects*, vol. 2 (1898), pp. 434–544. Also Sadler and Edwards, 'Public Elementary

Education in England and Wales 1870–1895', in *Special Reports on Educational Subjects* (1896–7), pp. 1–71.

2. See E. G. West, *Education and the Industrial Revolution* (1975), esp. Ch. 7. But also McCann, cited earlier, in *J.E.A.H.*

3. 'Statistics of Education in Bristol', *J.S.S.*, vol. 4 (1841), pp. 252–3. This was part of a critique of the approach of the Manchester Society; 'the Manchester Statistical Society, in their "Report on the State of Education" in the borough . . . state that "the whole number of children between the ages of 5 and 15 being estimated at 50,000 (or one-fourth of the whole population) whilst the number of children between the same ages under instruction amount only to 33,000, it would appear that one-third of the population between 5 and 15 *are receiving no instruction whatever*". The same mode of estimating the ratio of the instructed and uninstructed has been adopted by the Society in their Reports on Salford, Bury and Liverpool, but there is an obvious fallacy in it which vitiates the conclusion. It is implied (though not so expressed) that, because the number of children between the ages of 5 and 15 under instruction at any one time falls considerably short of the whole number of children between those ages, the residue . . . are at the same moment *altogether uninstructed*.'

4. P.R.O. H.O. 107/1951.

5. See Chapter 3.

6. *Select Committee*, p. vii.

7. P.P. 1843 [431] xiv, *C.E.C., Appendix to Second Report of the Commissioners. (Trades and Manufactures)*, Part 1, p. c69.

8. P.P. 1843 [432] xv, *C.E.C., Appendix to Second Report of Commissioners. (Trades and Manufactures*), Part 2, p. M29.

9. *Education Census*, pp. xliv–xlvi.

10. *The Times*, 28.3.1861.

11. *Newcastle*, vol. 1, p. 79. The total number of all private schools — of whatever social class — was 34,412. We can assume that the 68.95 per cent of this number in which the highest weekly fee was between 2d and 6d were utilised by the working class. To this must be added a proportion of the next 16.57 per cent in which the highest charge ranged between 7d and 1s. See p. 75. Horace Mann was not unaware of the wide gap between the Commission's findings on this subject and his own. 'The Royal Commissioners . . . compare the number of children in private schools (for the working class) at two-thirds of the whole, (i.e. 860,000), viz., 573,536. I have ventured to prefer an estimate based upon facts ascertained at the Census of 1851.' *J.S.S.*, (March 1862), p. 51. It is not clear from this what 'facts' Mann was referring to, but he probably had in mind his 'rough attempt to classify according to efficiency the 29,425 private schools which sent returns'. See *Education Census*, p. xxxiii.

12. *Hansard*, 18 October 1876, col. 933. Also see Sandon's comments on the same subject, 28 July 1876, col. 26. Here he is recorded as saying that there were 40,000 private adventure schools. This is almost certainly an error; the figure was more likely to be 4,000. It is also worth noting that he went on to say there were '1,450,000 children to be accounted for' (i.e. not at school). 'he thought they could not account for them even in the private adventure schools . . . .' In 1866, H. A. Bruce put attendance at schools outside public control — 'indifferent schools' — at 800,000. 'Address on Education' in *Transactions of the National Association for the Promotion of Social Science* (1867), p. 60.

13. The 1870 return was called for in Section 8 of the Act. See Chapter 6.

14. *Education Census*, p. clviii.

15. 'Statistics of Education in Bristol', *J.S.S.* (October 1841), pp. 250–63. See also an earlier publication, *Statistics of Popular Education in Bristol* (Bristol, 1837).

16. Cumin, *Newcastle*, vol. 3, pp. 21–212.

17. *Bristol Times and Mirror*, 24.12.1870, p. 2. Cited in R. Nutter, 'A Study of the Implementation of the 1870 Education Act in Bristol with a Special Reference to the Newfoundland Road Area', unpublished Bristol Dip. Ed., 1965, pp. 6–8.

18. See *Western Daily Press*, 30.10.1875, p. 8.

19. *Population Census (England and Wales) 1871*, vol. 3, pp. 332, 336. This number includes only teachers over 20.

20. For the methods employed in deriving these statistics, see Appendix A.

21. This point is made by Richard Johnson, in Sutherland *et al.*, *Education in Britain*, p. 10.

22. *Education Census*, p. xxxiii.

23. Hurt argues that nineteenth century bureaucrats calculated that the proportion of the population for whom education should not be supplied — the middle and upper classes — was one-seventh. *Elementary Schooling and the Working Classes* (1979), p. 5.

24. *Education Census*, p. xciv. See Goldstrom, 'Education in England and Wales in 1851: the Education Census of Great Britain', in R. Lawton (ed.), *The Census and Social Structure* (1978), pp. 224–40. Goldstrom sees the principal weakness of the Education Census as *over*-estimating the number of private schools, for many of them were 'little more than child-minding establishments . . . The enumerators must have had great difficulty in distinguishing between a school and such an establishment . . .', p. 227. But in all probability this qualitative prejudice against private schools would have led to a quantitative *under*-estimation.

25. See E. A. Wrigley (ed.), *Nineteenth Century Society: Essays in the use of Quantitative Methods for the Study of Social Data* (Cambridge, 1972), esp. M. Drake, 'The Census 1801–1891', pp. 7–46; P. M. Tillott, 'Sources of Inaccuracy in the 1851 and 1861 Censuses', pp. 82–133; M. Anderson, 'Standard Tabulation Procedues for the Census Enumerators' Books 1851–1891', pp. 134–45; B. I. Coleman, 'The Incidence of Education in Mid-century', pp. 397–410.

26. P.R.O. H.O. 107/1947.

27. P.R.O. H.O. 107/1951.

28. A copy of this form is reproduced in *Education Census*, pp. cii–civ.

29. P.R.O. R.G. 10/2524.

30. *Education Census*, p. xciv.

31. See *1851 Census (Great Britain) Report*, part 2, vol. 1, pp. ccxviii–ccxix. 'The return of scholars here given — derived from the statements of the householders respecting their children — will, from various causes, generally differ, more or less, from the returns of the *Educational* Census.' But also see p. lxxxix. Also Edward Baines, 'On our Past Educational Improvement and the Means of Future Progress, especially in Lengthening the Term of Education', in A. Hill, *Essays upon Educational Subjects* (1857, rep. 1971), p. 53. The shortfall in the numbers of scholars under 15 in the Population Census (2,046,848) — 135,893 — is about 6 per cent of the total. In reality it was rather greater. In the first place, the returns of scholars *under five* from the Population Census — and which are included in the above equation — are undoubtedly too small. This is because the Census Office's processing procedures did not take account of the instructions which it had itself issued to heads of households. The Schedule clearly instructs that, 'Against the names of children above 5 years of age, if daily attending school, or receiving tuition . . . at home, write "Scholar" and in the latter case add "at home".' *Report*, p. cxxxviii. Following this, many parents would not have returned scholars *under* five, as such. To allow for this, the under-five cohort needs to be deleted from both censuses to ensure that like is being compared with like. Comparison then of the 5 to 15 cohort gives 1,955,377 for the Population Census and 1,768,231 for the Education Census — a shortfall of 187,146, or about 10.5 per cent.

32. *Education Census*, p. xciv.

33. Ibid., Refusal was considerably more common in the Education Enquiry of 1870. See *Bristol Times and Mirror*, 24.12.1870.
34. *Education Census*, p. xiv.
35. Ibid.
36. Cumin, *Newcastle*, vol. 3, p. 4.
37. Ibid., pp. 38–9.
38. 'Bristol', *J.S.S.* (October 1841), p. 250.
39. Ibid. More generally, some nineteenth-century reporters were uneasy about the level of suspicion which their enquiries met, feeling perhaps that it reflected upon their own capacities. Most, however, seem to have interpreted it in the same way that they understood the schools themselves — that is, with a mixture of condescension and disgust. The degree of distrust on the part of school-keepers was often great. In Salford, for example, 'Many of the mistresses thought it necessary to consult a prudent neighbour, and sometimes required his presence, before they would venture to answer any questions, or suffer their School to be inspected.' 'Report of a Committee of the Manchester Statistical Society on the State of Education in the Borough of Salford in 1835', *M.S.S.* (1836), p. 11. Also 'Report of a Committee of the Manchester Statistical Society on the State of Education in the Borough of Liverpool in 1835–1836', *M.S.S.* (1836), p. 4. 'The difficulties alluded to were greater than those which had occurred in the case of Manchester and Salford, . . . almost all originated in the same cause, viz., a distrust, on the part of those from whom information was sought, on the motives and objects of the enquiries . . .' See also 'Report of a Committee of the Manchester Statistical Society on the State of Education in the Township of Pendleton', *J.S.S.*, vol. 2 (1839), p. 73; 'Report on the State of Education in the Borough of Kingston-upon-Hull', *J.S.S.*, vol. 4 (1841), p. 156; 'Report of the Education Committee of the Statistical Society of London on the Borough of Finsbury', *J.S.S.*, vol. 6 (1843), p. 28. It has to be pointed out that this lack of co-operation was not restricted just to school-keepers. Investigators often found the same reaction in parents and children. 'I could not induce some of them (pit-boys) to come near me; others replied to my questions, however good humouredly put, with sullen abruptness.' P.P. 1842 [382] xvii, *C.E.C., Appendix to First Report (Mines)*, Part II, p. 11. Also P.P. 1842 [381] xvi, *C.E.C., Appendix to First Report (Mines)*, Part I, p. 539. '. . . from the suspicion and ignorance of pit people, it appeared to them as a natural, and indeed inevitable, conclusion that a stranger . . . deputed by government to inquire into their earnings and the nature of their work, sojourning in their rarely-visited villages . . . and perpetually committing to writing the precise words of the putters . . . that all the evidence they gave would be turned against themselves. It was in vain that I went in the evenings from house to house, explained the objects of my mission, read to them my instructions, and combated [*sic*] their objections; vague suspicions still lurked in their minds . . .'; also ibid., p. 527. For some of the other practical problems faced by the Statistical Societies in the gathering of data, see 'Report on the State of Education in Birmingham, By the Birmingham Statistical Society for the Improvement of Education', *J.S.S.*, vol. 3 (1840), p. 25; 'Hull', *J.S.S.*, vol. 4 (1841), p. 156; 'Report of a Committee of the Manchester Statistical Society on the State of Education in the County of Rutland in the year 1838', *J.S.S.*, vol. 2 (1839), p. 303. 'It is impossible to expect accuracy in returns obtained by circulars, various constructions being put upon the same question by different individuals . . .'; 'Finsbury', *J.S.S.* (February 1843), p. 28, 'the extreme difficulty of procuring agents, at once sufficiently active and trustworthy for so confidential and laborious an employment'.
40. 'Bristol', *J.S.S.* (October 1841), p. 256.
41. Ibid., pp. 254, 259.
42. The more general designation for this type of school in other reports was

'middling school'.

43. *Education Census*, p. xx. But see J. Lawson and H. Silver, *A Social History of Education in England* (1973), p. 280. 'Dame and private-venture schools declined in numbers in the 1830's and 1840's, but continued to provide a large quantity of poor quality education.'

44. 'Fifth Report and Summary of the Education Committee of the Statistical Society of London', *J.S.S.* (August 1843), p. 216.

45. *Bristol Times and Mirror*, 24.12.1870. Two additional denominational schools were also included in this category. Also note this important remark by H. M. I. Barry on the 1870 returns in Somerset. '218 private schools, with very few exceptions under female teachers, were returned to the Department. Many more such schools were not returned . . . Some of these schools declined inspection, and several were mysteriously closed on the day of inspection.' *C.E.C.* (1873–4), p. 61.

46. P.R.O. R.G. 10/2509; R.G. 10/2520.

47. P.R.O. R.G. 10/2520.

48. P.R.O. R.G. 10/2560.

49. P.R.O. R.G. 9/1750.

50. See Chapter 4.

51. P.R.O. R.G. 10/2505.

52. P.R.O. R.G. 10/2557.

53. P.R.O. Ed. 3/23; R.G. 10/580–584.

54. P.R.O. Ed. 3/23; R.G. 10/583.

55. See Chapter 6.

56. Bristol School Board, *Review of Proceedings* (Jan.–Dec. 1875), p. 6

57. The theory of mushroom growth after the 1870 Act — and in particular with the powers of compulsory attendance which the Act placed in the hands of the School Boards — is an attractive one for opponents of the working-class private school. It conceives the large numbers of these schools as a desperate short-term response to the unwanted problems brought by compulsion. In other words, as an escape from the responsibilities of legitimate educational provision through a spurious surrogate. But the mushroom growth theory simply ignores that working-class private schooling was, as it had been throughout the century, an important and persistent educational force, immediately *before* as well as after the 1870 Act. See Chapter 6.

58. For instance, see G. Bartley, *The Schools for the People* (1871), p. 403.

59. P.R.O. Ed. 3/16.

60. *Education Census*, p. xxx. Also see David Vincent, *Bread, Knowledge and Freedom* (1981), p. 94.

61. 'Bristol', *J.S.S.* (October 1841), p. 259.

62. *Newcastle*, vol. 1, p. 79.

3 PARENT CULTURE

Thus far, we have considered the nomenclature and numerical extent of working-class private schooling in the nineteenth century. The present chapter will try to locate the tradition within the broader context of working-class culture, and to establish the links between the two, especially in terms of working-class educational demand. How did the working-class private school appear to those who made use of it? Why did many parents choose it in preference to the public alternative? How did the working-class private school accommodate itself to the daily exigencies of poverty, uncertainty and material deprivation?

The first point to be made is that for probably most working people, whether in town or village, the working-class private school — to a far greater extent than its public counterpart — was a very familiar part of everyday life. Where parents in the mid-nineteenth century had personal experience of schooling as children themselves, the likelihood was that it would have been gained at a small private school. For example, a witness to the Children's Employment Commission of 1842 commented of the state of popular education 50 years earlier, that 'then as now, the poor boy was sent down below at the age of 6 to 8 . . . Previous to going down the pit, his education, when he had any, generally consisted of a little reading got from the village school-mistress.'[1] And contemporary accounts speak repeatedly and despairingly of both the large numbers and the ubiquity of working-class private schools. Leonard Horner, a Factory Inspector with an abiding interest in popular education — which he frequently expressed in his reports — wrote in 1846 of, 'the ordinary run of those miserable mock schools, to be found everywhere, in which a mass of children of all ages . . . are crammed together . . . with an old man or an old woman sitting in the midst of them'.[2] Many of those who gave evidence to the earlier reports of the Children's Employment Commission refer to the existence of dames' schools in industrial centres as commonplace. The manager of Bilson Coal Works and Iron Mines, for example: 'There are numerous dames-schools in the neighbourhood';[3] 'In north Wales, Mr. H. H. Jones states that the children . . . "Have few opportunities of obtaining any education whatever''. There are indeed everywhere dame-schools, though under no guidance but that of the teachers.'[4] 'The means of education in Alston parish are extensive: there is the grammar school . . .; there is a charity-school, and a school kept by a master on his own account; there is the school of the London Lead Company at Nenthead . . . There is a school at Garrigill Gate, and one at Tynehead, and another at Leadgate; there are also many dame-schools and 10 Sunday-schools.'[5] At Oldham, 'There is only one small public day-school in the whole parish and neighbourhood for the labouring classes . . .; the only other day-schools being, with few exceptions, petty dame-schools of the poorest description . . .' At Willenhall, 'We have no schools in this part of the Parish except ordoniary [*sic*] Dame Schools for the week days . . .'[6] As late as 1870, George Bartley could write that 'There is scarcely an alley or court in the crowded districts of London and the larger towns in which a Dame may not be found'; 'the growth of Private Schools for the children of the working classes during the last half-century has been very great'.[7] Working-class private schools existed in numbers difficult or impossible to quantify, almost everywhere and frequently unknown other than by chance encounter, like that related by the traveller Paul Hawkins Fisher in 1871;

> When the writer was on horseback in a part of the Cotteswold range with which he was unacquainted, he dismounted at a cottage, to inquire his way; and on opening the door he found it was a school for children. The mistress was walking backward and forward, spinning some clothier's wool into yarn and performing her scholastic duties at the same time. A boy was in the act of reading his lesson aloud to her. . .'[8]

Such schools existed wherever and whenever there was a sufficient local demand for them. The nature of this demand was however a very specific one which middle-class investigators failed fully to appreciate. Most of them initially regarded it as a basically laudable quality. But underlying this was the implicit notion that as new provided public schools gradually spread throughout the country, their evident superiority over private schools would be universally recognised, and working-class demand would simply be converted away from an old and inefficient form to a new and progressive one. It was soon discovered however that the issue was not as straightforward as this. Working-class attachment to private schools was tenacious. In March 1861, *The Times* gave voice to the concern that this caused for middle-class opinion;

> It might have been supposed that the impetus given to education in the public schools belonging to the religious bodies would have been the means of reducing the number of scholars in private adventure schools . . . On the whole, however, the proportion of scholars in private schools to the total number of week-day scholars remains much the same as it was in 1818, 1833 and 1851.[9]

Patrick Cumin reported to the Newcastle Commission that in three of the five areas he examined, 'it seems a remarkable fact the [between 1851 and 1859] the proportion of children who attend public schools, as compared with those who attend private schools, instead of increasing, has actually diminished . . . Amongst the mass of the people, I found no great readiness to abandon the private for the public school.'[10] And even after the 1870 Act, George Bartley could write that 'In spite of the competition which must have existed since the creation of the Education Department between State-aided and Private Schools, the latter do not appear to have diminished as rapidly as might have been expected.'[11]

Investigators were therefore obliged to consider more deeply the exact nature of working-class demand for this type of schooling. It was an issue that would not simply go away, and which could not go on being ignored. But, given the dominant professional assumptions of working-class educational incompetence on the one hand, and the allegedly transparent superiority of the publicly provided schools on the other, it was a problem which commentators found hard to handle. The fact that this was a period before any form of general compulsion had been introduced — and that the fees at private schools were usually higher than those of public schools — compounded the difficulty further. Quite simply, for middle-class educationists, working-class attachment to the schools was a puzzle, and an embarrassing and inconvenient one. For a few writers, it was inexplicable: 'The colliers of Mold . . . are not in other repects a class of people who are regarded as slow to perceive what is to their interest, so I am at a loss how to account for the encouragement which they have been in the habit of giving to those nurseries of ignorance.'[12] Most, however, were not slow to offer their personal theories, however tenuous, speculative or generally unconvincing. These fall into two general categories which might be described as those adducing essentially negative reasons, and those highlighting more positive reasons. In practice, however, arguments from both categories were frequently jumbled together in a way which underlines the ignorance, uncertainty and cultural distance of investigators. These groups of explanatory theories need to be looked at closely.

Immeasurably the larger and more influential group was that founded upon negative explanations of working-class behaviour. There were three trump cards in the group, and they were played over and over again throughout the nineteenth-century official reports with such persistence and regularity that it is hard to believe that they were anything less than self-evident truths. The explanations offered by each of the three centred upon apathy, ignorance and status.

'Apathy' was a concept quite generally favoured in the middle-class comprehension of many forms of working-class behaviour. In so far as it could be made to fit the education issue, 'apathy' was most suited to explaining why public elementary schools were under-utilised by the working class. Such explanations naturally conceived this negatively, as a shortcoming of popular demand, rather than as a positive disenchantment with the quality and character of supply.[13] However, 'apathy' was clearly of limited appeal in the case of working-class private schools which demonstrated, by their very existence, the presence of a specific educational demand. This did not, however, entirely rule out its use by those who chose to ignore or disqualify such demand. David Stow, for example, argued that 'We have always advocated large government grants for the moral and intellectual training of the young, knowing that otherwise the people would never educate themselves.'[14] Bartley felt that to induce the working class to 'receive an advantage which now they do not appreciate and would in many cases rather be without, is one of the greatest difficulties which will have to be removed'.[15] Assistant Commissioner Coode held that middle-class philanthropy alone could advance the cause of popular education, 'forcing it and almost imposing it upon indifferent or reluctant recipients'. He continued: 'By no sudden process of self-development has any community ever been known to start from ignorance to knowledge — from brutality to civility . . . The working population has shown no inborn or spontaneous power of self-improvement.'[16] This particular generalisation does not seem to relate very well to Coode's own statistical return for his district, which showed that 42 per cent of children in regular attendance used private instead of public schools.[17] Neither do such views accord with the reports of parental concern and interest which many accounts indicate. Assistant Commissioner Winder, for example, felt that, 'Speaking generally . . . the poor are keenly anxious that their children should be "got on"';[18] Assistant Commissioner Hare talked of 'the anxiety of parents for the instruction of their children';[19] and Cumin 'found it difficult to get parents however poor, to say that education was of no use to their children'.[20] Some of the agents of the Statistical Societies made similar observations:

> With few exceptions, the working classes in Hull seem to have a just appreciation of the value of education, as well those parents who have been deprived of the advantages of instruction, as those who have been more favourably circumstanced. Even in cases where the children were not obtaining instruction, there were few parents who did not speak of the circumstance with regret.[21]

Where the direct voice of the working-class parent itself survives, such generalisations are not merely endorsed, but are returned to the real contexts of poverty and hardship within, and in spite of which, demand was generated.

> The wife of a dyer, mother of seven children, expressed herself thus:- 'We senden them to school a bit, when we can afford it; but there's too mony folk i' th' warld — poor folk canna live, let alone clothing and larning. I canna, for shame, to let children go out, let alone going to school. But it's a weary thing when people canna read. It's a blessed fine thing to be a good scholar'.[22]

And John Gordon, a Lancashire miner, spoke to the Children's Employment Commission of a general parental desire for the education of their children, 'but they are prevented by the scantiness of what they earn; and he himself has paid for the day-schooling of his children, each for a short time, when he could ill afford it. Thinks that there are more people than formerly who would make sacrifices to get "learning" for their children, to make them a comfort to their old age and not merely an advantage for their youth.'[23]

Explanations of the working-class private school solely through the concept of 'apathy' were clearly inadequate and were recognised as such by most contemporary commentators. Consequently, far greater explanatory weight was attached to the concept of 'ignorance', the close relative of 'apathy' in deprivation theory, though sometimes the two were harnessed together to form a powerful ritualistic insult; for example, 'Amidst much of apathy and ignorance, it is cheering to find occasional examples of a contrary character';[24] and again, 'undoubtedly the strongest reason for the continued existence of so many worthless private schools is the extraordinary ignorance and indifference of the parents'.[25]

'Ignorance' alone was in this context a less powerful notion than apathy, because it was obliged to concede partially the existence of a degree of independent working-class educational demand. But having acknowledged this, 'ignorance' theories achieved their impact by arguing that such demand, though perhaps praiseworthy in its initial expression, was not mature or intelligent enough to prevent itself from being tricked into disreputable and harmful practical forms. Thus for example, 'It was impossible not to respect the motives of several parents for sending their children to these schools in preference to the inspected ones; for, exhibiting often ignorance and prejudice, they at least equally showed parental care and thoughtfulness very pleasing to find.'[26] It is important to appreciate both the general explanatory pretension and the wide, talismanic appeal of the notion of working-class ignorance which lay behind this kind of analysis. Brougham, for example, warned that 'the ignorance of the people [is] the origin of all the worst ills that prey upon our social system'.[27] Similarly, Kay-Shuttleworth, though he saw the working class as 'victims of their own ignorance', was principally concerned with such ignorance as a contaminating disease 'capable of corrupting the whole body of society'.[28] Working-class ignorance, with all its anti-social behavioural manifestations and its ramifications for the whole of civilised society itself, could be dammed back only by a comprehensive programme of rational schooling as 'the means of rescuing the great body of the people from the slough of ignorance'.[29]

Ignorance in choosing a school was not a specific or separable cultural phenomenon to be rectified by limited corrective measures; rather it was a logical manifestation of a culture which was, in its totality, brutalised, deficient and dangerous. In the same way, accusations of juvenile ignorance were only partially concerned with the absence of basic knowledge and skills; their central thrust was against an entire moral culture. 'Ignorance' was, in this sense, not just an instrumental and resolvable obstacle in the path of the march of progress, but a blade at the throat of civilisation itself. This was evident whether commentators ostensibly confined themselves to 'education as knowledge' — 'I almost tremble . . . when I contemplate the fearful deficiency of knowledge existing throughout the district (the Potteries), and the consequences likely to result';[30] or more openly to 'education as moral regulation':

> A lower condition of morals, in the fullest sense of the term, could not, I think, be found. I do not mean by this that there are many more prominent vices among them, but that moral feelings and sentiments do not exist among the children and young persons of Willenhall. They *have* no morals . . . [They] are in a state of utter confusion on all religious subjects when not in absolute darkness. They do not display the remotest sign of comprehension as to what is meant by the term of morals.[31]

For most commentators, the evils of illiteracy and immorality were inextricably bound together in the pervasive notion of ignorance itself. In this understanding, neither the educative achievements of the private schools, nor the particular working-class demand which they answered, could diminish this ignorance, for both were indeed themselves products and symptoms of it. Conceived like this, ignorance could be treated only with a notion of 'education' on a broad scale which could go beyond 'mere instruction' to encompass the regulation of behaviour and attitude.

Once public education of this kind had been fully established, it would act both as an individual benefit for working people, and as a defence for society as a whole against future recontamination by an unregulated working-class moral culture. Most educationists in the mid-nineteenth century saw such a system as an attainable and realistic goal. Their writings are laden with anecdotal examples of the corrective powers of regular formal schooling, and are suffused with a general optimism for the properly schooled society of the future. But there was a weak link in this chain of prescribed educational progress. And that was the problem of inserting a formal education system with real regulatory power into a resisting working-class culture in the first place. To establish, in effect, the hegemony of the public school.

In this process, the key identified obstacle — against whom the experts waged an unending verbal war — was the working-class parent. Kay-Shuttleworth for instance told the Select Committee in 1838 that, 'I regret to say that the example of the parents is not such as those who hope for the improvement of the children would desire to exhibit as a model for them.' And the Manchester Statistical Society offered the opinion that, 'Much of all this evil must be charged on the parents who, ignorant themselves, and incompetent to appreciate the value of good instruction exercise little discrimination in their selection of a School, and are often the cause of the irregularity of their children.' The implication was clear. 'Ought', the report continued, 'the instruction of the rising generation to be left any longer to the sole caprice of such persons?'[32] Once in the classroom of the publicly provided school, the working-class child was, from the educationist's perspective, not seen as a great problem — though practising school teachers, then as now, would probably have disagreed. For the educational system-builders, the primary goal from which all else followed was to breach and to defeat the residual parental 'ignorance' which kept working-class children out of the public elementary schools; to break in on this particular vicious circle of working-class cultural deficiency.[33] And it was just this parental dereliction which allowed the private schools to exist in the first place. Such schools 'could not exist if the people . . . were capable of judging of the value of the article set up for sale, which they are not; for the parents of the children were themselves left to grow up in ignorance'.[34] The whole problem was very much 'the result of leaving education to voluntary exertions (with very insufficient assistance from the State) and to the "natural instinct and self-interest" of parents'.[35]

Educational improvement and expansion were then the inseparable companions of a profound and sustained drive towards moral and cultural reformation, without which 'it will be a long time, I fear, before the public mind is sufficiently advanced on the subject of education'.[36]

Between them, the notions of working-class apathy and ignorance did most of the work in the negative explanations of the popularity of the working-class private school — simply the miserable and misguided product of a miserable and misguided culture. The third — status — clearly operated from an opposite perspective to 'apathy' though it too could be made to fit quite well with 'ignorance'. For example, 'In spite of the evident inefficiency of these schools, they are undoubtedly popular with the poorer classes . . . Another reason why many patronise them is that, being styled "Private Seminaries", a strong opinion appears to be prevalent that they are "more genteel" than the National, or public Infant School.'[37] This is a persuasive and damning argument, as it was intended to be. Moreover, it strikes a familiar chord in our modern understanding of the *raison d'être* of the contemporary private school. But benefits of this kind were not the ones which working-class private schooling could offer. What the nineteenth-century working class sought was not something *more* than that offered by the publicly provided schools, but something *other* than it.

Until the 1870s, private schools existed for all social classes, but it would be a mistake to suppose that beyond the condition of their privateness, the various types of school had much in common. This study is centrally concerned with the most lowly of the schools — those used by the working class — and has already faced some of the difficulties of distinguishing these from other, more exalted types. The issue of 'status' presents a similar difficulty, most obviously in connection with the distinction that was drawn earlier between the working-class private school and the lower middle-class school into which it shaded around the 9d per week mark. In the latter type, the question of gentility and enhanced status and the necessity of maintaining a social distance from the educational institutions provided specifically for the working class, were likely to have been factors of considerable importance.[38] An article written in 1873 by 'A Riverside Visitor' illustrated this point forcibly. The author referred to 'the majority' of schools declared under the Enquiry of 1870 to be 'inefficient' as ' "Private Adventure Schools", which means, as a rule, Dames' Schools'.

> The schools are of various kinds, from the 'respectably situated' and genteel 'Establishment for Young Ladies', which boldly hangs its banner — in the shape of a brass plate — upon the outer wall . . . down to the humbler type, whose whereabouts is a bye street or a poor quarter, and whose modest announcement of 'A Da School Kep here', is scrawled upon a half-sheet of note-paper exhibited in the window . . . To the different types of the schools, go different classes of children . . . Unfortunately for the interests of popular education, there are many parents

> . . . who, sinking all reference to the essential question of the education to be obtained, and deciding solely upon grounds of what they choose to consider gentility, prefer low-priced and inefficient 'Adventure' Schools, simply that they may be able to say, 'My children go to a private, or 'a Young Ladies' School', not a public school that 'all sorts of *common* children go to'.[39]

However, schools trading on the aspirations of respectability and upward mobility in this way appear to have been a minority of those inspected for the Enquiry of 1870. This is evident from those returns which survive from that investigation.[40] Indirect evidence drawn from local directories also points in the same direction. Schools oriented towards the more status-conscious, lower middle-class end of the scale — 'brass plate schools' — would certainly have been the most likely to further enhance their appeal through a listing in local directories. In Bristol there were, in 1870, 61 recorded private adventure schools with fees of less than 9d per week; and of these, just eight, or slightly more than 13 per cent are to be found in the Kelly's Post Office Directory for that year. Of these, three are listed as 'Preparatory School', and one each day as 'Day School', 'Private School', 'Girls' School', 'Young Ladies' Establishment' and 'Seminary'. Certainly, the main body of lower middle-class schools was untouched by the 1870 Enquiry, and, unlike their working-class counterparts, they survived the storms of the 1870s and continued to flourish, substantially unmolested by local or central authority, well into the twentieth century. Their continuing role as a genteel alternative to public elementary schooling was a fundamentally different one to that carried out by the working-class private school. This is expressed, once more, in the words of 'A Riverside Visitor': 'The less pretentious kind of Dame's School chiefly differs from the brass-plate kind in that it *is* less pretentious, otherwise they are pretty equal in their inefficiency.' Far from associating working-class private schools with gentility, H.M.I. Kennedy felt indeed that they were more suited to the 'many poor children of the "residuum" who can hardly be received, with advantage to the school, among the decent and tidy scholars of many of the public elementary schools'.[41]

'Status', understood as genteel pretension, was never an important consideration in the functioning of the working-class private school. Its value to working-class culture was of an entirely practical kind. However, to middle-class investigators, the idea of an education founded upon gentility and refinement was one to which they themselves subscribed and adhered in the education of their own children. It was therefore a known and understood motivation, and it is not surprising that they should have sought to apply it in some way to account for a cultural phenomenon that was otherwise hard to explain. But the central problem with 'gentility' was that it simply did not fit with the other commonly favoured strands in conventional middle-class analyses of the working-class school — factors like squalor, overcrowding, carelessness, brutality and the general absence of facilties. How could the idea of gentility or enhanced social status be seriously linked with what Nassau Senior called 'these dens of ignorance and malaria' to which 'one-third of the labouring classes still send their children . . . although good and cheap public schools are at their doors'.[42] In truth, it could not be. What commentators were referring to when they talked of 'gentility' was the frustrating existence of a stubborn working-class spirit which capriciously rejected the officially prescribed forms of schooling. When Assistant Commissioner Wilkinson wrote: 'there is a strong and wide-spread preference among the poor of London for private over public schools partly because the former are more *genteel* . . .', he was, in effect, attempting to comprehend, through terms which were sensible to his own understanding, a current of working-class cultural independence which presented itself as a kind of class insubordination.[43]

Accusations of 'gentility' as an explanation of working-class behaviour were a particularly powerful and emotive leaven with which to strengthen otherwise unconvincing accounts, but beyond this, the concept was worth very little. This explains why it was so rarely used on its own. Instead, it was usually flung in as part of an ill-assorted explanatory catalogue. Thus, for example, Wilkinson's remarks, given above, continue: 'partly because the same regularity of attendance is not required'; and Senior's explanation, which begins, 'They (the labouring classes) think . . . the public school vulgar . . .', goes on, 'or their boy has been punished there, or he is required to be clean, or to be regular, or the private school is half a street nearer, or is kept by a friend, or by someone who will submit his teaching to their dictation'.[44]

The latter part of Senior's list begins to tackle the genuinely important reasons for working-class use of private schools — and by implication, for the rejection of the public alternative — but, as is often the case in such accounts, these are left unamplified and their considerable implications are left undeveloped.

'Apathy', 'ignorance', 'status' — these are the common negative explanations of working-class behaviour which, though flawed and inaccurate, confidently inhabit the pages of the official investigations of popular elementary education. The many *positive* explanations — those which do not unthinkingly ridicule or execrate an independent working-class culture — are buried or obscured. Nevertheless, even in the most hostile of reports, these can usually be unearthed, developed and evaluated, as they should have been at the time. These 'positive' explanations will now be considered.

What is particularly important about such explanations is their revelation of a coherent series of related educational demands. These challenge any easy or general assumption of a brutal and ignorant popular culture devoid of any independent educational character, upon — and into — which a corrective schooling system could be introduced only from above. Moreover, these demands were not the result of idealised programmes developed away from the economic constraints and outside the cultural experience of the working class. They were in fact shaped by these very contexts, and as such, they represented a genuinely alternative working-class approach to childhood learning to that prescribed by the education experts.

Above all, working-class private schooling offered to its users a degree of power and control over both the content and organisation of education, which was entirely absent in the publicly provided alternative. It was a matter of the greatest irritation to inspectors and investigators — the custodians of 'correct' educational theory — that the private schools were quite beyond their powers of regulation. They were, in fact, out of control. And it was clear where the control actually lay. 'In these schools, the teachers have no authority to consult, they have no one else to please . . . their faults and their merits alike arise from a desire to meet the exact demands which the parents make . . . Accordingly, they find out what parents like and how best to fill the school.'[45] Private schools were 'popular with the poorer classes . . . chiefly because they are kept by persons in their own station of life, and over whom they seem to exercise a certain amount of control'.[46]

An important element in determining this high level of control was a financial one. In a period before any legal general compulsion, school attendance of any kind was a matter of individual choice, but the private school, unlike its public rival, depended entirely on the payment of weekly fees and could not survive financially without responding closely to local demand. But it would be wrong to view the payment of fees as the only, or indeed the paramount link between teacher and parent, or, more accurately, between school and home. The school was by no means obliged, through financial dependence, to follow educational aims and methods which it might otherwise have abandoned for more enlightened or 'advanced' alternatives. The connection was more subtle and complex, the school, and usually the teacher, being themselves the products of the culture which they served. In the pit villages of Northumberland and Durham, for example,

> The schoolmaster . . . is generally one from the people themselves . . . His education and mental training have not been of that kind to raise him above the prejudices, passions, and moral feebleness (if the expression will be allowed) of his own class. From such a man, therefore, little improvement in the tone of thought and feeling of pitmen, can be expected. He cannot, because he does not know them, nor feel them himself, be expected to infuse into the minds of his pupils, those new feelings and principles which are essential for the improvement of this class of labourers.[47]

But as far as the working-class recipients of private schooling were concerned, such teachers represented familiar and trusted values. In most cases they were themselves local people, the friends and neighbours of those who used their schools. And as such they could often have significant value to local communities beyond simply the education of their children. References of this kind are difficult to find, and their typicality is impossible to establish. Some, however, are particularly interesting and are worth recording. In the rare instances when working people needed the skills of a practised scribe, it seems that a neighbourhood private teacher would have been likely to have been called upon. 'At Ipswich, for example, I became acquainted with one whose general intelligence enabled him, not only to keep a day and an evening school, but also to conduct the correspondence of persons who are no scholars, and to make the wills of testators.'[48] And of the 'dames' of Portsmouth, 'A few can write with a fair hand, and do write letters for the neighbours at 2d., or for a long letter 3d., or for an Admiralty letter

6d.'[49] As the possessor and transmitter of valued knowledge and skills, a teacher might be accorded a position of political or social esteem and influence within a local community. According to the Viewer of Killingsworth Colliery in the early 1840s, for example, 'In strikes the few men who may be educated may happen to be the most mischievous, and schoolmasters themselves have led the men on in strikes.'[50] Elsewhere, teachers might retain a local prominence as a sort of oracular authority — a repository of all kinds of scarce and valued knowledge. This was essentially a remnant of the social organisation of an older, pre-industrial age. In 1842, Jellinger Symons recorded that, 'a dame's school is the only school in the scattered and populous district of which Highgreen [Yorkshire] is the centre . . . The only additional instruction was afforded by an old cripple who is *wiseman* of the country, named West, and who not only tells fortunes but who is widely famed for supernatural craft touching missing bodies, stolen goods and stray pigs.'[51]

Close and informal relationships between parents and private teachers were viewed with particular concern by the experts. They were seen at best as irrelevant, and at worst, as intensely damaging to the cause of 'real' or 'genuine' education. 'Frequently, the preference [in choosing a school] is determined by friendship for the master or mistress . . .'[52] 'Some [parents] would rather help and trust a neighbour of their own grade, than place their children under the care of a stranger and superior.'[53] 'The teacher of the adventure school has a personal following. She is probably related to half her neighbours.'[54] Fee-paying — the only formal link between teacher and parent — was itself mediated by their social and cultural closeness. This might involve the individual alteration, or occasionally suspension, of set fees, the extension of credit, or sometimes schooling in exchange for goods or services in kind. An arrangement of particular interest was described by G. R. Porter in 1837:

> The sum paid for schooling [by working families in a district of St Marylebone] appears to be unusually large considering the condition of the parents; the average weekly payment for each scholar, where regular payments are made, being 5¼d. There is a school in the court, attended by about fifty scholars, held in a room twelve feet square, and eight and half feet high, which is the sole dwelling of the schoolmaster, his wife, and six children . . . The mode of payment to the teacher of this school is

> remarkable and characteristic. A kind of club, which does not consist exclusively of the parents of the scholars, meets every Saturday evening at a public-house; when, after some hours spent in drinking and smoking, a subscription is raised and handed over to the schoolmaster, who forms one of the company, and who is expected to spend a part of the money in regaling the subscribers.[55]

Working-class control over the schools had an important impact on the style and content of teaching and learning. But it also ensured that the schools were organised to accommodate other demands which had less to do with the development of cognitive skills themselves, than with the context in which they were gained. This required that the schools should be able to respond flexibly to the fluctuating though always constrained economic circumstances of everyday living and above all, that they should concentrate learning-time, when it could be afforded, upon basic instrumental skills, without the unwelcome and time-consuming element of moral regulation which formed a crucial part of the public school curriculum. Particularly valued, then, was the private school's characteristic absence of demands for formal discipline, regularity and order. The school fitted itself to the daily needs of family life and work by tolerating attendance of the most erratic and spasmodic kind. Thus: 'My own impression is that the vitality of these schools is owing, in great measure to the fact, as I believe, that the children can come and go when their parents choose.'[56] 'Above all, the liberty of sending or detaining the children when they like is much appreciated by many parents. To a poor and ignorant woman living in an irregular hand-to-mouth way, and accustomed to employ her children on trifling errands, or to yield weakly to their wishes, the discipline of a good public school, and the persistent enquiries after absentees are very irritating; she escapes all this by sending the children now and then whenever she can easily spare the money, to a so-called private school where no questions will be asked . . .'[57] 'Though in these as in other schools nine o'clock in the morning is nominally the time at which children should come in . . . they are dropping in all morning long, . . . while it is an hourly occurrence for mother unceremoniously to throw open the school door, and call out Johnny or Polly to run an errand.'[58]

For the teachers and managers of public schools, for whom regularity was one of the necessary conditions for an 'efficient' elementary education, this stuttering and unpredictable pattern of attendance was a cause of continual protest.[59] And most concentrated, once more, on a familiar target. 'Our chief hindrances are the neglect of parents, in not enabling the children to be punctual, and their evil example by which, for the most part, the best instructions, and even the most favourable impressions are quickly effaced.'[60] Robert Roberts, a teacher at a public school in the 1850s, recorded 'a great deal to fight against . . . Big boys, thoroughly ignorant, brutal in their manners, and disgusting in their habits; parents as ignorant and brutal who looked upon the schoolmaster as their natural enemy and resented his attempts at correcting their children's evil habits.'[61]

The close physical proximity of the school to its users — in the same street or court, or one within a minute or two's walking distance — clearly facilitated the subordination of the school to the demands of the local community. But more than this, it epitomised the close cultural link between home and school which the public system sought to break down. The traditions upon which the working-class private school was based did not seek to separate learning activity from other spheres of daily life. In the schools, learning was instead done within familiar domestic contexts and the daily transition from home to school required none of the disruptive changes of behaviour, demeanour and appearance which the public schools felt were essential preliminaries to effective education. Thus, 'attendance at private adventure schools is useless, not only because the children learn nothing, but also because discipline, order, cleanliness and decency are unknown'.[62] 'I have visited schools in which there has been a total absence of all attempt to introduce method or discipline — where constant disorder prevails, and where the children are permitted to attend without the slightest regulation as to cleanliness of dress or person.'[63] However, 'There is a distinct preference for the private school because the restraints of the public school, the attempt to enforce regular attendance and cleanliness are found to interfere inconveniently with the liberty of a disorderly home.'[64] 'Some [parents] obviously have a lazy liking for places where punctuality and cleanliness are not rigidly enforced, and to which an unwashed urchin may be sent without cap or bonnet.'[65] '. . . the parents will, in their ignorance, not value the schools according to the kind of instruction they give, but they will take into account whether they are allowed to break the rules or not. They resist the discipline of our schools to a surprising extent; they do not like the obligation of attending at fixed hours, and conforming to rules, having clean dress and short or tidy hair.'[66]

The popular attraction of the working-class private schools which disturbed commentators even more, was perhaps not so much the lack of physical, as of moral, hygiene, though in practice, the two were inseparably joined. This important issue will be considered at length in a later chapter which will concentrate on educational activity within the schools.

For the moment, it is sufficient to note that most working-class parents demanded an education for their children that was free of irrelevant or intrusive regulation. 'Parents have no idea that there is any advantage in children spending so many years at school if the same amount of learning can be acquired in a shorter time. In short, they regard schooling, not as a course of discipline, but only as a means of acquiring reading, writing and arithmetic, sewing and knitting, as a preparation for the main business of life — earning a livelihood.'[67] 'I regret . . . that for each parent who expresses an earnest wish for the moral and religious improvement of his children, there are at least twenty who evince no such feeling, but appear, on the contrary, to be wholly indifferent to the subject.'[68]

In the working-class private school, the relationship between teacher and pupil was very similar to that between parent and child at home. The two agencies operated with moral and cultural expectations that were substantially the same. But the links between home and school went beyond this. Just as the school was virtually an extension of the values and physical environment of the home, the family and the local community, so the private domestic household often complemented the educational work of the school, in however humble a fashion. Literate and concerned working-class parents who taught their children in the home are familiar from the pages of many of the better-known working-class autobiographies. But the experience of such authors was not exceptional. Indications of this, on a considerable scale, come from two sources. First, from the returns of Bristol Population Censuses, and, more colourfully, from the reports of the Children's Employment Commission.

Analysis of the Bristol returns has shown that the occupational designation 'Scholar at Home' was by no means entirely restricted to the children of the wealthy in households employing a resident governess or tutor. In many working-class districts, children were recorded as receiving their education at home, presumably from the mother or an elder sibling. This arrangement must have been very similar to the private school itself, which was, after all, a 'home school'. Indeed, it must be likely that many schools started in this small, entirely domestic way before expanding to take in the children of a few neighbours. Several working-class private schools in Bristol are indicated by the returns of the Population Censuses as having 'Scholars at Home'. A further example is that of the widowed mother of Robert Bloomfield, the shoemaker-poet, 'who managed by her own, unaided efforts, not only to maintain her little family, but to give each of her children the rudiments of an education. This she accomplished by opening a school and teaching her own children along with the rest. With the exception of a few months' instruction in writing from a schoolmaster at Ixworth, the future poet learnt from his mother all he knew . . .'[69] Education at home cannot have been an easy option, especially where both parents had to work to support the family, but the clear advantage must have been in the saving made on school fees.

The chief historical problem with the scholar at home is the familiar one of quantification. For the most part, the working-class scholar at home is a comparative rarity in the census returns and it would be easy to conclude that attempts at a systematic education within the family were quite unusual. And yet occasionally, through the instrumentality of an individual enumerator, a different picture emerges. Take, for example, the enumerator who covered part of the Hotwells Road area in 1851.[70] His district comprised a narrow ribbon of mean working-class dwellings and lodging houses running alongside the docks; it was among the poorest areas in the city. His colleagues who enumerated the neighbouring dockland districts returned not a single scholar at home but his own results were immediately and obviously different. His district contained 331 children of nominal school age — that is, from 3 to 14. Of these, just 134 — 40 per cent — were returned as scholars. But 23 of these — 17 per cent of all the scholars — attended no school, for they were 'scholars at home'. Seven out of every 100 children in the solidly working-class corner of the city were being self-consciously taught within their own families. These families were ten in number; the heads of each household were a solitary married woman with no declared occupation, a shipwright, a carpenter, two labourers, a sawyer, a shoemaker, a sailor, a groom and a painter. These were not the exalted kinds of vocation which generally presided over the households containing domestic scholars.[71]

The earlier reports of the Children's Employment Commission contain numerous brief insights into the struggles of individual working families to gain basic literacy for their children — insights which put some flesh on the dry bones of the census enumerator's 'Scholar at Home'. John Kinsler, for example, was a pit-boy at Fawdon Colliery in Northumberland: 'can read (very well); writes his name; his father taught him. Went to school for 2 years or so before he went down the pit.'[72] William Arnold, 'aged 12 . . . [was] 9 years of age when I went to the pits . . . I can read and write a little . . . and have been taught by my parents and at school.'[73] William Flewit, 'went to day-school afore I worked in the pit . . . I can read (very well) and write but very little; I am learning now in a copy-book at home . . .'[74] Eleanor Scrowther, a 14-year-old pottery worker, 'goes to no school now . . . Was at day school a good bit before she came to work, but learnt most reading at home.'[75] Charles Gregory, a chemical worker, 'was at school 3 years, paying 2d. a week at some . . . father (a bricklayer) learns him sometimes.'[76] The father of John Robson, an engineer's boy in a paper mill, himself kept a school; John 'reads fairly, writes his name. Father is a schoolmaster and teaches him at night, and keeps a night-school in winter-time.'[77] And the pattern is much the same in the Commission's later reports in the 1860s; thus Annie Burton, an eleven-year-old, 'At lace work nearly 4 years . . . was at day school for a short time when "going 5". Can read (does). Father taught her and is going to teach her to write. (Is miserably thin and pale).'[78] And Sarah Pearce, a young munitions worker, 'Went regularly to a week school, since she was four or five years old, till she came to work here . . . Can read "very well", quite long words in the Bible. Can write on the slate very well. Mother is just teaching her to write a letter on paper in the evenings after work.'[79]

Intra-familial learning was not confined to parent and child. Siblings also helped one another: Maria Hook, recorded in 1833, 'I am a spinner . . . I used to go to school. I can read. I can write very little; what I can my brother learnt me.'[80] And miner Henry Barnett: 'I am 19 years of age . . . I can read middling and I write a little . . . I have refreshed my memory by teaching my sisters at home.'[81] Occasionally, young people might help each other in this way on an informal basis outside the family. An overlooker at a Nottingham lace warehouse in the early 1860s reported, for example, that she, 'Thinks most of her girls can read pretty well, because she sees them reading at tea time and sometimes a bigger girl gets a few round her and helps them to read in the scriptures etc.'[82]

Examples of the above kind are not isolated and many others could be cited. There is no need to extend the catalogue unduly, though no apology is offered for setting out a long and fundamentally repetitive list, for it helps to underline the widespread presence of an indigenous educative element in nineteenth-century working-class culture which history has monumentally failed to acknowledge. Though hard to evaluate, difficult to trace and impossible to quantify, the educational contribution of domestic working-class culture cannot be overlooked.

Finally, there is some evidence that the interpenetration of school and home could operate in reverse, as the educational resources of the private school — in the shape of its teacher, together with a few books — might be brought into the working-class home for a few hours. The curate of St Mary's, Barnsley, reported in 1842 that, 'There are a few schoolmasters who go about from house to house, and give an hour's instruction in the family, and then proceed to another . . .'[83] And D. R. Fearon gave a similar individual example from Liverpool in the late 1860s. 'The master says he can keep his school here in warm and dry weather only . . . so when bad weather comes, he dismisses his scholars to their homes and goes round to the different houses teaching them. The neighbours say he often has over twenty children at school in the cellar. I sent for him from a neighbouring house and he said he was now visiting 6 houses in this alley, and teaching reading and spelling.'[84]

This chapter has raised the question of why large sections of the nineteenth-century working class maintained their support for the private school in the decades before the 1870s. The officially favoured explanations, which concentrated on the allegedly deficient or negative characteristics of working-class behaviour, have been challenged as either partially or wholly misleading, and in their place, a series of positive class-cultural explanations have been offered. The working-class private school was a product of a broader working-class culture, and as such it was attuned, in personnel and in atmosphere and organisation, to the demands of that culture. It was an education that was fully under the control of its users; it was an education truly 'of' the working class and not 'for' it. And it is in these terms that the close and often complementary relationship between the working-class home and the working-class school has to be set.

Notes

1. P.P. 1842 [381] xvi, *C.E.C.*, p. 675.
2. P.P. 1843 [429] xxvii. *Reports by Factory Inspectors*, p. 6. Also see H.M.I. Norris, *C.C.E.*, 1852, pp. 380–2.
3. P.P. 1842 [382] xvii, *C.E.C.*, p. 17.
4. P.P. 1843 [430] xiii, *C.E.C.*, p. 145.
5. P.P. 1842 [382], xvii, *C.E.C.*, p. 753.
6. Ibid., p. 833; P.P. 1843 [432] xv, *C.E.C.*, p. Q51.
7. Bartley, *Schools for the People*, p. 404. 409.
8. P. H. Fisher, *Notes and Recollections of Stroud, Gloucs.* (1871), p. 291.
9. *The Times*, 28.3.1861.
10. Cumin, *Newcastle*, vol. 3, p. 29.
11. Bartley, *Schools for the People*, p. 409.
12. H.M.I. Rhys, *C.C.E.*, 1875–6, p. 395.
13. For a valuable appraisal of the concept of 'apathy' as a problem of supply rather than demand, see S. Yeo, 'On the Uses of Apathy', *European Journal of Sociology*, XV (1974), pp. 279–311.
14. Stow, *National Education: The Duty of England* (1847), p. 2.
15. Bartley, *Schools for the People*, p. 19.
16. Coode, *Newcastle*, vol. 2, p. 262. Also see Tremenheere, *C.C.E.*, 1839–40, p. 162; Blakiston, *C.C.E.*, 1874–5, p. 48; P.P. 1843 [431] xiv, *C.E.C.*, p. C10.
17. Coode, *Newcastle*, vol. 2, p. 297.
18. Winder, *Newcastle*, vol. 2, p. 206.
19. Hare, *Newcastle*, vol. 3, p. 312. He explains this anxiety — slightingly — in terms of, 'motherly tenderness that . . . the object of their fond affection will be less exposed to danger or neglect'.
20. Cumin, *Newcastle*, vol. 3, p. 62.
21. *J.S.S.*, vol. 4 (1841), p. 161. Also, 'On the Condition of the Working Classes in the Inner Ward of St. George's Parish, Hanover Square', *J.S.S.*, vol. 6 (1843), p. 141.
22. 'Report of a Committee of the Manchester Statistical Society, on the State of Education in the Township of Pendleton, 1838', *J.S.S.*, vol. 2 (1839), p. 68.
23. P.P. 1842 [382] xvii, *C.E.C.*, p. 851. The father of pit-boy Jonathan Clayton 'used to make me read and said I should see the day when I should wish I had practised reading . . .'. P.P. 1842 [381] xvi, *C.E.C.*, p. 227.
24. '. . . Pendleton . . .', *J.S.S.*, vol. 2 (1839), p. 70.
25. *Special Reports*, p. 106. H.M.I. Blakiston's formulation is yet more interesting for the unrealised paradox it establishes: 'most of the parents . . . are ignorant and apathetic, tenacious of their parental rights . . . they indignantly resent any attempt at coercion'. *C.C.E.*, 1874–5, p. 48.
26. H.M.I. Brodie, *C.C.E.*, 1872–3, pp. 54–5.
27. Brougham, *Practical Observations on the Education of the People* (1825), p. 9. For working-class responses to such allegations, see *Northern Star*, 17.10.1840; 25.12.1847; quoted in Brian Simon, *Studies in the History of Education, 1780–1870* (1960), pp. 244, 257.
28. Quoted in Silver, *English Education and the Radicals, 1780–1850* (1975), p. 96. See also T. Tholfsen (ed.), *James Kay-Shuttleworth on Popular Education* (1974), Introduction.
29. J. A. St John, *The Education of the People* (1858), p. 2.
30. P.P. 1843 [431] xiv, *C.E.C.*, p. C10.
31. P.P. 1843 [432], p. Q49; see also p. Q51.
32. *Select Committee*, pp. 23–4; 'Report on the State of Education in the Borough of Salford in 1835', *M.S.S.*, (1836), p. 21.

33. 'The most destitute and immoral marry to increase their claim on the stipend appointed for them by law, which thus acts as a bounty on the increase of a squalid and debilitated race who inherit from their parents disease, sometimes deformity, often vice, and always beggary.' J. Kay-Shuttleworth, *The Moral and Physical Condition of the Working Classes Employed in the Cotton Manufacture in Manchester* (1832, 2nd edn), p. 47; also pp. 5–6. For a discussion of subsequent developments in the highly influential theories of deprivation and cultural inadequacy, see Humphries, *Hooligans or Rebels?* Ch. 1.

34. P.P. 1847 [828] xv. *Reports by Factory Inspectors*, p. 5. Also P.P. 1851 [1304]xxiii. *Reports* . . ., p. 53.

35. P.P. 1844 [523] xxvii. *Reports by Factory Inspectors*, pp. 25–6.

36. P.P. 1847 [828] xv. *Reports* . . ., p. 6.

37. Bartley, *Schools for the People*, p. 402; also Bartley, *One Square Mile in the East End of London* (1870, 2nd edn), esp. p. 15; Cumin, *Newcastle*, vol. 3, p. 29. Also Frederick Rogers, *Labour, Life and Leisure* (1913, rep. 1973 with an introduction by D. Rubinstein), pp. 58–9.

38. See for example, Eileen Elias, *On Sundays We Wore White* (1978), esp. p. 19. From an analytical point of view, the Taunton Commissioners found considerable difficulty in establishing a clear definition of the middle-class private school. See G. Sutherland, 'Secondary Education: The Education of the Middle Classes', in Sutherland *et al.*, *Education in Britain* (1975), pp. 137–95, 145. Also useful on the middle-class private school is Margaret Bryant, 'Topographical Resources: Private and Secondary Education in Middlesex from the Sixteenth Century to the Twentieth Century', in T. G. Cook (ed.), *Local Studies and the History of Education* (1972), pp. 99–122. Interesting for the negotiation of the public elementary schools by some sections of the lower middle class is, W. E. Marsden, 'Education and the Social Geography of Nineteenth Century Towns and Cities', in D. Reeder, *Urban Education*, esp. pp. 58–66. Also see p. 70. See too, J. Hurt, *Elementary Schooling* (1979), pp. 8–9.

39. 'A Condemned Institution', *Good Words*, vol. 14 (1873), pp. 745–8. This useful source is cited by Rubinstein, *School Attendance in East London, 1870–1904: A Social History* (Hull, 1969). See also, 'An Assistant Master', *Private Schools and Schoolmasters* (1982), esp. pp. 5–8; also H.M.I. Routledge, *C.C.E.*, 1874–5, p. 142, 'The pride engendered by paying ten shillings a quarter . . . the vulgar passion for "gentility" '; H.M.I. Alderson, *C.C.E.*, 1873–4, p. 25.

40. Unfortunately, only those returns from London survive at the P.R.O.

41. *C.C.E.*, 1875–6, p. 319.

42. Senior, *Suggestions on Popular Education*, p. 29. This volume contains Senior's papers as one of the Newcastle Commissioners.

43. Wilkinson, *Newcastle*, vol. 3, p. 420.

44. Senior, *Suggestions*, pp. 29–30.

45. *Special Reports*, p. 54. Also see Foster, *Newcastle*, vol. 2, pp. 337–8.

46. Bartley, *Schools for the People*, p. 402. For the popularity of the schools, also see Laquer in L. Stone, *Schooling and Society*, pp. 192–205. Also see Fitch, *Special Reports*, 'a large number of the poor who cannot be said to neglect their children undoubtedly prefer . . . the private to the public school', p. 107; also P.P. 1842 [381] xvi, *C.E.C.*, 'In connection with the boy's [sic] school at Wingate Grange Colliery, a striking example of the peculiar jealousy and independent pride of pitmen may be adduced. The owners, anxious that the education of the boys should be as much an act of benevolence as possible, professed to exact only one penny a week from the men, as an acknowledgement, and subsequently became very lax and indifferent in this exaction. The schoolmaster also was a man of superior education and gentlemanly address . . . An under-clerk, possessing physical defects, was discharged from the service of the colliery, he established a school in the Methodist

chapel, and in six weeks obtained 70 pupils at the usual rates of charges, sliding between 2d. and 6d. per week — the owners' school having diminished in this time nearly in the ratio of the increase of the other . . . This person possesses the usual qualifications of a pit village schoolmaster, and is, doubtless, desirous of effecting good. Neither his ability, nor his system can for one moment be compared to those of his competitor . . .', p. 728. A useful summary list of reasons accounting for 'the fact that in neighbourhoods where there are good infant schools under inspection, many parents still prefer to send their young children to a dame's school?', is given by one of Cumin's witnesses (*Newcastle*, vol. 3, pp. 144–5), and is reproduced in Appendix C.

47. P.P. 1842 [381] xvi, *C.E.C.*, p. 726.

48. Hare, *Newcastle*, vol. 3, p. 295.

49. Cumin, *Newcastle*, vol. 3, p. 143. See also E. P. Thompson, *Making of the English Working Class* (1968 edn), p. 786.

50. P.P. 1842 [381] xvi, *C.E.C.*, p. 588. Links between school-keeping and political radicalism existed but are difficult to establish. In London in 1843, 'there was one master who kept a school for Socialist principles; and there might be in the whole ten or twelve men who spoke upon serious things in a manner which indicated that their principles were more or less infidel', 'Fifth Report . . . London', *J.S.S.* (1843), p. 214.

51. P.P. 1842 [381] xvi, *C.E.C.*, p. 199.

52. Howson, *Newcastle*, vol. 4, p. 378. Also Fitch, *Special Reports*, p. 54; H.M.I. Smith, *C.C.E.*, 1876–7, p. 565. Howson also pointed out that 'very frequently, the preference of the child determines the consent of the parent'. The same point is made more graphically in William Scarratt, *Old Times in the Potteries* (1906, rep. 1969), p. 80, 'A companion . . . persuaded me to leave the Church School I had attended and go to a private one he attended.'

53. Hare, *Newcastle*, vol. 3, p. 253; also see Winder, *Newcastle*, vol. 2, p. 183.

54. H.M.I. Smith, *C.C.E.*, 1876–7, p. 565. Also Fitch, *Special Reports*, p. 54; 'Much of the success of some of the most worthless of the schools arises out of the sympathy which the poor feel for one another.'

55. Porter, 'Statistical Inquiries into the Social Condition of the Working Classes, and into the Means Provided for the Education of their Children', *C.S.E. Second Publication* (1838), p. 254. Also see 'Liverpool', *M.S.S.* (1836), p. 23. 'One master, whose school is in a cellar, being asked what his terms were, replied, "Why, I only charge sixpence for the readers, ninepence for the writers and one shilling for the counters". Surprise being expressed that his terms were so high compared with those of his neighbours, he explained by saying, "It's very true they're above the common, but then we're good creditors — the weeks they have it they pay, and the weeks they haven't it, why we look over it".' Joseph Blacket, the youngest son of a large, poor family, was sent to school, 'early in youth, owing to the village schoolmistress being very partial to me, and giving me a free education'. *Specimens of the Poetry of Joseph Blacket, with an account of his Life*, p. 13.

56. H.M.I. Watson, *C.C.E.*, 1874–5, p. 192.

57. Fitch, *Special Reports*, p. 54.

58. 'A Condemned Institution', *Good Words* (1873), p. 746. For a similar example from the early twentieth century, see R. Roberts, *The Classic Slum* (1971), pp. 136–7.

59. A graphic indication of diverse and shifting patterns of attendance can be derived from Admissions Registers, especially where they have been properly kept. See for instance North St Wesleyan (Infants) Admissions Book, 1858–1863 (Bristol). Particularly interesting are some of the reasons for withdrawal: 'Too far to come'; 'Mother going to teach them'; 'Mother keeps a school'; 'He was kept in'; 'Would not pay'; 'To go to school near home'; 'Did not like monitors to teach

them'; 'Wanted at home'; 'Gone with his sister to a private school'. Respective length of attendance in these individual cases was 3 months, 10 months, 9 months, 4 months, 20 months, 9 months, 8 months, and not given. Also see Chapter 1, note 77.

60. Rev. Mr Farish, vicar of St Mary's, Sheffield, in P.P. 1843 [431] xiv, *C.E.C.*, p. e3.

61. Quoted in Sturt, *The Education of the People*, pp. 36–7; Ann Smith Goodger, the mistress of Killingworth Colliery Infant School, felt that 'bad language . . . might be checked and suppressed by the parents, who, instead of doing this, frequently abuse her for punishing the children'. P.P. 1842 [381] xvi, *C.E.C.*, p. 713.

62. H.M.I. King, *C.C.E.*, 1875–6, p. 329.

63. P.P. 1851 [1304] xxiii. *Reports by the Factory Inspectors*, p. 55.

64. Fitch, *Special Reports*, p. 106.

65. Hare, *Newcastle*, vol. 3, p. 254; also see, 'Third Report . . . Westminster', *J.S.S.*, vol. 1 (1839), p. 455.

66. J. C. Wigram of the National Society in, *Select Committee*, p. 77; also see Frith, 'Socialisation and Rational Schooling', who quotes a public school teacher, 'Such is the *animus* of these people; that the arrangements of the Committee and the interests of the School are nothing to them if they may not have their own way', p. 86. Symons reported Mrs ______, a member of the Visiting and Bettering Society of Sheffield, 'The parents make it quite a favour to send their children to school. Pride is a great and very prevailing vice among them; the least thing said to a child is taken as offence.' P.P. 1843 [431] xiv *C.E.C.*, p. e8. The continuous battles against pupil and parent resistance to the regulatory claims of the public school are best seen in log books. The following extracts are taken from the *Log Book of St Augustine's (National) Boys' School* (Bristol):

19. 6.65: 'Visited by Mrs. Bale who complained of her boy being beaten.'

28.11.65: 'Gave the boys a good drilling in order to enforce *immediate obedience*.'

13. 2.66: 'Shrove Tuesday — many boys ask for holiday and stay away in the afternoon because I refuse to give it.'

22. 5.67: 'A punishment to Fitzgerald is followed by a threat from him that he would heave a chisel at me the next time I thrashed him.'

29. 5.67: 'Evans late in the afternoon and as he had no excuse, I sent him back to see if that would cure him of his bad habit. This however only brought his mother down to tell me that he should not come again.'

26.10.70: 'John Davey brought to school and after receiving a thrashing, his hands and feet were tied together and remained tied from 10 to 4'.

6.11.74: 'Was met again by Mr. Gardiner in street and told not to cane his boy again'.

10. 3.76: 'Yesterday seemed one of the most unfortunate days I have spent here. Reed sent W. Nash out of his class because he had been playing all the morning and done no work at all. I gave him *one slight* stroke with the cane on his hand. Soon after dismissing school, Mrs. Naish [sic] was heard at the door using the most foul language and calling me all she could think of. She told me her boy was dying from my cruelty and threatened to summon me. Boy expelled. In the afternoon a man named Bailey came up to to school in a beastly state of intoxication and invited me "to have a round with him". After he had gone into a fit, I managed to get rid of him without a broken neck.'

More generally, see S. J. Humphries, *Hooligans or Rebels?* esp. Ch. 3.

67. Foster, *Newcastle*, vol. 2, p. 351.

68. P.P. 1844 [523] xxvii. *Reports by Factory Inspectors*, p. 24.

69. W. E. Winks, *Lives of Illustrious Shoemakers* (1883), p. 103. Thomas Chatterton's mother set up a school in much the same way as Mrs Bloomfield. See J. H. Ingram, *The True Chatterton* (1910), p. 30.

70. P.R.O. H.O. 107/1952.

71. In a private survey of east London in 1870, Bartley recorded, 'A Cottage behind Shoreditch Church; 4 children: 1 goes to school, 2 make match boxes. The mother . . . said she "taught them at home", but judging from the filthy, neglected and miserable look of the parent and the children, the teaching could not have amounted to very much.' G. Bartley, *One Square Mile in the East End of London*, Appendix III, no. 87. The 1851 Census gave a total of 44,625 scholars at home. Edward Baines, the Voluntaryist, felt that 'probably there is a greater number educated by mothers, sisters, or other relatives'. 'On our past Educational Improvement and the Means of Future Progress, especially in lengthening the Term of Education', in Alfred Hill (ed.), *Essays upon Educational Subjects*, p. 53. Also see J. Hurt, *Elementary Schooling* (1979), p. 38. 'Before the age of mass compulsory education, parents may have been a more important educative influence with their offspring than historians of education, taking a rigidly institutional approach, have yet conceded.' For an opposing view, 'I should think there are very few who are educated at home in their parents' houses', see Caldwell, *Select Committee*, pp. 29, 30.

72. P.P. 1842 [381] xvi, *C.E.C.*, p. 605.

73. Ibid., p. 677.

74. P.P. 1842 [382] xvii, *C.E.C.*, p. 140.

75. P.P. 1843 [432] xv, *C.E.C.*, p. 119.

76. Ibid., p. 131.

77. Ibid., p. 137.

78. P.P. 1863 [3170] xviii, *C.E.C.*, p. 232.

79. Ibid., p. 115. Also see p. 198.

80. P.P. 1833 (450). *Reports from Commissioners (Factories Inquiry Committee)*, p. 22.

81. P.P. 1842 [381] xvi, *C.E.C.*, p. 72.

82. P.P. 1863 [3170] xviii, *C.E.C.*, p. 214. Also note the singular experience of Sam Shaw in Birmingham in the 1880s: 'My education, however, had begun before I was five, for I had attended an "amateur school" held in the yard near the Brew-house, where little Nellie, a neighbour's child, acted as a school teacher. I was employed chiefly as one of the pupils to be caned, nevertheless, I was a good pupil and by the time I graduated to Summer Lane School I already had a fair smattering of the three R's, could read simple letters of the alphabet and knew figures by sight.' *Guttersnipe* (1946), p. 14. Also see J. Hogg, *The Mountain Bard* (1807), p. xii.

83. P.P. 1842 [381], *C.E.C.*, p. 263. Also see Neuburg, *Popular Education in Eighteenth Century England* (1971), for 'Tim Bobbin', the Lancashire poet-schoolmaster who, at fourteen, 'and young as he then was, . . . commenced itinerant school-master, going about the country from one village to another . . . teaching reading, writing and accounts', quoted p. 30. These examples are fascinating parallels with the predominantly itinerant hedge schoolmasters of Ireland, whose schools have much in common with the English working-class private school. Indeed, 'Glassford, who was a member of the Commission of Inquiry into the State of Education in Ireland in 1824, declares that the Hedge Schools would be called "dames' schools" in England', Dowling, *The Hedge Schools of Ireland* (Dublin, n.d.), p. 107. Dowling denies the similarity because he, like other writers, is easily persuaded by the confident dismissal of the dame's school by other historians. In his case, it is Frank Smith, whom he quotes as saying that

such schools were 'baby-minding institutions', whose 'educational importance is slight'. This is something which Dowling amply demonstrates is not the case for the hedge school and from which only continuing historical carelessness can fail to rescue the 'dame's school'. Perhaps Glassford's original association was not far wide of the mark, and attention should be fixed more closely on the process of official distortion with which he sought to discredit both forms of school. See also, Dowling, *A History of Irish Education* (Cork, 1971), Ch. 6; N. Atkinson, *Irish Education* (Dublin, 1969), pp. 45–8. There is at least one reference in the official literature to English versions of hedge schools. In Warrington in the early 1840s, the number of children attending 'Private dame schools, or hedge-schools, may be reckoned as 100', P.P. 1843 [432] xv, *C.E.C.*, p. M22.

84. *Special Reports*, p. 152.

4 TEACHERS

Who were the keepers of the working-class private school? Of all the questions relating to the schools, evidence on this point is perhaps among the slightest. Few working-class autobiographies have been left by such teachers, and once again therefore, it is with the official middle-class record that any investigation has to begin.[1] In this chapter we will assess the recurring themes which dominate this record, using as a principal comparative source the analysis of working-class private teachers in the city of Bristol, which was described in Chapter 2, and which covers the period 1851 to 1871.

The first and most notable theme was that the teachers were simply ordinary members of the working community — 'from the people themselves . . .'. In theory, anyone could establish himself or herself as the teacher of a school at any time and in any place. A central implication of this was that the working-class users of private schools acknowledged no fixed or inflexible distinction demarcating the skill of 'teaching' as a specialised quality distinct from, and above those commonly possessed by other working people. To be the teacher of a working-class private school implied no more than the mastery of the basic skills of literacy and some ability — whether great or small — to communicate them.[2] Indeed, the close relationship which we have noted between education in the private schools and education at home demonstrates this. The school-keeper might have had more extensive knowledge than the parent, and certainly had greater teaching experience and time to teach, but essentially, the educative roles of the two were harmonised. The working-class teacher was in most respects an educational extension of an existing working-class domestic culture. And it was precisely this cultural consonance which education experts felt obliged to erode and ultimately to fracture. How, after all, could working-class culture be reformed and refined through the medium of popular education, if a substantial part of that education was itself a product of that very culture, and ultimately under its control?

It was in this context that the elevation of 'teaching' to a professionalised status could take place. Teaching could be mystified as a secret preserve with special skills which were distinguished from those needed or generated in other areas of daily life. It became a facility which was self-evidently beyond the resources of ordinary people. Crucially, it came to denote a body of skills which could not be casually acquired, but for which a coherent programme of specialist *training* was an unavoidable prerequisite. This was summed up by H.M.I. Morrell: 'Where good qualifications are secured in the teachers themselves everything else will follow; where they are not secured everything else will fail.'[3] These words encapsulate one of the nineteenth-century educationist's most strenuously supported objectives — the control and regulation of the 'teachers of the people'.

Without formal training, the private teachers had 'picked up their knowledge promiscuously'.[4] They were consequently 'much less highly educated than the public [teachers]; generally speaking, they seemed very ordinary persons, and to have been recruited from various sources'.[5] The implications of the distinction between trained and untrained teachers will be considered from an educational and organisational perspective elsewhere. What is important to note here is the symbolic significance of training as a legitimate distinction between 'teachers' and 'ordinary persons' as well as its practical importance in the regulation of working-class education.

The former tendency comprised a central part of the hegemony of the publicly provided school which developed progressively throughout the nineteenth century, being consolidated particularly in the 1870s and 1880s following the destruction of the working-class private schools.[6] From this point on, though the activities of the public teacher continued to be challenged or resisted in significant ways by working-class parents and children, his or her exclusive expertise as a teacher, based on formal professional training, was increasingly acknowledged.

The second theme — training and inspection as necessary processes for the effective control of the teaching force and its work — was axiomatic in all nineteenth-century educational writing. The Manchester Statistical Society provides an early and characteristic example of this in a report of 1836;

> It is the belief of your Committee that in the establishment of Normal schools, the funds devoted to educational purposes would be more usefully employed than in any other manner; for they consider it hopeless to expect an extensive improvement in the conduct of the schools, until the teachers have first been

> qualified for the task of education.[7]

And the absence of formal training furnished a strong negative indictment of working-class private schools;

> To consider as receiving efficient education children who 'get some schooling' at the will of a teacher, whose ignorance or results of instruction are not subject to any test seems to me to be throwing the cold water of contempt on recent efforts to improve the education of the people.[8]

Private schools

> subject to no inspection are consequently in great measure beyond the reach of those beneficial influences which could not fail to be produced by intercourse with persons of superior intelligence.[9]

> The [private] schools are conducted according to the particular view of the teacher . . . the result is that . . . educational efficiency suffers.[10]

Public teachers could be relied upon not only to be more 'efficient', but more important, to abstain from 'particular' views of their own — views which were likely to be in harmony with those of a deficient and unreformed parent culture. Thus it was that private teachers were 'far more thought of than duly qualified teachers'. [11] This dangerous closeness of parent and teacher was recognised but could be accounted for only in terms which, however deprecatory, were always obliged to come back again to cultural consonance:

> Their ideas were on a par with the parents' ideas; they were metal that anyone could work upon; were pliant to every whim — sycophancy their virtue, hypocrisy their faith; could be snubbed and rebuked at pleasure, and gave way to every illiterate prejudice.[12]

Such closeness highlighted a particularly vivid distinction between the private and the public school. As the influence of the latter extended, it brought with it a new and more distinct teacher-parent relation. Burnett for example points out that a 'theme which emerges clearly from [working-class] autobiographies is the lack of contact between home and school', suggesting that this represents 'the little interest which many working-class parents took in the education of their offspring'.[13] In fact, it would be more accurate to talk of the low level of parental involvement in, or identification with, publicly provided schools, rather than with the education of their children *per se*.

The generality of working-class private teachers were an integrated part of a broader popular culture — of 'the people'. But what sort of *individual* would be most commonly involved in teaching?

The feature which emerges most clearly and immediately is that the teachers of working-class private schools were, in overwhelming numbers, female.[14] In Finsbury in the early 1840s for instance,

> The first thing which strikes a visitor with respect to the proprietors of these schools is *the immense preponderance of female teachers*; the schoolmistresses being to the schoolmasters in the ratio of nine to one, although the children placed under their care are in respect of sex nearly equal.[15]

This ratio represents the male teaching strength at just over 11 per cent of the total. This corresponds very closely with those derived from the Population Census for Bristol in the years 1851, 1861 and 1871; respectively, these are 11 per cent, 11 per cent and 9 per cent.

Such a persistent sexual imbalance should not be surprising, for working-class private schools were the products of a domestic organisation that was traditional and patriarchal. Women's biological child-bearing role, along with the associated sexual division of labour within the family, meant that the function of instructing the children tended to devolve disproportionately upon mothers and elder daughters. Teaching was, in other words, a particular specialisation within an enduring pattern of traditionally legitimised domestic female labour. We might note, however, that teaching was anomalous to the extent that it was one area of domiciliary labour which was not officially encouraged and celebrated as a bulwark of the structure and stability of the family itself.[16] Although it contributed to the maintenance of the traditional domestic division of labour, its product notably lacked the critical regulative and reformative capacity of formal schooling.

In many ways, the occupation reflects wider changes in women's labour patterns. On the one hand, it represented a traditional unified emphasis on the home as workplace, on the integration of labour and life, and on the family as a productive unit; on the other, it offered a source of independent remunerative employment for the woman who was progressively denied an outlet for her labour other than through its complete constriction into 'housework' in the gradual privatisation of domestic life.[17] In the former case, teaching could be inserted into or deleted from the resources of the domestic economy virtually as need demanded or circumstances allowed. It represented a viable and valuable supplement to weekly income which could be achieved with the minimum disruption of domestic routine and without undertaking outside employment.[18] In the latter case — and in Bristol, the majority of women teachers were independent of direct male support — teaching might assume a greater and more lasting importance.

But the sexual imbalance cannot be reduced simply to traditional structural features of this kind. Of equal significance was the persistence, noted and sometimes endorsed by observers, of a powerful and clearly related conception of women as the 'natural' teachers of the young. In part, this resulted from the acceptance of assumed behavioural determinants which were judged particularly to suit women to the demands of working with children. In particular, it was widely held that women were kinder, more tolerant and more sympathetic to children than were men. Kay-Shuttleworth observed that, 'I do not attribute [kindness of temper and demeanour] so much to any system adopted by the dames as to the natural feelings which prompt them to behave more kindly to young children.'[19] J. R. Leifchild of the Children's Employment Commission felt that 'it occasionally appeared that the children derived some benefit from their attendance when the preceptress tempered her authority with an approach to maternal solicitude'.[20] The London Statistical Society itself supposed that the best and most suitable of teachers was 'an able, active middle-aged, motherly female, of mild temper, and accustomed to children'.[21] And though schools kept by women and men alike could be castigated as educationally 'inefficient', men's schools were in addition 'devoid of that appearance of cheerfulness and domestic comfort which belongs to schools kept by females'.[22] J. R. Wood, the

Manchester Statistical Society's principal agent, clearly surprised the members of the 1837 Select Committee with some of his replies which rated the dame's school as ideally above the Infant School because of its teachers: 'I am strongly of opinion that dame schools are the best for young children . . . I think placing young children under a female is better than under a male; the influence of the female character is very much felt at that age.'[23] The implication of this point was developed in the London Statistical Society's Finsbury investigation. Here it was suggested that the large numbers of male teachers in public schools represented a central distinction between them and their private counterparts;

> The circumstance of so large a proportion of boys being under female superintendence according to the private . . . system of education is worthy of remark, because the opinion of the promoters of charitable education at the present moment is much in favour of employing male teachers in preference to females . . .[24]

Such alleged differences in teaching capability — women gentler and more 'maternal'; men firmer and less familiar — were sometimes held to lead to distinctions in curriculum. In particular, the tendency to regard the teaching of writing as being most effectively carried out by male teachers seems to have been quite common. In the early eighteenth century it had been

> commonly thought so tiresome an Undertaking, to teach Children to Spell and read English, that a peevish Schoolmaster is not judged to have Patience enough to do it. And therefore, they are sent to a Mistress, supposing she may be more fit to deal with them in their tender Years . . .[25]

And over 100 years later, J. R. Wood could charge that male teachers were continuing to treat the teaching of writing as their specialism. They

> generally establish in the eyes of the public a false criterion of their qualifications; that is, the art of writing, which is the great criterion with schoolmasters. You generally see exhibited some few specimens of fine writing, and a schoolmaster who can write well is almost sure of a large school . . .[26]

In Westminster in the late 1830s, for example, though the majority of pupils kept by men were boys 'in some instances girls are also sent there to learn to write and cipher — a general notion seeming to exist that men alone can teach these subjects'.[27] It seems likely that the minority of male teachers sought actively to accentuate this impression. In so doing, they endeavoured to monopolise the more lucrative end of the market in basic skills. It is clear, however, that popular perceptions of the connection between writing and gender, though perhaps strong, were very far from universal. As the reports of the Statistical Societies make clear, many 'writing schools' were operated by women.

What can be safely said in sum, is that for both structural and residual cultural reasons, working-class private education relied overwhelmingly upon women. Further, though both men and women might work in the same basic subjects and with the same age groups, men may well have tended to concentrate to a disproportionate extent on the business of writing, and therefore on slightly older children.

Analysis of Bristol's Population Census returns can shed a little more light on the categories of women most involved in teaching in that city, though there does not exist, as yet, evidence from other localities to allow comparative study. The number of married women in Bristol who declared themselves as teachers fell from 21.8 per cent of the total in 1851, to 15.3 per cent in 1861 and recovered to 18.2 per cent in 1871. Over the same period, the number of widows was constant at 23 per cent and 22.8 per cent and then tumbled to 14.8 per cent in 1871. Married women with no husband at home remained fairly constant at 5.1 per cent, 3.3 per cent and 4.4 per cent, as did unmarried women at 20.5 per cent, 25.1 per cent and 22.6 per cent. But the proportion of unmarried daughters still living in the parental home showed a dramatic increase, particularly from 1861 to 1871 — 18.4 per cent, 22.3 per cent and 31.5 per cent.[28] This may suggest that a wave of new young private teachers were embarking on school-keeping as teachers from the previous generation dropped out. H.M.I. Morell's 1871 report on London schools suggests that such a pattern might well have been more general. He offered an internal differentiation of the categories of working-class private school, based chiefly on teacher age.

> These 240 [adventure] schools, although all of one general type, yet are various in point of efficiency. On the lowest scale stand

> what may be regarded as the few remaining relics of the old-fashioned dame school. These are kept by old women, mostly in the back rooms of their cottages . . . They seldom attempt to teach anything except the alphabet and the most elementary kind of reading . . . Another class of adventure schools, not much superior to those just described, is kept by a number of middle-aged women, some of whom are widows, some of whom have husbands that earn a small pittance, but all of whom strive to eke out a livelihood and keep themselves from the parish by collecting a few of the neighbouring children and *pretending* to instruct them . . . Many of these adventure schools, again, are kept by young women who have had a fair amount of education, and . . . can . . . impart some useful information.[29]

The emphasis on age, far more than marital status, was a central element in the official critique of the teachers of working-class private schools, and we will return to it shortly.

As well as differentiation by gender, the official evidence also stresses the business of school-keeping as the special preserve of a particular social category — the 'unfortunate' and the destitute. The particular characteristics identified with this group were principally ignorance; poverty; extreme age; and personal disability, both physical and moral. Each of these will be considered separately in a moment. Before this, however, there are some more general observations to be made on the linkage of school-keeping with personal failure or inadequacy.

Such assertions have formed the basis of an arresting and enduring current of criticism. Not only do they add spice to the catalogue of specifically educational condemnation, but they permit school-keeping to be presented very dramatically as a 'last resort'. And as such, it has been assumed that the educational effectiveness of any such practitioners would necessarily be minimal. More significantly still, the argument implies that the status ascribed to the teachers by their customers was low: 'This employment, requiring no great talents, usually fell to the lot of old women, or men of mean capacities';[30] 'to become a schoolmaster or teacher can never be to rise and may be to descend in station'.[31] Sometimes indeed, the argument could be pushed as far as characterising school-keeping as a thinly disguised form of popular charity with an entirely spurious educational connection. From this point of view, the private teacher was supported by her neighbours, 'not because of the education she professes to give, but from mixed motives of regard and pity'.[32]

How justifiable were such assertions? Any defence of them must confront two central objections.

In the first place, it has to be remembered that the concept of 'status' was already an important one in middle-class theories of the working-class private school. It was widely employed to explain working-class usage of such schools as an unworthy striving for 'gentility'. In this argument, the working-class private school was, by implication, associated with high ascribed popular status. It is ironic that when the origin rather than the usage of the schools came to be considered, the stress was switched to *low* ascribed status, with teachers conceived as pitiable failures and misfits. Thus could the same concept, casually employed, be adduced in two opposed senses.

Once again, it can be seen that both types of 'status' explanation were the products of an essentially middle-class perception of the close and informal links between home and school, user and teacher, which we have already noted. In reality, such explanations were of little value. Certainly private teachers did not seek and were not accorded the inflated status sometimes sought by those in public schools.[33] 'Low teacher status', as it appears in middle-class accounts, might be interpreted more constructively as the expression of a low level of occupational differentiation, together with a high degree of social integration, access and control on the part of clients. In other words, there was much which teacher and users shared in common. Teaching was not understood as an exclusive skill, qualitatively superior to other areas of working life. Though valued and respected, it was not exalted or shrouded in the mystique of professionalisation. We can see something of this by the way in which working people could move in and out of some kind of teaching role in a quite casual and unself-conscious way. A good example is the experience of Joseph Gutteridge in the 1830s,

> To eke out my earnings still further I taught at night to some few friends the rudiments of reading and writing, but this mode of raising money was more pleasure than profit. It at least kept me from worse company, and was the means of increasing my circle of friends.[34]

There can be little doubt that the ascription of low status to the private teachers was conferred by the observers and not by the observed. Moreover, the more extreme conception of teachers as the desperate recipients of popular pity and charity is even harder to sustain. The weakness of such an argument must be that it fails to comprehend the full implications of the contexts of economic and social deprivation within which both teacher and user had to operate. Working-class private schools were without doubt run as a source of weekly income for their proprietors. To suppose anything other than this is absurdly unrealistic. The teachers were not, like some of the wives or unmarried daughters of the wealthy middle class, keeping schools for diversion or amusement. For some working-class teachers, their schools comprised their only financial support, their entire livelihoods. To look for motives beyond economic ones for the keeping of a working-class private school is unnecessary. It is like asking why other workers 'became' miners or factory operatives. They did so to earn a living and because it was a job they were skilled in. In this sense, the modern notion of 'professional vocation' is inapposite. Any prospective private teacher had to satisfy more practical criteria — those of ability, aptitude and proven achievement in teaching. And such criteria had to be satisfied rapidly. For whilst personal economic circumstances made the need for a school to pay its way a critical one, the prospective users of the school were, as much as the teachers, victims of similar social and economic inequalities.

From the perspective of the user, the expenditure of scarce resources on education had to show a quick and useful return in accordance with expressed educational demand. Costly fees could not be paid out to schools which failed to conform to these demands. It was in this sense that, in the words of Patrick Cumin, 'there is abundant evidence to show that the parents thoroughly understand the difference between a good and a bad school'.[35] A school which failed to measure up to demand could not be kept going simply as a gesture of communal charity towards an individual with no teaching ability or skill. Instead, the school would be likely to be abandoned for another, more effective one. And when this happened, a deserted teacher could find herself in desperate straits, having to turn to the parish to eke out her livelihood. Though there are references in the official reports to pauper school mistresses, they were not common in Bristol. Here, the study of the Population Census has discovered few confirmed examples in a 20-year period.[36] A failing school was more likely to disappear altogether. There is no reliable way of tracking failed schools though the Population Census can give us some clues. A good example is that of Harriet Uphill from Redcliff. In 1861 she was a solitary 57-year-old widow, sharing humble lodgings with a young married couple — a labourer and a charwoman — and keeping a 'Cottage School'.[37] Ten years later, she was still alone, but her school-keeping struggles were evidently over, for she was recorded as 'Schoolmistress Formerly'.[38] She was probably unable to meet satisfactorily the educational demands of her customers and simply gave up. She was however more fortunate than many of her contemporaries in their declining years, for in 1871, she had found a place in the almshouses of Fry's House of Mercy.

The view expressed by a recent writer that many private teachers were 'ruthlessly exploiting a situation in which an increasing number of mothers went out to work', whilst highlighting the general context of economic constraint, under-estimates the genuine nature of working-class educational demand and the response which it was given by the schools.[39] The ramifications of poverty and hardship were indeed likely to bear as heavily on the schools as they were on parents. These did not spring only from the failure of a particular school to satisfy demand, but could also result from the day-to-day attrition of defaults in the payment of fees. Whilst it is clear that many teachers were remarkably tolerant in this respect — as indeed they had to be — relatively large sums had to be entirely written off each week. Kay-Shuttleworth, responding to the 1837 Select Committee, estimated the probable loss at about 20 per cent.[40] Working-class schooling had of necessity to be a highly marginal commodity, and in times of real material hardship, 'the school money [was] the first to be saved in the calculations of the parents . . .'.[41] The London Statistical Society highlighted this issue in a discussion of the alleged 'gentility' of working-class private schools which was supposed to be revealed in a parental desire to pay as much as possible for their children's education.

> This is no doubt true in many cases, but your Committee, judging from the frequent complaints which they heard during the progress of their enquiries of the difficulty of obtaining the money due from the parents, have great doubts whether it is so universal as is supposed.[42]

Support for a working-class private school was therefore far from being a form of popular charity for an incapable teacher. Financial hardship affected teacher and parent alike and within the limits of such constraint, education was provided and paid for as best as the two parties could manage.

We can now look more closely at the specific claims of theories of teaching as 'a last resort'. Such claims are encapsulated in a celebrated and much-quoted passage from the report of one of the Newcastle Commission's London agents, Dr W. B. Hodgson. It can serve as a model of its kind.

> '. . . none are too old, too poor, too ignorant, too feeble, too sickly, too unqualified in any or every way to regard themselves, and to be regarded by others, as unfit for school-keeping. Nay, there are few, if any, occupations regarded as incompatible with school-keeping, if not as simultaneous, at least as preparatory employments. Domestic servants out of place, discharged barmaids, vendors of toys or lollipops, keepers of small eating-houses, of mangles, or of small lodging-houses, needlewomen who take in plain or slop work; consumptive patients in an advanced stage; cripples almost bedridden; persons of at least doubtful temperance; outdoor paupers; men and women of 70 or even 80 years of age; persons who spell badly (mostly women, I grieve to say), who can scarcely write, and who cannot cipher at all.[43]

The charge that school-keeping was frequently combined with other occupations will be considered later. For the moment our analysis can concentrate on the specific social groups to which Hodgson's claims relate; namely the ignorant — particularly the illiterate — the poor; the aged; the physically and morally unfit.

To the extent that the working-class users of the private schools sought particular — if limited — educational demands, the teachers had to be able to offer particular instrumental skills and the ability to communicate them. Precisely because such teachers were responsive only to the pressure of demand, the absence of basic skills was a disqualification from teaching. Despite the more lurid claims of middle-class investigators, the illiterate simply could not operate as school-keepers. Working-class educational demand was too sensitive to allow this.

And where the skills of teachers were subject to an objective test, rather than to individual subjective assessment, their abilities were not easy to fault. This is most apparent in the reports of the Factory Inspectorate who possessed statutory powers extending to those private schools operating within the Factory Act. Under Section 39 of the Act, inspectors had powers of closure over schools kept by incompetent teachers; that is, by teachers who were

> unfit to instruct children by reason of (his or her) incapacity to teach them to *read and write* . . . the Inspector cannot reject the certificate of any schoolmaster who is able to teach (and who has the books and materials necessary for teaching children) to read and write.[44]

Cases where the certificate could be rejected under the Act appear to have been few.[45] Inspector T. J. Howell wrote in his report for 1845 that,

> I found with regret that a great number of the children attended private schools kept by masters who just came up to the statutory standard of capacity to teach reading and writing, but where the education was of course far inferior to that of any of the public institutions in the place.[46]

And 30 years later, the Factory and Workshops Acts Commission heard that the situation was unchanged;

> those private adventure schools we have very little power of abolishing, because our authority over schools is very limited. If a schoolmaster is unable to teach reading or writing, or has not the materials for teaching reading and writing, or is of immoral conduct, we may annul his certificate, but beyond that we have no power. There are very few of those private adventure schoolmasters and schoolmistresses who do not come up to the qualifications laid down.[47]

In other words, though without formal training, certification and approbation, such teachers were qualified in the eyes of their clients to satisfy a particular demand. The degree to which such demand was satisfied in practice will be considered in Chapter 5.

Perhaps the most popular and influential component of the 'last resort' theory was the stress laid on the advanced age of teachers, and in particular, women. Many writers habitually reinforced the derogatory impact of the label 'dame' by expanding it to 'aged dame' or 'poor old dame', conveying the impression that teaching belonged to the desperation of an unprotected old age.[48] The concept of old age was in fact a vivid metaphor both for the worthlessness of private teaching and for the 'last resort' which it was supposed to represent.

There were indeed some teachers of great age, but in fact these were relatively few and were likely to have been as exceptional as were those who were very young. In Liverpool, in 1835, for example, 'Two teachers of Dame Schools were girls of thirteen years of age, one of whom had been left by her father, after his wife's death, to support herself and an infant brother; others of the respective ages of seventy-five, eighty and eighty-three were met with.'[49] But the conclusion of the London Statistical Society's study of Westminster — 'The number of persons advanced in life was very small' — seems to be one which can be applied generally.[50] Certainly this is true of the results derived from the census returns in Bristol. In this city, for the years 1851, 1861 and 1871, the numbers of private school teachers over the age of 60, expressed as a percentage of the total, were respectively 10.7 per cent, 14.8 per cent and 11.5 per cent. Those who were under 20 comprised 9.5 per cent, 6 per cent and 8.9 per cent respectively. And the average age of female teachers at each of these dates was 40.3, 43.5 and 37.1 respectively.[51] School-keeping was therefore a common occupation at virtually any given point in a normal working life and cannot be characterised as primarily a refuge from the economic difficulties of old age.

School-keeping was never a very remunerative activity and teachers were as likely to suffer as much as were their clients from economic hardship. The financial return from teaching was always likely to be low and certain to be unpredictable. Teachers of working-class private schools seldom made much profit from their labour. The average weekly receipts of Birmingham's dames in 1840 was estimated to be as low as 4s 3½d. In Bury, in 1835, the corresponding figure was given as 7s 4d, or about £19 a year. For teachers of 'common day' schools, the same enquiry suggested that 'their yearly annual receipts amount to £62, a smaller sum than common industry would procure for them in many mechanical and manufacturing employments'.[52]

It cannot be denied that many private school teachers, like other workers, were poor, though there is no necessary connection between this and bad teaching. But the main emphasis of the official record is not so much on the poverty of practising teachers as the poverty of those who *became* teachers in the first place. In other words, that teaching was turned to only when all else had failed — the 'last resort'. Thus could the London Statistical Society allege, for example, that male teachers 'were men in distressed circumstances, or who had, at some time or another, failed in trade, and seemed to have taken up the profession as a last resource'.[53] H.M.I. Johnstone argued that 'The dame is an old woman, disabled for all else, who ekes out a scanty livelihood and just manages to avoid the workhouse.'[54] And according to Factory Inspector Horner, 'Private schools . . . are, in general, small assemblages of children in cottages, brought together by indigent old men or old women, who nominally keep a school, they being incapable of earning a livelihood in any other way.'[55] George Bartley, as he frequently did, made the same point more colourfully. 'The great number [of private schools] are kept by broken-down dressmakers, widows and such persons who, having failed in everything else take to "keeping school" like the Irishman who was put to teach the children when too old to look after the pigs.'[56]

It is important to remember that such arguments were informed by the conviction that teaching should be a vocation and a trained profession. The apparently casual and unprepared manner in which some working people could turn to teaching was, for the educational expert, profoundly disconcerting. It was therefore a tendency which needed to be discredited as 'a last resort'. In fact, teaching was simply a skill which many men and women discovered that they possessed, and which they exercised from time to time with various degrees of regularity, when it suited them and when they needed the income. In some circumstances, this might indeed be when some other form of activity — possibly more profitable — had come to an end. But to assume that this was usually the case is seriously misleading. Some might well begin their working lives as teachers and remain so for many years. Just as the official accounts failed to grasp the working-class conception of school-keeping as an unremarkable activity, relatively undifferentiated from other working-class employments, so they misunderstood the role of school-keeping within the domestic economy. The meagre financial return from teaching often meant that the activity was an integrated part of overall family income and not its only component.

In this sense, teaching did not present itself in the simplistic and dramatic terms of a desperate last chance against destitution. School-keeping did not always insert itself into working-class culture in general, or the domestic economy in particular, in quite this all-or-nothing way.

The generally low level of remuneration from teaching — especially from the teaching of reading — together with its fundamentally domestic character, must have contributed to the numerical preponderance of female teachers over male. However, some male workers precluded from physically demanding — and potentially more profitable — labour, found they could still contribute to the domestic economy through teaching. This frequently seems to have been the case where workers were confined to the home through industrial injury.[57] For such men, teaching was a useful second skill to fall back on.

Such teachers were always a small minority of the total, but they were singled out for particularly bitter attack by some writers, largely because their overt physical disability fitted well with a theory of general condemnation. The Manchester Statistical Society, for example, spoke of 'ignorant and uneducated men, who are often destitute of every qualification for their office, and have undertaken it only because they found this the easiest means of gaining a subsistence, and frequently in consequence of accident or bodily infirmity'.[58]

In reality, the association between physical handicap and bad teaching was once more not a necessary one. Some of the official reports themselves acknowledge this. The Manchester Statistical Society itself found that

> . . . one of the best of these [private] schools is kept by a blind man, who hears his scholars their lessons, and explains them with great simplicity; he is, however, liable to interruption in his academic labours, as his wife keeps a mangle, and he is obliged to turn it for her.[59]

The most well-known example of a disabled worker setting up a school must however be that of Thomas Cooper, whom no one could describe as an incompetent teacher. In his case, it was not a physical handicap, but a serious nervous breakdown which temporarily kept him from manual work.

> I was very weak for some time; and when I attempted a little manual labour, it brought on a particular nervous tremor that almost frightened me, and which compelled me to desist, time after time. [My friends] took counsel together, and proposed to me that I should try the profession of a schoolmaster. I agreed, for I felt I could not work again on the stall . . . My school was a perfect passion with me for a time.[60]

It was not only physical or mental handicaps which were commonly deemed to force an individual to keep school as a last resort. Identified moral disabilities were also adduced in much the same way. J. R. Wood sought to distinguish such individuals in terms of broad personality-type; 'frequently, their tempers, dispositions and habits have occasioned the very misfortunes that have driven them to [teaching]'.[61] But by far the most common charge of this kind was the specific one of intemperance. In Manchester in 1834, for example, 'The Committee met with two instances of schools kept by Masters of some abilities, but much given to drinking . . .'. To their dismay, the Committee was obliged to notice further that this deficiency evidently was not viewed with equal displeasure by the schools' clients; the two

> had however gained such a reputation in their neighbourhood that after spending a week or fortnight in this pastime they could always fill their school-rooms again as soon as they returned to their work. The children during the absence of the Masters go to other schools for the week or play in the streets, or are employed by their parents in running errands, etc. On another occasion, one of these Instructors and Guardians of the morals of our youth was met issuing from his school at the head of his scholars to see a fight in the neighbourhood; and instead of stopping to reply to any educational queries, only uttered a breathless invitation to come along and see this sport.[62]

And William Scarratt recalled of his brief time at a private school in 1850 that, 'the "mentor" was absent from duty the greater part of the afternoon, and one of my last visions of the "don" was his being brought up home from the Staff of Life with the assistance of two other "buveurs" '.[63]

The argument that some working men became teachers because they were physically or morally incapable of any other employment is a spurious one — though undoubtedly colourful. For a small minority of the total private teaching strength, school-keeping was indeed an enforced alternative to a manual trade. This did not make such teachers necessarily incompetent or inferior to the others. They, no less than the others, were subject to the need to satisfy the expressed educational demand of their working-class clients.

What, in sum, can be said of the view that school-keeping was a 'last resort'? Essentially, it was a false conception produced in the first place by the efforts of the official record to tarnish working-class private schooling. Teaching in such schools was no more a 'last resort' than any other working-class employment, though it was characterised by a high degree of flexibility and compatability with daily domestic life. The majority of teachers were neither illiterate, nor destitute, nor aged, nor incapable of carrying out their work effectively. School-keeping was a valued and traditional occupation, rooted in the cultural and social life of the working class. It was undertaken by those members of the class seen as most suited to the task, and most likely to accomplish it successfully.

We have already seen that school-keeping, though based in the home, was frequently not the only source of household income. Indeed, the occupation of school-keeper itself was often combined with other forms of employment; thus was the modest financial return from teaching augmented. Additional labour of this kind might be domestic or remunerative. The former variety helps to explain further the predominance of female teachers. Daily domestic labour could be combined with teaching without great organisational difficulty. Expert commentators however found the arrangement deeply unsatisfactory.

Assistant Commissioner Winder, for example, commented that 'The usual scene of one of these schools is a cottage kitchen, in which the mistress divides her time between her pupils and her domestic duties.'[64] And Assistant Commissioner Foster held that 'the worst of the private adventure schools are those in which 30 or 40 children are crowded into the kitchen of a collier's dwelling, and the mistress divides her attention between teaching them, nursing her own baby, and cooking for her husband and sons'.[65]

Other reports widened out the scope of dual employment. In London in the early 1840s for instance, the Statistical Society found that

> Of 540 schoolmasters and mistresses who were asked whether they had any other occupation than their schools, 260 [or 48.1%] answered that they kept a shop or took in washing or needlework, or had other occupation than in their schools. But although they might not have any other ostensible occupation, it can hardly be supposed that they were in a condition to devote their whole energies to their scholastic duties. On the contrary, the mistresses of the common day schools were sometimes young persons unable to go to service from ill-health, or desirous of staying at home with a sick or aged parent, and glad to add something to their means of maintenance; some again were mothers of large families; and in all cases, even the most favourable, the female teachers had their own household work to do.[66]

And in Birmingham in the same period, 'Out of 267 [mistresses of dame schools], there were 190, or 71.6% following some other employment, frequently trenching largely on the teacher's time'.[67]

The most widespread form of additional remunerative activity for women teachers was the taking in of washing and the sale of sweets and snacks. The latter activity was obviously well suited to a situation in which a stream of children came and left the house. Henry Althans reported to the 1837 Select Committee that the dames of east London 'often keep toy-shops and cake-shops, and they make something by the children who buy their cakes'.[68] Assistant Commissioner Fletcher found that,

> Frequently the little room in the teacher's house, perhaps not more than nine or twelve feet square, and seldom exceeding fourteen feet, serves also as a shop for the sale of pins, needles, tapes, and other little huckstery, and sometimes is the weaving shop of the mistress of the school.[69]

The Education Enquiry of 1870 discovered individual cases of this type, such as Sarah McQuin's school in Hackney, '. . . a back room, a dame school. In the front room sweets are sold.'[70] And other examples come to light in the recollections of scholars, such as Frederick Hobley from Thame in Oxfordshire,

> . . . I was sent to another Dame's School, kept by Ma'am Lund . . . [she] eked out her living by selling Bulls'-eyes and Brandy-balls. These were at that time the chief sweets for children to buy. Every Tuesday, she replenished her stock. On that day, each week, an old man named Jackson called on her, he had a good sized oblong tin box, which was strapped on his back, and this was filled with Bulls'-eyes etc. He used to give one to the child who sat near the door as he went out. I remember I sat there more than once.[71]

William Howitt remembered one of his teachers, 'William Woodcock, more familiarly called Billy Bingo — a little, jolly man, who united the two vocations of schoolmaster and baker, while his wife boiled toffee and barley-sugar for the children.'[72] The uniting of two occupations was less common among male teachers than female, though Billy Bingo was certainly not unusual. John Jones, the working-class poet, relates that in his Gloucestershire village, 'the only person . . . who taught writing at that time was an old man, by trade a stone-cutter, and he only on winter evenings — after his return from his daily labour . . .'[73] John Palmer, who kept a school in Bristol in 1871, returned his occupation as 'School Master/Greengrocer'. And in Bury in 1835, of 17 common day teachers, 'six follow other occupations, among which we find enumerated those of a pawnbroker, a hatter and a dyer.'[74]

The mixing of teaching with other tasks, whether domestic or remunerative, was therefore extremely common, despite the condemnation of education experts. They found the practice both educationally inefficient and morally dangerous. But for the users of the schools, teachers of this kind were quite natural, presenting one more aspect of the lack of differentiation between everyday working life and schooling. Indeed, such teachers might be particularly highly thought of by their users, as the words of an anonymous 'Working Man' testify.

> My first schoolmaster was an admirable type of the class that flourished in our village when I was young. He was a man of some ingenuity, and a little original in his manner. Like most schoolmasters who were above the ordinary mark in those days, he had another employment, making account books, and this was carried on in school hours and in the schoolroom.[75]

A major charge against the teachers, and one which was closely linked to the view of school-keeping as a last resort, was that their schools were ephemeral. In the following discussion, we will therefore concentrate on the issue of institutional ephemerality; on the allegedly high rate of turnover in individual schools. Before we do so, it is however worth considering that the ephemerality of institutions is but one dimension of a more complex pattern, and not necessarily the most significant one. Ephemerality can be charged against other elements in this pattern. The ephemerality of the learning relationship itself, for instance — of the interaction of pupil and teacher — needs particularly to be stressed. In working-class private schools, the relationship was always closer, more co-operative and probably more productive than in the publicly provided schools. Though the latter possessed the physical longevity of formal institutions, the effectiveness of the rigidified, distanced and authoritarian learning environment they provided cannot be assumed as a necessary consequence of this. Indeed, there is considerable evidence to suggest that the opposite was true. Working-class private schools on the other hand, however short-lived, did not share such ephemerality of daily interaction. We will return to this theme in the next chapter.

Let us now however consider in some depth the issue of institutional ephemerality. How justified was the claim, made by one of the Statistical Societies in 1840, and since unchallenged, that 'Few circumstances tend more fully to reveal the defective character of this class of schools than that of their very ephemeral nature.'?[76]

From the outset, we must set the question within the broader frame of working-class social and cultural life as a whole. It cannot be approached very meaningfully through comparison of private and publicly provided schools. Public schools clearly possessed a degree of permanency which was independent of the lives of their teachers. But in the case of the working-class private school, the institution was synonymous with the individual teacher and vice versa. Moreover, such teachers were themselves likely to share the high degree of geographical mobility of their clients and of the urban working class in general.[77] This fluidity makes individual schools enormously difficult to track. It is generally impossible to say whether the movement from one town or district to another of a family in which a school was kept might lead to the total disappearance of the school, or to its reappearance in the family's new location. Indeed, it is not easy to trace positively individual schools over a period of time even where they remained in the same locations. There have been some recent attempts to do this through the columns of local street directories, but these are largely futile because the great majority of working-class private schools simply were not listed.[78] Where schools *can* be tracked in a single urban location — through the Population Census — it is clear that removal within the same city within a ten-year period was extremely common. In Bristol, of 69 known examples of working-class private schools surviving over such a period, only 18 (26 per cent) were kept at the same address throughout, though of these, two were maintained at the same address for at least 20 years — that is, over the course of three Population Censuses. A further 18 schools — if the accuracy of the census can be relied upon — moved to new premises within the same street or an adjoining street. This leaves 33 cases (48 per cent of the total) where a school was removed from one area of the city to another over a ten-year period. This finding is of great significance. The failure to trace a known private school at two points in time at the same address cannot be taken to indicate the effective disappearance of that school. Still more, part of the reality of the working-class private school is lost if this element of movement is overlooked; in truth, the idea of the school in this culture resided not in a particular, purpose-specific building, but in the person of the teacher.[79]

This is a major difficulty in sustaining an unequivocal charge of ephemerality against the schools. It may be possible to show that this or that school was not in existence in a particular location for very long, but it is far more difficult to demonstrate that particular individuals did not offer their skills in various locations over long sustained periods. And where this was the case, it is is unjust to say that such a school was ephemeral; more accurately, it was mobile.

By no means does this imply the wholesale rejection of the notion of ephemerality, but rather the need for its restatement in more informed terms. Undoubtedly, there must have been some teachers who 'turned' to school-keeping only to fail rapidly. Such schools would have been genuinely ephemeral; over and done with in a few weeks or months, and the skill of teaching unproved and undeveloped. As such, they would have been highly unlikely ever to have been documented in any way at all. But it seems that such cases were comparatively few. Most school-keepers would have come to the occupation as a natural extension of teaching their own children or as a sideline which could be fitted in with other work.

In this context, teaching activity might be woven into the domestic economy in a relatively unstructured and possibly sporadic pattern. Teachers might keep school only for a few years when necessity, opportunity and demand coincided, or for a long unbroken period. Susannah Lewis from Bristol, who ran a school from at least 1851 to 1881, and almost certainly longer, is an example of the latter. In 1881, she was an

> old lady, now paying one shilling and threepence for a single room, [who] for many years . . . kept a large school in a cottage in Unity Street; and even now, in her one room with bare furniture, and a humble pallet covering half the space, she has a 'school for infants'.[80]

Joseph Tittle, on the other hand, kept a humble school in the city in 1851, had disappeared from the educational scene by 1861, and surfaced once more ten years later at the age of 71 as a school master again.[81] This kind of episodic teaching career was more likely to stem from the personal circumstances of the teacher, rather than from a failure to satisfy popular demand.

The critical point is that neither pattern of school-keeping might be accurately or fairly labelled as 'ephemeral'. Whilst many schools were not operated by men and women who devoted their whole working life to teaching, the majority were run seriously, practically and purposefully by people drawing on some years of teaching experience and demonstrated ability. The categorisation as 'ephemeral' of schools which had a known continuous and stable existence over a period of years is both an injustice and a misunderstanding of the culture of the working-class private school. With these thoughts in mind, we can now look at the available statistical evidence on longevity.

A recent writer has argued that,

> From the reports of the statistical societies of the 1830's and the Report of the Newcastle Commissioners, published in 1861, it is apparent that dame and common day schools were often set up by their proprietors as a desperate last resort. The precarious income they earned kept them out of the workhouse. Since little or no capital was required, these schools were ephemeral institutions.[82]

This assertion rests primarily upon findings of the Manchester Statistical Society's two separate investigations of Pendleton — 'one of the few occasions, possibly the only one, on which two investigations were made in the same area over a short period of time'.[83] These investigations took place in 1835 and 1838. This evidence 'gives us some idea of the rate of turnover'.[84] Its most powerful finding among other examples of high turnover rates in private schools was 'that only one of the eight dames met with in 1835 is now keeping school in the township and she is not in her former abode. The remaining six dame schools are all new.'[85] This implies a striking pattern. It suggests a very large number of individuals turning in succession for a characteristically very short period to school-keeping, though the total number of schools over time might remain stable. A survey at any given moment would therefore be no more than a snapshot, capturing only those handful of individuals briefly operating schools at that particular moment. A short time before or after that moment, the personnel of the schools would be highly likely to be quite different. This massive circulatory pattern is belied by the static picture which momentary surveys inevitably convey and which imply an appearance of longevity which did not, in reality, exist.

However, the Pendleton sample was on a very small scale, and it cannot reasonably be made the basis for large generalisations. We need to search for better evidence than this.

Relatively few of the reports of the various Statistical Societies make direct references to the question of longevity. Where they do, it appears that the very high turnover rate in the small Pendleton sample — only 12.5 per cent of dame schools managing to survive in a period of less than three years — was unusual. The London Statistical Society's 1839 investigation of Finsbury found, for example, 'Of the 317 schools, one-seventh had commenced before 1820, one-sixth between 1820 and 1830, and the rest (214) between 1830 and 1839.'[86] And for the same period, the Manchester Society found that, 'Out of the 267 dame schools in Birmingham, 73 or 27.34 per cent, were established in 1830, while 194, or 72.66 per cent, have been established since.'[87]

Whilst not referring directly to the question of longevity in the text of their reports, some other investigations — notably those of Bristol and Rutland — have a tabular appendix on the subject. Together, these seem to accord reasonably closely with the pattern in Finsbury and Birmingham.[88] (See Table 4.1.)

Table 4.1: Working-class Private Schools: Findings of Statistical Societies

Location	Year of survey	Type of school	No.	Date of establishment				
				Before 1801	1801–10	1811–20	1821–30	1830–8
Birmingham	1838	Dame	267	2 (0.7%)	4 (1.5%)	16 (6%)	51 (19.1%)	194* (72.7%)
		Common Day (Boys)	54	3 (5.6%)	2 (3.7%)	8 (14.8%)	12 (22.2%)	29 (53.7%)
		Common Day (Girls)	123	2 (1.6%)	7 (5.7%)	5 (4.1%)	29 (23.6%)	79 (64.2%)
Rutland	1838	Dame	50	—	5 (10%)	6 (12%)	12 (24%)	27 (54%)
		Common Day (Boys)	8	—	—	—	3 (37.5%)	5 (62.5%)
		Common Day (Girls)	17	2 (11.8%)	—	3 (17.6%)	5 (29.4%)	7 (41.2%)
					Before 1820			
Finsbury	1839	Dame	180		26 (14.4%)		29 (16.1%)	125 (69.5%)
		Common Day	137		17 (12.4%)		31 (22.6%)	89 (65%)
Bristol	1841	Dame	211		18 (8.5%)		40 (19%)	153 (72.5%)
		Common Day	171		23 (13.4%)		40 (23.4%)	108 (63.2%)

* Of this figure, 127 (47.7%) commenced during the period 1830–7; 67 (25%), in the year 1838.

We should however note that the figures do not make it clear what they mean by 'date of establishment'. As we have seen, school-keepers changed dwellings as frequently as other members of the working class. It is therefore of central importance whether the 'date of establishment' is understood to relate to present address only, or to the existence of the same school over time at different addresses. Unfortunately we have no way of knowing which meaning was used, and by whom. But it is as well to bear the issue in mind. For the purposes of the following discussion, we will assume the least favourable option: that the 'date of establishment' refers to the total life of the school and incorporates any changes of address.

To the extent that they were accurate, these figures present several interesting features. In the first place they suggest that the rural dame's school might well have been typically more long-lived than its urban counterpart; and second, in the large urban centres, the turnover rate of 'dames' schools' was likely to have been higher than that of the common day schools. It is in the shifting and unstable environment of the nineteenth-century city that we would therefore expect to find the theory of ephemerality most amply demonstrated, and particularly among the more modest varieties of the 'woman's school'.

But the demonstration is by no means clear. Even if we take the most favourable figure — that for the 'dames' schools' of Birmingham — we find that 27.3 per cent of such schools had been in existence for at least eight years and sometimes much longer. The theory of ephemerality ignores these schools and concentrates on those with a life span of eight years or less. It would argue that most of these schools would run for perhaps just a few months and therefore artificially inflate the real significance of working-class private schooling at the time of the enquiry. In this view, probably most of the 194 dames' schools in Birmingham dating their existence from 1830 would in fact have been opened as late as 1837 or 1838, the very year of the survey. Even if this were the case, the theory of ephemerality would have to acknowledge the existence of two layers of working-class private schooling in terms of longevity. Even if all the 194 schools were proved satisfactorily to be 'ephemeral', there remain 73 (27.3 per cent) that were not. However, the Birmingham report — unusually — does supply some further detail on the 194 shorter term schools: 'of the 194 schools, 67 or 34.53%, have been opened during the last 12 months'.[89] It is in this number that the classic 'ephemeral' school is likely to be found. However, without comparative totals from earlier periods and without figures of permanent closure, it is possible that such schools might represent not the tip of an ephemerality iceberg, but, rather, part of a long-term expansion in total provision as indicated by the Education Census of 1851.[90] In other words, though there was indeed a substantial number of young schools in 1838, the total demand for such schools was increasing, making the existence of some new schools inevitable. These need not therefore have closed down rapidly, but might have lastingly augmented total available provision.

The best therefore that the theory of ephemerality can achieve among the figures most apparently favourable to it — Birmingham's 'dames' schools' — is that 67 schools out of 267 (25 per cent) were *potentially* 'ephemeral'. Moreover, as we shall now see, the Birmingham report also suggests that not all of the teachers of these 67 schools were new to teaching itself.

The reports of the Statistical Societies often contained valuable though limited evidence on the careers of private school-keepers as distinct from their schools. Such evidence clearly bears directly on the question of longevity. In this connection, the most useful information is the length of teaching experience. The available figures from the various reports are set out in Table 4.2.[91] From them we can deduce that though 25 per cent of Birmingham's dames' schools had been functioning for less than one year, just 19.9 per cent of the dames themselves had less than one year's teaching experience. The discrepancy can only be accounted for by assuming that a proportion of the 'new' dames had run schools — either in Birmingham or in other locations — before.

Of its various enquiries in London, the London Statistical Society reported in 1843 that,

> Of 500 [private teachers] who were asked how long they had been engaged in teaching, 194 (38.8%) answered that they had been engaged in that occupation for a period of less than 5 years; 99 (19.8%) had been engaged for a period between 5 and 10 years; 111 (22.2%) between 10 and 20 years, and 96 (19.2%) more than 20 years.[92]

Thus, 61.2 per cent of the teachers of London's working-class private schools had been teaching continuously for at least a

Table 4.2: Part 1. Teachers of Working-class Private Schools: Findings of Statistical Societies

Location	Date	No. of teachers	Number of years teaching experience							
			Less than 1	1–2	2–3	3–4	4–5	5–6	6–7	7+
			%	%	%	%	%	%	%	%
Dames' Schools										
Manchester	1834	230	44 (19.1)	24 (10.4)	31 (13.6)	20 (8.7)	21 (9.1)	12 (5.2)	8 (3.5)	70 (30.4)
Salford	1835	64	12 (18.8)	6 (9.3)	7 (10.9)	13 (20.3)	3 (4.7)	3 (4.7)	1 (1.6)	19 (29.7)
Bury	1835	30	3 (10.0)	1 (3.3)	2 (6.6)	4 (13.3)	1 (3.3)	3 (10.0)	5 (16.7)	11 (36.8)
Liverpool	1835–6	244	24 (9.8)	31 (12.7)	34 (13.9)	27 (11.1)	21 (8.6)	15 (6.1)	11 (4.6)	81 (33.2)
York	1836–7	37	3 (8.1)	1 (2.7)	4 (10.8)	2 (5.4)	4 (10.8)	3 (8.1)	1 (2.7)	19 (51.4)
Birmingham	1838	266	53 (19.9)	33 (12.4)	32 (12.1)	20 (7.5)	18 (6.8)	16 (6.0)	7 (2.6)	87 (32.7)
Rutland	1838	50	2 (4.0)	7 (14.0)	4 (8.0)	2 (2.0)	3 (6.0)	6 (12.0)	4 (8.0)	23 (46.0)
			Less than 1	1–2	2–3	3–4	4–5	5–10	10–20	20+
			%	%	%	%	%	%	%	%
Westminster	1838	63	18 (28.6)	3 (4.8)	6 (9.5)	6 (9.5)	4 (6.3)	14 (22.2)	7 (11.2)	5 (7.9)
Westminster	1838	46	11 (23.9)	9 (19.7)	6 (13.0)	3 (6.5)	3 (6.5)	7 (15.2)	6 (13.0)	1 (2.2)
Finsbury	1839	166	17 (10.3)	19 (11.4)	12 (7.2)	10 (6.0)	12 (7.2)	35 (21.1)	30 (18.1)	31 (18.7)

Table 4.2: Part 2

Location	Date	No. of teachers	Number of years teaching experience							
			Less than 1	1–2	2–3	3–4	4–5	5–6	6–7	7+
			%	%	%	%	%	%	%	%
Common Day Schools										
Manchester	1834	177	20 (11.3)	11 (6.2)	26 (14.7)	14 (7.9)	16 (9.0)	6 (3.4)	9 (5.1)	75 (42.4)
Salford	1835	39	4 (10.2)	1 (2.6)	6 (15.4)	3 (7.7)	5 (12.8)	3 (7.7)	12 (30.8)	5 (12.8)
Bury	1835	17	2 (11.8)	1 (5.9)	3 (17.6)	1 (5.9)	0	1 (5.9)	3 (17.6)	6 (35.3)
Liverpool	1835–6	186	7 (3.8)	20 (10.8)	17 (9.1)	21 (11.3)	14 (7.5)	11 (5.9)	13 (7.0)	83 (44.6)
York	1836–7	23	0	0	1 (4.3)	7 (30.4)	0	2 (8.7)	0	13 (56.6)
Birmingham	1838	199	20 (10.0)	9 (4.5)	14 (7.0)	7 (3.6)	10 (5.0)	11 (5.5)	7 (3.6)	121 (60.8)
Rutland	1838	24	0	3 (12.5)	0	0	0	2 (8.3)	2 (8.3)	17 (70.9)
			Less than 1	1–2	2–3	3–4	4–5	5–10	10–20	20+
			%	%	%	%	%	%	%	%
Westminster	1838	41	5 (12.2)	3 (7.3)	1 (2.4)	1 (2.4)	2 (4.9)	5 (12.2)	15 (16.6)	9 (22.0)
Westminster	1838	54	5 (9.2)	7 (13.0)	2 (3.7)	4 (7.4)	4 (7.4)	11 (20.4)	13 (24.1)	8 (14.8)
Finsbury	1839	130	2 (1.5)	3 (2.3)	6 (4.6)	3 (2.3)	7 (5.4)	27 (20.8)	40 (30.8)	42 (32.3)

period of five years, and often considerably longer. And if we take an average of all the reports, we find that 54.8 per cent of all teachers had been teaching for at least five years in a period of educational expansion. These are not figures which sit very easily alongside the notions of 'last resort' and 'ephemerality'.

We need to note however that if we break these figures down further, they do indicate a significant difference between 'dames' and 'common day' teachers. Dames with more than five years' continuous experience comprise an average of 48.1 per cent of those so described, whilst of common day teachers, 61.4 per cent had been teaching for five years continuously. But only in some of the larger urban centres, it must be stressed, is there evidence of a disproportionate number of teachers — and in particular, dames — with less than one year's experience. Once more then, we can see that it is in this category, if anywhere, that the classic 'ephemeral private school' appears to lie. But it is crucial to note that such a school was not, on the strength of the available figures, the dominant form of the working-class private school.

What can be said in summary? In most areas, large numbers of schools, varying from a fifth to a half of the total, probably had an existence in excess of seven years, with most of the remainder lasting — at one or more locations — about two to seven years. There were some ephemeral schools, possibly lasting only for a few months, but these were not numerous and appear to have mainly comprised some of the 'dames' schools' in the larger urban centres.

There are two further sources which give useful information on the question of the length of teaching experience of individual teachers and the longevity of their schools.

The first comes from the returns of the Education Enquiry required by the Act of 1870. These returns were supposed to indicate, among much else, the length of time that an individual school-teacher had been in the business of teaching. Frequently, the information was not given, though in some areas it was generally supplied. One such area was the parish of St James, Bermondsey. Full details of the returns from this parish have been set out elsewhere; here it need only be noted that 59 of 63 private teachers gave information relating to the length of their teaching experience.[93] The local pattern which their responses suggests is broadly compatible with that indicated by the Statistical Societies, with 46 per cent of the total having more than five years' experience. This is best seen in the form of a graph (See Figure 4.1).

Figure 4.1: Teachers of Working-Class Private Schools: St James' Bermondsey. Length of teaching experience

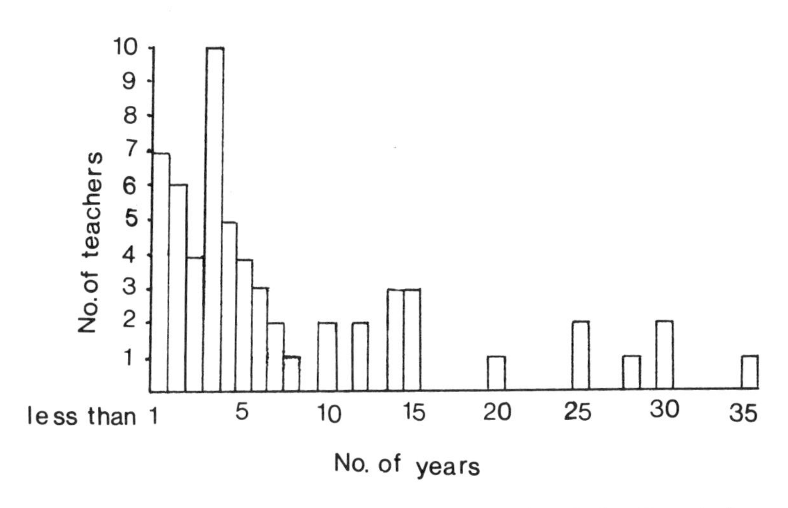

The second source derives from the study of the Population Censuses in Bristol from 1851 to 1871. This at first appears to indicate levels of longevity rather lower than those suggested by the reports of the Statistical Societies. The levels are however very constant; 11.5 per cent of working-class private schools found in 1851 were present in 1861 and 12.1 per cent of the 1861 total survived until 1871. In 1871, 5 per cent of the 1851 schools were still in existence. What do these lower rates of overall longevity suggest? How can they be explained?

The explanation in fact came from a chance observation. In 1851, a school was kept in Camplin's Court, St Augustine's by Sarah Smallcorn, the 27-year-old unmarried daughter of George Smallcorn, a tailor.[94] A limited investigation of the 1841 Census revealed that the school was in existence in exactly the same location at this earlier date.[95] Sarah was returned at this census as 'School Assistant' to her elder sister, Ann, in whose hands the school apparently then was. By 1851, though, Ann had disappeared, leaving Sarah in sole charge. In 1861, a school is recorded in Prince's Street, St Augustine's, where a certain Sarah Dunn returned herself as 'Schoolmistress'.[96] Her husband, John, a carpenter, was given the relatively unusual familial status of 'son-in-law', and this prompted a passing glance at his father-in-law, who would otherwise have gone unnoticed. The father-in-law turned out to be George Smallcorn, now 70 and still a tailor. His daughter had clearly married at some point after 1851, brought her husband to live in the parental home, and continued her school there under her new name. The schools of Sarah Smallcorn and Sarah Dunn were one and the same, but if it had not been for a chance observation and the singularity of the surname 'Smallcorn', no connection would have been made, and the two schools would have been recorded as being kept for relatively short periods by separate individuals. In fact, Sarah Smallcorn-Dunn's school was still functioning in 1871 when she was just 47.[97] She had been keeping the same school continuously, though at different addresses, for at least 30 years. Her case cannot have been unique, but most schools which were kept before marriage and continued after it are, because of change of name, and probably also of address, quite impossible to track. Hence the apparently lower longevity rate revealed by the Population Census.

One more point needs yet to be made on the issue of longevity. It has been argued above that the working-class private school was synonymous with a single individual, and when that individual ceased to teach, the school simply died. Whilst this was true in the majority of cases, there are exceptions which need to be recorded.

The returns required by the 1870 Act show that, very rarely, a school might be purchased as a going concern and passed on to a new keeper. It is not clear whether such transfers involved simply the pupils of a particular school, or its premises as well. On the few occasions where such a change had taken place, the fee involved was — at least in London — invariably £3, the equivalent of between three weeks' or three months' income.[98] Such a transfer might explain the comment made in 1871, by an inspector upon a school kept by 60-year-old Catharine Cornish in Viaduct Street, Bethnal Green. She had 'held this school for eleven years and was once a scholar in it'.[99]

A more common practice was the passing of an individual school to another, generally younger, member of the existing teacher's family. A good example is the school kept by Sarah Ellis in the parish of Bedminster, Bristol.[100] In 1851, Sarah was 37; she was married to a tanner and had three children including Charlotte, who was four. Sarah gave her occupation as 'Governess'. Ten years later, the family had fallen on harder times. Sarah was now widowed and shared a house in Hillgrove Street, Bedminster, with the family of a young chain-maker.[101] She gave her occupation as 'Schoolmistress', with her two youngest children as 'Scholars' whilst Charlotte, now 14, was a 'Tailoress', probably working at home. Times for the Ellis family were still hard in 1871, for they now occupied 'Rooms over Timber Yard' in Doveton Street, Bedminster.[102] But Sarah, now given as 60 years old, was fortunate to retain the support of two unmarried daughters at home. One of these was a 'Machinist', whilst Charlotte had been elevated to run the school as 'Governess'. Her mother, probably enjoying a kind of semi-retirement, was now given as 'Formerly Governess'. The school, which was recorded in 1871 as having 30 scholars, had been a continuous and doubtless crucial source of income for Sarah Ellis as a wife with a young family, as a struggling widow and — though it was now in the hands of her daughter — on the threshold of an uncertain old age.

Sometimes the census records the very moment at which a daughter first began formally to share with her mother the duties of teaching the school. Such is the case of 13-year-old Susannah Fisher from Bedminster, whose initial entry in the 1861 Census of 'Scholar' was deleted by the enumerator and replaced by 'Teacher at School' — that is, at the school kept by her mother, Emma Fisher.[103] A similar instance was recorded ten years later when Julia, the 15-year-old daughter of Martha Minty, 'Governess', was recorded variously as 'Scholar', 'School Keeper' (deleted) and finally as 'Assistant to ditto', that is, to her mother.[104]

Far more difficult to trace are cases where the skills of school-keeping, though not an individual school, were learned and passed on within a single family or household. In 1851, for example, a school was kept by William Ashton in a house in the parish of St Andrew's.[105] He shared the house with his wife, Fanny, their young daughter, Mary, and a number of lodgers. By 1861, William Ashton was dead, and his widow and daughter had moved to St Paul's, where Fanny herself, no doubt drawing on her husband's skills, set up a new school.[106] To augment her income, she continued as before to take in lodgers, one of whom was a local woman, Elizabeth Breeding, a widowed needlewoman. If Fanny Ashton's school conformed to the common pattern, then Elizabeth Breeding was, as a member of the immediate household, likely to have been drawn into some aspects of its day-to-day organisation and operation. It seems that this was indeed the case, for whatever lessons she picked up from her landlady, Elizabeth Breeding had by 1871 given up her needle and, as a lodger in another St Paul's household, declared herself as 'Schoolmistress'.[104]

How common the kinds of informal 'apprenticeships' which both Fanny Ashton and Elizabeth Breeding in their turn served were, it is impossible to say, but both cases show how new schools might be set up by individuals who were not ignorant of what school-keeping involved.

Finally, it is worth pointing out that the evidence from the Bristol censuses shows relatively little sign of significant changes in the social status of individual schools over long periods of time. Of Bristol schools with an ascertained life-span of ten or twenty years, just 20 per cent showed — on the basis of assigned gradings — significant changes in status. Of these, about two-thirds were upwardly mobile, probably seeking to cater for a more exclusive lower middle-class clientele (see Table 4.3).

Table 4.3: Working-class Private Schools in Bristol: Changes in Status, 1851–71

	Assigned grade		
Initial ref. no. of school	1851	1861	1871
51/343	B	B/C	B
51/34	C	B	A/B
51/117	A	A	A
51/133	A	A	A
51/689	A/B	A/B	A/B
51/791	B	A/B	B
51/793	A/B	A/B	A/B
51/92–3	C	A/B	A/B
51/774	C/D	B	B
51/823	A/B	B	B
51/160	A/B	C/D	C/D
51/829	A	—	A
51/96	A	A	
51/7	C	A	
51/31	A	A	
51/42	C	B	
51/39	A	A	
51/46	B/C	B/C	
51/59	A	A	
51/60	A	B	
51/252	B	A/B	
51/406	C	B/C	
51/664–6	B/C	D	
51/691	A/B	A/B	

Table 4.3 – continued

Initial ref. no. of school	Assigned grade 1851	1861	1871
51/715	A	B	
51/728	B	B/C	
51/162	B	A	
51/300	C/D	B/C	
51/520–1	C/D	A/B	
51/652	A	B	
51/706	C	B	
51/794	B/C	B/C	
51/795	B/C	B	
51/817	A/B	A/B	
51/825	A/B	A/B	
51/826	A/B	A/B	
51/831	A/B	A/B	
61/8		A/B	A
61/25		B	A/B
61/28–9		A/B	C/D
61/37		A/B	B/C
61/60		A/B	B
61/75		B	B
61/83		B	C/D
61/102		C/D	B
61/117		A/B	A
61/121		A/B	A
61/157		A/B	A/B
61/167		B	B/C
61/174		C	C
61/177		B/C	A/B
61/182		A/B	A
61/184		A	A
51/187		A/B	B
61/214		A/B	A/B
61/226		A/B	A/B
61/229		A	A
61/239		A	A
61/254		B	B/C
61/256		B	C/D
61/15		C/D	B

The keeper of the working-class private school remains a figure as elusive as any other in the unrecorded daily lives of the nineteenth-century working class. This chapter has tried to offer some indications of the sort of people they were and to challenge the prevailing impression that they were careless or desperate incompetents whose involvement in teaching the children of the working class was 'ephemeral'.

Notes

1. For some useful references, see D. Vincent, *Bread, Knowledge and Freedom* (1981), pp. 100–4. It is noteworthy that the few existing autobiographies are written exclusively by males. Of the great majority — the female teachers — there is no record.
2. See for example, Saunders in P.P. 1851 [1304] xxiii, *Reports of Inspectors of Factories*, p. 54: 'provided the party be able to read and write, he is forthwith appointed schoolmaster, without any reference to his ability to convey instruction to others, or to introduce and support the necessary discipline of a school'.
3. H.M.I. Morell, *C.C.E.*, 1871–2, p. 64.
4. Fraser, *Newcastle*, vol. 2, p. 38. Private teachers have 'no special fitness . . . that is the fruit of preparation or training'.
5. Winder, *Newcastle*, vol. 2, p. 219. But see also, 'Finsbury . . .', *J.S.S.* (February 1843). Also *Select Committee*, p. 137.
6. In particular, see H. Silver, *Nothing but the Present or Nothing but the Past?* (1977), p. 8. For the development of teacher training see A. Tropp, *The Schoolteachers* (1957); R. W. Rich, *The Training of Teachers in the Nineteenth Century* (1933; rep. 1972); H. C. Dent, 'An Historical Perspective', in S. Hewett, *The Training of Teachers* (1971); G. F. Bartle, *History of Borough Road College* (1976); some interesting recollections of individual student teachers in the nineteenth and early twentieth centuries are in *Annals of the College of St Matthias* (Bristol, 1975). A valuable treatment from a more theoretical perspective is G. Grace, *Teachers, Ideology and Control* (1978).
7. 'Report of the Manchester Statistical Society on the State of Education in the Borough of Salford in 1835', *M.S.S.* (1836), p. 22.
8. H.M.I. Watson, *C.C.E.*, 1874–5, p. 193.
9. H.M.I. Allen, *C.C.E.*, 1840–1, p. 127. Also see Bartley, *Schools for the People*, p. 134. The inferiority of private against public schools 'is to be attributed to the regular and systematic inspection of the latter'. Also 'Liverpool', *M.S.S.* (1836), pp. 38–9.
10. H.M.I. Bowstead, *C.C.E.*, 1872–3, p. 41. Also H.M.I. Boyle, *C.C.E.*, 1880–1, p. 262.
11. From a 'very spirited letter' written by a public schoolmaster, quoted by Foster, *Newcastle*, vol. 2, pp. 337–8.
12. Ibid.
13. J. Burnett, *Destiny Obscure*, (1982), p. 155.
14. F. Widdowson, *Going up into the Next Class* (1983), p. 8.
15. 'Finsbury', *J.S.S.* (February 1843), p. 31.
16. See Sally Alexander, 'Women's Work in Nineteenth Century London', in A. Oakley and J. Mitchell (eds.), *The Rights and Wrongs of Women* (1976), pp. 59–111.
17. See A. Oakley, *Housewife* (1974), esp. Chs. 1–2.
18. See 'Fifth Report . . . London', *J.S.S.* (August 1843), p. 215.
19. *Select Committee*, p. 4.

20. P.P. 1842 [381] xvi, *C.E.C.*, p. 532.
21. 'Fifth Report . . . London', *J.S.S.* (August 1843), p. 213.
22. 'Third Report . . . Westminster', *J.S.S.* (December 1838), p. 456.
23. *Select Committee*, p. 121.
24. 'Finsbury', *J.S.S.*, p. 31.
25. Quoted in Neuburg, *Popular Education*, p. 17.
26. *Select Committee*, p. 119.
27. 'Third Report . . . Westminster', *J.S.S.* (December 1838), p. 452. Also see Joseph Blacket's brief autobiography in Blacket, *Specimens of the Poetry of Joseph Blacket*. He attended a woman's school in Tunstall until, 'another school being opened, by a man who my parents thought better able to instruct, I was placed by them under his tuition, and continued to write and learn arithmetic till the age of eleven', p. 13.
28. Also see Appendix B.
29. *C.C.E.*, 1871–2, pp. 66–7.
30. Quoted in Neuburg, *Popular Education*, p. 18.
31. 'Liverpool . . .', *M.S.S.* (1836), p. 20.
32. H.M.I. Smith, *C.C.E.*, 1876–7, p. 565. Also *Special Reports*, p. 54. 'Much of the success of some of the most worthless of the schools arises out of the sympathy which the poor feel for one another'.
33. See G. Crossick (ed.), *The Lower Middle Class in Britain 1870–1914* (1977); also, R. Roberts, *The Classic Slum* (1971), pp. 133–4.
34. V. Chancellor, *Master and Artisan*, p. 117.
35. Cumin, *Newcastle*, vol. 3, p. 57. See also J. Hurt, *Elementary Schooling*, p. 31.
36. But see Tremenheere for example, 'Of the dame schools, 11 are kept by poor widows, who derive their sole subsistence from them. One of these appeared to be in a state of extreme poverty and solicited charity'. 'Agricultural and Educational Statistics of several Parishes in the County of Middlesex', *J.S.S.*, vol. 6 (1843), p. 130.
37. P.R.O. R.G. 9/1712. Also see Appendix E.
38. P.R.O. R.G. 10/2520.
39. Sutherland, *Elementary Education in the Nineteenth Century*, p. 12.
40. *Select Committee*, p. 31.
41. P.P. 1863 [3170] xviii, *C.E.C.*, p. 176.
42. 'Third Report . . . Westminster', *J.S.S.* (December 1838), p. 455.
43. See Report, *Newcastle*, vol. 1, p. 93. It is worth noting that such attacks on independent working-class schooling also came from all political quarters. Engels's vision for instance was rooted in provision by the state of education for the working class. 'The few day schools *at the command of the working-class* are available only for the smallest minority, and are bad besides. The teachers, worn-out workers, and other unsuitable persons, who only turn to teaching in order to live, are usually without the indispensable elementary knowledge, without the moral discipline so needful for the teacher, and relieved of all public supervision' (my emphasis). *The Condition of the Working Class in England* (1892; rep. 1969), p. 140.
44. See P.P. 1846 [681] xx, *Reports . . .*, p. 20; P.P. 1851 [1304] xxiii, *Reports . . .*, p. 55; P.P. 1851 [1396] xxiii, *Reports . . .*, p. 13.
45. But see for example, Horner, P.P. 1847 [828] xv, *Reports . . .* 'Another case was reported to me by Mr. Ewings, Sub-Inspector, where the children employed in a factory near Haslingden, were attending a Dame school, kept by a person named Mary Wilkinson, in which, as Mr. Ewings stated, the schooling was a mockery. There being a good school within a mile, and Mary Wilkinson's school not affording the means of the children being taught to write, it was brought within my power of interference; and I served the occupier of the factory with a notice, that Mary

Wilkinson's certificate would not in future be valid for the purpose of the Factory Act. I report this annulment of a schoolmistress's certificate in conformity with the provision to that effect contained in the 39th section of the Act 7 Vic., c. 15', p. 6. See also P.P. 1849 [1017] xxii, *Reports* . . ., p. 18; P.P. 1851 [1304] xxiii, *Reports* . . ., p. 29.

46. P.P. 1846 [681] xx, *Reports* . . ., p. 20.

47. P.P. 1876 [1443 — I] xxx. *Factory and Workshops Act Commission . . . Minutes of Evidence*, p. 8. More generally, see E. and R. Frow, *A Survey of the Half-time System in Education* (Manchester, 1970); A. H. Robson, *The Education of Children Engaged in Industry in England, 1833–1876* (1931); M. Sanderson, 'Education and the Factory in Industrial Lancashire, 1780–1840', *Economic History Review*, vol. 20 (1967), pp. 266–79.

48. Also see the definition given in Widdowson, *Going up into the Next Class* (1983), p. 94.

49. 'Liverpool', *M.S.S.* (1836), p. 22.

50. 'Third Report . . . Westminster', *J.S.S.* (1839), p. 452.

51. See Appendix B.

52. 'Birmingham', *J.S.S.* (1840), p. 31. Based on 'the average terms charged in dame schools, viz. 3d. per week, with the mean number of scholars to a school, viz. 14.6.'; also 'Bury', *M.S.S.* (1835), pp. 5, 7. Some 50 years earlier, David Love had found that the return even on a thriving school was meagre: 'the first week I got more than twenty scholars, increasing each week, till I had above fifty; but I got no more than a penny each week for readers, and three halfpence for writers, so that my wages were but very small and ill paid. My abode there was short, about five months. I then took to my old trade of travelling . . .' *The Life, Adventures and Experiences of David Love* (1824), p. 14.

53. 'Fifth Report . . . London', *J.S.S.* (August 1843), p. 216.

54. *C.C.E.*, 1872–3, p. 94.

55. P.P. 1844 [523] xxviii, *Reports* . . ., p. 12. More recently, see J. L. Field, 'Private Schools in Portsmouth and Southampton, 1850–1870', *J.E.A.H.*, vol. X (1978), pp. 8–14.

56. *One Square Mile* (1870), Appendix III, no. 126. Also *Select Committee*, pp. 116, 137. Note also a more recent assessment '"Dames" and private schoolmasters were simply people who had acquired some teachable and marketable skill, rarely more than a basic literacy, or who found in child-minding or teaching, full-time or as a by-employment, some support in old age, infirmity, unemployment or other time of need.' Johnson, 'Notes', in Dale *et al.* (ed.), *Schooling and Capitalism,* p. 44. Johnson does at least add that 'This account of private schooling is based mainly on official or philanthropic nineteenth-century sources, notably the reports of the Manchester Statistical Society', ibid., p. 52. As Johnson himself makes clear in a later work, such sources need to be critically rather than literally interpreted. Johnson, 'Elementary Education: the Education of the Working Class', in G. Sutherland *et al.*, *Education in Britain*.

57. The survey of the Population Census revealed no teachers with declared handicaps in Bristol from 1851 to 1871.

58. Manchester . . .', *M.S.S.* (1873), p. 19.

59. 'Manchester', *M.S.S.* (1837), p. 6. Also see examples in P.P. 1851 [1396] xxiii, *Reports by Factory Inspectors*, p. 13. 'This school is in the upper room of a cottage, 18 feet by 15, in which 33 children were assembled . . . The master had lost his right arm. The children read tolerably well'; 'This school is in a room 15 feet square. The master had been a labourer, but being in bad health, turned schoolmaster. His wife assists, attending at the same time to her domestic duties'. Alexander Somerville attended a school kept by one who was, 'a teacher only because he was lame'. Nevertheless, 'he had a local fame as a good teacher.' *The*

Autobiography of Working Man (1848), p. 19.

60. Cooper, *Life of Thomas Cooper*, p. 73.

61. *Select Committee*, p. 116. This remark incidentally serves also to demonstrate the astonishing degree to which the Committee's questions were loaded. The question to which Wood was responding was, 'In consequence of so many of these persons having been driven to keep schools as a resource from adverse circumstances, bodily infirmity, age, and misfortune, do you not consider that those circumstances are likely to have influenced their temper, to have given them rather a dark view, and to have rendered them in many instances unfit for an occupation which requires particular patience, gentleness and perseverance?' Another example, 'Are the children in these schools in fact receiving any instruction or are they allowed to amuse themselves . . . or are they passing their time in a state of listlessness and coercion?' — 'In a state of listlessness and coercion . . .', p. 117. Also p. 135.

62. 'Manchester', *M.S.S.* (1837), p. 10.

63. Scarratt, *Old Times in the Potteries*, p. 3.

64. Winder, *Newcastle*, vol. 2, p. 182; also Cumin, *Newcastle*, vol. 3, pp. 83–4.

65. Foster, *Newcastle*, vol. 2, p. 336.

66. 'Fifth Report . . . London', *J.S.S.* (August 1843), p. 215.

67. 'Birmingham', *J.S.S.* (April 1840), p. 31. Also 'Second Report . . . Westminster', *J.S.S.* (August 1838), p. 196; 'Manchester', *M.S.S.* (1837), p. 55; *M.S.S.* (1835), p. 5.

68. *Select Committee*, p. 136.

69. Fletcher in P.P. 1840 [220] xxiv, *Reports from Commissioners* . . ., p. 85.

70. P.R.O. Ed. 3/11.

71. Hobley, quoted in Burnett, *Destiny Obscure*, p. 178.

72. Quoted in F. Smith, *A History of English Elementary Education*, p. 40.

73. John Jones, in *Attempts in Verse . . . With Some Account of the Writer, Written by Himself* (1831), p. 171.

74. 'Bury', *M.S.S.* (1835), p. 5. For John Palmer, see P.R.O. R.G. 10/2530.

75. 'A Working Man', *S.B.C.*, 9.11.1872, pp. 401–2.

76. 'Birmingham', *J.S.S.* (April 1840), p. 30. Also, *Newcastle*, vol. 1, p. 94.

77. This is in part illustrated by the declared birthplaces of teachers in the Bristol Population Census. See Appendix D. Also see Bartley, *One Square Mile*, 'That which gives the teachers great trouble in this part of London is the migratory character of a large section of the population . . .', p. 27. Also W. E. Marsden, 'Education and Social Geography', p. 56. Also 'Conditions of the Working Classes in St. George's . . .', *J.S.S.* (1843), p. 22; Report, *Newcastle*, vol. 1, pp. 659–60. 41.65 per cent of scholars in public elementary school had been in the same school for less than one year.

78. See for example D. Leinster-Mackay, 'The English Private School', vol. 1, p. 217. Also the same author's article in *J.E.A.H.*, cited earlier. See also M. J. Board, 'A History of the Private Adventure School', p. 78.

79. This was most graphically so in the case of the Irish hedge schools. See Chapter 3, note 83.

80. P.R.O. R.G. 10/2524; *The Homes of the Bristol Poor* (1884), Ch. 8, p. 44. For her earlier schools, see P.R.O. H.O. 107/1949; P.R.O. R.G. 9/1717; P.R.O. R.G. 10/2524.

81. P.R.O. H.O. 107/1954; P.R.O. R.G. 10/2524.

82. J. Hurt, in *Economic History Review*, p. 627.

83. Ibid.

84. Ibid.

85. Ibid.

86. 'Finsbury', *J.S.S.* (February 1843), p. 32. See the slightly different wording

relating to the same figures in a subsequent report. 'Fifth Report . . . London', *J.S.S.* (August 1843), p. 215.

87. 'Birmingham', *J.S.S.* (April 1840), p. 30.

88. 'Rutland', *J.S.S.* (October 1839), p. 311. 'Bristol', *J.S.S.* (October 1841), p. 257.

89. 'Birmingham', *J.S.S.* (April 1840), p. 30.

90. See *Education Census*, p. xx.

91. *M.S.S.*, 'Manchester', p. 36; 'Salford', p. 36; 'Bury', p. 20; 'Liverpool', p. vii; 'York', p. vi; *J.S.S.*, 'Birmingham' (April 1843), p. 42; 'Rutland' (October 1839), p. 311; 'Westminster' (August 1838), p. 209; 'Westminster' (December 1838), p. 464; 'Finsbury' (February 1843), p. 40. Also see Chapter 1, pp. 36–8.

92. *J.S.S.* (August 1843), 'London', p. 215.

93. P.R.O. Ed. 3/20. See Chapter 1, pp. 36–8.

94. P.R.O. H.O. 107/1951.

95. P.R.O. H.O. 107/371.

96. P.R.O. R.G. 9/1716.

97. P.R.O. R.G. 10/2509.

98. See for example, P.R.O. Ed. 3/12, Church Ward, Shoreditch. Also see *Newcastle*, vol. 1, p. 94.

99. P.R.O. Ed. 3/11.

100. P.R.O. H.O. 107/1953. Also see 'Finsbury', *J.S.S.* (February 1843), p. 30. In the common day schools, 'two sisters, or a mother and daughter sometimes conducted them together'.

101. P.R.O. R.G. 9/1705.

102. P.R.O. R.G. 10/2508.

103. P.R.O. R.G. 9/1706.

104. P.R.O. R.G. 10/2559.

105. P.R.O. H.O. 107/1953.

106. P.R.O. R.G. 9/1719.

107. P.R.O. R.G. 10/2527.

5 SCHOOLS

What of the working-class private schools themselves? What sort of places were they? The question requires two types of answer. The first needs to concentrate on physical descriptions of locations, interiors and equipment; the second on a consideration of internal organisation and method, and on an assessment of educational activity. We can deal with these as analytical separates, though in practice, their interconnections would have been very close.

Our first answer is likely to be more straightforward than our second. In the latter case the problems of analysis and evaluation impinge in a very direct way on description. Nevertheless, it is particularly important to focus on the issue of the educational effectiveness of the working-class private school, for the question itself, let alone any answer, has not yet been deemed a valid or serious one. Historically, there has been no question of this kind to answer. How, after all, can places which were not genuinely 'schools' at all be described or analysed in the terms reserved for authentic educational institutions? In effect, the unregulated and informal nature of the working-class private school is precisely the characteristic which has disqualified it from admission to the very terminology of educational analysis.

We have already noted some of the ways in which the legitimate definition of this terminology has been ever in the hands of the suppliers of publicly sponsored schooling for the working class. But only if the limits of this terminology are identified with some universal definition of 'education' itself is the status of the working-class private school invalidated. Though assumed by many educational historians, such an identification cannot be carelessly supported. The concept of 'education' cannot be universally linked only to the particular varieties of officially sanctioned schooling as they emerged in the nineteenth century. Education, as it was comprehended by nineteenth-century working-class culture, was a diffuse and flexible process which could be furthered through a range of agencies, of which formal public schooling was but one.[1] But this particular variety was understood by nineteenth-century educationists as the only legitimate channel of popular education. As such, it was increasingly conceived as a neutral, though beneficial social process, operating above, and independently of, broader social and economic conflicts. To the extent that educational history has accepted and operated within this rubric, it has been unable to come to terms with working-class private schooling as it was practised in the nineteenth century. The principal theoretical failure of such an approach has been its unwillingness to relate education to the wider contexts of class and culture. There is much to be learned from comparative analysis of the private and public varieties of elementary schooling so long as the primacy and legitimacy of the latter is not automatically conceded. So long, in other words, as the concept of education is not narrowed into that of formal schooling. The avoidance of such conceptual conflation allows us the possibility of understanding some of the complex and powerful linkages between 'education' and 'society' — between 'culture' and 'class'. It allows us both to examine the working-class private school as a serious and genuine educational alternative, and to ask why the public and private varieties were so different in style, objective and emphasis.

We have seen that modern historical assessments of the working-class private school would, for the most part, do little to offend the original official commentators. Their judgements remain effectively unimpugned, confidently maintaining their dominance to the point where a recent writer can argue that, 'Modern defenders of "the much maligned dame school" need to prove their thesis in the face of the testimony of contemporary investigators.'[2]

The time has come to mount such a defence — though not of the 'dame's' school, but of working-class private schooling as a whole. We will concentrate particularly on learning — but our attention must first be directed at the schools as physical units.

If the concept of the school in its nineteenth-century context is taken to include of necessity very specific physical requirements of design, construction and equipment, as opposed merely to a place where teaching and learning within defined practical limits are effectively done, then perhaps the description of the working-class private school as a non-school is legitimate. Perhaps it should be re-styled as a working-class 'place of learning'. But this kind of purely physical qualification surely cannot be allowed to stand as a sufficient definition, just as 'school' itself cannot define 'education'. The real significance of schools rests more with the people who use them than with the buildings themselves. The traditional 'hedge schools' of Ireland frequently operated out of doors and had no fixed physical home at all. Physical contexts undoubtedly impinge upon the quality and ease of learning but they cannot, by themselves, fully comprise the meaning of 'school'. This would be like rejecting the products of domestic industry because they were not fashioned in a building called a factory and by the techniques associated with such a building. If the detractors of working-class private schooling, old and new, wish to withold or confer the title 'school' purely on physical grounds, then their allegations can be conceded with no real loss. Schooling, after all, can only take place in a 'school'; education can happen anywhere. On other and more important grounds, any claimed exclusivity of definition can be disputed.

Attacks on the physical setting of the working-class private school were as much concerned with what it was not as with what it actually was. And what it emphatically was not, was a purpose-built construction specifically designed for the cheap and effective dissemination of rational schooling to concentrated numbers of pupils. This was the standard against which the working-class private school was held to be so 'inefficient'. The public school for the working class and the private school of the working class in fact represented two distinct cultures of popular education, and in each, the physical context of the school was in part a working expression of the differences of approach and objective.

Though scarcely any of the private schools were held in buildings exclusively designed for the purpose, a few of the larger ones made use of relatively spacious rented accommodation which could be turned to the purpose without difficulty. Most commonly, this would have been a local hall or chapel. Factory Inspector Saunders wrote, for example, that, ' "Private, or dame schools", include . . . schools held in the residence of the teacher, or in any Sunday school-room hired for the purpose.'[3]

And in Battersea in 1871, Matilda Cooper kept a school for 82 children at the Nine Elms Lecture Room, rented on a yearly basis from Mr Sellars of Wandsworth.[4] James Williams's school in Victoria Road, Deptford, which, with 106 pupils, was a particularly large enterprise, was, in the words of H.M.I., 'held in a good room, hired from the Methodist New Connexion Congregation'.[5]

But such a school was not typical, presenting an example of a working-class private school that was unusual in the degree of its physical specialisation for the purpose.

By far the most common location for the working-class private school was the working-class home itself. The Education Return provided by the 1870 Act distinguished such schools by including a question concerning the room where actual teaching was done:

> Is each of the above Rooms (or will it be) exclusively *appropriated* to Education? If the Answer is No, specify the other use. Answer NO if the Teacher sleeps, takes meals, or follows any trade in the room for teaching, or if Divine worship, or any occupation except teaching (or is to be) carried on in it'.[6]

Some were clearly what might be called 'one-room' schools. That is, schools held in a room which was also the sole dwelling space of the teacher. One of the witnesses quoted in Patrick Cumin's Bristol survey held that 'The dames most commonly have only one room for every purpose, and their scholars may often be seen sitting round the sides of a four-post bed, on low forms, the sides of the bed forming a back to the seat; sometimes on the side of the bed.'[7]

H.M.I. Wingate, in his valuable summary of adventure schools in the Chelsea Division in 1871, did not find the one-room domestic school as prevalent as this. But where he did, his description is in most respects similar.

> In rooms where the teacher lives wholly in the room, a bed is seldom met with, the teacher sleeping on an old sofa, in a wardrobe, or on the floor, as convenience suggests. The washing apparatus is generally limited to a bason [sic], the remaining furniture consisting of a table and one or two chairs, more or less broken. Where the means of the teacher admit of it, a low form is obtained, and on this, ranged against the wall, the children sit . . . Where the teacher only partly lives in the room, matters are a shade better, but there, furniture generally takes up all available space, and the children are huddled out of the way into a dark corner, seated upon the traditional low form, or else upon the floor.[8]

This latter group — that is, schools held in a room where the household itself consisted of more than one room — appears to have been the more common. But in such cases the teaching room was seldom fitted up exlusively as a school and reserved solely for the purpose.[9] Generally, the room served a dual function.

Sometimes the second function might relate to another remunerative activity. In Cambridge Street, Bethnal Green, for example, Eliza Anderson gathered the 28 children of her school in 'A very miserable place — school is held in a weaver's upper shed who in part looks after it while at his work . . . It is in no respect efficient.'[10] But more generally the function was domestic — the school was held in rooms which were also kitchens or living rooms. Such was Mrs Lay's school in Limehouse; her 16 pupils met in a room 16 feet by 9, which she declared was also 'used as a living room' and was 'furnished as a dwelling'.[11] Mrs Nichol's school in Bethnal Green, which she had held continuously for 27 years, was castigated by H.M.I.: 'Front parlour — a miserable dame school . . . Teaching room used for living in.'[12] A school in Lambeth was a 'Dirty cottage room in which the schoolmistress was engaged in cooking';[13] another at Streatham was 'A cottage living room destitute of school furniture or apparatus . . .'[14] More sympathetically, Charles Shaw recalled, 'old Betty W's school', as

> the only room on the ground floor of her little cottage. It was about four yards square, with a winding, narrow staircase leading to the bedroom above. The furniture was very scant, consisting of a small table, two chairs, and two or three little forms about eight inches high for the children to sit upon.[15]

The picture which these examples together create is substantially similar to that set down by the London Statistical Society over 30 years earlier;

> The rooms in which these schools are held appear to be for the most part tolerably clean, but they are rarely used exclusively as schools; in 34 cases (of 63) they serve as bed-rooms, and in many for the general purposes of the family, while in several even the business of a shop is conducted. The size of the rooms is generally insufficient; the mean length being 13 feet, the width 11 feet, and the height 8 feet. The largest was 20 feet in length, 8 in width and 9 in height.[16]

The theme of the chaotic interpenetration of educational activity and domestic life within the 'classroom' is one which much occupied the attention of expert observers. Assistant Commissioner

Foster, for instance, reported that,

> the worst of the private-adventure schools are those in which 30 or 40 children are crowded into the kitchen of a collier's dwelling, and the mistress divides her attention between teaching them, nursing her own baby, and cooking for her husband and sons. In one such school, the collier and two lodgers, just from the pit, were at dinner, and it is to be feared, afterwards undressed and washed themselves in the same apartment.[17]

Perhaps one of the most common cases of dual-purpose classrooms, and one which united three roles in one person — teacher, housewife and wage-earner — was the classroom/laundry.[18] This was so in the case of Eliza Drake of Battersea. Her school was dismissed by H.M.I. Swettenham: 'Premises consist of an underground mangling and living room. 6 children. Inefficient premises.'[19] Wingate offered a more detailed general example of such a school:

> The visitor descends some steps to an area and finds himself in a kitchen. The floor and furniture are covered with baskets and bundles of newly washed clothes. At one side of the room, stands a large mangle, which the teacher, with bared arms, works and turns, while amid the noise and clatter, the children, seated on two low forms at the other side, mumble out their reading or draw upon their slates.[20]

However, even in the dual-purpose classroom, it is clear that teachers did make efforts to furnish the room to make learning possible. Such rooms were more than just places where children congregated with no consideration to the ostensible reason for their being there. 'Apparatus', in the shape of wall maps or globes might have been rare, but all sought to provide the long, low forms where children sat to read, and a table at which writing could be done. Even Eliza Drake's poor mangling school provided these, together with, in the Inspector's judgement, 'moderate furniture (cupboards, grates and other fixtures), and a 'moderate' supply of books. What was lacking were more extraneous features — 'Registers' — 'None'; 'Apparatus' — 'None'; 'Properly lighted for a school' — 'No'; 'Properly drained' — 'No'; 'Properly ventilated' — 'No'; 'Properly supplied with Offices' — 'No'. Like the overwhelming majority of working-class private schools inspected through 1870–1, Eliza Drake's school was declared inefficient 'In respect of the Premises', thereby rendering judgement on the second prescribed criterion, efficiency 'In terms of the Instruction' superfluous. In Liverpool, 35 years earlier, the internal appearance of such teaching rooms seems to have conformed to a similar pattern. Here, of 244 schools, only four were returned as being 'without any forms'.[21] Rooms which made no visible concession to their teaching function were rare. But one such was recorded in Manchester in 1834,

> In another school, all the children to the number of twenty were squatted upon the bare floor, there being no benches, chairs, or furniture of any kind in the room. The Master said his terms would not yet allow him to provide forms, but he hoped that as his school increased, and his circumstances thereby improved, he should be able sometime or other to afford this luxury.[22]

Contemporary reports indicate some broad variation by region in physical environment. In Manchester in 1834 for example, 'These [dame] schools are generally found in very dirty unwholesome rooms — frequently in close damp cellars, or old dilapidated garrets.'[23] And in Liverpool a few years later,

> With few exceptions, the Dame Schools are dark and confined; many are damp and dirty, more than one-half of them are used as dwelling, dormitory, and school-room, accommodating, in many cases, families of seven or eight persons. Above forty of them are cellars.[24]

But in Birmingham in 1840,

> The physical condition of the dame schools . . . is much more satisfactory than could have been anticipated. None of them are kept in cellars, very few in garrets or bed-rooms, and they are generally more cleanly and better lighted than schools of the same description in Manchester and Liverpool. They are, however, ill-ventilated, and particularly in those districts in which the resident population is chiefly of the poorer classes.[25]

A more detailed discussion of the physical characteristics of the schools in the city of Bristol can be found in Appendix B.

Away from the crowded pressures of the industrial city, conditions were likely to have been better, on the whole. In the dames' schools of Rutland, for example, 'it was very gratifying to observe the marked difference in general appearance and order, as compared with schools of a similar class in large towns'.[26] The fact however remains that here too, ill-designed buildings, often dirty, dark, damp and insanitary, were frequently hosts to working-class private schools. These are not conditions which would be acceptable in a modern school, or to a modern educationist. This is certainly a point which has influenced many historians. But we do not have to romanticise or ignore the squalor and general inadequacy of nineteenth-century working-class housing in order to celebrate the schools which such buildings supported. On the contrary, the achievements of this domestic educational culture are rendered more remarkable by the material constraints with which they were ceaselessly engaged. The assumption of a narrow determining linkage between material and cultural deprivation has actually helped to obscure from us even the possibility of indigenously generated working-class education. Our understanding of such education must have a relativist element. Whatever might be the objective desirability of this or that material facility, the argument does not reflect sound historical analysis. If working-class private schools continued to exist today, they would not operate in the domestic conditions of the nineteenth century. And it is as extensions of existing domestic environments at any given point that the schools have to be seen. In terms of physical definition, home and school were one and the same, and the privations and discomforts of the latter would have been reproduced in the former. Moreover, this familiarity of environment was what the public school — cold, draughty, joyless and severe — could not offer. It represented a fracture of place as well as of tradition and procedure. Moreover, there was no substantial part of the prescribed curriculum of the public elementary school — save drill — which the domestic environment of the private school of itself precluded.[27] The basic skills of literacy could, given the necessary materials, be learned here as well as anywhere. The 'efficiency' provided by the larger, purpose-built school did not relate so much to the learning of these skills, as to the ways in which they were learnt and to the organisational and behavioural context in which learning took place. Above all, the disadvantaged physical environment of the working-class private school was alluded to by nineteenth-century commentators only to the degree that such allusions were seen to advance the cause of the fundamentally different public versions of elementary schooling. The thrust of the argument was not — at least until the 1880s — centrally against squalor and deprivation *per se*, but more against their contribution to a working-class moral culture that was straying beyond effective regulation.[28] The critique of the physical environment of the working-class private school was seldom, from this perspective, part of a wider condemnation of the patterns of exploitation and poverty which governed the entire cycle of working-class life — not just at school. This represents in effect a rather specific aspect of the prescribed separation of home and school. In its very building as well as its organisation and processes, the public school for the working class was to be above, apart from and visibly distinct from the working-class home.

Though unobjectionable in themselves, middle-class accusations of the deprivation of educational environment usually had little independent impetus then, being more a particularly lurid element in the broader attack on independent working-class education as a whole. This is why the argument was especially in evidence when attacks based on levels of educational achievement alone were felt to be ineffective. In Bristol, for example, H.M.I. Bowstead,

> visited a great number of private adventure schools . . . we have found only two or three that have any reasonable pretensions to be regarded as efficient. It is not that the rest are all under the charge of ignorant or incompetent teachers; it is rather that the premises in which they are carried on are altogether unsuited for the purpose. The rooms are generally . . . common living rooms.[29]

H.M.I. Watkins made the point more forcefully,

> It will be needful that all *efficient* schools be registered and publicly recognised as such, or some parents will continue to send their children to the miserable places where so many of them go, and will represent them to the inquiring officer as 'at school'. But their statement must not be accepted. It certainly will be very difficult at first to convince a Yorkshire father that the school is not '*efficient*' when his child is 'getting on' very

> well in it. It will be very difficult to convince him of the slow but sure mischief caused by crowded, ill-ventilated rooms, by want of light, want of drainage, by filthy offices and by unhealthy 'surroundings'.[30]

There is nothing in the reports of the nineteenth-century experts that establishes a necessary link between place — as distinct from method — and a low level of learning in the basic skills of literacy. There is indeed considerable evidence that effective learning could and did take place in the working-class private school. And if the ambient domestic activity of such a school is to be adduced as a potential diversion from learning, so the superfluous discipline, drill and religious instruction of the public school could be seen — as indeed they were by many of their working-class clients — as unwarranted and unwanted distractions.[31]

Increasingly after 1850, official criticisms of the environment provided by the working-class private school did not concern just its physical limitations as such, but also the way that these were exposed by its sheer popularity. Whilst the Statistical Societies had attacked the schools on almost every conceivable ground, the issue of overcrowding was not a particularly prominent one.[32] But subsequent investigators — especially from the Newcastle Commission onwards — highlighted it as a central problem, perhaps gambling the admission of popularity against its propaganda value as an adjunct of general squalor.

H.M.I. Turnbull reported in 1875 that *'The rooms are often crowded to excess'*; in one case, 'there was not area . . . for an average attendance of fifteen and there was not volume for an average of eleven. The number of children found present in the room was *sixty-six*.'[33] One of Cumin's witnesses related that in some dames' schools, 'I have seen the children as closely packed as birds in a nest, and tumbling over each other like puppies in a kennel.'[34] In Wales, the schools 'are generally well attended — much beyond the means of their accommodation . . . the school-room is often a nest of squalor; in these human cages, the atmosphere is so foul as to be absolutely repulsive'.[35]

But whilst it is beyond doubt that the physical environment of the working-class private school was commonly shocking and offensive to middle-class sensibilities, it is by no means clear that the majority of such schools — though popular — were over-crowded to the point where effective individual learning was impaired. The nature of working-class demand, with its accent on a rapid and visible educational return from an expensive short-term investment, makes this unlikely. High local demand and the pressure of pupil numbers tended instead to stimulate the opening of more schools to cope, and sometimes, in the case of particularly successful individual schools, the pressing into service of more accommodation. This was so, for example, in the case of Harriett Longley whose school in Battersea Park contained 52 children in 1871. Her classroom was described as being 14 feet by 11 feet and was, according to the Inspector, 'A fair room but without school furniture; there is however another room which Miss Longley says she will use as well to prevent the great overcrowding which exists at present.'[36] But schools of this size were always comparatively rare. Most were restricted to the 20 or 30 who could fit into an average sized family room.[37] Moreover, however numerous the pupils, and even if some degree of overcrowding was sometimes the case, it must not be forgotten — for working-class parents certainly did not forget it — that numerically, such a school would always be very much smaller than its public counterpart, and that its scholars would receive far more individual attention from the teacher.

The physical environment provided by a school was not just a matter of the building which housed it or the cubic space which its dimensions afforded. It was also determined by organisation and by atmosphere. These were of course dependent in part on the constraints of physical environment, but more importantly, they were shaped by the degree to which schools of different types tried to differentiate education from other areas of daily life. In the working-class private school, learning did not demand a dislocation of this kind, as evidenced in the descriptive account of a rural Somerset school reproduced in Appendix D.[38] Learning took place in rooms which were otherwise kitchens, living-rooms and bed-rooms, and, apart from the usual addition of a few long forms as additional seating, existing domestic furniture and equipment was pressed into use. Characteristically, such a school would have looked like this: the teacher seated in a chair, possibly with a table, either in a corner of the room, or more likely towards the centre; children of all ages clustering around in a rough circle or horseshoe pattern, some seated on forms and others where they could; 'writers' gathered around the table shared by the teacher, or possibly at a second table. When school ended, very little reorganisation of furniture was needed for the room to revert to its other function.

The public schoolroom, specifically designed and set aside for a single particular purpose, presented an altogether different appearance and represented a similarly different aim. Furniture and internal organisation were designed for a very particular relationship of teaching and learning. Seating arrangements, whether in the gallery or in rows of parallel desks, were rigidly organised, facing mutely towards the source of knowledge — the teacher on his or her raised dais. This marked an approach to learning which drew enthusiastic praise from commentators. Assistance Commissioner Winder for instance, reported that 'The system of parallel desks is swallowing up all other forms of school arrangement . . . The appearance of neatness and order which it has is captivating.'[39] From the pupil's point of view, the reality accompanying this organisation was less attractive. Joseph Ashby remembered that,

> All the children as a class came out together to a series of commands. One! and you stood in your desk. Two! and you put your left leg over the seat. Three! and the right joined it. Four! you faced the lane between the classes. Five! you marched in the spot. Six! you stepped forward and the pupil-teacher chanted, 'left right, left right, left right'.[40]

The regulative function of the highly formalised organisation of the public school was clear, sometimes being expressed as part of a critique of other, older organisational forms, including that of the working-class private school. H.M.I. Smith, for example, knew 'of nothing more painful than to pass from a well-ordered Government school into a small, overcrowded, unventilated cottage room, where a number of children of all ages are huddled together learning almost absolutely nothing' [*sic*].[41] H.M.I. Bowstead felt that,

> Where there are 'vis-a-vis' desks, the children sit talking or playing . . . a teacher cannot tell whether the children are working when their backs alone are visible. The children know this well enough, and so ensue listlessness and apathy . . . the only proper arrangement of desks is the parallel arrangement which enables the teacher by one glance down the line to tell who is idle and who is doing honest work.[42]

And Matthew Arnold castigated those National Schools which retained

> What I must call *dame-school methods*, in the use of loose benches put in squares on the floor for classes that are neither in desks nor in the gallery. Now in general, when the floor is not occupied either by gallery or desk-group, it should be clear; and the class which is neither in the gallery nor in the desk-group should stand. It is often well to have a class standing; but a class sitting on loose benches has neither the smartness of a class standing nor has it the rest and convenience for work of a class seated at desks.[43]

We can now turn from the purely physical environment of the working-class private school to the related patterns of teaching and learning which went on within it. Official rejections of these rested on two contentions. First, that the working-class private school did not and indeed could not provide a full and suitable 'education' for the working class; and second, that even within the restricted pedagogic compass of which such a school was nominally capable, it was normally chronically deficient.

It has already been seen that the official disqualification of working-class educational activity rested in part on the lack of formal teacher training and in part of the deficiencies of physical environment. To these can be added a third complaint, centring upon curriculum and method; on the production and legitimation of knowledge and on the relations of its production; on what was learnt and how it was learnt.

The working-class accent on the mastery of the basic skills of literacy and especially reading was universal. In the middle-class view, literacy for the working class was certainly desirable, but by itself, it constituted no more than 'mere instruction', being simply an instrumental component of a process in which moral reformation was the primary object. This view was regularly expressed:

> we are compelled to confess that, although the rudiments of useful learning are taught in an efficient manner, the range of instruction . . . is very limited. How long reading, writing and ciphering will continue to receive the name of education we will not predict; but the time must come when the training of

> children shall have a more full relation to the business, duties and happiness of life. They shall then be taught not only the symbols of knowledge, but the elements of those useful arts and sciences which are likely to be connected with their future employments, and above all they will be made acquainted with the powers of their own nature, and with those laws, physical, mental, moral and religious, the observance of which is, by their Creator, rendered necessary to their happiness.[44]

The Manchester Statistical Society argued that,

> generally throughout this country, the acquisition of Reading, Writing and Arithmetic seems to be considered as constituting the finished education of the children of the lower classes of the people . . . the real cultivation of the mental powers, the softening of the manners, the improvement of the character, instruction on moral and religious subjects, and all the more valuable *objects* of education, are totally neglected and forgotten.[45]

The tone of the official consensus on this point can be glimpsed in Henry Althans's dialogue with the 1837 Select Committee.

> Do you not consider that religious and moral training of the early minds of youth is one of the most important points of education? — I should consider it ought to be the basis of all education.
>
> Do you consider that these day and dame schools which you have described are effective for the important parts of education? — There is not much attention paid to religious instruction in these schools.
>
> Nor moral training? — No.
>
> Is there any system of moral training observed in these schools, which might have its effect in the conduct of children as they gradually grow up? — I consider there is very little effort for that purpose; the time is chiefly devoted to teaching reading, writing and arithmetic.
>
> It appears that the general view of the system of education, in these day and dame schools for the children of the working

classes, is, that it is very inefficient for good purposes? — Decidedly so.[46]

The goal was the promotion of social order by the management of 'ignorant' working-class behaviour and attitude through the medium of provided schooling. For political conservatives, emphasis was laid chiefly on discipline and obedience through religious indoctrination, whilst for liberals, the accent was more on the winning of a working-class assent to their own subordination through an understanding of the laws of political economy.[47]

However, in the same way that there was widespread and enduring working-class resistance to the efforts made by the public schools to regulate patterns of dress, attendance and general behaviour, so the intrusions of a moralistic curriculum and an authoritarian pedagogy were also resented. In the later decades of the nineteenth century this took the form of overt resistance by both pupil and parent alike against the daily operation of public schooling which was by then the sole agency of popular education.[48] Earlier in the century, the range of working-class options was wider. Not only was the authority of the public school subject to daily challenge but, in the absence of general compulsion, such challenges could, and frequently did, take the form of permanent withdrawal. But above all, there was an alternative supply of education to turn to; a supply with none of the problems which the public school presented.

Private schools offered the education which the working class demanded for themselves and not that which the middle class provided for them. And nowhere was this more apparent than in the popular rejection of the schools which experts saw as the leading edge of the moral assault on working-class values and behaviour — the Infant Schools. Brougham believed that,

> the unwillingness of the poor to contribute even a penny a week in Westminster [to an Infant School] when they used to give fourpence and even sixpence to the most wretched Dame Schools, is truly astonishing, and presents no very favourable picture of their good sense or feeling. The superiority of the institution over the Dame Schools is so plain as to strike every eye.[49]

Kay-Shuttleworth saw the primary value of the Infant School as

> separating the children from the contamination of the street play-ground, and conveying to them combined amusement and instruction in associations from which all moral contamination is excluded, and where they live in an atmosphere of much greater purity.[50]

The Manchester Statistical Society argued that 'The system is admirably adapted to awaken the mental powers, and to instil a moral and religious principle; in this the Infant Schools form a striking contrast with the dame and common schools . . .'[51] And that 'The system . . . has been the means of proving that it is possible to implant, in the minds even of infants, some of the leading principles of morality and to give them habits of order and obedience.'[52] In more practical terms, one of the Sub-Commissioners of the Children's Employment Commission felt that 'A boy, eight years old, who had been trained at a well-conducted infant-school, would be better taught, than many boys of twelve, after several years tuition at the common dame-school of a village.'[53]

This was not the way that parents saw it. They did not welcome the subversion of cultural and domestic authority which such schools represented.

> An infant school in a colliery village is such an entire novelty that the advantages . . . for the women . . . is not at all understood by them. The first impression of the idea of removing their young children from under their own eye, is doubtless revolting to their strong maternal feelings, and comes into very powerful collision with their very peculiar and ungovernable prejudices.[54]

'Maternal feelings' were not, however, similarly revolted when children were sent to local private schools. Undoubtedly, part of the popular appeal of the private school lay precisely in what Nassau Senior called 'the kind of semi-parental care which the dames bestow upon the children entrusted to them'.[55] Here the goals of parent and teacher were harmonised. And this represents a particular manifestation of the working-class view, that the distinctive reformation of moral behaviour was not the business of the school. This helps to explain why, of the publicly provided institutions, the Infant School was particularly condemned by parents. Thus the Manchester Statistical Society, in attacking the educational standards of the private schools, could muse in a footnote, 'Yet it is curious that a very frequent objection made against Infant Schools both by the parents and the teachers, was that the children *learn nothing* there . . .'[56] And at Pendleton, 'the peculiar training which mainly creates the value of the [Infant School] system was rarely appreciated'.[57] Indeed, parents here expressed their dislike of the schools in terms which ironically mirror those used by experts to dismiss the private schools. One

> female said she had sent her child a few times, but had taken her away again, and should like to send her 'to a gradely school, where they teach 'em summut'. A collier's wife said she had taken her child away, adding, 'So how long they goon to this infant schoo' they do larn nothin'.'[58]

J. R. Wood was himself obliged to register that,

> I have heard complaints [on the subject of Infant Schools] from the parents of the children that the children do not come on so well . . . they wanted to see something, like sewing or reading, that they might have a test of the child's progress . . .[59]

And when the 1837 Select Committee demanded of him 'how is it that the children do not come from the dame schools and go to the infant schools?', Wood replied, 'One reason is, the impression that is abroad amongst the mothers of the lower classes against those schools; they do not like the infant schools generally.' But, the Committee asked, probing this paradox,

> Do they also get moral instruction, and in their relative duties are they better instructed than in the dame schools? — Yes, that is one of the great beauties of the infant school system, that it consists in a great measure of instruction in moral duties and their duties to their parents.'[60]

As always, the problem was rationalised as one of 'ignorant' demand rather than inappropriate supply. Such an argument did not always depend solely on parental gullibility but could be reinforced with allusions to the guile and obstructiveness of school-keepers themselves. Bartley felt that 'to [the dames'] opposition may be attributed, to a considerable extent, the comparative slowness of the development of the regular Infant School system'.[61] H.M.I. Morell told how the dames,

> look upon themselves . . . as the lawful instructors of the neighbourhood in which they are situated, claim a kind of vested interest in it, and sometimes speak with considerable indignation of the way in which the 'new-fangled' Government Schools have invaded their territory.[62]

Brougham spoke in more sinister terms, of 'the arts of those old women, who, of course, set themselves against the [Infant] school, both misrepresenting it and cajoling the parents'.[63] Such explanations, however, do not comprehend the nature and depth of popular resentment towards curricula dominated by religious or moral teaching and designed to 'break through the dense crust of ignorance . . . to rub off the outer coating of stolidity and civilized barbarism [despite] the frequent counteracting influences of bad homes . . .'.[64]

In Liverpool, in 1836, 'Some [private] teachers object to give religious instruction at all . . . In the poorest schools, no pretence is made to teach morals, and many masters have no idea what teaching morals can possibly mean.'[65] At Bury, to the dismay of the investigator, one private teacher answered, 'to the question, how he taught morals, "I tell 'em to be good lads, you know, and mind what I say to 'em and so on".'[66] In Birmingham,

> very few [mistresses] appeared to think it was part of their duty to instruct the children in morals . . . One in particular insisted with much warmth, that to teach morals was the duty of the parents, not hers.[67]

In the West Riding, where

> Moral condition [was] . . . as bad as it is possible to be . . . Before entering the pits some few children attend day-schools, but they are of the most inefficient and ordinary kinds, and presided over by some goodly dame of the village; the education therefore does not extend beyond spelling and 'Reading made Easy'. No provision of any sort is made for religious instruction or moral training, neither are there any means imparted to the girls for acquiring habits of modesty, prudence, domestic economy or fore-thought.[68]

Elsewhere in Yorkshire, 'in almost all the "private or dame-schools", it may be said that no religious instruction whatever is attempted to be conveyed.'[69] In the mining areas of Northumberland and Durham, private schools 'must be considered, I fear, in the worst sense of the words, merely *secular schools*'.[70] In Wales, 'religious instruction, as a General rule, is not given in private day schools'.[71] In Rochdale and Bradford, according to Assistant Commissioner Winder, 'Religious instruction is for the most part totally ignored.'[72] In Leeds and Birmingham, J. G. Fitch found the same.

> I am certainly doing these schools no injustice when I say that as a class they possess no distinctive religious character whatever. None of the teachers considers it his business . . .[73]

> Nor [he went on] must I conceal the fact that there are many parents who object to the religious character so strongly impressed upon most of the State-aided schools. I attended a large meeting of working people in Leeds, including many of unusual intelligence, and in the course of the discussion, I asked how it was that, notwithstanding the existence of so many institutions on a public basis, so many parents seemed to prefer the private school. One speaker said strongly, that for his part he thought 'it was because there was too much religion in the aided school' and the remark was very loudly and generally cheered.[74]

Having no genuine or controlled element of moral regulation, the educational legitimacy of the working-class private school was consequently denied. They could not be true schools; they could 'answer few of the purposes of education. They may teach some of the children reading, writing and arithmetic . . . But the mass of the children cannot there learn their duties.'[75]

In itself, the dismissal of such schools by middle-class experts on these grounds is not surprising, but our present acceptance of it as a valid and conclusive judgement certainly is. Such dismissiveness was the result of measuring the intellectual product of one educational tradition by the expressed aims of a distinctive alternative. Relatively, genuine measurement of this product has to be made, at least in part, against the particular goals which the working-class tradition itself set. And in this respect, the identified intent of working-class schooling was in fact more successfully realised as a product than was that of the competing provided schools. The extent of this realisation will be considered shortly. But some attention must first be directed at the official rejection of the working-class private school as inadequate in pedagogy rather than curriculum.

Part of the novelty of the publicly provided elementary school in the early decades of the nineteenth century lay in its emphasis on a new role for the trained teacher. His or her control lay not merely in the management of pupils, but in the framing and production of particular forms of legitimate classroom knowledge to be transmitted in discrete blocks to an entire class-group which received and digested the information as a single passive unit. Within this unit, the response of each individual pupil was ideally identical to all the others. Mechanistic or military analogies were applied with approval; one Assistant Commissioner, for example,

> was fortunate in having the opportunity of frequently observing one of the noblest specimens of [public inspected] schools in Rochdale. There could hardly be a more striking sight to the understanding eye than the interior of this school, in which I have seen 600 children present at one time, all under the most perfect command, moving with the rapidity and precision of a machine, and learning as though they were learning for their lives . . .[76]

In this perspective, successive new teaching techniques were accorded the status almost of scientific discoveries — monitorial, mutual, simultaneous, suggestive, interrogative, elliptical — and the 'efficiency' of schools was judged by the extent of their adoption.[77]

These new methods were never found to be practised in the working-class private schools. They were in fact technically impossible in such schools because pupil classification, the corollary of the new methods, was seldom attempted. As Fitch pointed out:

> It is needless to say that classification is well nigh unknown in the schools. The fact that the schools are generally small, and that they comprise children of all ages from three and four up to thirteen or fourteen, would alone account for the difficulty of grouping them into classes, even if the confined area and clumsy fittings did not furnish a physical hindrance.[78]

But the new techniques were ignored by the private teachers principally because of their positive preference for the old, officially scorned 'individual method'. This was a preference which rested on tradition, experience and exigency, and not on formal training. In the private school, not only were the children of mixed ages and abilities, but their attendance was often irregular. And even when they were present, the lack of resources or the particular wishes of the parents meant that most pupils would be working from different books. In practice then, each child in attendance was given a particular 'task' to prepare, whether learning the alphabet, reading a passage or writing a copy. From time to time, each pupil would come up to the teacher's chair and they would work through the task together.[79] While each child periodically received a few minutes of the teacher's time, the remainder of the group would be working on their individual exercises. This, in effect, was the 'individual method', and it was ceaselessly attacked by experts as chaotic, inefficient and unsystematic. As class work was virtually unknown, so therefore were all the new methods which between them rapidly annexed the entire territory of 'teaching' to themselves.[80] What went on in the private schools was thus, by definition, not genuine teaching; 'Instead of the master exerting himself to teach, the scholars are expected to learn';[81] '. . . of *teaching* I could find no evidence'.[82]

Though the individual method in reality represented a coherent, effective and appropriate approach to working-class learning, it was officially portrayed as formless and disorganised. The private teachers 'have no acquaintance whatever with any correct methods of conveying religious and secular instruction; they have no idea whatsoever of the proper mode of conducting the moral and industrial training of children'.[83] The schools 'are usually arranged on no kind of system . . . the general character of private schools is that of individual and unsystematic teaching'.[84] 'The system of teaching . . . is generally the old system, without monitors and without interrogation.'[85] 'In the great majority of these schools there seems to be a complete want of order and system.'[86]

Far from seeking to embrace the new methods, private teachers viewed them with distaste and contempt. One such claimed that parents 'like a private school better than one of those large twopenny schools, where boys are only taught . . .'[87] And the Manchester Statistical Society found that,

> Most of the Masters and Mistresses of these schools seemed to be strongly impressed with the superiority of their plans to those of any other school, and were very little inclined to listen to any suggestions respecting improvements in the system of education that had been made in other places — 'The old road is the best', they would sometimes say. One master stated, that he had adopted a system which he thought would at once supply the great desiderata in education — 'it is simply', he said, 'in watching the dispositions of the children, and putting them especially to that particular thing which they take to'. In illustration of this system, he called upon a boy about ten years of age, who had *taken* to Hebrew, and was just beginning to learn it: the Master acknowledging that he himself was learning too, in order to teach his pupil.[88]

What was particularly objectionable to the experts about the individual method was not just the failure of the teacher sufficiently to regulate and direct the production of knowledge, but the accent which the method put on uncontrolled learning. In the official view, such learning was inevitably wasteful, dangerous and invalid.

> It is certain that these private schools cannot compare in efficiency with a good public school . . . the scholars are half their time doing nothing. The system of teaching being almost wholly individual, each child can command but a very minute fraction of the master's attention.

In the public schools, 'the children are never left a moment to themselves; every minute is economized and turned to use'.[89] Any time during which the pupil's learning was not under the direct control of the teacher was disqualified from having any possible educative value.

> 'We use the individual method', said one of the more ambitious governesses to me; and this method consists in calling up one or two in turn to say their tasks. It is obviously very difficult to secure employment for the rest, and as a rule they do nothing but con over the task before they come up and relapse into idleness afterwards. This idleness is partly disguised no doubt . . .[90]

Pupils brought up on this method could cause serious problems if they were subsequently transferred to the public school system; such transfers were 'to the dismay of the [public] teacher, [for] badly taught or hardly taught at all, and wholly undisciplined, it is easy to conceive what a serious drawback they are to efficiency. They are enough to drive the teacher to despair.'[91] Working-class parents, on the other hand, valued the method for the degree of control over learning which it brought and for the individual contact between teacher and pupil in the private school; 'it is often believed that better attention is given to individual children when the numbers in the school are comparatively small'.[92]

Discrimination in favour of the private school on pedagogical grounds was particularly pronounced at the height of the period of the monitorial system in the public schools. The remote, mechanical organisation of this system was deeply disliked and resented. 'Parents . . . have a stong objection to pay the weekly 2d., 3d., or 4d. for their children to be made the monitors of others, or to their receiving instruction from other as such . . .'[93] Pupils remembered their experiences of the system without pleasure or profit; 'I cannot read at all or write; I did go to Old Church-school, but 'twas not much good, there was nothing but boys to teach us, they did us more harm than good, they used to get us down and punish us . . . .'[94]

Between them, the individual method, the absence of teacher professionalisation, and the domestic atmosphere of the working-class private school allowed enormous pedagogical and organisational flexibility. One aspect of this was that the individual method did not have necessarily to restrict the access of individual learner to teacher to just a few minutes. Others could share the teacher's work from time to time. Generally, this would have been a member of the same family or household; at Mrs Reynolds's school in Carmarthen, for example, an inspector 'found Mrs. Reynolds sitting by the fire, and her husband busily engaged in giving lessons to a group of children one by one'.[95] At a school in Leeds, 'the teacher, formerly a shoemaker . . . is assisted by his wife in the care of the younger children, and has in all 35 scholars, varying in age from 2 to 11 years'.[96] Not infrequently, older scholars might help with the teaching of younger ones, though in this respect, as in most others, Thomas Cooper was something of an exception; 'at three years old I used to be set on a stool, to teach one Master Bodley, who was seven years old, his letters'.[97] Of lesser celebrity was Mary Ann Lancashire, a matchgirl: 'age 11 . . . went [to school] on a week day when she never worked. Went since she was 4 years old. That was "in another country", in Blackburn. Had to teach scholars herself when she was about 7, because there was only one teacher. "I had about 7 on me".'[98]

In pedagogy as in curriculum then, the working-class private school was disqualified by the educational experts from constituting a genuine 'school' at all. But from the point of view of working-class educational demand, satisfaction on both counts was far greater than it was with the publicly provided alternative. We now have to see how far the private schools met the primary element in this demand — the quick and effective learning of basic skills.

The central ascribed role of the working-class private school in working-class culture was to transmit the tools of literacy — reading above all; 'the standard aimed at by parents for their children [is] only a little writing, a very little ciphering, and the power of "reading", however imperfectly . . .'.[99] It is these expressed criteria that any historical judgement of the schools must follow. We might simply argue that, given such criteria, together with the capacity of parents to assess the extent of their realisation, and given the constraints of economic hardship, it would have been unlikely for any unsuccessful school to have remained in business for long.[100]

But the available evidence permits us to develop the argument a little further than this. Because most middle-class commentators did not accept the validity of the instrumental working-class view of education, they rarely made assessments of its effectiveness on just this narrow ground.[101] Instead, they concentrated, as we have seen, on physical squalor and deficiency, on moral unsuitability and on professional incapacity. Judgements which would have conveyed any real meaning to the understanding of the users of the schools were rare, and were usually immersed in extraneous moral condemnation. Frequently indeed, the assertion that the schools taught merely the basic skills of literacy forms in itself an element of condemnation, and many reporters did not particularly see the need to go further and judge the success or failure of such instruction on its own terms. Thus; 'Very few of the dames pretend to do more than they are competent to perform. They labour, with the few books they possess, to initiate the scholars in the mystery of spelling, or even carry them so far as to read a little, but here they stop.'[102]

Where commentators did try more forcefully to decry the schools on the basis of declared rather than prescribed curriculum, they found themselves on shaky ground. This is well illustrated by Henry Althans's responses to the 1837 Select Committee.

> Have you had any opportunity of knowing what has been the result of what is called a dame school education? — I have never met with any of those children who could read unless they had been taught in public infant schools.
>
> Have you had any opportunity of ascertaining that? — I am quite satisfied in the dame schools they cannot teach reading.
>
> What can they teach? — I do not know.[103]

Under challenge, Althans's rapid descent from confident assertion to lame and ignorant uncertainty exposes the indefensibility of his position which, even for the most hostile opponent of the working-class private school, was a rather rare one. Most writers, whilst attacking the narrowness of the private curriculum, were less certain that it was always unfulfilled. Some were even impressed despite themselves.

> The reading in dame schools is often tolerably good.[104]
>
> I very much doubt if any public school could teach [reading] so quickly as was done in some small schools of this class which I visited.[105]
>
> In a blundering and unsatisfactory way the children are really learning to read a little by the governess's method of hearing reading and little tasks one by one, and to write letters on broken scraps of slates.[106]
>
> I have been surprised at the capacity for teaching which I have met, where the antecedents have been apparently so unfavourable. In one of the most wretched corners of St. George-in-the-East I found the widow of a petty warrant naval officer keeping a mixed school of 35, from 6 to 12, in perfect order, and the reading, writing and arithmetic were all up to the average

> of any ordinary inspected public school.[107]

> It is almost the universal opinion of parents that children are taught to read quicker and better in the dames' schools than in the lower classes of the public schools.[108]

Joseph Fletcher attempted to devalue his acknowledgement of this sort of success with a petty criticism; 'In some of the dame schools, the teacher, instructing the children one by one, frequently enables them to read pretty well, though with very uncouth pronunciation . . .'[109]

And if the meagre evidence relating to parental responses to the level of educational results is examined, it appears that it was the public rather than the private school which was often found wanting. One private teacher 'told me very gravely that she had several scholars from the National schools, because their parents said they learnt nothing there by clapping hands and singing.' Another

> has had children frequently returned to her from public schools on the alleged ground of expense and bad teaching. When the parents are out of work they remove their children, and send them to the schools where they get taught free, and when in work again they bring them back to her.

> Mrs. N. has had several children taken away and sent to the public schools because they could be taught cheaper, and occasionally they are brought back, the parents being dissatisfied with the instruction.[110]

Assistant Commissioner Fraser 'continually found in the private schools young children who had been removed from the public schools because, as the dames informed me, "they learn nothing there".'[111] And Fitch reported of one elderly private school keeper, 'of the neighbouring National school she speaks with considerable irritation not unmixed with contempt. She has known some children to be nine months in such a school and never to have learned a single task.'[112]

Experiences related by former scholars at private schools frequently follow a similar pattern. Thomas Cooper recalled his teacher in Gainsborough — 'Old Gatty' — as 'an expert and laborious teacher of the art of reading and spelling . . . I soon became her favourite scholar, and could read the tenth chapter of Nehemiah, with all its hard names . . . and could spell wondrously.'[113] Charles Shaw's teacher at Tunstall in the 1830s was 'old Betty W.'; 'though she never taught writing, her scholars were generally noted for their ability to read while very young. I know I could read my Bible with remarkable ease when I left school, when seven years old.'[114] 'G.J.', an apprentice in the 'House of Correction, Middlesex' in 1840, was,

> aged 17 . . . went once to a national school in Cowper St.; stayed there half a year; did not get on well there; only boys set to teach you, who cannot teach you so well as you can teach yourself; left it because I did not get on; went then to a private school where I paid 8d. per week; got on there faster.[115]

The same conclusion was reached by an anonymous working man writing in *The School Board Chronicle* in 1872;

> I remember very well that I . . . was kept fairly to work . . . My life at a dame school was happy and I believe it was profitable . . . I cannot take my leave of the dame school without expressing my obligations to that primitive institution . . . Perhaps my subsequent experiences of National and other schools was a little unfortunate — I do not think it was particularly so — but I know I have frequently had cause to contrast this early experience with that I had of more pretentious schools, unfavourably to the latter.[116]

The classrooms of the working-class private school were the true focuses of an alternative educational culture, physically and financially constrained but effectively unregulated by middle-class morality. They were places where the basic skills of literacy could be quickly and conveniently picked up at times and in ways which suited the user and not the provider. And whilst they were not devoid of the day-to-day problems of working with children with which all teachers, then and now, are familiar, they were entirely free of the endemic class resistance which blighted the efforts of the publicly provided schools. These were places of simple and straightforward learning where cultural incompatibility, subversion of the curriculum and truancy were not problems, and where attendance registers, uniformity of appearance, classification and 'standards' were unknown.

What, finally, can we say of the typical patterns of activity which must have daily gone on in thousands of classrooms of this kind, in both town and country, for the greater part of the nineteenth century? And how did such activity impinge on working-class life outside the classroom?

The most striking feature within the schools was perhaps the absence of regular or settled attendance. Dependent on a range of seasonal and economic factors, the classroom might contain only a handful of scholars, or it might be crowded to excess.[117] But large numerical fluctuations could occur in the course of a single day as well. School hours were nominal and pupils came and went at all times during the day, generally as the result of domestic or familial duties.[118] Frequently, this could involve the care of a younger brother or sister, though private schools were always willing for a scholar to bring such an infant to school.[119] In part, this helps to explain the large proportion of under-fives in many schools, which, it was often claimed, were sent merely to be 'out of the way' or 'kept safe'.[120] On its own, this would have been an expensive form of simple child-minding when other alternatives, like the care of an older sibling for example, were generally available.[121] In fact, even the youngest children in the classroom would usually have been started on 'saying their letters'. The age range in most schools was therefore likely to have been wide, probably ranging from about two years old to eleven or twelve.

The large majority of these would have been occupied, in one way or another, with learning to read:

> for a dame school you must imagine a square room, with about four or five forms of children; they are seated there, and the particular business of the mistress is to keep the children quiet; they have their books in their hands, and they are required to be learning their lessons, with nobody to teach them; they go up, one at a time, to the mistress, and they try to read, by repeating the words after her.[122]

The probable success of the teachers in teaching reading has already been indicated, but the precise methods which they employed are very hard to determine. Certainly, the repetition of words after the teacher was an important element, but most appear to have relied also on a traditional progression from alphabet — 'learning your letters'; to construction of syllables — 'I learn a, b, abs'; to three-letter words, then to little phrases, longer words, short paragraphs and finally to short stories.[123] Charles Shaw, who first went to school at three years old, remembered that

> There was an alphabet, with rude pictures, for beginners. There must have been something intensively vivid about these letters in the alphabet, for to this day when I see the letters Q and S as single capitals I see them rather as when I first saw them in old Betty's alphabet.[124]

Such an alphabet, possibly alongside an apposite drawing of an animal or object, would have been learned either from an old horn book or, more likely, from one of the numerous cheap spelling books much favoured by private teachers as introductory readers.[125] These ranged from little penny booklets containing an alphabet, some reading and spelling lessons and a few short stories and poems, to more substantial works like the popular 'Mavor's' which ran, in some of its hundreds of editions, to many pages.[126] The 1826 publication for example, was 168 pages long and contained an illustrated alphabet, progressive lists of syllables, words, phrases and paragraphs, and a jumble of longer reading material and information: Lessons in Natural History, Select Fables, Moral and Practical Observations, Lists of Proper Names, Poetry, Directions for Reading, writing copy, an almanac, an outline of geography and history, and so on.

The adherence of the private school to such old-fashioned works in preference to the inexpensive publications of the Education Societies was viewed with the same official disdain as was the traditional pedagogy of working-class educational culture.

> Generally speaking there seems to be no wish on the part of the proprietors of private schools to avail themselves of those helps to education which are furnished so cheaply by various Societies . . . This disposition to continue in the old routine of school keeping is particularly observable with respect to the books used . . . A dame, when asked by one of your Committee what was the reason she did not supply herself with some of the 'Society's

> Cards', in preference to the torn leaves of a Dictionary, from which the children were learning to spell, replied that such a measure would immediately be followed by the removal of all the children from the school.[127]

Once more, this kind of criticism was informed, above all else, by the fear of the characteristically unsystematic and uncontrolled approach in the private school. In Westminster dames' schools in the 1830s, 'Frequently there was seen a shelf of old dusty books . . . the Bible, carefully preserved in a green-baize cover; the old newspaper seldom failed.'[128] In Liverpool, 'In many of those schools which are not wholly destitute, the books are of such a mixed character as to defy enumeration, consisting of old magazines, of parts of novels or sermons, and sometimes even of political pamphlets.'[129] John Pounds apparently had

> next to no books, of any sort, for them to read out of. He'd take a hand-bill, with large letters, and let them read that; or a bit of a newspaper; anything he happened to have ready; sometimes a stray leaf out of an old worn-out book, that he happened to pick up.
>
> I said, 'I think, Mr. Pounds, you want some new books'. 'Why so?' he said. 'Because those just under that bird-cage seem to be coming to pieces'. 'So much the better'. 'How can that be, Mr. Pounds?'. 'Why, ye see, Sir, when a book's new like, an' all tight together, it sarves for only one at a time; but when it comes to pieces, every leaf sarves for one'.[130]

Whilst it might indeed have been the case that 'It is a very rare occurrence that a *private or dame school* is found to have an adequate supply of books', most had a stock of this heterogeneous kind.[131]

Such deficiencies were not as absolute as might be supposed, for it was a very common practice for children to bring reading material to school with them, thereby relieving the teacher's stock for the minority who were not so supplied. 'The teacher has no power to determine what class books shall be used . . . he is therefore dependent on the books the parents choose to send.'[132] In some schools,

> any book brought by the children was made use of; indeed, this

latter practice appears to be generally adopted.[133]

> The children are sent to these schools mainly with the view of being 'kept out of the streets', and in general read from any book which they happen to bring with them from home.[134]

In the working-class private school therefore, group teaching would have been rendered impossible by the enormous variety and diversity of reading matter, even had it been thought desirable. In practice, 'no two children . . . have books alike, and so, there are almost as many classes as scholars'.[135] The works which came closest to being generally available were the Bible and the Testament, both of which were frequently used — especially in 'common day' schools — for learning to read or for reading practice.[136] Observers were particularly critical of this purely instrumental use of sacred texts — 'desecrated by such a use' — and feared that their moral impact would be debased.[137]

It is particularly difficult to say how activity in the classroom affected subsequent life and in particular, how the skill of reading, once mastered, was exercised. In some cases, individual attendance was so abbreviated that little of lasting use was achieved. James Lackington, for example, 'was sent to a dame-school and began to learn to read; but before he could learn anything worth knowing, his mother, who was obliged to maintain her children as best she could, found it impossible to pay the twopence a week for his schooling'.[138] For others, reading skill atrophied after schooling, when the exigencies of earning a living were faced. George Wilde, a 17-year-old Lancashire collier in the early 1840s, admitted that he could read, 'not much, I have forgotten how; when I was 12 years old I could read, but since then, I have been my own master, and I have never done much in that way'.[139] And John Watson, aged 16, 'Only knows his a, b, c; cannot write at all. Goes to no school now . . . Was at school before he went down the pit for a year and could read the Bible then; now he has forgotten everything.'[140] For many others though, reading continued to play a significant part in their lives, despite the brevity of intial schooling. Richard Hampton, the itinerant Cornish preacher, related that, at the age of eight,

> my parents then sent me to a raiding school, kept by a poor owld man caaled Stephen Martin. My schoolin' cost three a'pence a-week. I was keept theere for seven months and so my edication

> was wurth no less than three shellin' and sexpence — theere's for 'ee! When me edication was fenished, as they do say, I was took hum,seven months' larnin' bein' aall that my poor paarents cud affoord for me. But I shall have to bless God to aall eternaty for that edication. At that dear owld man's school I larnt to raid a book they caaled a Psalter; an', havin' larnt so fur, when I got hum I gove myself to raidin', and kept on keepin' on tell I cud raid a chapter in the Testament or Bible.[141]

For some, subsequent reading might go no further than the kind of material with which they had become familiar at school. Thus, 'I can read the Testament; I can read the spelling book and the sixpenny book. I have never read anything else.'[142] 'I do not know exactly what age I am. It is 16, 17 or 18 . . . I cannot read much, some little. I have read the Testament. I have read the Spelling-book and Ready-ma-daisy.'[143]

But frequently, reading was taken further, sometimes for the acquisition of knowledge but probably more often for the kind, of light amusement and entertainment which middle-class moralists deplored.

> I am 19. I am a moulder . . . I can read and write a little . . . I read the Bible. I also read books about Turpin and Jack Sheppard. I also read Bell's Life in London; it is much read in this part . . .[144]

> I am 16 years of age . . . I read middling . . . I read the Bible sometimes . . . I have read Reading Made Easy. I have read about Turpin and Jack Sheppard; I have read about Robin Hood. I read song-books . . . I have read a bit of Robinson Crusoe. I have read about the pigs and cows dying of distemper.[145]

For some, of course, literacy was the key to much more extensive learning. Such were individuals like William Lovett, John Clare or John Jones.[146] The numbers of those launched into the autodidactic tradition by the acquisition of basic literacy however went far beyond such classic examples. One such unnamed scholar was recorded by Sub-Commissioner Kennedy:

> At Todmorden . . . at the house of a man who is now a

> gardener, but who had previously been a hand-loom weaver, I found a well-selected library of literary and scientific works; a small laboratory; a tin telescope made by himself; a superior electrical machine of his own construction; and a collection of geological and botanical specimens. I found that, whilst this man was a hand-loom weaver and earnings only 7s. to 8s. per week, he had contrived to travel over the whole of Craven, in Yorkshire, and has made a collection of the indigenous plants and geological specimens . . . His conversation, like his pursuits, was of a superior order.[147]

Finally, it may have been that the greatest valuation placed on reading was often for its worth to the family as a whole, rather than simply to the individual reader. At Ramsbottom in Lancashire, for instance, with a reported illiteracy rate of over 50 per cent in 1839, only 11 families of a total of 309 had no single reader among their number.[148] And it is perhaps with this image of the young literate scholar, conveying the fruit of his or her dearly-won skill to the rest of the family that this chapter on the working-class private classroom — a true extension of the domestic environment — can come to a close.

> I likes 'em to read well. It's a good thing for 'em at home. A little girl as reads clear and pleasant like, can read to 'em at home, whiles they's all at work round their candle, on a winter's night; and it makes work go on light and quick like; and all's cheerful and happy.[149]

Notes

1. See S. Frith, 'Socialization and Rational Schooling: Elementary Education in Leeds before 1870', in P. McCann, *Popular Education and Socialization in the Nineteenth Century* (1977), pp. 67–92, esp. pp. 79–80. Whilst all forms of publicly provided schooling were disliked by the working class, the monitorial system was the most universally hated. See n. 94 for references.
2. U. R. Q. Henriques, *Before the Welfare State* (1979), p. 230. Also see J. Hurt, 'Education and the Working Class', in *Society for the Study of Labour History Bulletin*, no. 30 (1975), p. 46.
3. P.P. 1847 [779] xv, *Reports by Inspectors*, p. 22.
4. P.R.O. Ed. 3/15. Fees ranged from 2d and 4d, pupil ages from under 3 to 13.
5. P.R.O. Ed. 3/9. Fees from 2d to 9d.

6. See School Form (No. 74L), January 1871, p. 2.
7. Cumin, *Newcastle*, vol. 3, p. 83.
8. P.R.O. Ed. 3/2.
9. Where a room was so fitted, it usually contained 'a few forms, a table or desk, and perhaps a map on the wall', ibid., p. 5.
10. P.R.O. Ed. 3/11.
11. P.R.O. Ed. 3/24.
12. P.R.O. Ed. 3/11.
13. P.R.O. Ed. 3/15.
14. P.R.O. Ed. 3/16.
15. Charles Shaw ('An Old Potter'), *When I was a Child* (1903), p. 1.
16. 'Second Report . . . Westminster', *J.S.S.*, vol. 2 (1839), p. 196.
17. Foster, *Newcastle*, vol. 2, p. 336.
18. See *Select Committee*, pp. 102–3.
19. P.R.O. Ed. 3/15.
20. P.R.O. Ed. 3/2.
21. 'Liverpool', *M.S.S.* (1836), p. 24. Schools run by women, the report continued, 'have generally a neater and more comfortable appearance than the Boys' Schools of the class. In the latter, there is generally a total disregard of external appearance, which gives an air of poverty and discomfort all around. In the former, greater pains seem to be taken to make everything appear to the best advantage . . .'.
22. 'Manchester', *M.S.S.* (1837), p. 6.
23. 'Manchester', *M.S.S.* (1837), p. 6
24. 'Liverpool', *M.S.S.* (1836), p. 11. But note that on p. 24, a tabulated list indicates that of 244 dames' schools, 45 were 'generally of a poor description', 13 were 'very close', 15 were 'very dark', 18 were 'very damp', 32 were 'very filthy' and 7 were 'very crowded and disorderly'.
25. 'Birmingham', *J.S.S.*, vol. 3 (1840), p. 30. Also see 'Finsbury', *J.S.S.* (February 1843), p. 31; 'Fifth Report . . . London', *J.S.S.* (August 1843), p. 216; 'Hull', *J.S.S.*, vol. 4 (1841), p. 158.
26. 'Rutland', *J.S.S.*, vol. 2 (1839), p. 305.
27. On drill in the public school, see in particular, J. Hurt, 'Drill, discipline and the Elementary School Ethos', in P. McCann (ed.), *Popular Education*, pp. 167–91. Also Noble, P.P. 1878 (236), *London School Board (Inspectors' Reports)*, pp. 5–6. 'Drill is so important an aid to securing and maintaining discipline, that, unless good reason could be shown to the contrary, every master of a school ought to be required to render himself a thoroughly efficient drill master. I have noticed a very great improvement in the behaviour and carriage of the boys of many of our schools, and drill may fairly claim the credit of this. I should like to see all movements in school, as well as in the drill-ground, executed at the word of command; and further, that girls as well as boys should participate in the benefits of drill.'
28. See J. Kay-Shuttleworth, *The Moral and Physical Condition of the Working Classes Employed in the Cotton Manufacture in Manchester* (1832; rep. 1970).
29. H.M.I. Bowstead, *C.C.E.*, 1871–2, p. 47.
30. H.M.I. Watkins, *C.C.E.*, 1871–2, p. 80. But notice how *exactly* those physical and organisational characteristics of the working-class private school which were usually castigated as impossible educational deficiencies could, in very special circumstances, be quite differently assessed. The clearest example is the case of John Pounds, the Portsmouth cobbler celebrated as the founder of the ragged school movement to which middle-class philanthropy rapidly became associated. (See for example, Mary Carpenter, 'Neglected Children', in *National Association for the Promotion of Social Science* (1865), pp. 313–25.) Henry Hawkes was the Unitarian

minister of Pounds' local chapel, and in 1884, he wrote his hagiographical *Recollections of John Pounds*. Compare these interpretations of Pounds' school with those relating to the generality of working-class private schools — all of them contemplating fundamentally similar phenomena. ' " When I consider the room available in that little shop for his keeping his school; with himself sitting on his bench at the window, working at his trade, with his tools and materials about him; it seems astonishing he could have done so much in it". "From front to back . . . not quite five yards; from side to side, about two yards; as to height, a man six feet high could only just stand straight up in it". "Scarcely anything for the children to sit on: — some old broken boxes; a little form or two; and the lower steps of the very little stairs . . .". "Not a desk, or a table: — and such poor meagre means for teaching with".' (p. 242). 'His personal appearance is altogether against him; so dark, and coarse, and not clean . . . And that loud harsh voice was at times shocking; revolting . . . But what a poor bit of a place for a school: — And so many crowded into it! — scarcely room for them to turn about: — the roof, so low; the walls so dark and dirty; and crowded with bird-cages, and other things . . . all meagre and poverty-stricken. Still, there was an air of happiness and comfort in all that busy group' (pp. 33–4).'And on the hearth you might see the cat and some kittens sleeping before the fire; and a bird asleep on the cat's back; and two or three young birds nestling with the kittens; and some young guinea pigs in a basket in the corner' (p. 249). '"I could scarcely have fancied sometimes that there were so many in [the shop]; they were all so comfortable and pleasant together. It was a beautiful sight to stand looking at them, over the little half-door"' (p. 317).'"Mr. Pounds often went out suddenly during school hours; and he'd leave us all alone — boys and girls together; and say to us, 'Now, you bide here, while I come back; and mind you be good'. And then he'd tell one of the oldest boys, perhaps, to take care of us"' (p. 337). '"There was always a prevailing life and pleasantness in your school. The children seemed to be doing their work as a delight; not as a drudgery"' (p. 135). Also, pp. 64, 169, 307, 317.

31. In the clamour to denounce working-class private schools precisely because they did not separate school from life, either physically or practically, the question of the possible advantages — educational as well as social — of this kind of schooling has scarcely been raised. For the physical characteristics of public schools, see Jellinger Symons *School Economy: A Practical Book on the Best Modes of Establishing and Teaching Schools, and of Making them Thoroughly Useful to the Working Classes by Means of Moral and Industrial Training* (1858; rep. 1971), Part 2, Ch. 1; E. Robson, *School Architecture* (1874; rep. 1972); Malcolm Seaborne, *The English School, Its Architecture and Organization 1370–1870* (1971), Chs. 8–10; Seaborne and Roy Lowe, *The English School, Its Architecture and Organization, Vol. II, 1870–1970* (1971), Part 1.

32. See for instance, 'Liverpool', *M.S.S.* (1836), p. 24.

33. *C.C.E.*, 1875–6, p. 415.

34. Quoted by Cumin, *Newcastle*, vol. 3, p. 84.

35. Jenkins, *Newcastle*, vol. 2, p. 529. Complaints about ill-ventilated rooms were common and investigators frequently remarked on the over-heating which resulted. This was a characteristic working-class practice, by no means confined to schoolrooms. In his enquiry into the fustian cutters of Lymm, for example, H. W. Lord remarked on 'the almost invincible objection to fresh air which I found among the work-people . . .'. P.P. 1863 [3170] xviii, p. 169. What this in fact represented was the valuation which was put on the potentially expensive business of staying warm. This luxury was not afforded by the draughty public schools, but was usually present in the private schools where an extra ½d or 1d might sometimes be charged for 'coals'. See H.M.I. Smith, *C.C.E.*, 1875–6, p. 565. 'The cottage school is thought to be warmer than the school.'

36. P.R.O. Ed. 3/15.
37. *Select Committee*, p. 136.
38. See E. Horne, *Somerset Folk* (1938), pp. 51–62.
39. *Newcastle*, vol. 2, p. 221.
40. M. K. Ashby, *Joseph Ashby of Tysoe 1859–1919*, (1961), quoted in P. Gosden, *How They Were Taught* (1969), p. 44. Also see Johnson, 'Education and Popular Politics', p. 25.
41. *C.C.E.*, 1876–7, p. 565. Also see Hare, *Newcastle*, vol. 3, p. 275.
42. H.M.I. Bowstead, *C.C.E.*, 1872–3, p. 26. Also see H.M.I. Allen, *C.C.E.*, 1840–1, p. 128.
43. H.M.I. Mathew Arnold, *C.C.E.*, 1872–3, p. 26.
44. 'State of Agricultural Labourers in Northumberland', *J.S.S.*, vol. 1 (1838), p. 403.
45. 'Manchester', *M.S.S.* (1837), p. 22.
46. *Select Committee*, p. 135. Also see Fraser, quoted in *Newcastle*, vol. 1, p. 243; P.P. 1842 [382] xvii, *C.E.C.*, p. H8; P.P. 1843 [430] xiii, *C.E.C.*, p. 182; P.P. 1843 [432] xv, *C.E.C.*, p. Q16.
47. For an example of the latter, see Coode, quoted in J. W. Adamson, *English Education 1789–1902*, p. 206. 'Inspected schools . . . surpassed general expectation . . . the principles of political economy with especial reference to questions which touch on the employment and remuneration of labour, principles of taxation, uses of capital, etc., affects of strikes on wages, etc., are taught with great clearness and admirable adaptation to the wants and capacities of the children of artisans . . .' Also see Kay-Shuttleworth's answers to the *Select Committee*, esp. pp. 23, 41–2, 77. For the later development of liberal and conservative educational ideologies, see S. Humphries, 'Schooling and the Working Class in Bristol, 1870–1914', in *Southern History*, vol. 1 (1979), pp. 171–207, esp. pp. 176–80.
48. See Frith, 'Socialisation and Rational Schooling', esp. pp. 85–7. Also T. Tholfsen, *Kay-Shuttleworth on Popular Education*, Introduction. Reaching forward to some of the implications for the educational policy of the Labour Party in the early twentieth century, see Dan Finn *et al.*, 'Social Democracy, Education and the Crisis', in *On Ideology*, D. Coffey *et al.*, (1978) C.C.C.S., cited earlier. Also see P. Corrigan and S. Frith, 'The Politics of Youth Culture', in *Resistance Through Rituals*, Working Papers in Cultural Studies 7 and 8 (1975), pp. 231–9.
49. *Edinburgh Review*, vol. 38 (1823), p. 444. Cited by McCann. Also, Thomas Pole, *Observations Relative to Infant Schools (designed to point out their usefulness to the Children of the Poor)* (Bristol, 1823).
50. *Select Committee*, p. 15. Also Pole, *Observations*, p. 4. Infant Schools 'are especially requisite at the present period, when juvenile delinquency prevails to a lamentable extent; arising in a great measure, there is reason to believe, from very defective moral and religious instruction at an early age, the deplorable effects of bad examples, and the children being suffered to range at large, and associate in groups, where they corrupt each other by improper conversation and yield to the impulse of evil propensisities.'
51. 'Salford', *M.S.S.* (1836), p. 14.
52. 'Liverpool', *M.S.S.* (1836), p. 34.
53. P.P. 1842 [382] xvii, *C.E.C.*, p. 36. For other comparisons — unfavourable to the dame's school — see *Newcastle*, vol. 1, pp. 28–31. Also H.M.I. Noel, *C.C.E.*, 1840–1, p. 16. Note also how Pole could enthuse over Infant Schools for just the reason for which dames' schools were condemned — child-minding. 'The education of very young children is but a secondary consideration in the establishment of Infant Schools — The two great objects are, first, that of relieving their mothers from the care and attention which their children's presence would demand, and to leave them at liberty to do what may be needful at home, or to go out to daily

labour in other families, or places, for their comfortable maintenance . . .' The reason for this paradox is clearly expressed by Pole's second consideration; 'and secondly, that of taking the children from the influence of pernicious examples, for the purpose of cultivating far better dispositions and habits, than what we see prevalent amongst the children of the poor . . .'.

54. P.P. 1842 [381] xvi, *C.E.C.*, p. 727.
55. Senior, *Suggestions on Popular Education*, p. 371.
56. 'Manchester', *M.S.S.* (1837), p. 5.
57. 'Pendleton', *J.S.S.*, vol. 2 (1839), p. 70.
58. Ibid., p. 68.
59. *Select Committee*, p. 118.
60. Ibid., p. 122.
61. Bartley, *The Schools for the People*, pp. 107–8.
62. *C.C.E.*, 1871–2, p. 67.
63. Brougham, *Edingburgh Review* (1823), p. 445.
64. H.M.I. Morrell, *C.C.E.*, 1873–4, p. 129.
65. 'Liverpool', *M.S.S.* (1836), p. 14.
66. 'Bury', *M.S.S.* (1835), p. 6.
67. P.P. 1843 [430] xviii, *C.E.C.*, pp. 168–9.
68. P.P. 1842 [382] xvii, *C.E.C.*, p. 73. Also see P.P. 1843 [431] xiv, *C.E.C.*, p. d30.
69. P.P. 1844 [523] xxvii, *Reports by Factory Inspectors*, p. 25. Also P.P. 1847 [828] xv, *Reports*, p. 5.
70. H.M.I. Allen, *C.C.E.*, 1840–1, p. 127.
71. P.P. [1847] 870 xxvii, *Education in Wales*. R. Comm., Pt. 1, p. 29.
72. *Newcastle*, vol. 3, p. 224.
73. *Special Reports*, p. 56.
74. Ibid., p. 107.
75. Noel, *C.C.E.*, 1840–1, p. 163.
76. Winder, *Newcastle*, vol. 2, pp. 224–5. Also see Ricks, P.P. 1876, (75) lix. *London School Board (Inspectors' Reports)*.
77. See Symons, *School Economy*, esp. Part 2, Chs. 2 and 3. Also *Select Committee*, p. 6; P.P. 1843 [431] xiv, *C.E.C.*, p. E22.
78. *Special Reports*, p. 55; also pp. 40, 43, 52. Also 'Second Report . . . Westminster', *J.S.S.*, vol. 2 (1839), p. 196.
79. More generally, see E. P. Thompson, 'Time, Work Discipline and Industrial Capitalism', *Past and Present*, no. 38 (1967), pp. 56–97.
80. The closest approximation to 'classwork' would have been story-telling. See for example, Christopher Thomson, *The Autobiography of an Artisan* (1847). Thomson attended a school run by a woman who 'had the reputation of "keeping a good school", which goodness consisted mainly in having a large number of pupils — so large, that the "letter learning" was all she could afford time for, except drilling into the young mind a goodly array of ghost stories.' In retrospect, Thomson, like several other working-class intellectuals, did not approve of such frivolousness. 'This mode of "shooting young ideas"', he went on, 'is out of fashion. Our infant schools, gymnasiums and Wilhelm have come to the rescue . . . The play-grounds, the picture cards and singing, are better companions for the tender things, than barguests and fairies', pp. 35–7. Also see Charles Shaw, *When I was a Child*, p. 2.
81. 'Birmingham', *J.S.S.*, vol. 3 (1840), p. 34.
82. *Special Reports*, p. 51.
83. *Select Committee*, p. 2.
84. Winder, *Newcastle*, vol. 2, p. 222. Also Jenkins, *Newcastle*, p. 563; P.P. 1847 [870] xxvii, *Wales*, Pt. 1, p. 25.

85. *Special Reports*, p. 107.
86. 'Manchester', *M.S.S.* (1837), p. 9; also 'Liverpool', *M.S.S.* (1836), pp. 18, 38.
87. Quoted in *Special Reports*, p. 50.
88. 'Manchester', *M.S.S.* (1837), p. 8. Also *Select Committee*, p. 102.
89. Winder, *Newcastle*, vol. 2, p. 227.
90. *Special Reports*, p. 56. Glimpses of the day-to-day classroom problems at some schools show that they were not devoid of the familiar strains of teaching which many modern practitioners will recognise. William Lovett for example, seems to have been a difficult pupil, 'when very young, my love of play was far greater than that of learning, for I was sent to all the dame-schools of the town before I could master the alphabet'. *Life and Struggles of William Lovett* (1876), pp. 3–4. And an unnamed Manchester school-keeper had a school of 'about 130 children, [where] the noise and confusion was so great as to render the replies of the Master to the enquiries put to him totally inaudible; he made several attempts to obtain silence but without effect; at length, as a last effort, he ascended his desk, and striking it forcibly with a ruler, said in a strong Hiberian accent, "I'll tell you what it is boys, the first I hear make a noise, I'll call him up and kill him entirely;" and then perceiving probably on the countenance of his visitor some expression of dismay at this murderous threat, he added quickly in a more subdued tone, "almost I will".' 'Manchester', *M.S.S.* (1837), p. 9. See also Ben Brierley, *Job Thatcher's School* (1889); also Jocelyne Goodman (ed,), *Victorian Cabinet Maker, The Memoirs of James Hopkinson* (1968), p. 6.
91. H.M.I. Smith, *C.C.E.*, 1876–7, p. 565.
92. Howson, *Newcastle*, vol. 4, p. 378. Also Winder, *Newcastle*, vol. 2, p. 183. There is 'an impression which some parents entertain that more individual attention is paid in [the private school] to the scholars'.
93. P.P. 1843 [431] xiv, *C.E.C.*, p. C11.
94. P.P. 1843 [431] xiv, *C.E.C.*, p. c110; also p. f284. Also P.P. 1863 [3170] xviii, *C.E.C.*, p. 277; 'Hull', *J.S.S.*, vol. 4 (1841), p. 161; 'Schools for the Industrious Classes', *C.S.E. Second Publication* (1838), pp. 366–7.
95. P.P. 1847 [870] xxvii, *Wales*, Pt. 1, p. 293.
96. *Special Reports*, p. 100.
97. Thomas Cooper, *The Life of Thomas Cooper*, p. 5.
98. P.P. 1863 [3170] xviii, *C.E.C.*, pp. 87–8.
99. See P.P. 1852 [1525] xxi, *State of the Population in Mining Districts*, p. 27.
100. See T. Laquer, 'Working Class Demand', p. 198.
101. See for instance Mr. Tancred's report on the mining districts of South Staffordshire in 1843. 'I cannot confine the term *education* to the instruction merely of a few years of childhood.' P.P. 1843 [508] xii, p. cxxxviii.
102. 'Rutland', *J.S.S.*, vol. 2 (1839), p. 305. With the physical difficulties under which the working-class private school operated in mind, it is perhaps worth mentioning Philpott's generous tribute to the relatively well-supplied and funded public school in the pre-School Board era. In commending their 'truly patriotic work', he felt that, 'when we remember the difficulties under which they laboured, the wonder is that they accomplished any really effective educational work at all'. *London at School*, p. 6.
103. *Select Committee*, p. 136.
104. Hedley, *Newcastle*, vol. 2, p. 159.
105. Winder, *Newcastle*, vol. 2, p. 227.
106. *Special Reports*, p. 53. See also H.M.I. Barrington-Ward, *C.C.E.*, 1881–2, p. 196. 'In the great majority of the schools the work is exceedingly bad. The ordinary dame schoolmistress can teach reading very fairly . . .'
107. Wilkinson, *Newcastle*, vol. 3, p. 394.

108. Fraser, *Newcastle*, vol. 2, p. 36. See also Hedley, *Newcastle*, vol 2, p. 158; Hare, *Newcastle*, vol. 3, p. 276.

109. P.P. 1840 [220] xxiv, *Hand Loom Weavers*, p. 84. Also see Wingate, P.R.O. Ed. 3/2, 'In reading, decidedly the subject best taught, the children will generally follow the often extraordinary pronunciation and accent of the teacher . . .'

110. Wilkinson, *Newcastle*, vol. 3, p. 379.

111. Fraser, *Newcastle*, vol. 2, p. 36. See also P. McCann, 'Spitfalfields', in P. McCann, *Popular Education*, p. 29.

112. *Special Reports*, p. 105.

113. Cooper, *The Life of Thomas Cooper*, p. 7.

114. Shaw, *When I was a Child*, p. 2.

115. P.P. 1840 (639) xxxiv, *Report by Mr. Hickson on the Condition of the Handloom Weavers*, p. 24.

116. 'The Dame School Forty Years Ago', by 'A Working Man', *School Board Chronicle*, 11.5.1872, pp. 409–10. Also see Master William Morris, *Reminiscences, Notes and Relics of ye Old Wiltshire Towne. Swindon Fifty Years Ago (More or Less)* (1885), p. 285.

117. For examples of fluctuations due to season or epidemic, see 'Birmingham', *J.S.S.*, vol. 3 (1840), p. 29. For those due to economic recession, see 'Pendleton', *J.S.S.*, vol. 2 (1839), p. 66.

118. H.M.I. Barrington-Ward, *C.C.E.*, 1881–2, p. 196. Also H.M.I. Boyle, *C.C.E.*, 1876–7, p. 437.

119. P.P. 1843 [431] xiv, *C.E.C.*, p. e3. Also Frith, in McCann, *Popular Education*, p. 85.

120. See 'Liverpool', *M.S.S.* (1836), p. 95; 'Birmingham', *J.S.S.*, vol. 3 (1840), p. 25; 'Hull', *J.S.S.*, vol. 4 (1841), p. 158; 'Leeds', *J.S.S.*, vol. 2 (1840), p. 417. Also *Newcastle*, vol. 1, p. 28; Winder, *Newcastle*, vol. 2, p. 183; *Special Reports*, p. 51; H.M.I. Barrington-Ward, *C.C.E.*, 1881–2, p. 196. 'Do nothing' or 'out of the way' explanations of infant attendance have much impressed historians. Less well known are accounts which speak disparagingly of 'delicateness' or 'maternal concern' — see for instance, Hare, *Newcastle*, vol. 3, p. 312 — and those which speak of particularly 'difficult' children. Duppa, for instance, spoke of dames' schools as 'asylums for mischievous or troublesome children [rather] than actual seminaries of instruction'. 'Analysis of the Reports of the . . . Manchester Statistical Society', *C.S.E. First Publication* (1837), p. 295. 'Do nothings', 'delicate infants', 'troublesome children', all were attempts to detract from the educative element of the working-class private school.

121. After James Lackington was taken from school, 'for several years his time was divided between nursing his younger brothers and sisters and getting into mischief'. W.E. Winks, *Lives of Illustrious Shoemakers* (1883), p. 21. Also see P.P. 1863 [3170] xviii, *C.E.C.*, p. 208. Harriet Brown, a ten-year-old lace worker was at 'week day school for a year once, but mother wanted her at home to "mind the baby"'.

122. *Select Committee*, p. 136.

123. See P.P. 1841 [382] xvii, *C.E.C.*, p. 113. For the pattern of such progressions, see the spelling books mentioned below.

124. Shaw, *When I was a Child*, p. 2. See also P.P. 1842 [381] xvi, *C.E.C.*, p. 617; J. Symons, *School Economy*, pp. 79–88.

125. See Neuburg, *Popular Education*, p. 59. Also Edward Clodd, *Memories*(1916), quoted in D. Leinster-Mackay (Ph. D. Thesis), pp. 43–4.

126. For a typical example of a penny spelling-book, see J. Page's *Tom Thumb's Alphabet or Reading Made Easy* (1843).

127. 'Fifth Report . . . London', *J.S.S.* (August 1843), p. 88. For books used in

individual schools, see 'Third Report . . . Westminster', *J.S.S.*, vol. 1 (1839), pp. 457, 464; also 'Second Report . . . Westminster', *J.S.S.*, vol. 2 (1839), pp. 210–11; 'Finsbury', *J.S.S.* (February 1843), p. 41. Useful secondary sources are J. M. Goldstrom, *The Social Content of Education, 1808–1870* (1972), and T. Laquer, *Religion and Respectability: Sunday Schools and Working Class Culture, 1780–1850* (1976), particularly pp. 113–19.

128. 'Third Report . . . Westminster', *J.S.S.*, vol. 1 (1839), p. 452.

129. 'Liverpool', *M.S.S.* (1836), p. 18.

130. Henry Hawkes, *Recollections of John Pounds* (1884), pp. 309, 64.

131. P.P. 1844 [523] xxvii, *Reports by Factory Inspectors*, p. 21. Also 'Birmingham', *J.S.S.*, vol. 3 (1840), p. 30; 'Finsbury', *J.S.S.* (February 1843), p. 30.

132. *Special Reports*, p. 55; also p. 54.

133. 'Second Report . . . Westminster', *J.S.S.*, vol. 2 (1839), p. 195.

134. 'Third Report . . . Westminster', *J.S.S.*, vol. 1 (1839), p. 451. Also 'Rutland', *J.S.S.*, vol. 2 (1839), p. 310; 'Manchester', *M.S.S.* (1837), p. 6. For some indication of the likely extent of reading material in the working-class home, see particularly P.P. 1842 [381] xvi, *C.E.C.*, pp. 218–19; P.P. 1842 [382] xvii, *C.E.C.*, p. 238; F. Liardet, 'State of the Peasantry in the County of Kent'. *C.S.E. Third Publication* (1839), pp. 17–139; 'Hanover Square', *J.S.S.*, vol. 6 (1843), pp. 20–1; 'Report of an Inquiry into the Condition of the Working Classes of the City of Bristol', *J.S.S.*, vol. 2 (1839), p. 371; 'Report on the State of Education among the Working Classes in the Parish of West Bromwich', *J.S.S.*, vol. 2 (1839), p. 377.

135. Foster, *Newcastle*, vol. 2, p. 337.

136. 'Third Report . . . Westminster', *J.S.S.*, vol. 1 (1839), p. 452.

137. P.P. 1851 [1304] xxiii, *Reports by Inspectors of Factories*, p. 14. Also P.P. 1851 [1396] xxiii, *Reports* . . ., p. 9; P.P. 1844 [523] xxvii, *Reports* . . ., p. 25. See also *Select Committee*, pp. 112, 125.

138. W.E. Winks, *Lives of Illustrious Shoemakers*, p. 21.

139. P.P. 1842 [382] xvii, *C.E.C.*, p. 208.

140. P.P. 1842 [381] xvi, *C.E.C.*, p. 617. Also ibid, 594, 805. Also P.P. 1843 [432] xv, *C.E.C.*, p. 123; P.P. 1863 [3170]xviii, *C.E.C.*, p. 288; *Select Committee*, p. 106; 'Hull', *J.S.S.*, vol. 4 (1841), p. 161; 'Pendleton', *J.S.S.*, vol. 2 (1839), pp. 67–8.

141. *Foolish Dick: An Autobiography of Richard Hampton, the Cornish Pilgrim Preacher*, ed. S. W. Christophers (1873), p. 16.

142. P.P. 1842 [381] xvi, *C.E.C.*, p. 73. Those investigations in this volume undertaken by Sub-Commissioner Mitchell show a particular interest in individual reading habits.

143. Ibid., p. 86. 'Ready-ma-daisy' was a colloquial corruption of 'Reading Made Easy'. Also see p. 72.

144. Ibid., p. 71.

145. Ibid., p. 84. Also pp. 66–7, 87, 162–3. See too P.P. 1843 [431] xiv, *C.E.C.*, p. b42, for the developed reading habits of the Midlands hatters. Also P.P. 1843 [432] xv, *C.E.C.*, p. q10; ibid., p. q11. Note also this frequently made claim, 'it is to be especially remarked that among all those who had never even heard such names as St. Paul, Moses or Solomon, there was a general knowledge of the characters and course of life of Dick Turpin the highwayman, and more particularly of Jack Sheppard, the robber and prison breaker'. P.P. 1843 [430] xiii, *C.E.C.*, p. 170.

146. Lovett, *Life and Struggles of William Lovett* (1876), p. 29; John Clare, *Sketches in the Life of John Clare* (1821), pp. 50–4; Jones, *Attempts in Verse*, pp. 171–2.

147. P.P. 1842[382] xvii, *C.E.C.*, p. 187.

148. 'Statistics of the Parish of Ramsbottom, near Bury in Lancashire', *J.S.S.*,

vol. 1 (1839), p. 539. It has been outside the scope of this study to make a contribution to the debate on the extent of working-class literacy — and in particular the ability to read. Such enterprises are notoriously difficult, though the implication of this study is that, because of the existence of many uncounted private schools, and because of other varieties of domestic learning, literacy was significantly greater than the numerical extent of publicly provided schooling at any given point would suggest. There are many important local indications of the extent of literacy in the reports, though the picture they draw is patchy and uneven. See for example, P.P. 1833 (450), *Reports . . . Factories Inquiry Commission*, p. 30, and especially p. 42. P.P. 1842 [381] xvi, *C.E.C.*, pp. 240, 527, 538, 714, 717, 719, 627, 629, 633, 704, 758, 829, 798–9; P.P. 1842 [382] xvii, *C.E.C.*, pp. 19, 138, 187, 752, 835; P.P. 1843 [431] xiv, *C.E.C.*, p. F35; P.P. 1843 [432] xv, *C.E.C.*, p. Q35; 'Results of some Inquiries into the Condition and Education of the Poorer Classes in the Parish of Marylebone in 1838', *J.S.S.* (February 1843), p. 46; 'Leeds', *J.S.S.*, vol. 2 (1840), p. 418; 'Hull', *J.S.S.*, vol. 4 (1841), p. 159; 'Working Classes of Bristol', *J.S.S.*, vol. 2 (1839), p. 372; 'West Bromwich', *J.S.S.*, vol. 2 (1839), p. 377; 'Mandron', *J.S.S.*, vol. 2 (1839), p. 228; 'Pendleton', *J.S.S.*, vol. 2 (1839), p. 73, pp. 80–1. More generally see W. L. Sargant, 'On the Progress of Elementary Education', *J.S.S.*, vol. 30 (1867), pp. 80–137. R. D. Altick, *The English Common Reader* (1957); R. K. Webb, *The British Working Class Reader, 1790–1848* (1955); V. Neuburg, *Popular Education*, Ch. 4, esp. p. 97; also Appendix (iii), 'A Statistical Approach to Literacy', p. 170. See also the same author's *Literacy and Society* (ed.), (1971), Introduction; L. Stone, 'Literacy and Education in England, 1640–1900', *Past and Present*, no. 42 (1969), pp. 69–139; M. Sanderson, 'Literacy and Social Mobility in the Industrial Revolution in England', *Past and Present*, vol. lxi (1972); R. S. Schofield, 'The Measurement of Literacy in Pre-Industrial England', in J. Goody (ed.), *Literacy in Traditional Societies* (1968), pp. 311–25; W. B. Stephens, 'Illiteracy and Schooling in the Provincial Towns 1640–1870', in D. Reeder (ed.), *Urban Education in the Nineteenth Century* (1977), pp. 27–47; D. Levine, 'Illiteracy and Family Life during the First Industrial Revolution', *Journal of Social History*, vol. 4 (1980), pp. 25–44; E. P. Thompson, *Making of the English Working Class*, pp. 782–7; G. Sutherland, *Elementary Education* (1971), pp. 13–14.

149. H. Hawkes, *Recollections of John Pounds*, p. 140. See also examples from the Children's Employment Commission — P.P. 1842 [381] xvi, *C.E.C.*, p. 83; P.P. 1842 [382] xvii, *C.E.C.*, p. 242.

6 DESTRUCTION

At the passing of the Education Act of 1870, it does not seem fanciful to suppose that something like a quarter of all working-class childen at elementary school were attending private schools. In any judgement, this was a very substantial presence. But by the 1880s, such schools were becoming few and far between. Some years later, Philpott could write that 'private schools of this type have long been practically extinct all over England'.[1]

The schools themselves were not all that the working class lost. The link between the working class and a network of independent schools under their direct control was severed not only in fact, but also in popular perception. Thereafter, the legitimacy of the concept of the 'private school' was annexed in a very short space of time as an exclusively middle-class educational preserve. Indeed, the association came to be somehow inappropriate, even unnatural or illogical. In effect, working-class private schooling disappeared from history almost as if it had never been. In 1913, Joseph Thornton could confidently assert that which, 50 years earlier, would have made no sense, 'in all elementary education, in comparison with the public school, the argument for the private school amounts to very little, and the tendency of modern educational evolution is all against it', whilst 'the case with the secondary schools is far different. A brief survey of the field of education will show that this is the special home of the private school.'[2] The triumph of provided elementary schooling and the ideological capture of 'private schooling' was complete. What then happened to the working-class private schools in the years following the 1870 Act? Why did they disappear?

The generally accepted historical answer — where one has been thought to be necessary — has been identical to the pre-1870 official prognosis. Such schools would not, or did not, survive the competition of the vastly more 'efficient' public sector once it was finally made nationally accessible. They were simply abandoned by their customers for an obviously superior — more 'efficient' — and cheaper product. Like the disappearance of some old country craft, death was by entirely natural causes.

> Originally, there were a good many [private schools] that provided an elementary education for children of the poorer part of the populace, by payment of small fees, and which were independent of the establishments which came to be accepted as schools to be carried on at public expense; the development of the public system has put such schools almost completely out of being, and the private schools now remaining normally require the payment of considerable sums for the privilege of the school attendance they provide.[3]

The anticipation and the subsequent analysis of the disappearance of working-class private schooling are therefore clear enough. But like every other aspect of the official, or officially-based accounts, their certainty does not survive closer investigation. Such investigation must centre upon the decade of the 1870s — a period of widespread official concern about the problem of the working-class private school and the means of its resolution.

The 1870 Act has commonly been seen as a step — long overdue — in bringing effective elementary schooling within the reach of all; as the exercise of the moral duty of a benevolent state on behalf of its citizens in an under-developed area of social policy.[4] It is a measure which has been alluded to in the language of progress, democracy and civilisation.[5] But any serious analysis has to be more critically aware and cannot proceed as if the provisions of the Act advanced into some kind of social and political vacuum.[6] And this is the position towards which any treatment of the 1870 Act which passes over its ramifications for working-class private schooling is led. History has accentuated those features of the Act which can be presented as the culmination of an advancing, putatively consensual 'education'. But to the keepers and users of working-class private schools, the Act represented a vast and unknown threat and an uncertain future. For them, it meant the beginning of the end of a long cultural tradition. For us, it represents the beginning of a system which is recognisably ours. This is why we have been content to extol the expansion of publicly provided schooling after 1870 while we have remained ignorant of the catastrophic decline in private elementary schooling in the same period. Such is the extent of the shaping of our perception by our own experience.

The details of the destruction of the working-class private schools are complex. There was nothing in the 1870 Act which simply banned or outlawed them, however much educationists might have wished for it. Such a measure would have been unthinkable for many reasons, not least of which was the unavoidable comparison with an unregulated middle-class private sector which such a clumsy and explicit manoeuvre would have involved. What was sought was the regulation of a particular sector of private schooling, and not the rejection in total of privateness in education. State interference into middle-class private schooling was rejected as an infringement of valued, though clearly not universal, liberal freedoms. Indeed, differential attitudes to the role of the state in education in this period are like a litmus test to distinguish working-class from middle-class schooling. And the Manchester Statistical Society's view that, 'If superior Private Schools are in any respect defective, those whose children are educated in them may, perhaps, safely be left to discover the defects, and have ample means and leisure to provide for their improvement',[7] remained dominant throughout the century and beyond. F. S. Marvin, for example, writing in 1933, echoes this still familiar theme. He speaks of private schools as 'typically and historically English'. They 'certainly demonstrate', he goes on, 'the unabated vitality and love of freedom in the British middle classes . . . It would be intolerable for the State to control the schools in the sense of prescribing who shall teach or what they shall say.'[8]

The goal, therefore, was the regulation of working-class private schools through discreet and preferably indirect mechanisms. The report of the Newcastle Commission had recommended that the best — the most 'efficient' — of such schools should be drawn into the public orbit, conform to the requirements laid down for state-sponsored schools and submit themselves to inspection, in return for financial aid from the public purse.[9] For most educationists, however, the notion of financial support for a class of schools whose complete destruction was sought, was out of the question, and the idea received little further attention. The possibility of some form of indirect regulation which would confer no benefits to individual schools was however explored more energetically.

One way of doing this — albeit a rather involved one — was to proceed against individual schools through the agency of local sanitary authorities. That is, to approach the issue as one of public health rather than private schooling.[10] Such a solution could however only be applied in situations where schools were seriously overcrowded. Besides, what was needed was a more unambiguous, less costly and universally applicable answer. George Bartley, through the *School Board Chronicle*, suggested the idea of some form of licensing of teachers as a legal prerequisite for school-keeping. Without enacting compulsory training, this kind of certification should concern the grasp of instrumental skills. 'Perhaps the simplest way . . . would be to require that all who undertake to teach "the three R's" should pass, at least, an examination in reading, writing and arithmetic.'[11] But despite his claim that 'the carrying out of such a simple test would, it is to be feared, close not a few schools', it had already been shown that most private teachers of half-timers, for whom such certification was required, had proved themselves to be instrumentally competent. Besides, excessive pressure on the teachers themselves was seen as politically risky. Few educationists welcolmed the popular opprobrium which a frontal assault on the livelihoods of individual teachers would have brought.[12]

Much expert opinion at first took the view that the mere passing of the Act would obviate further troublesome legislative manoeuvring. Enthused by the transparent superiority of public over private school, officials expected private schooling to evaporate before the overwhelming competition of an enhanced public supply. The problem would resolve itself naturally. H.M.I. Gream for instance argued that 'where school boards are elected these schools soon disappear . . .'.[13] His optimism was ill-founded. Like his spiritual predecessors in the 1850s and 1860s, his understanding of working-class support for the schools was misplaced.[14] As we shall see in a moment, working-class private schools did not suffer this kind of immediate collapse after the passing of the Act.

If the teachers were not to be regulated, and if public competition could not by itself destroy working-class support for the schools, then only one realistic target remained. This was the working-class parent himself or herself. Throughout the 1870s, such parents were subjected to a long and wearing war of attrition to break down their traditional allegiances. Such a strategy would outflank the teachers by destroying their popular support. And once this was eroded, individual teachers would go to the wall without the direct intervention of central or local public authorities.

This phase of the story is very difficult to re-create. This was no grand political battle fought out to a climax between two well-organised interest groups in the glare of the public spotlight. It was instead a fitful, intensely localised process of harrassment, warning and threat, in which representatives of local educational authorities sought to redirect working-class preference from private to public schools. In this, they utilised a range of indirect sanctions passed down through successive legislative action. Against these, parents who were faced with many other material problems, and who had no organised support, must have found sustained resistance very hard. There were to be no celebrated set-piece encounters in this long and often bitter fight, but only a numberless succession of isolated skirmishes. The vast majority of these have no record. They mostly comprised the fierce street or doorstep confrontations between parents and attendance officers which were such a mark of the years following the 1870 Act.[15] Frequently, these ended in victory for the officials, though where informal pressure or threat was insufficient, individual cases found their way before the magistrates. Of these, there is some record, though they were a very small minority. We can now consider in detail the pattern of this assault on the parents, from legislative instrument to local implementation.

The first stage in the process was bound up in the popular conception of the 1870 Act rather than its actual provisions — that which people believed, or were persuaded to believe, the Act would do. Among parents and teachers alike, it is clear that the sheer scale of the Act, as well as widespread uncertainty about its precise objectives and provisions, initially caused considerable confusion and demoralisation. Some did indeed understand it to mean that private schooling had actually become illegal at this point. In Birmingham, for instance, large numbers of schools were closed in 1870–1 as a result. The keepers 'imagined that they would not be permitted to continue and many even believed themselves liable to punishment if they did so . . . the poor people who kept [the schools] did not understand the law'.[16]

This kind of uncertainty was compounded by the flurry of official activity which followed the Act, and particularly by the surveys of local educational provision for which it provided. The purpose of these surveys was to determine the extent of the deficiency of school places region by region, and thence to ascertain those 'gaps' which needed to be 'filled'. It was argued in Chapter 2 that many working-class private schools were overlooked in this exercise. Certainly the methods for discovering their whereabouts were not very rigorous.

> To discover these, the [London School] Board inserted advertisements in local papers, and posted notices at the doors of churches, chapels and in other conspicuous positions likely to attract attention, inviting . . . teachers to make application for copies of Form 74L. The agents for collecting returns were further instructed to consult all rating authorities, ministers, teachers, Scripture readers, missionaries and others likely to possess information on the subject, for lists of all schools known to them.[17]

And even when tracked down, such schools frequently refused to make a return.[18] This was important because non-co-operative schools were not reckoned in the final calculation of acceptable local school accommodation.[19]

> If the teacher of any school refuse or neglect to fill up the form required for the said return, or refuse to allow the inspector to inspect the schoolhouse or examine any scholar, or examine the school books and registers . . . such school shall not be taken into consideration among the schools giving efficient elementary education to the district.[20]

But the final total of working-class schools which were not taken into consideration was very much greater than this.

Having completed their returns, schools had to await formal inspection in the course of 1870–71. If the inspector was satisfied that a school was satisfactory in both instruction and premises, it could then, and only then, be placed on the list of schools recognised by the Education Department, or by the School Board, as efficient.[21] Those schools which refused inspection at this point were added to the list of those summarily declared to be inefficient. In Birmingham, for example, such schools comprised 10 per cent of the total.[22] Schools which actually underwent inspection did not fare a great deal better. The instructions to inspectors outlined precise criteria for recognition as efficient. These focused on well-established qualitative differences between public and private schooling. Tests were to be made in respect of:

> 1. The premises in which the school is held . . . You will recommend no school to be recognised as efficient in point of accomodation which you would not at present recommend as

fitted to receive annual grants.

2. The qualifications of the teacher as shown by the results of the secular instruction given in the school.[23]

The majority of working-class private schools clearly had little hope of being judged 'efficient' when they were measured by the very different standards of the public school. Most failed immediately on the criterion of 'accommodation' and evaluation on the second criterion was seldom undertaken. The inspections therefore resulted in another large crop of 'inefficient' schools to be added to those which had not made returns in the first place, and those which had refused inspection. Education experts were jubilant. Their long-standing complaints about the schools seemed amply demonstrated. In London,

> The outcome of the inquiry was a fearful separating of wheat from the tares, followed, so far as the private adventure schools were concerned, by the garnering of marvellous little wheat . . . only 8.4% were efficient, 4.2% were semi-efficient, and no less than 87.4% were condemned.[24]

The inspection discounted, at a stroke, most of the school places occupied by over 44,000 of London's children.[25] These 44,000, along with most of the others at private adventure schools in the rest of the country, were simply placed on the lists of children recorded as being without schooling and for whom new public schools would have to be supplied.

The 1870 Act had therefore at last established a formal relationship between working-class private schools and the state. Though the state continued to have no direct educational jurisdiction over the schools, it had succeeded in cataloguing, inspecting and labelling them. It could now refer to such schools officially as 'not recognised by the Board as efficient'. Here was a real stick with which to beat the recalcitrant parent. And with the advent of the School Boards, there was an effective and determined local agency through which the message could be continuously hammered home. Attendance officers could warn parents that the attendance of their children at working-class private schools was 'not recognised' by the local School Board, and where compulsory attendance bye-laws were implemented, recourse to the courts might be taken if such children were not removed to public schools.

Such threats cannot have been without effect, and, given their superficial understanding of the nature of working-class private schooling, officials might be forgiven for supposing that the 1870 Act and its attendant activity would have despatched the problem once and for all. This was not the case. Considerable parental support weathered the storms of 1870–1 and many of the schools went on. This was because there was nothing in the Act which directly banned working-class private schools, nothing which explicitly outlawed their use, and nothing which disallowed their 'inefficiency'. Non-recognition by the School Board or by the Education Department itself, did not in fact matter. The disapproval of such authorities carried no legal weight; and mere disapproval, though now more systematically directed than ever before, was insufficient to destroy a resilient cultural tradition which had never known anything other than official hostility. So whilst the Education Department made its calculations as if working-class private schooling hardly existed, many of the schools themselves continued to function.

The blows of this first assault of 1870–1 undoubtedly weakened the tradition, but it soon became apparent that a second, more effective attack would be needed finally to kill it. This second offensive began in 1875.

In the intervening few years, the attrition of the School Boards continued to achieve only limited success, and official frustration became more intense. H.M.I. Boyle, for example, found that in Somerset, private adventure schools were 'frequently being newly established, and [I] am consulted as to the probability of anything being done by the managers of public elementary schools, when I have to confess my helplessness . . .'.[26] Increasingly, this frustration was directed at the 1870 Act itself which was seen to be unable finally to resolve the problem. At root, this was principally a matter of the imprecise legal definition of the two key terms which the educational experts themselves had always been very clear about — 'school' itself, and 'inefficient'. Chapter 5 showed some of the contexts in which the experts habitually denied the title 'school' to working-class private schools and the particular failings which were taken to demonstrate their 'inefficiency' — accommodation, pedagogy, curriculum. But the Act, whilst sympathetic to these subjective judgements, failed to elevate them to the status of legal definition. And it was this which educationists blamed for facilitating continuing parental non-compliance. Moreover, without terminological clarification, School Boards found that where individual cases came to court — on charges either of failing to attend 'school' or of not receiving an 'efficient' education — a successful outcome was by no means assured.

George Bartley was one of the first to point out the problems of leaving the term 'school' too vaguely defined. He observed in 1871 that 'there is a slight flaw in the Elementary Education Act. It enacts that all may, by a bye-law, be compelled "to attend school" but what a school is, is not defined. The worthy dames and the inferior private schools teachers will of course consider that their pupils fulfill this condition.'[27] A contributor to the *School Board Chronicle* identified only as 'T.' pointed out in more detail the potential confusion of the three-fold definition with which the Act worked. 'In the Act we have the three terms, "school", "elementary school", and "public elementary school", each differing in scope from the other two.'[28] Some Boards literally took the law into their own hands by ignoring the second of these definitions and conflating the other two. In the bye-laws of the Liverpool Board, for example,

> The term 'elementary school' [is] absent . . . but we find . . . the two extreme terms 'school' and 'public elementary school' used with so widely different a meaning in the [1870] Act, violently and unnaturally made to mean the same thing, the broad generic term being narrowed down to mean the same as the specific and technical one.[29]

This meant that in theory, the Liverpool Board could summon parents, not merely on the grounds that their children were not receiving an 'efficient' education, but also on the unassailable ground — if the legality of the bye-laws was accepted — that they were not receiving their education, efficient or not, at a *public* elementary school. In a subsequent article, 'T.' offered the likely scenario of such a case; it is worth quoting at length, and the relevant passages can be found in Appendix G.[30] Within the Act, however, as distinct from bye-laws, the working-class private school could clearly be comprehended as an 'elementary school', as defined in Section 3; that is, 'a school . . . at which elementary education is the principal part of the education there given . . . and does not include any school . . . at which the ordinary payments . . . exceed ninepence a week.'[31]

Problems of a similar kind were encountered when Boards moved against parents on the lesser ground that although their children were nominally at school, they were receiving an 'inefficient' education. Such actions drew their logic from two sources. First, from Section 74 of the Act, which provided that though School Boards could make bye-laws for the compulsory 'obligation to attend school', there were allowable exceptions based on 'reasonable excuse'. One of these was 'that the child is under efficient instruction in some other manner'.[32] And secondly, from the operation of the 1870–71 inspections which had established, according to the criteria of the Education Department, the efficiency or non-efficiency of individual schools. Boards commonly felt that such judgements, having been made by professional experts, should be automatically endorsed in the courts. But the magistrates — often locally hostile to the new Boards — were not always impressed by the fact that a particular school had not been officially recognised as efficient. Frequently, they preferred to judge each case on the evidence presented, often examining children from unrecognised schools for themselves in court. This led to an uncomfortably high number of acquittals, and a rising frustration among the slighted educational experts. H.M.I. Faber, for example, reported

> At North Creake in the [Walsingham] Union, a dame's school seems to have seriously injured the attendance of the children at the national school. It was condemned by my predecessor some nine or ten years ago, but has gone on and flourished ever since in blissful contempt of the Inspector's ban . . . The . . . Committee lately prosecuted the parents of the girl who was attending this school, and the magistrates, after examining the child, decided that she was being sufficiently educated . . . so far as I can see, the dame remains master, or rather mistress of the situation.[33]

And in more general terms, H.M.I. Barrington-Ward charged that

> the justices of the peace are too often inclined . . . to side with the parent, and they are perhaps satisfied with a mere minimum of proficiency if they test the child's knowledge themselves. It is an anomalous thing to constitute the magistrate a discerner of educational standards . . . Some magistrates are willing to

> accept the statement of the school board officials as regards . . . efficiency . . . But there is no guarantee that such a statement will be accepted, and consequently the local authority is reluctant to prosecute in dame school cases, knowing that the risk of failure is great, and that if the prosecution fails, the influence of the authority . . . is certain to be impaired. I greatly wish that compulsory inspection could be applied to every school attended by the children of the working class.[34]

In practice, of course, the issue of 'efficiency' was an integral component of the experts' conception of 'school' itself. The two were inextricably bound together, and it was really only the ambivalence of the Act which permitted their theoretical separation. In the courts, this could lead to bizarre results. Prosecutions for failing to attend (public) 'school', or for failing to receive 'efficient instruction in some other manner' might be unsuccessful on their own terms, but more than this, a prosecution on the latter ground could be invalidated by the implication of the former. That is to say, even in spite of a successful prosecution that a child was not receiving 'efficient instruction in some other manner', a magistrate could still rule that the child was within the law because it was at 'school'. At Southwark in 1873, for example,

> The presiding magistrate . . . had a case of attendance at an inefficient school before him, and, acting according to the best of his judgement, while admitting the school in question was inefficient, he dismissed the summons on the ground that the child could not be said to be 'not attending school'.[35]

An 'inefficient' school might yet then be understood as a 'school' within the meaning of the Act. The problem appeared intractable. A letter to *The Times* in April 1871 complained that

> cases will very often arise in which these 'dames' schools' or 'private schools' will be far from efficient. Yet, as it appears, the excuse will be a valid one — 'The child goes to such and such a dame's school'. Does the power of the School Boards end there? Or have they the power, in cases in which they have good reason to know, through their local officers, that the said 'dame school' is utterly inefficient, to test either the school or the scholar?
>
> It seems difficult to devise any means of doing either of these

> two things without an interference with personal liberty which will be resented and resisted. Yet if it be not done, some thousands of children will be left under most inefficient instruction — instruction which will be a name and a sham only.
>
> There may be some means of testing the individual scholar; but as to the school, the good dame will fall back upon the principle that her house is her castle, and will set inspectors, truant officers and School Boards at defiance.[36]

The complex and confused legal position following the 1870 Act can be summarised as follows. After the unique inspection implemented during that year, neither the Education Department nor the School Boards had any right of subsequent inspection in private schools. Meanwhile, many parents continued to use private schools, risking the wrath of the local authorities. Such authorities however had no statutory authority to prevent attendance at any private school, whether recognised as efficient or not. At the same time, there was widespread and recurring disagreement between local educational authorities and magistrates as to what constituted 'efficient' or 'inefficient' education. And above all, the law itself gave no unequivocal definition of 'school'.

This final, crucial point was not an oversight. The *School Board Chronicle* explained that 'the Government, in this peculiarly permissive and tentative Bill, hestitated so to frame the clauses as to peremptorily close inefficient schools . . .'.[37] Lord Sandon himself, the Vice-President of the Committee of Council in 1875, was more explicit;

> the whole question resolved itself into the wording of Clause 74 of the Act of 1870 — that the word 'school' in that clause should be defined. He believed that the word 'school' was left undefined in the Act from a feeling of caution at the time, as it was felt they were introducing a great novelty by introducing compulsion, and so the magistrates were left to put their own definition upon the word 'school' . . . he believed that the Act was passed in that way to ease its working in the first stage.[38]

By 1875, this first stage was over. Moreover, the frustration of ambitious School Boards was reaching a climax. Their urgent need was for legislative clarification to strengthen their hand against the wayward educational preferences of working-class parents. What they sought was a sure and exclusive definition of 'school' with a built-in element of specified 'efficiency'.

During the course of 1875, a campaign, led by the School Board of Hull, gave organised expression to this demand. In this city, the *School Board Chronicle* reported, 'the dame schools had proved a gigantic obstruction to the work of the Board'.[39] At the end of 1874, there were 'probably from 2,000 to 3,000 [children] at dames' schools' in the town.[40] At its meeting of 2 December 1874, the Hull Board was told that on the subject of 'dames' schools'; 'there was a good deal of correspondence going on with other Boards'.[41]

In Bristol, a letter from Hull had been read at the meeting of the Board on 25 September. The letter related to a proposal for 'a deputation to the Education Department on the subject of Dame Schools', and was similar to that sent to the other major School Boards. The Bristol Board ordered, 'that the Clerk be instructed to state in reply to the letter that the Board feel the importance of the matter and will be glad to join in the deputation'.[42] Two members of the Board 'were requested to join the deputation as representatives of this Board'.[43] Similar correspndence went on with other Boards, and ultimately, 113 other bodies emulated Bristol and joined Hull's projected deputation. A total of 200 Boards sent in memorials to the Education Department on the subject of the problems which working-class private schools were almost everywhere continuing to present.[44] One such memorial is reproduced in Appendix G.

The primary objective of the deputation was an unequivocal legal redefinition of the working-class private school in the terms sought by the Boards; measures which would redesignate attendance at such schools not just — as it had been seen before 1870 — as ignorant and misguided, but now as a purposeful criminal evasion of compulsory attendance bye-laws. The fact that working-class private schools had been functioning on a large scale long before 1870, before even the first steps of the state's involvement in elementary education in 1833, was ignored. Working-class educational behaviour was now exposed to the hostility, not just of the educational experts, but also to the equally unsubtle understanding of local bureaucracies.

Sandon received the deputation on 29 January 1875.[45] *The Times* reported the following day that:

A numerous deputation waited on Lord Sandon, Vice-President

> of the Committee of Council on Education, yesterday, for the purpose of laying before Parliament the difficulties experienced by School Boards in enforcing their bye-laws, especially with reference to dame and other private adventure schools.[46]

The deputation described the physical and educational characteristics of the schools in familiar terms — squalid, inefficient, irregular. But to these, they added a newer complaint;

> the magistrates seldom, if ever, convict if the parents show that the child is in attendance (even irregularly) at a dame or adventure school; and they appear to hold the opinion that the parent should have free choice of any school, and that the dames' schools are efficient for the class of children attending them.

The deputation's solution was,

> a more clearly-stated law, as to what is an efficient school [which] will greatly facilitate the operations of the School Board generally, as well as have the effect of causing the decisions of the magistrates to be more uniform. . .
>
> the remedy proposed is an annual inspection and registration of all schools through the Education Department, so that the question of efficiency shall be decided by a competent Government official . . .

and not by magisterial whim.[47] This was a request to place the private schools as firmly under the authority of local officials as were the public schools. Only a handful of private schools could, as the inspection of 1870–71 showed, hope to gain a place on the list of 'efficient' schools. And by the proposed new legislation, attendance at a non-listed school would automatically be seen as truancy.

Sandon listened to the deputation sympathetically. He declared himself 'thoroughly convinced' that the 'evil [of the private schools] was a most serious matter'. He suggested that the less extreme measure of requiring such schools to keep regular attendance registers might be effective; the deputation felt this would be wholly insufficient. They held out for more comprehensive action.

In concurring, Sandon made it clear that, 'In order to carry out what they were driving at, they must have fresh legislation, for the Education Department could not cope with this evil under the present law.'[48]

Consequently, the *School Board Chronicle* hoped, in January 1876, to 'see an effectual and satisfactory remedy applied to the inefficient school nuisance early in the coming session of Parliament'.[49] The *Chronicle* was not to be disappointed, though when the legislation appeared, it took an unexpected form.

Sandon's first action following his meeting with the deputation was to contact all the Boards for detailed local information on the existing state of working-class private schooling, together with suggestions for tackling the problem.[50] Circular 103 — reproduced in Appendix G — went out to the Boards on 1 September 1875.

In Bristol, the document was discussed at the meeting on 24 September. Four members of the Board were 'appointed a Committee to consider and reply to the letter'.[51] On 29 October the *ad hoc* Committee delivered its report, which was approved by the Board and sent into the Education Department.[52] Their enquiry had 'ascertained that the number of schools of this class was 160, which were said to be attended by 4,280 scholars . . . in 98 of these schools, there was sufficient accommodation for 1,782 children only, while the children said to be attending them numbers no less than 3,176 . . .'.[53] In that month, comparative attendance at public elementary schools in Bristol was 18,446. The Board recommended the control of the problem through regular inspection and powers of recognition by the Board which were legally binding. In this respect, the Bristol Board was echoing the prescription of all the others. Their replies to Circular 103 came in steadily during the last months of 1875; their recommendations were invariably the same — 'that a child in attendance at an unregistered school be not considered to be receiving efficient instruction within the meaning of the Elementary Education Act of 1870.[54]

For the Education Department, the solution did not seem this simple. The suggestion of the Boards implied the kind of direct attack on the working-class private schools which the Department had previously tried to avoid. On the one hand, regular inspection would have been costly; and it 'would put upon the Department an amount of work which it could not well undertake . . . the Department would have to inspect all private adventure schools'.[55] On the other hand, a statutory right of inspection for private schools could create potentially embarrassing and unpleasant local confrontations, as well as unwelcome precedents which might begin to threaten the independence of middle-class schools. Sandon had already told the House in April 1875 that

> the subject is a very serious one, and I am bound to say that many authorities on education matters . . . consider that premature interference with these schools and additional interference with the choice of school by a parent would largely increase the difficulties of carrying out the bye-laws for compulsory attendance.[56]

In July 1876, he remained circumspect, still warning against measures which were aimed too directly at school-keepers: 'inspection . . . would be very delicate . . . to undertake . . . in many cases it would destroy, by Government action, the livelihood of the persons who owned private adventure schools, which would lead to serious difficulties'.[57]

The solution eventually worked out by the Department therefore rejected direct action against schools in favour of renewed pressure on parents of the kind had had some effect in 1870–1. In those years, many parents had been warned away from the private schools by the confusion over non-recognition and by the associated bullying and misrepresentation by School Board officers. To answer the problem of the working-class private school once and for all, the Department needed to find a more effective and lasting way of breaking down parental support, whilst safeguarding itself against any charges of directly attacking the schools themselves. The demise of the schools could then be more plausibly presented as a natural process.

The measure which the Department felt would achieve such a result was inserted into the Act of 1876. The main significance of this legislation has traditionally been seen as a step in the progress towards general compulsion and as an attempt by the Conservative Party to keep rural areas free from unwanted School Boards.[58] In such areas, the Act permitted the formation of new School Attendance Committees. These, together with the Boards themselves, were empowered to introduce a form of indirect compulsion by forbidding the employment of uninstructed children. Section 5 of the Act specified that,

> A person shall not, after the commencement of this Act, take into his employment . . . any child —
> (1) Who is under the age of ten years; or
> (2) Who, being over the age of ten years or upwards, has not obtained such certificate either of his proficiency in reading, writing and elementary arithmetic, or of previous due attendance at a certified efficient school . . .[59]

To obtain a 'certificate of proficiency' a child of ten or over had to qualify in reading, writing and arithmetic at least to the level of Standard II of the 1876 Code; to obtain a 'certificate of attendance' — the 'dunce's certificate' as it came to be known — a child was required to make at least 250 attendances, 'in not more than two schools during each year for two years'.[60] Without one or other of these certificates, no child, having reached the age of ten, could legally leave school for employment.

Four years later, Mundella's Education Act introduced general compulsion between the ages of five and ten. However, as William Mackenzie, in his *Elementary Education Acts*, explained, the 1880 Act 'did not repeal the indirect methods of getting children to school which had been enacted in 1876. [The certificates of proficiency and attendance]. These remain side by side with the local bye-laws as a collateral security for attendance . . .'[61] The significance of the certificates was, however, considerably greater than this. They had a central role to play in the final destruction of the working-class private schools.

In this respect, the critical point about the 1876 Act was that it introduced a wholly new category of school — the 'certified efficient school'.[62] This was just the kind of unambiguous label for which the deputation of 1875 had been lobbying. But the label was not to be linked, as the deputation had further hoped, to regular inspection and the subsequent compilation of a register of schools so designated. The articulation was instead less direct and more subtle. What the Act simply did, was to make access to the early-leaving certificates through working-class private schools either wholly impossible or effectively so.

Section 48 of the 1876 Act stated that,

> The term 'certified efficient school' in this Act means a public elementary school . . . and also any elementary school which is not conducted for private profit, and is open . . . to the

> inspection of Her Majesty's Inspectors, and requires the like attendance from its scholars as is required in a public elementary school, and keeps such registers of those attendances as may be for the time being required by the Education Department, and is certified by the Education Department to be an efficient school.[63]

This could hardly be more explicit. Not only did the definition exclude private schools in some aspects of their well-known characteristics, such as the failure to keep registers, but it ruled out any possibility of doubt by specifying, 'not conducted for private profit'.[64] And as Section 5 of the Act, given above, also made clear, the attendances necessary for achieving an attendance certificate *had* to be made in a certified efficient school — that is, a school 'not conducted for private profit'. Therefore, a child attending a private school was precluded from gaining an attendance certificate.

The proficiency certificate was not in theory so directly ruled out, though it was virtually so in practice. Scholars from private schools could only obtain this certificate by attending their nearest *public* school at one of the periodic examinations conducted by H.M.I. Even then, this procedure could only take place after a formal application to the local education authority, and only if 'allowed by the managers' of the public school concerned. Neither of these agencies, and particularly the latter — in direct competition with local private schools — could be expected to respond sympathetically in this circumstance.[65] For private scholars, the certificate of proficiency was therefore effectively almost as unattainable as the attendance certificate.

These enactments constituted a decisive blow against the parents of children at working-class private schools. They were now faced with a stark choice between two unwelcome alternatives. If they continued to keep their children at a private school, the likelihood of a 'labour certificate' was virtually nil. This meant that between the ages of 10 and 13, such children were legally unemployable. Such a sacrifice could hardly be made by poor families who depended on the maximisation of familial income at the earliest practicable point. Nevertheless a few were prepared to make such a sacrifice. In the Warwick district in 1881, for example, H.M.I. Faber still found some surviving parental support for local private schools. But 'the policy is shortsighted and recoils upon themselves, for the child attending the dame school does not obtain a labour certificate and must continue at school until 13 years of age'.[66] For most, the only realistic alternative was finally to accept the regime of the public school, trading the losses in preference, convenience and cultural consonance against the guaranteed retention of the right to early employment.

The effect on the working-class private schools was not immediate. It took some years before the full effect of the 1876 Act began to work through, but once parents began to understand the implications, the life-blood drained away quickly. There was no effective way of fighting back. It was not as though attendance at working-class private schools had been made in itself illegal. Parents were still nominally free to send their children to schools which were not 'certified efficient' if they chose. But finally, the price had, for the majority, become too high — their children could not get jobs. This was something which Sandon had clearly anticipated. To a questioner in the House who favoured the blunt instrument of inspection and registration of private schools, he replied that,

> the hon. Member [should] be content to leave the private adventure schools to the sure but slower and more indirect action of the [1876] Bill, which, as it confined certificates of school attendance to certified efficient schools, not kept for private profit, must tell upon these schools . . .[67]

And to H.M.I.s, he could write, early in 1878,

> it has now become evident that, by the operation of recent legislation, the great majority of the labouring classes will be virtually compelled to send their children to public elementary schools . . . in which these children will be obliged to spend all their school life.[68]

From 1876, the days of the working-class private school as the central product of an independent tradition of education were numbered, and by the 1880s only a handful of schools remained. Mostly, these were those few schools which had been declared 'efficient' in the general inspection of 1870 and which were allowed by some Boards to function unharrassed as a stop-gap measure until new public schools were built.[69] The position of this small category of schools was made extremely uncertain by the Act of 1876. How could they remain on the lists of schools recognised as efficient, when the Act specifically disqualified private schools from the status of 'certified efficient schools'? This was precisely the question which the London School Board was to ask of the Education Department.[70] After a good deal of confusion and uncertainty, the Department came to the conclusion that, 'the School Board must exercise their own discretion as to the schools not being "Certified Efficient" which they will allow children to attend, remembering always that the ultimate decision as to the efficiency of the instruction . . . rests with the magistrate'.[71] However, by the mid-1880s, even this tiny rump of officially acceptable private schools was jettisoned by the Board as their short-term usefulness declined.[72]

The issue of working-class private schooling rapidly evaporated from the columns of the educational press after 1876. Silently and unrecorded, individual schools were disbanded and given up. Their distinctive style, character and achievements had been swept aside by the forward march of a different kind of 'education'. We might conclude by referring to a story — possibly apocryphal — in *The Times* of 7 May 1932; a 'terse protest against bureaucracy', which conveyed its own comment on the destruction of the private schools;

> an old-world 'school-marm' . . . taught the 3 R's to all the lads and lasses of her village for countless years, to their great, and to her small, advantage. Progress, however, intervened, even in Cornwall; her establishment was taken over by the local authority, and at her final session she wrote an epitaph on the blackboard; 'Blast all eddication'.[73]

For other variants of private education, specifically middle or lower middle class, the last quarter of the nineteenth century brought no similar threat. The legislation of 1870–1 and 1875–6 did not concern them, and they continued, effectively unmolested. For such schools, and for the classes which utilised them, the encounter with the state was to come in the next century.[74]

Notes

1. Philpott, *London at School*, p. 11.
2. Thornton in, *A Cyclopedia of Education*, vol. 5 (1912), ed. P. Monroe, pp. 41–2.
3. J. H. Garrett, *Mass Education in England* (1928), p. 76.
4. This was most evidently the view of the spate of books and articles published to commemorate the centenary of the Act. See for example, *The Struggle for Education* (1970), published by the NUT.
5. But also see E. G. West's right-wing anti-statist argument, which sees state involvement simply as a corollary of increasing and unnecessary bureaucracy and centralisation. See *Education and the state. A Study in Political Economy* (1965) and *Education and the Industrial Revolution* (1975).
6. A valuable collection of theoretical essays on the capitalist state is, Philip Corrigan (ed.), *Capitalism, State Formation and Marxist Theory* (1980).
7. 'Liverpool', *M.S.S.* (1836), p. 26.
8. F. S. Marvin, *The Nation at School* (1933), p. 63.
9. *Newcastle*, vol. 1, p. 96.
10. For local examples, see the *School Board Chronicle* (hereafter *S.B.C.*), vol. 23 (1880), pp. 294, 495.
11. *S.B.C.*, 22.4.1871, p. 313. Also see H.M.I. Smith, *C.C.E.*, 1876–7.
12. See for example, H.M.I. Faber, *C.C.E.*, 1881–2, p. 271. Also Sandon himself in *Hansard*, 28 July 1876, col. 26.
13. *C.C.E.*, 1874–5, p. 90.
14. See for instance the report in *The Times* of 8 November 1859, dealing with a speech given at a meeting of the East Lancashire Union of Mechanics' Institutes. The speaker was Richson, who claimed that 'We had destroyed the dame-schools and adventure-schools and gathered the children from those wretched places of instruction into schools well systematized and under capable teachers. It was a glorious thing to see the vast numbers of schools of all denominations springing up in every direction.' p. 4.
15. See D. Rubinstein, 'Socialization and the London School Board 1870–1904: Aims, Methods and Public Opinion', in McCann, *Popular Education*, pp. 231–64. Also G. Sutherland, *Policy-Making in Elementary Education, 1870–1895* (1973), Ch. 5.
16. *S.B.C.*, 20.11.1875, p. 500.
17. T. Spalding, *The Work of the London School Board* (1900), p. 42.
18. See Chapter 2, above, p. 66.
19. 1870 Act, Section 72. Also see *C.C.E.*, 1870–1, p. xli.
20. These words from Section 72 were reproduced on the front of School Form (No. 74L) which was issued to all known schools with fees of less than ninepence.
21. See Chapter 5.
22. *S.B.C.*, 20.11.1875, p. 499.
23. P.P. 1883 [3602] liii, *Instructions to H.M. Inspectors of Schools, issued in May, 1871, relative to the Inquiries into the School Supply of their respective Districts.*
24. Spalding, *Work of the London School Board*, p. 44. 'Semi-efficient' schools were judged acceptable either in accomodation or teaching, but not both. They were given a short period in which to rectify any deficiency before being considered once more. Some aspects of the short history of the 'semi-efficient' school in London can be traced in the documents of the London School Board in P.R.O. Ed. 14/42. Particularly detailed results of the 1871 enquiry also survive for Sheffield. See P.R.O. Ed. 16/370, 'Report presented by the Clerk of the Sheffield School Board to the Statistical Enquiry Committee'. This report is also reproduced in the *Sheffield*

and Rotherham Independent, 24.3.1871, p. 4. Also see J. H. Bingham, *The Period of the Sheffield School Board* (1949).

25. G.L.C. Record Office, S.B.L. 1518, *Tables of the Elementary Schools within the District of the Metropolis. August, 1871*, pp. 263–4.

26. H.M.I. Boyle, *C.C.E.*, 1876–7, p. 437.

27. *S.B.C.*, 22.4.1871, p. 313.

28. *S.B.C.*, 5.8.1871, p. 376. 'Public Elementary School' was defined in Section 7 of the Act, and 'Elementary School' in Section 3.

29. Loc. cit. Also see 'Definition of the Word "School"', *S.B.C.*, 1.7.1871, p. 217. The Liverpool bye-laws were not exceptional. Bristol's bye-laws stated that, 'The term "School" or "Public Elementary School", means a Public Elementary School as defined by the Elementary Education Act 1870'. Moreover, 'the parent of every child not less than 5 years of age, and residing within the City of Bristol, shall cause such child to attend school'. *Bristol School Board Minutes*, 7.7.1871.

30. *S.B.C.*, 12.8.1871, pp. 407–8.

31. Education Act, 1870. Section 3.

32. Education Act, 1870. Section 74.

33. *C.C.E.*, 1881–2, pp. 430–1; 'the Inspector's ban', was, of course, without any legal power.

34. *C.C.E.*, 1881–2, p. 195.

35. *S.B.C.*, 5.4.1871, p. 187.

36. John Miller, *The Times*, 24.4.1871.

37. *S.B.C.*, 5.4.1873, p. 187.

38. *S.B.C.*, 6.2.1875, p. 142.

39. *S.B.C.*, 18.9.1875, p. 282. Also see *The Hull Packet and East Riding Times*, 18.12.1874, p. 5.

40. *S.B.C.*, 26.12.1874, p. 616. Also see *S.B.C.*, 5.9.1874; *S.B.C.*, 12.9.1874, p. 252.

41. *S.B.C.*, 26.12.1874, p. 616. Inter-Board communication of this kind was common. Boards contacted each other on a range of problems which they encountered. See Sutherland, *Policy Making in Elementary Education*, p. 109.

42. *Bristol School Board Minutes*, 1873–6, p. 652.

43. Ibid., 15.1.1875, p. 696.

44. *The Times*, 30.1.1875, p. 7.

45. The deputation was led by seven MPs including Mundella and Roebuck from Sheffield, Norwood from Hull, and Hodson from Bristol and by Sir Henry Cooper, Chairman of the Hull Board. *S.B.C.*, 6.2.1875, p. 142.

46. *The Times*, 30.1.1875, p. 7.

47. Ibid.

48. *S.B.C.*, 6.2.1875, p. 142. Also see *The Times*, 30.1.1875, p. 7.

49. *S.B.C.*, 1.1.1876, p. 16.

50. Ibid.; also, *Hansard*, 16.4.1875, col. 1114; also *School Board Directory* (1876), pp. 61–3.

51. *Bristol School Board Minutes*, 24.9.1875, p. 794.

52. Ibid., 29.9.1875, p. 802.

53. *Bristol School Board Review of Proceedings, Jan.–Dec., 1875*, p. 6; also, *Western Daily Press*, 30.10.1875, p. 8.

54. Croydon School Board, *S.B.C.*, 27.11.1875, p. 539. Also see the article 'Compulsion and Registration' by the Clerk to the Sunderland School Board, *S.B.C.*, 8.1.1875, pp. 39–41.

55. *Hansard*, 28.7.1876, col. 26.

56. Ibid., 16.4.1876, cols. 1113–1114.

57. Ibid., 28.7.1876, col. 26.

58. See for example, Sutherland, *Policy Making in Elementary Education*, Ch. 5.

Also D. K. Jones, *The Making of the English Education System, 1851–81* (1977), pp. 78–9; Peter Gordon, 'Lord Sandon and the Centenary of Compulsory Education', in *History of Education Society Bulletin*, no. 18 (1976), pp. 53–6.

59. Education Act, 1876, Section 5. Also see 'Regulations as to Certificates of Age, School Attendance and Proficiency . . .', *C.C.E.*, 1876–7, pp. 254–6.

60. See First Schedule of 1876 Act. *C.C.E.*, 1876–7, p. 17. The requirements for exemption were soon made more stringent. See W. Mackenzie, *A Treatise on the Elementary Education Acts* (1892), Ch. IX. Also, *School Board Directory* (1877), pp. 27–35.

61. Mackenzie, *Elementary Education Acts*, p. 80.

62. See *S.B.C.*, 24.2.1877, p. 219. Also *The Times*, 3.3.1877, p. 4.

63. Education Act, 1876, Section 48. See *C.C.E.*, 1876–7, pp. 1–16.

64. See 'Circular to Her Majesty's Inspectors, conveying Regulations as to Certified Efficient Schools', *C.C.E.*, 1876–7, pp. 249–53.

65. 'Regulations . . .', *C.C.E.*, 1876–7, pp. 255–6. Subject to certain conditions, a local authority could apply for a 'special examination' to be held if there were more than 15 candidates 'not being scholars in a certified effeicient school' put forward for certificates of proficiency.

66. *C.C.E.*, 1881–2, p. 271.

67. *Hansard*, 28.7.1876, col. 26.

68. 'Circular to Her Majesty's Inspectors', 16.1.1878. P.P. 1878 [1964] lx.

69. One member of the Hull Board indeed pointed out that 'it was no use seeking to exercise powers over dames' schools unless they had places of their own to put the children'. *S.B.C.*, 26.12.1874, p. 616.

70. P.R.O. Ed. 14/12. Letter from the Board to the Department, 9 March 1877.

71. P.R.O. Ed. 14/12, Education Department Minute, 3.7.1877. Also see *The Times*, 18.4.1877, p. 11; *School Board Chronicle*, 21.4.1877, p. 417; 'In truth . . . there can be no such thing as a certified adventure school; but in practice the school that might without impropriety be known by that name becomes now an institution in London by virtue of the action of the London School Board.' Also see *The Gloucestershire Chronicle*, 19.2.1881, 'Regulation of Private Adventure Schools'.

72. P.R.O. Ed. 14/12. Letter from the Board to the Department, 24 October 1884.

73. *The Times*, 7.5.1932, p. 32.

74. The details of this encounter are outside the compass of this study, and certainly merit detailed separate investigation. Useful starting points are Chuter-Ede's Departmental Report on *Private Schools and other Schools not in receipt of Grants from Public Funds* (1932); *The School Government Chronicle*, June 1932, p. 362; *The Journal of Education*, June 1932, p. 374; *The Saturday Review*, 21.5.1932, p. 513; *Education*, 12.10.1928, pp. 315–16, 322–3; 19.10.1928, p. 345; 26.10.1928, p. 372; 2.11.1928, p. 398; 29.3.1929, p. 343; 21.6.1929, pp. 712–14; 5.7.1929, pp. 4–5; 3.1.1930, p. 6; 3.10.1930, pp. 295–6, 297; 31.10.1930, p. 405; 7.11.1930, p. 425; 6.2.1931, p. 154; 8.5.1931, pp. 533–5; *The Times Educational Supplement*, 12.2.1920, p. 89; 14.10.1920, p. 551; 16.7.1921, p. 326; 2.1.1926, p. 1; 6.3.1926, p. 109; 13.3.1926, p. 127; 26.2.1927, p. 102; 5.3.1927, p. 115; 30.6.1934, p. 17. Also see P.R.O. Ed. 15: *Private Schools not recognised for Grant or Efficiency: Returns 1919–1944*. Also Lord Carlingford in 1882; the middle class 'did not find itself subject to the paternal care of the State, either in the matter of favour or chastisement'. *The Macclesfield Advertiser*, 23.12.1882. Demands for some form of public financial assistance for middle-class education became increasingly vocal in the last quarter of the century.

7 ECHOES

The paucity of detailed evidence originating from genuinely working-class sources has been a considerable restriction in this study. It is undoubtedly one of the reasons why such areas of working-class cultural life as independent schooling have been so under-researched.

It seems as though any attempt to reconstruct working-class experience must founder on this difficulty, and all that has so far been achieved is a definition of the parameters of this experience. The experience itself went to the grave with the last pupil cohorts of the 1870s and 1880s. It is now just beyond our reach, in an age when the educational experience of most living members of the working class has been institutionally incorporated.[1]

One possibility of recovering some scraps of evidence of the working-class private school as it was experienced by its users is oral recollection. This did not however seem an approach which could yield much of value for this study. Any appeal for recollections through the columns of the local press needed to have been made sometime before the Second World War if it were likely to have borne much fruit. Nevertheless, such an appeal was made. As expected, this met with little success. The overwhelming mass of responses whilst indeed coming from former pupils at private schools referred to lower middle-class schools which flourished in their thousands up to the 1930s. Whilst a large number of these had been kept, like the working-class schools, in private houses, the norm in this case was the spacious suburban villa. These were the 'brass-plate schools' par excellence — titling themselves as preparatory schools, High Schools and Colleges. Untouched by the state because of the level of fees charged — generally from around 2s a week to 4 guineas a quarter — these schools existed to keep their charges out of the contaminating clutches of the public elementary schools. This was a clear recollection of the majority of respondents: 'very genteel'; 'taught good manners and respect'; 'a better class'; 'thought better than a Council School'; 'a nicer type of child'; 'a slight snob value'; 'did not have to mix with rough children'.

However, among a crowd of responses of this kind, there was the occasional example that was clearly anomalous. The profiles of these few schools, so far as they can be drawn, indicate that here and there, isolated schools which truly belong in the earlier working-class tradition were surviving after the turn of the century. Before turning to individual examples, the value of this kind of evidence needs to be weighed.

In the first place, it needs to be recognised that any working-class private school surviving into the early years of the twentieth century would have been exceptional simply in terms of its capacity for survival. This could well token other areas of atypicality. Indeed, such a school might well have started its existence after 1876. This would not necessarily impugn its authenticity as a working-class private school, but clearly, the earlier its inception, the stronger would be its claim as a genuine residual expression of the mainstream tradition. Moreover, such a school would be operating in a materially changed educational environment to the schools of the 1870s. And then comes the question of how any such school managed to survive the operation of those restrictive measures which, as we have seen, effectively destroyed the tradition itself. There can be no adequate answer to this. However, it seems likely that as the mass of working-class private schools disappeared, so the intensity of official pressure eased, attention was diverted to other pressing problems, enabling an occasional school to slip through the net. The likelihood of this occurring depends on the local combination of three factors: first, on the character and motivation of individual school-keepers; second, on the degree of severity with which different education authorities exercised their powers; and third, on the risks which parents were prepared to run in flouting the law on 'labour certificates'.[2]

The examples which follow, then, cannot be offered as necessarily representative of nineteenth-century private schools. Nevertheless, they are those examples closest to us in time which display many of the characteristics of those schools, and which were, for the early twentieth century, plainly of extraordinary unusualness. But even for these few survivors, the recoverable evidence is often slight. That which is known will be set out below. It will need to be measured against the larger though less specific body of material which relates to the mainstream nineteenth-century tradition, and which was considered in earlier chapters. If these individual examples of the early twentieth century are not perceived to be a vestige or a relative of that tradition, then their existence will continue to await a better or more convincing explanation.

Oxford Street, in the Totterdown district of Bristol, was the site of two working-class private schools according to the general enquiry of 1870. Fifty years later, this narrow street of small terraced houses still supported one similar school, though no more like it have been traced elsewhere in the entire city in this period.

The school was kept by Miss Margaret Hughes, who shared the house with her sister and a younger man, Ernest Somers, apparently a nephew. He is listed in Wright's Bristol Directory for 1919 as a 'wholesale stationer' — a business which he reportedly carried out from the first floor of the house — though no occupations are recorded for his aunts. No school under the name of Hughes is at any time listed in the commercial section of the Directory. The house — number 52 — was destroyed by a bomb in the last war, and there is no evidence as to what happened to Miss Hughes after this; at this time, she was apparently in her late sixties or seventies. The dates at which she began her school and when she eventually gave it up are not known, but former pupils have been traced for the period 1914–28. These are Ellen Martin, Dorothy Martin, Rachel Wells and George Day.[3] In 1914, the weekly fee was 7½d; by 1925, it had risen to 10d.[4]

Totterdown was predominantly inhabited by railway workers. Rachel's father 'was on the railway . . . He was a checker on the goods . . . Nearly all the people round that area worked on the railway then.' Though unsure of the fee he paid, George felt 'it couldn't have been very high because my father was . . . a railway engine driver, and there wasn't . . . that much money about in those days'. And the general background of the pupils as a whole 'was very working class . . . yes, certainly. They were, you know, reasonably well clothed, most of them, and that sort of thing, but you know, not very well off, no.' Dorothy was asked if the pupils 'were a cut above the ordinary people in the neighbourhood?' 'Well no, no, we were all sort of . . . working class, you know, all the same . . . We were only working-class people . . . though my dad always worked, you know . . . and my mother was a very good manager . . . My dad was a motor driver.' Ellen was particularly clear about the reasons why she and her sister were sent to Miss Hughes':

> Well I know my mother's reason. She was not happy at the school where she went — she went to St Mark's School, and she didn't get on very well at school. She wasn't a very good scholar and she always vowed and declared that her children would never . . . sort, of, go through what she went through . . . But I think her mother was always keeping her home to look after the other children and things like that, you see, so mother didn't get very much chance . . . She said she used to put her tongue out at the teacher . . . No, she didn't like it.

Like many others recalling long-distant school days, Rachel had no real idea of why she was sent to Miss Hughes' instead of to the Council School; 'Well . . . I think possibly it was because they would rather they went to a little school like that than to to the bigger schools . . . I don't know why my mother-in-law and her sister went, but of course they lived only a few doors away.' But for George, 'Well, as far as my case was, it was purely, as I recall, a sort of introduction to school, prior to going into the State system . . . breaking the ice as it were to going to school.' Ellen remembered that the school was held in a small downstairs back-room; 'there was an oven grate in the room, and always a fire there in the winter . . . I don't know if she did any cooking there when we'd gone home'. Rachel recalls that 'we weren't in various classes, we were all ages in the one room', and Ellen, once more, 'I don't know how she got them all into the one room . . .'cos it wasn't a very big room'. Dorothy remembers about 20 to 25 scholars; 'it was very crowded'. Rachel thought 'there was about 18 to 20 of us', and George 'probably . . . somewhere between 12 and 20'.

> It was a smallish room, yes . . . It was pleasant and comfortable . . . I certainly regarded it as a house with a school in it. It certainly had a more homely atmosphere.

> well, it was a normal . . . house room as opposed to a class-room, you know . . . it was very different.

Dorothy was more apologetic, 'I know it wasn't a proper school like really . . . but everybody seemed to do well.'

The room was set out in much the same way as were the earlier private schools. 'Miss Hughes used to sit at a . . . a, I think it was a sort of cane-work type desk . . . out in the front by the window.'

There was an ordinary dining table in one corner at which older pupils could write, whilst for the younger ones, 'there were ordinary wooden bench forms . . . we certainly didn't have backs on the forms, no. I recall being more or less hunched over your slate.'[5] Other features of the school also echo those of its nineteenth-century forerunners. Regular attendance, though normal, was not strictly enforced;

> you could stay home if you weren't . . . if you had a bad cold or anything . . . or a slight cold . . . Whereas you couldn't . . . you'd be chased up by the . . . what they used to call the School Board Man.[6]

> if she [Miss Hughes] wanted something — shopping or anything — she'd say, 'Oh, will you go and get so-and-so for me . . .'.[7]

And occasionally, Miss Hughes' place was taken by others;

> as I recall, on a rare occasion this man . . . possibly her brother, I'm not sure, he used to sit in. He certainly was in no way a teacher . . . I recall somebody, an older girl, by the name of Ruby . . . she would have been . . . I don't know, I would have thought somewhere about 14-ish . . . As I recall, she was a pupil, but she used to help out with the younger people.[8]

All seemed to remember Miss Hughes as a kind person and a capable teacher.

> she wasn't very hard . . . she used to keep order but . . . she was never very hard, and . . . quite pleasant . . . yes . . . The Council School was harder, yes. She was a softer person I would have said than the people who taught in the State . . .[9]

> we had quite a good education there. She was quite a good teacher . . . I mean, we shouldn't have stayed there if she hadn't have been . . . she was kind and we could go to her and ask her anything, you know, and we weren't afraid of her.[10]

> I was very happy . . . I didn't want to leave.[11]

Apart from the fact that they all got on well with their learning, all four found it hard to recall precise details about day-to-day routine in the school.

> I mean, we all more or less had the same lessons, only in a varying degree to suit the ages . . . unless it was history or something like that . . . she'd take us all together then.[12]

> She used to call out children to read, and . . . if you couldn't do your sums right, she'd have you out and show you how to do it . . . on your own.[13]

> We used to go and stand at her desk and she used to point to a book, you know, with a knitting needle, C-A-T spells cat and this sort of thing, and . . . we used to sort of . . . you know, an introduction to spelling and reading and that sort of thing . . . We mainly went up to her. We certainly went up to her to spell and read, and we just sort of sat on the forms with slates, perhaps doing mainly . . . simple sums . . . She sort of used to teach individually to a certain extent. Certainly one of the strongest memories is . . . sort of . . . her at the desk and me standing by her side, and she, sort of pointing to letters . . . making words.[14]

> She used to have us all out, you know, the same age all round her, reading . . . she'd give us our lessons, what we had to do, then she'd give the others, and then she'd have a class out reading, and then they'd go back and do what they had to do, and another class reading. She had it really good you know . . . She was well organised . . . all different ages she had to teach you see.[15]

A similar school was kept until 1927 by Miss Lucy Besant in Lewis Street, Newport. A number of former pupils have been traced; of these, the clearest memories are recalled by Bill Evans.[16] He remembers that the school 'was in a working class area, most of the people, certainly in my childhood, being employed on the railway, docks or the local steelworks'. His own father was a lengthman on the Great Western Railway.[17] He goes on:

> Miss Besant ran the school for many years. My mother, who was

> born in 1892, says that she was a pupil there from the age of three until starting at the local Council School when she was about five. This means that she was at Miss Besant's from about 1895 to 1897. I also started at the school at the age of three in 1926. I was only there for about a year, for in 1927 Miss Besant, who by that time was probably approaching seventy . . . closed the school. My mother thinks that when she went, the weekly fee was 6d. Certainly I can remember in my time it was a shilling, and I can recall taking it every Monday morning . . . The classes were held in the back room of the house, the room which when I was young was always known in these houses as the kitchen . . . When I attended I should think there were probably about 20 pupils, rather more girls than boys. Some were quite old, possibly about 14 years of age . . . the pupils were . . . from Lewis Street or the streets adjoining. The pupils sat round three sides of the room at long desks which could take four or five pupils. As far as I remember there were two rows on each of the three sides. The youngest pupils, such as I, sat in the front row facing the teacher at rather low desks or possibly little tables. I don't know if the older children used exercise books, but we small ones wrote, drew and did our sums on slates. I can still hear the awful squeak that the slate pencils used to make. I can't say what was the full extent of the curriculum; I suspect that the 3 Rs was a substantial part of it, although I do recall that some afternoons Miss Besant taught some history, geography and so on . . . It is difficult after so many years and because I was very young to assess how good the education was. Certainly I learned to read at a very early age — I could read reasonably fluently when I left Miss Besant's . . . One of my abiding memories was that it was a very happy place, and I know that I was very upset when it closed.

The experience of Bill Evans at Miss Besant's and George Day at Miss Hughes' illustrates that some parents used the schools in the nineteenth-century tradition of starting school as early as was practically possible.[18] Neither of these schools was however solely for infants — that is, a classical 'dame's school'.[19]

A particularly interesting survivor of that species was attended very briefly by Mary Howard, 70 years ago, in East London.

This school was kept by a solitary widow in a small terraced house in Forest Gate, where 'no one was very well-off'. Mary's father was an electrician, though in her childhood, he was often without work. 'Things were very, very difficult.' Mary went to the school only for a few weeks in 1912, when she was six, to enable her to change from one state elementary school to another; direct removals were not permitted by the local authority. The reason for the change was an undeserved punishment;

> A teacher upset me . . . I went home weeping my heart out . . . I had a good slap and I didn't deserve it . . . Yes, I think there was a good bit of slapping . . . plenty of slaps . . . We were not allowed to speak, you know. You sat with your arms behind you and nobody even whispered or anything you see . . . very strict . . . My parents decided that I must change schools . . . You weren't allowed to change from one Council School to another . . . They wouldn't take you. Whichever one you were in, there you were stuck.

Mary's little school 'was just around the corner'. She had no idea how her parents knew of it, nor can she remember them mentioning the teacher. As regards fees, 'I shouldn't think it was much more than 6d a week, 'cos I don't know how my parents could have afforded it'. The school was held in the front living room; 'it was very small'. There were only half a dozen pupils, all very young. 'All six of us sat round this table . . . just an ordinary sort of . . . probably a sort of kitchen type of table . . . with a cloth on.' Clearly, Mary's teacher — her name now forgotten — did not make much from her school. To eke out her living, she also seems to have taken in washing, and Mary's account has echoes of the laundry-schools of half a century earlier.

> I can visualise her with her . . . you know . . .they . . . they had skirts down to their ankles in those days, sweeping the floor probably. I can . . . I know that hers was always bundled up round her waist . . . with an apron sort of to keep it up, and . . . she sometimes brought the wash-tub into the passage, you know . . . by the front door, and we were in the best front room, so that she could hear us better, you know . . . She did her work and she popped in to see us from time to time and gave us something to read or write . . .She came to us, we never left that room . . . She never sat down with us . . . All I can remember is

> reading to her . . . She wouldn't come in and hear me read, she'd be out in the hall or . . . or doing her work or mopping or sweeping and I'd have to read . . . 'Read louder dear!'; sweep, sweep.

Such recollections are both interesting and valuable. They breathe the descriptive colour of experience into the carcass of working-class private schooling. But as examples they remain partial and incomplete. They convey only passing glimpses seen through the eyes of a young child, and now distantly remembered. What is lacking is the wider local context within which these glimpses were set. We want to know of the other sides of the story of each of these schools — why did the parents use them?; how did local authorities respond to them?; and what of the teachers themselves? The problem is actually the reverse of that which we faced in earlier chapters. Then there was an abundance of 'downward' evidence — though biased — which was not effectively matched by the voice of working-class experience. Now there is a source of 'upward' evidence, but without supporting documentary context, it is a source composed of lonely voices and isolated anecdote — high in terms of individual interest, but low in analytical utility. It seems that the two blocks have to remain spatially distanced. They cannot quite be made to enter the same arena at the same time. The links between the two are obvious, but they lack the sureness of direct and genuine contact which only a single, detailed case-study, in which all competing voices are represented, can offer. Happily, a case-study with something approaching this completeness can be attempted for what is surely one of the most remarkable working-class private schools of all — Miss Beetlestone's.

The school is best introduced in the words of the Walsall Town Clerk's Office in a letter to the Board of Education in 1917:

> I am directed by the Education Committee of this Borough to lay before your Board the following facts in connection with a private school kept by a Miss Beetlestone, and to ask if the Board will give the matter their consideration and observations thereon.
>
> For some 30 years Miss Beetlestone has kept a private school

> in Walsall of the 'Dame School' character. The Education Committee have for some time past been concerned with the poor character of the education given therein and have formed the opinion that it was developing into a refuge for parents desirous of evading the provisions of the Education Acts and Byelaws.[20]

There was a considerable background to this letter. It is clear that, late in 1916, the Education Committee decided to terminate the existence of this school, which had stood out in Walsall as a stubborn survivor of a vanished tradition. Throughout the winter, officers of the Local Authority gathered information on the school, 'which was then carried on in two separate houses in West Bromwich Road and Weston Street'.[21] These were both small terraced buildings standing in narrow parallel streets of working-class houses 50 yards apart. One reason why the Committee were particularly irritated by the school is that Miss Beetlestone's house stood directly opposite Whitehall Council School, on the other side of West Bromwich Road, visibly drawing pupils away from it.

In particular, the school was visited on several occasions by Arthur Hibbett, the Borough Inspector of Schools, and by Doctor Carroll, the local Schools Medical Inspector.

Hibbett first visited the school on 29 November 1916.[22] His report was not favourable.[23] The teaching staff, he wrote, consisted of the 'Teacher in charge (unqualified). Assisted by two elder girls (scholars), neither of whom are 14 years of age.' The premises were, '(a) Front bedroom of house, 15 ft. × 10 ft. × 10 ft. (b) Front ground floor room of another house . . . 10 ft. × 10 ft × 10 ft.' The school had 'no desks but a few forms of various sizes and conditions of dilapidation. One broken blackboard supported by two chair legs . . .' Hibbett complained that there was no sign of any effective organisation of the school into classes; the instruction he dismissed as 'solely of the mechanical type . . . there is no existing syllabus of work nor is instruction graduated . . . Children work on broken pieces of slate, there being no facilities for paper work.' In his concluding remarks, he wrote:

> In answer to questions it appears that this school is chosen by the parents because of the 'go easy' rules both as regards regularity and punctuality — parents on being pressed by the Attendance Officers as to their children's irregularity and by the teachers for

> unpunctuality, remove their children from this inconvenient pressure and send them to a school of the 'go easy' kind.
>
> On the date of the visit, four children arrived at 10.30 a.m. This practice is common as is also the practice of allowing children to leave at an early hour, both morning and afternoon.'

Dr Carroll accompanied Hibbett on this visit. His report concentrated on the physical condition of the school, and in particular, the main classroom in West Bromwich Road, which was the upstairs front bedroom of Miss Beetlestone's home.

> The cubic contents of this room is 1,500 feet . . . At the time of our visit 10.25 a.m. this room was occupied by 47 children. The Board of Education prescribe a minimum of 10 square feet for sitting per scholar and 100 to 140 cubic for ventilation etc. . . . This room is regarded as the 'assembly room' but on the occasion of our visit children were coming to school even at 10.30 a.m. although the prescribed time for their attendance is 9.30. A great number of children are, therefore, crushed together for a variable time of the school session before any of them are drafted to the second classroom . . . The air was very foul . . . [The] general condition of the room . . . was filthy . . . To reach this room the children entered the house through a scullery littered with rubbish . . . along a dark passage the walls of which were in the same dilapidated condition as the schoolroom . . .[24]

With these damning documents in hand,

> the Education Committee thereupon intimated to Miss Beetlestone that in consequence of the serious conditions disclosed in the reports . . . both from an educational and medical standpoint, they would not recognise the attendance of any child at her school after the 28th February, 1917. Notice was also given to the parents of the children attending the school that the children should be sent to a Public Elementary School after the above mentioned date.[25]

And there the history of Miss Beetlestone's school might well have ended, had the dictates of the local authority been heeded. However, the actions of refusing 'recognition' and demanding the removal of pupils to public schools, were — as they had been in the 1870s — without legal basis. The authority was in fact exceeding its powers, and when its demands and threats were ignored, its only recourse was to the courts.

However, it was not the authority, but Miss Beetlestone herself who first seized the legal initiative.[26] Refusing to accept what must have seemed ultimately inevitable, she took legal advice, and through her solicitor communicated to the Education Committee that she 'would be willing to take more commodious premises [for her school], and asked that the Committee should grant an interview . . . to allow her to state her case'.[27]

The Committee were disdainful:

> The Committee did not see that any useful purpose would be served by a personal interview between themselves and Miss Bettlestone, and . . . intimated . . . that if Miss Beetlestone submitted a scheme for the establishment of an improved private school, covering buildings, equipment and teaching staff, the Committee would be prepared to consider it, but that they desired that Miss Beetlestone should not incur any expenses in regard to alterations in her school, prior to their consideration of, and their subsequent decision on any scheme she might put forward.[28]

This, clearly, was to be an act of destruction with a reasonable face. The offer of a plan for controlled improvement was made only in the sure knowledge that Miss Beetlestone's resources could never support a school of the kind which would be deemed officially acceptable. But once again, she replied to the Committee with direct and positive action in defence of her school.

> Miss Beetlestone submitted no scheme for the consideration of the Education Committee, but on her own responsibility took the Church Hall, Palfrey, for the purposes of her school . . . she was prepared to limit the number of her pupils to 50 until such time as she could 'obtain adequate assistance for her teaching staff' . . . 71 pupils were on the Register of Attendance at her school in West Bromwich Road and Weston Street.[29]

What was intended to have been a quiet and straightforward closure was developing into a war of attrition. Miss Beetlestone once more made the next move, instructing her solicitors to apply for an injunction to restrain the Committee from the action they had taken in notifying parents to remove their children to public schools. These notifications had not been without effect. By the middle of May, attendance had fallen to just 21.[30] For the majority of parents, the threat of official sanctions had been enough.

In late April, before Miss Beetlestone's application for an injunction had been heard, the Committee decided to take proceedings against the parents of twelve pupils, 'for habitually and without reasonable excuse neglecting to provide efficient elementary education'.[31] Summonses were issued under Section 11 of the 1876 Act, which empowered magistrates to make attendance orders in respect of children who were not receiving 'efficient elementary education'.[32]

The cases came before the Borough magistrates on 17 May 1917. The Committee were clearly confident of a quick and straightforward victory, and the prosecution, conducted by the Deputy Town Clerk, Victor Crooke, opened in a spirit of regretful self-righteousness. 'It was', according to Crooke,

> a rather painful case, but the Education Committee had gone to the utmost extremity in giving leniency to the lady who kept the school, and had no other course but to bring these cases . . . The Education Committee had done everything to meet her in every way . . . possibly some sympathy would be felt for the proprietress of the school, and he would endeavour to take the case in as fair and as reasonable a way as he knew how.[33]

However, on this occasion, the case was rapidly dismissed on a point of law, the prosecution having been unable to produce 'evidence as to the state of affairs on the dates to which the summonses related'.[34] In other words, they could not successfully demonstrate that the children of the accused parents had been at Miss Beetlestone's on the specific dates in question. The evidence of Samuel Bates, the Borough's Chief Attendance Officer, was in this respect inadequate. Though he had been despatched to spy on the school (now meeting in Palfrey Park) over a period of four days, his record of comings and goings of pupils and teacher was too vague. A copy of his brief report of this period of 'observation' is in Appendix H. In fact the most notable feature of this brief hearing was a bitter clash between the magistrates and the local authority, as represented by Victor Crooke. For Crooke, with his handful of expert reports from Hibbett, Carroll and Bates, this was a straightforward issue upon which magistrates should defer to expert officials and simply wave through whatever complaints were alleged. The local paper reported this clash as follows:

> During Mr. Crooke's opening statement, there had been several interruptions as to what was or was not relevant, and Mr. Crooke asked the bench to let him open his case in his own way. He could not do so because of the interruptions which were taking place.
>
> **Mr. E. J. Shaw** (magistrate): This is the first time, and I have sat more than twenty years, that a remark of that sort has been made to the magistrates.
>
> **Mr. Crooke**: I hope I shall show every respect to the Bench.
>
> **Mr. Shaw**: Pardon me sir, I hope you will, and we are entitled to some respect, and you must not say the Bench has interrupted you.
>
> **Mr. Crooke**: I don't think there is any necessity to lecture me on my conduct. I am perfectly willing . . .
>
> **Mr. Shaw**: But you must not say we were interrupting you.
>
> **Mr. Crooke**: You administer punishment to me and reproof without giving me an opportunity to reply. I said I had been interrupted, but I did not say the interruptions were by the Bench.
>
> **Mr. Muncaster** (Deputy Clerk): Do you refer to me?
>
> **Mr. Shaw** (to Mr. Crooke): Well, it seemed to me that you meant the Bench.
>
> The incident then closed.[35]

After this setback, the Committee withdrew to refine its case before returning to court. Hibbett and Carroll were once again called in to compile extra reports to supplement those already drawn up.

During a visit made on 22 May, Hibbett examined several pupils, 'asking questions requiring a little thought and some general knowledge before being answered . . . I found that the children were entirely mute'.[36] And if the standard of scholarship was poor, then that of the teaching was worse; 'With the exception of the time that I had charge of the class myself, I cannot say that there was anything useful in the way of Instruction given . . .'

On 25 May, the Committee issued six summonses against parents.[37] The first case heard was that of Charles Leeder, a fancy leather worker, in respect of his ten-year-old son Harry.[38] Once more the prosecution, again conducted by Crooke, was confident:

> Mr. Crooke, in opening the case . . . said that the officials of the Education Committee, by their reports, showed that the education given at Miss Beetlestone's private school was a travesty of education. There were children attending there of very tender age up to boys of 13 and 14 years old, and the only mistress who gave any instruction there was Miss Beetlestone herself . . . Samuel Bates (Chief Visiting Officer) gave evidence as to the school and the education there . . . A legal argument followed, raised by Mr. S. E. Loxton (Clerk) as to whether the school was or was not a 'certified school' within the meaning of the Act . . . Mr. A. Hibbett, the Inspector of Schools, gave evidence and said there was 'practically no equipment'. There were a few forms, but no desks, blackboards or maps, or anything they would find in an ordinary school . . . Asked what impression the schools had made on his mind, he replied 'an utter farce' . . . Dr. Carroll, School Medical Inspector said the conditions at Miss Beetlestone's were not such as were required by the Board of Education at a certified school.[39]

As Mr J. F. Addison, appearing for the parents, opened the defence, Crooke evidently became increasingly agitated and annoyed. In his judgement, there could be no legitimate defence in what was plainly an open-and-shut case. Nevertheless, 'Mr. Addison contended that the Education Committee's action was arbitrary, and that instead of giving Miss Beetlestone any opportunity of rectifying complaints, they were determined to close the school. The magistrates were the authority to decide the point at issue.'[40]

This was precisely the point which the prosecution, appearing on behalf of 'education experts', found hard to accept. Crooke was plainly beginning to feel that the conclusion of the case was not as foregone as he and the Committee had supposed. And when 'Mrs. Alice Leeder gave evidence to show that she was satisfied with the education her children received at the school', Crooke decided it was time to intervene in order to nudge the Bench back in the direction of the prosecution.[41]

After hearing Mrs Leeder, he 'asked for an adjournment in order that [His Majesty's] Inspector might make a report on this school, and the Education Committee would be quite prepared to abide by the result'.[42] In other words, the final judgement should be effectively taken out of the hands of the magistrates and placed in those of H.M.I. The magistrates were clearly incensed by the implication of this suggestion. The judgement was indeed, in law, in their hands alone, and they elected to reject the adjournment appeal and to conduct their own examination of those of Miss Beetlestone's children in court. This decision reawakened the acrimonious spirit of the previous hearing, and a further exchange followed:

> **Mr. Shaw**: You have tried the patience of the Bench almost beyond forebearance. Please do not presume on that forebearance any longer.
>
> **Mr. Crooke**: I decline to-day, as I declined a fortnight ago, to have you speak to me in those terms. I object to being lectured by you.
>
> **Mr. Shaw**: We are here to try this case. You are trying to distort it. We shall have no more.
>
> **Mr. Crooke**: I shall not permit you to speak to me like that. I am not here to bandy words with you.
>
> **Mr. Shaw**: Mr. Crooke, the Bench have been very patient with you. We have decided to hear the children.
>
> **Mr. Crooke**: You can have the children. I only made a suggestion, and I am put forward as if I insulted the Bench.[43]

Some of the 13 children in court were then examined by the magistrates in basic skills. This examination was observed by 'a member of the Education Committee who was present [Mr. J. Arnold] . . . [who] describes it as being farcical'. The Committee had no doubts as to Arnold's competence in such matters; he was 'a Bachelor of Arts and a retired Schoolmaster'.[44] A copy of his report of the examination can be found in Appendix H.

> Asked if he wished to examine the children, Mr. Crooke said: After what has happened I decline to have anything to do with the matter. I wash my hands of it.

Mr. Shaw: You must not talk like that. Do behave in a proper manner.
Mr. Crooke: If your worships would listen, there is a perfectly competent authority . . .
Mr. Shaw: We are competent.[45]

The unanimous decision of the magistrates was to dismiss the case against Leeder. Whilst this indicated that they were satisfied with the level of education his son was receiving, they added that 'Although they were not dealing with Miss Beetlestone, they could not forbear expressing the opinion that she should make such alterations as would bring her school up to modern requirements.'[46] The other cases were adjourned for one week.

The decision brought consternation to the Education Committee and they were stung into further action. At a meeting on 4 June, the Committee decided to set in motion an appeal in the Leeder case, to request that the remaining five cases be deferred *sine die*, and urgently to contact the Board of Education for its help and advice.[47] Communications on the subject of Miss Beetlestone's school began to flow out of the Town Clerk's Office in Walsall in a steady stream. More now than ever, the humiliated authority was determined that the school should be destroyed. But official disappointment had not yet reached its lowest point. Worse was yet to come.

On 7 June, the Committee made a formal request for the magistrates to state a case for an appeal to be heard in a higher court.[48] On 22 June, the Clerk to the Justices informed the Town Clerk, Herbert Lee, that the magistrates, having considered the application, had declined to state a case.[49] The Education Committee were considerably embarrassed by this decision, which they endeavoured to conceal from public attention.[50] The fortuitous death of Harry Leeder's father a few weeks later provided a convenient public excuse for not pursuing the appeal.[51]

Meanwhile, though action through the courts had ground to a halt for the moment, the Committee still expected the Board of Education itself to come to the rescue. On 11 June, all the material relating to the case was bundled off, together with a long covering letter, to the Board. The letter warned that,

> If the decision of the Local Bench as to the standard of efficient education is admitted, it may lead to schools of the character

> described to be opened in other parts of the Borough, and will prove a great obstacle to the Education Committee in getting parents to send their children to the Public Elementary Schools . . . [the] Committee respectfully suggest that your Board should take this matter into their consideration in connection with any further Education Bill; and also that the Board should consider the practicability of obtaining statutory powers making the establishment or continuance of private schools subject to the sanction of either the Board of Education or the Local Education Authority.[52]

The Board's reaction to this excited appeal was distinctly cool. Working-class private schools had long since ceased to be a serious national problem, and the Walsall authority's zeal in this isolated case threatened to stir up those delicate and troublesome issues which had so exercised the minds of the Education Department in the 1870s. The Board had considerably more to lose in becoming involved in the affair than they had to gain. The particular point on which the Walsall Committee sought the Board's support was an inspection by H.M.I., which, as Crooke's performance in court had shown, was held directly to challenge the magistrates.

> In connection with the summonses, the hearing of which has been adjourned, it would, I think, be desirable before they are heard, that the school should be inspected by H.M. Inspector. Miss Beetlestone can, of course, decline to permit such inspection, but I think if the Board expressed their desire for such inspection, she would have a difficulty in refusing.[53]

It is ironical that the position of the Board to Miss Beetlestone's school is analagous to that of the contemporary historian to the generality of working-class private schools in the nineteenth century. As an official at the Board put it:

> The Authority are much annoyed . . . and send us a mass of material intending to prove that Miss Beetlestone's school is a public scandal . . . It must be remembered however, that we have only got the case for prosecution and that three magistrates were unanimous in dismissing the summons.[54]

In other words, the Board was aware that it had before it that which was evidently highly biased. Certainly, the Board were not prepared that either it, or 'H.M. Inspector should be involved in acute local controversy'.[55] A sympathetic but firmly negative response was sent by G. N. Richardson, Secretary to the Board, to Walsall on 11 July:

> I am directed by the Board of Education to state that they do not consider that they can properly express any opinion on the matter or review or criticize the decision of the magistrates.
>
> Having regard to the course which the proceedings took, the Board do not consider that any advantage would be gained by requesting H.M. Inspector to inspect the school even if Miss Beetlestone were prepared to allow this.[56]

The Walsall Education Committee was beginning to run out of options, but it clung to the ideas of an inspection by H.M.I. as constituting the only remaining possibility of success in the five remaining adjourned cases. It turned to a new form of pressure behind the Board's back. On 15 July, H.M.I. Jackson contacted the Board:

> I have reason to believe that the Town Clerk is going to ask me to visit the school with the local inspector, and to write a confidential report for the use of the Education Committee. I quite understand that I cannot act in an official capacity, but is there any reason why I should not grant the Town Clerk's request . . . Will you please let me have your advice as early as possible? I know that they want the school to be visited before the summer holidays, and I should like to be prepared.[57]

On 18 July, Richardson told Jackson:

> The Board do not consider it desirable that H.M.I.'s should undertake the inspection of private elementary schools even if the owners consent . . . On all grounds it seems that your wisest course is not to go near the school.[58]

On 19 July, the Local Authority, through Herbert Lee, the Town Clerk, made its final direct appeal to the Board: 'I have brought your letter of the 11th. instant before the Education Committee, to whom it came as a disappointment, and I am instructed to approach you again with a view to your Board allowing H.M. Inspector to inspect Miss Beetlestone's School . . .'

An attempt was made to make this request more plausible by taking a softer and more conciliatory line on the magistrates' original decision in the Leeder case. With the appeal now completely dropped, the ruling was accepted, but the Authority felt that the magistrates' rider exhorting Miss Beetlestone to modernise her school might yet, in conjunction with an unfavourable report by H.M.I., afford a renewed line of attack in the future.

> The Education Committee have decided, in view of the strong expression of opinion by the Magistrates that Miss Beetlestone should make such alterations as would bring her School up to modern requirements, to defer any further action before the Magistrates till the end of the present year, to see whether Miss Beetlestone carries out the recommendation of the Justices. If she does, of course that would be an end of the matter, but if she does not, my Committee would of course bring the matter again before the Magistrates, and I am to point out that it would be a great help, not only to the Local Education Authority but also to the Magistrates, who may then adjudicate, if the opinion of H.M. Inspector were available. My Committee think they are not unreasonable in expecting the Board to assist them and the Magistrates in securing efficient elementary education in the Borough, and they trust that in view of the changed circumstances since I first wrote to you, the Board will now permit H.M. Inspector to inspect the school . . .[59]

The Authority, certain that the school could not be brought up to standards that would be deemed acceptable without prohibitive capital outlay, were clearly trying to prepare the ground for a final and successful prosecution in a few months. But the Board was not to be drawn like this. They preserved the view that 'it is undesirable to put H.M.I. in the position of an expert witness in the Courts . . . a refusal by the Magistrates to accept his evidence as conclusive would probably weaken his authority in his district'.[60]

One of the most interesting features of the Beetlestone case is the way in which it reproduces in microcosm so many of the issues which were so prevalent in the 1870s; the zeal of local authorities to eliminate working-class private schools, the clashes with local magistrates over the concept of the 'efficient school', and the anxiety of the central authority to avoid direct confrontations. And it was this final characteristic which briefly drew yet another hallmark of the 1870s into the debate — the 'certified efficient school'. It was this device which had originally circumvented all the problems surrounding the continued existence of the working-class private school, and it is interesting that, in a last attempt to afford some comfort to the Walsall Authority, the Board's officials raised it in connection with Miss Beetlestone's. Having rejected the Authority's final, anxious appeal for the intervention of H.M.I., Richardson asked of one of his officials,

> Do you think it would be any use to suggest that Miss Beetlestone should consider the desirability of applying for the recognition of her school as a Certified Efficient School . . .? If she refused to entertain the idea (assuming that the Town Clerk passed it on to her), her position would be weakened — if she consented, H.M.I. would visit and the Board would grant or refuse a certificate on his report.[61]

This would have been a neat solution apart from the fact that the category of 'certified efficient school' had originally been devised for the express purpose of disqualifying working-class private schools. The reply to Richardson's query reminded him,

> Is not your suggestion impracticable? Under Sec. 48 of the Elementary Education Act, 1876, a certified efficient school is a school which is not conducted for private profit. I think we must assume Miss Beetlestone's school is conducted for private profit.[62]

Richardson noted, 'Yes, it is: I had overlooked the point . . .' It was a disappointment. There was apparently nothing left to offer to the Walsall Authority, and the Board could only admit this. 'I suppose', Richardson's note continued, 'we must send some reply to this letter?'

When the reply did arrive at the Council House in Walsall, it was brief and final:

> I am directed to inform the Local Education Authority that the decision of the Board not to undertake the inspection of private elementary schools was arrived at some years ago . . . and that

they feel unable to depart from this rule. The Board regret that they cannot therefore meet the wishes of the Authority in the matter.[63]

The Local Authority was now entirely without support. Neither the courts, nor the Board of Education considered that anything further should, or could, be done. Powerless, the Authority had no alternative but to let the adjourned cases drop, and to allow the whole question quietly to fade out of the public eye. But local officials continued to watch the school and to await another, more favourable opportunity. 1917 was not the last year in which Miss Beetlestone's school would find its way into the courts and into the press.

In the meantime, the school went on. The Church Hall at Palfrey was given up, and another similar hall on the Delves Common, just outside the town, became the school's new home. This new location too was gradually deserted, and the school eventually gravitated back to Miss Beetlestone's own house in West Bromwich Road, where it had started.

Miss Beetlestone herself said nothing during the court cases. Even to her neighbours at the time, she was a rather mysterious character, and she remains so; she left no records. But there are those in and around Walsall who remember her and her work. Their voices can now be set beside those official judgements and declarations which we have already seen. It is important to note the marked similarity of the official accounts of Miss Beetlestone's school with those more general records dating from the nineteenth century. In all respects the documentary evidence proclaims the school as a legitimate survivor of the broad tradition; labelled a 'dames' school'; a single untrained teacher; children of all ages, unclassified and inefficiently registered if at all; unsuitable school accommodation; lack of equipment and facilities; overcrowding; careless parents and complete flexibility of attendance.[64] This is the official way of characterising the school. But what do those who, as local working people, remember the school well, have to say?

Nine such respondents were contacted and interviewed. They are John Emerson, born in 1912, whose sisters went to the school; Mary Fenn, born in 1904, who lived close to the school in the 1920s; Bertha White, born in 1910, who grew up on the Delves Common; George Halliday, who moved to West Bromwich Road in 1913 — an amateur local historian; Will Baker, born in 1908, who has lived most of his life in West Bromwich Road; Edith Henderson, born in 1902, who went to the school for a short period; Ada Carver, born in 1895, who started at the school in 1903; Alice Conway, born in 1908, and her sister, Betty Ringland, born in 1915, who received most of their education at the school.

Some of them were aware of the problems which the school faced from the Local Authority. Alice remembered an atmosphere of continuous and general harassment,

> They were never off Miss Beetlestone's back . . . the Education . . . Well, there was always something going on wasn't there, somehow . . . and she used to say to us, 'Now you must try, you must learn, you must this, you must that, you know, because if you don't, you won't have a Miss Beetlestone's to go to . . .'

Edith recalls the attitude of her public elementary school when she left to go to Miss Beetlestone's:

> The headmaster of Chuckery [Council] School, he was really annoyed . . . when he found 6 or 7 of us left Chuckery. And he had all the children in the Hall and he said, 'I hope no-body else was going to this babies' school' — he called it a babies' school.

John recalled that,

> There used to be a lot . . . a lot of controversy with the Education Committee see. They tried to . . . stop Miss Beetlestone from . . . holding a school, you see . . . The Education Committee tried to stop her . . . like, from having this school, because they didn't think she was suitable to teach . . . up to the standard of teaching them. But they . . . I'm afraid they were wrong.

Within the local community, Miss Beetlestone was a well-liked though little-known character. She had few visitors apart from her pupils and generally kept herself to herself. George Halliday recalls that,

> She had a reputation off the local lads who were always willing to run errands for her, because she never paid them in money,

> but she was more inclined to give them a couple of eggs — she kept some hens in the back garden — she was likely to give them a couple of new laid eggs or send them home for a cup and give them a cup of home-made jam. And I always remember that the front room of her house was lined with . . . bookcases and she was . . . fairly well off as regarded those days for reading material, and probably they were all school books . . .

She took in stray cats and dogs, of which there were always a large number in her house, or following her down the street. In the evenings, she often worked at a large table in the back room of the house. At these times, she always read or wrote by candlelight. John Emerson was a boy of five at the time of her trial in 1917, and he remembers looking out from his bedroom window which backed onto West Bromwich Road, and seeing her at work, illuminated only by candles, and with the dim figure of one of the cats sat alongside her on the table.

George Halliday recalls her physical appearance,

> Miss Beetlestone, as I remember her when she lived in West Bromwich Road, and we lived nearby, was a little body. I should say she was about 5′ 2″ . . . 5′ 3″, and most of the time she wore one of these old-fashioned fur coats . . . up round her ears and down to her ankles, and what we used to call a . . . sort of pot hat or a cloche type of hat.

Will Barker remembers her as,

> . . . very nice . . . but very old, very Victorian in her dress . . . the house was not over-clean . . . she'd always got two or three dogs hanging round her . . . she wasn't posh by any manner or means . . . she was a nice old lady, that's all you could say . . .

All the respondents were clear about the sort of people who used Miss Beetlestone's. Bertha White remembers 'Just ordinary working class . . .'; John Emerson, 'Working-class people . . .'; Will Barker, 'They was exactly the same, they lived in the same houses, lived next door to people as went to the Council School . . .'; George Halliday, 'The people that I knew went there were just ordinary . . . sort of working-class people . . .'; and Alice Conway, 'It wasn't a private school like the private schools are now

. . . they all seem . . . up in the world, don't they?'

The weekly fees were not much greater than might have been paid in such a school 50 years earlier. Edith Henderson remembers, 'Sixpence . . .sixpence. Then in the winter, a halfpenny extra for the coal for the fire . . .'; Bertha, 'Well, I sometimes tell my daughters, I say, "Yeah, we had a little school on the Delves . . . they only used to pay sixpence a week". "Never, Mum!"'; and John recalls that those at the school were

> well, the poorer people round here, that were what you call . . . scraping sixpence together . . . It wasn't a wealthy school, 'cos wealthy people, naturally they'd look at the place and they wouldn't send their children to it . . . it wouldn't make sense, would it?

Though she could not have made much of a living from the school, Miss Beetlestone was flexible about the payment of fees. Betty remembers that 'If they hit hard times . . . she'd say you can bring it next week, you know . . . then the next week, she'd perhaps say, give me the one this week, and then . . . that sort of thing, you know.'

When asked why such a school should be chosen when a free and ostensibly 'efficient' Council School was to hand, respondents gave answers which might have come directly from the 1870s. Most frequently mentioned was the closeness and flexibility of the home-school articulation, and the ferocious discipline of the local state schools.

Edith Henderson:

> You see, I was one of a large family and I was useful to me mother in various ways . . . So, if she wanted me to run errands before I went to school, I used to . . . which meant sometimes we never got there 'til ten o'clock or after, but she never used to bother. But she had a register . . . I remember that register on the desk. But . . . if we didn't go to school, it didn't matter . . . Although I remember the School Board Man coming to see her, but I only saw him once . . . I was very useful in lots of ways, you see, to me mother. If she'd got to go anywhere special where I couldn't go for her, I used to stay away from school to look after me younger brothers and sisters . . . Never any trouble over that, no.

John Emerson,

> You see, some of the mothers used to go out cleaning and all that, you know . . . domestics. Well, they could sneak an hour off . . . this is the . . . this is the method. They used to be able to sneak an hour off you see, or perhaps get away with half a day truant . . . you know, helping in the home sort of business. That's where paying to go to that school . . . what it meant paying to go to that school.

Ada Carver,

> There was a lot used to come and pay their threepence, and they'd go back home and they had to look after the other children at home . . . 'cos they was all big families around there . . . No, you could go any time you liked and you could leave any time you liked.[65]

Mary Fenn,

> People used to pay sixpence a week . . . now that enabled them to get the kids out of going to school ordinary. And . . . I remember hearing one man say, although it's so long ago . . . he was taking a little . . . I think it was a little girl . . . He was saying to someone, 'Well, he thought it best she went to Beetlestone's, because she doesn't like the ordinary school, so he'd taken her way and sent her to Beetlestone's'.

Will Barker,

> I know they used to say they were so lax [at Beetlestone's] . . . She allowed a lot of leeway, you know . . . [At the Council School], it was very strict, very strict, yeah . . . I had the tawse many times . . . We had a master . . . and by gum, he could belt it as well . . . [At Beetlestone's] they went when they liked . . . there was no restriction at all . . . Oh, yes, they could go in late, or they could go in when they liked . . . No, she wasn't strict at all . . . And her hours weren't as strict as the . . . ordinary school. But I cannot understand why she had a school where she lived, because it was straight opposite the Council School . . . but they didn't have the same hours . . . the hours were far different . . .

Edith Henderson: 'Definitely [Beetlestone's] was a different school altogether . . .different type of school altogether. I mean, they were strict at Chuckery [Council] School, very strict.' And finally, Alice Conway and Betty Ringland in conversation with each other:

> [At the Council School,]
> **A.C.:** . . .we used to have terrible punishments . . .
> **B.R.:** She [Miss Beetlestone] never, never gave anyone the cane or anything like that. But there was never any unruliness . . .
> **A.C.:** No, never . . . I mean, we was terrified at [the Council] School, wasn't we . . . I was anyway.
> **B.R.:** And I was.
> **A.C.:** But that . . . I think that's why we went.
> **B.R.:** It was more like being at home. She was very good and very kind, you know . . . but we had to do as we were told and . . . it sort of went from home to school and it was the same sort of discipline, you know.
> **A.C.:** I was too frightened to learn . . . at the other school.

John Emerson,

> Well, I don't think there was so much . . . discipline [at Miss Beetlestone's] . . . there was a certain amount of discipline, but the atmosphere was more jovial I'd say . . . you know, free and easy . . . [In the Council Schools, discipline was] very serious. I mean, if you was to speak in class when you should have been studying, the teacher'd come round and the next thing you know, you got a right whack up your ear'ole . . . because it happened to me more than once . . . yeah . . . in fact, it affected my hearing . . . a teacher could get away with that . . . If you was to speak in ranks outside, you know, when they collected you together . . . there used to be a schoolteacher there, I won't mention his name, but he was noted for it, as minute you got in, 'Bend over!', and you used to get that tawse boy, near to cut your trousers in half nearly. He was a sadist.

Within the school itself, the atmosphere was relaxed and pleasant. John's sisters 'enjoyed it . . . Well, they were happy there.' Will remembered his friend, 'Tom Farr . . . we were boys together, and he went to Miss Beetlestone's. He used to say he enjoyed it.' After leaving the Council School, Edith found that, 'it was much easier for me somehow at Miss Beetlestone's'. And in Ada's recollection, 'Well, everybody seemed to like it . . . She was more like your mother would be to the children, you know . . . You had to behave. Yes . . . but she'd talk on . . . talk to you like your mother would, you know.'

Alice and Betty remember the school with particular affection,

B.R.: She was lovely to go to . . . we never had to be made to go . . .
A.C.: We were happy.
B.R.: We were always ready to go, we loved it . . . Because we always was . . . like one big family . . .

The curriculum was basic, with the addition of some of Miss Beetlestone's particular interests, which seem chiefly to have been astronomy and natural history. When the school was on the Delves, Bertha White remembers that the curriculum was 'Arithmetic, history, geography . . . they did a proper school . . . an ordinary school . . . education. She used to take them on nature walks . . . She didn't keep more or less to a strict timetable like the Council School . . . She used to teach more or less a bit of everything.' George Halliday felt that 'one of the things that Miss Beetlestone could teach them was a fairly good hand at writing, and I'm told that some of them wrote excellent copper-plate'.

Former pupils found it hard to remember much about the ways that they learnt, though Betty recalls the normal teaching format as a circle of scholars of all ages, with Miss Beetlestone in the middle. She was, by Betty's account, an interesting and entertaining teacher. 'You could hear a pin drop . . . I've never been able to understand why we were all so good . . . I've never known how she controlled us.'

But all were agreed that however it came about, and despite all deficiencies or irregularities, Miss Beetlestone's pupils received a sound education. Bertha White claims that 'they all turned out that went there, wonderful scholars . . . They were all good scholars . . . equal to the Council School at that time.' And Alice Conway 'can't understand if she didn't learn them properly why so many of those got on so well'. In fact Alice felt that it was the Council School which had been inadequate,

I went . . . I went to the ordinary school for about three years, would it be? . . . and what I can remember of Tantarra Street — that's the ordinary school — I learnt simply nothing at all . . . I can't remember a thing of what I learnt those three years. [At this school] they weren't good teachers to my knowledge . . . to what Miss Beetlestone was . . . I wouldn't want any better . . . not now in these modern days.

John Emerson,

I mean, she did her job well, because I . . . I mean the people that I knew — there's lots of my friends went there — and they, I mean, there was none of them dunces. I mean, later on in life, none of them lacked getting a decent job . . . [The Education Committee] didn't like her being in existence shall I say, holding the school, but . . . you see, I don't think there was anything they could do about it because . . . I mean, if you went to check up on any of the pupils, they found they were all up to the same standard as the people that weren't paying.

And George Halliday: 'I did know one or two [of Miss Beetlestone's scholars], yes, and as far as I can remember, they seemed to get on as well as anybody who'd been to a normal Council School, or even Grammar School.'

Will Barker remembers Miss Beetlestone and her school most vividly two or three years after the 1917 court case, when he was a boy of eleven or twelve. This was the period when Miss Beetlestone was alternating the school between the house in West Bromwich Road, and the little church hall on the Delves, about a mile distant, down a country lane.

I saw them every day . . . If you went over the Delves, they were . . . outside more than anything. They were round this little school. I remember it ever so well, we used to play round there when . . . during the holidays, you know . . . If it was wet and she couldn't go [to the Delves], she'd have it in the house . . . in this little house down here. The children used to go to her house if the weather was very bad . . . and then I've seen them going down the road, past our house in West Bromwich Road . . . and going to the Delves, over to this little school . . . and the children, they used to run errands for her and go out for her if she wanted anything. Well I wish I could have found that

> photograph my brother took . . . going down the street, past our house, with the dogs and with . . . 'bout four children going to the school down over the Delves.

Where then is the truth of Miss Beetlestone's school? Like the two blocks of evidence considered here — official document and spoken recollection — it depends on the broader context of preconception, expectation and experience in which the question is rooted. But what the juxtaposition of the two sources has demonstrated is that, for this school, the confident voice of public authority has a serious opponent. This opposing voice is local, personal and private. It does not set itself before the public eye unless it is chased out and set there. Some small part of this private voice has been salvaged in the case of this single school; but for thousands of others, there can be no such rescue. And though the public and private voices have the same subject, they do not tell the same story. There is no way in which the two can legitimately be unified to form a single, acceptable composite 'truth'. The real truth lies in the nature of the chasm which separates them as versions of a single reality. The two accounts are much more than 'opposing views' of an identified social phenomenon. They are themselves the product of broader differences of class and of culture.

If the two blocks of evidence cannot agree on the purpose, the quality and the effectiveness of Miss Beetlestone's school, they clearly both proclaim it an authentic working-class private school, however judged. As such, it must have been among the last of the survivors of the nineteenth-century tradition. And the school was not yet finished.

In the later inter-war years, the school is hard to track, though it clearly continued to function. At some time in the 1920s, Miss Beetlestone shifted her nominal classroom base from the Delves to a large hut in Sandwell Street. It was in this location that the final act in the long story of her school was played out. The details, briefly, were as follows.

Twenty years after their unsuccessful prosecution, the Local Education Authority returned to the attack once more.

> At Walsall Police Court recently, forty-five parents were summoned under the Education Act, 1921, for failing to provide efficient elementary instruction in reading, writing and

arithmetic. They were the parents of children who attended a private school carried on by a Miss Beetlestone in Sandwell Street, Walsall.[66]

In 1937, Miss Beetlestone must have been in her seventies or eighties. She had been keeping her school continuously in south Walsall for at least 50 years. It is clear from the evidence given at this new trial that the character of the school had not changed. The prosecution's chief witness was H.M.I. Frank Taylor, who was called in to inspect the school on 8 and 9 April 1937. He testified that,

> The hut in which the school meets is about 300 square feet in area and has been allowed to fall into a state of disrepair. Facilities for ablution and the hanging of cloaks are lacking and the offices consist of one pail closet, for which there was no key in the school. Limited space for activities out of doors is available. The lighting is not good, the ventilation inadequate, and the only means of heating ineffective.
>
> On the roll are between 40 and 50 children, about equally divided between the sexes, the ages ranging from 6 to 14 years. The furniture provided is inadequate . . . When the children attend well, the room is overcrowded . . .
>
> The staff consists of the proprietoress, who has had no training in the accepted sense of the term, and has carried on the school at various addresses for about fifty years.
>
> No written timetable, schemes of work or records of progress are made, and the children are made responsible for bringing their own material and equipment, which consisted generally of an exercise book, a Bible and a pencil.
>
> Although in the absence of text books and syllabus there is no evidence of an ordered curriculum or of aims, work appears to proceed in a regular succession of activities . . .
>
> An attendance register is kept, but the registration is faulty . . . There is no reliable check on punctuality.[67]

The magistrates then subjected four pupils to tests of basic skills. The *Walsall Observer* reported,

> Four pupils from Miss Beetlestone's school were called before the magistrates in succession — Mary Jones (13), Winifred Jean

> Tomkinson (13), Betty Perrins and Norman Holt (14). All submitted to reading and writing tests and Mary and Winifred were commended for the clearness and fluency with which they read the oath. Both girls admitted . . . that they had been through Council Schools before attending Miss Beetlestone's.
>
> Norman Holt, who said he had been attending Miss Beetlestone's for the past five years, was unable to read the oath, but wrote his name and address in script characters.
>
> The boy's father told the magistrates that when at Croft Street School, Norman, 'was always under the doctor for headaches', but his health had been much better since he had been at Miss Beetlestone's.[68]

Having selected Norman Holt as a test case, the magistrates,

> announced that they had come to the conclusion that the authorities had satisfied them, beyond doubt, that the parent of the child had not fulfilled his duty of providing the child with efficient elementary education as required by law. That being so, a school attendance order would be made.[69]

In the changed circumstances of 1937, with enhanced legal powers, the Local Education Authority had exacted its revenge on Miss Beetlestone. Parental support was finally broken, and the school could not go on. After 50 years, Miss Beetlestone and her school — one of the last links with a redundant working-class tradition — disappeared from history.

Notes

1. See Paul Corrigan and Simon Frith, 'The Politics of Youth Culture', in *Resistance Through Rituals*, T. Jefferson (ed.) (1975), pp. 231–9, esp. p. 235.
2. The majority of the interview evidence considered below relates to the period after 1918 — the year in which the 'labour certificate' was finally abolished.
3. Dorothy Martin was born in 1908, attending the school from 1913 to 1922. Ellen was six years younger and did not leave the school until 1928. Rachel Wells was born in 1914 and was at the school from 1923 to 1928. George Day attended for about a year in 1927–8, when he was just five years old.
4. Dorothy Martin interview; Rachel Wells interview.
5. George Day interview.
6. Ellen Martin.
7. Rachel Wells.
8. George Day.

9. George Day.
10. Dorothy Martin.
11. Ellen Martin.
12. Rachel Wells.
13. Ellen Martin.
14. George Day.
15. Dorothy Martin.
16. The following memories are from a letter from Bill Evans (February 1981).
17. Two additional former pupils were contacted. Paternal occupations were coal trimmer and factory worker.
18. See A. Roberts, 'A New View of the Infant School Movement', *B.J.E.S.* (1972), pp. 154–64. Also P.P. 1908 [4259] vol. lxxxii, *Report of the Consultative Committee upon the School Attendance of Children below the age of five.*
19. See A. Roberts, 'A New View'. Also see Chapter 1 above.
20. P.R.O. Ed. 18/217. Letter dated 11.6.1917. A copy of this letter can also be found in the Walsall Record Office.
21. Ibid.
22. It is worth pointing out that such a visit could only have taken place with the prior consent of Miss Beetlestone.
23. P.R.O. Ed 18/217. Report of Visit . . . Hibbett.
24. Ibid. Report of Visit . . . Carroll.
25. Ibid. Letter to the Board, 11.6.1917.
26. Miss Beetlestone's resilience was uncommon. There are a few other cases of private teachers trying to resist closure of their schools with less success. The best documented of these concerns a school in Birmingham kept by a Miss Duckworth, which was closed following a court case in 1910. See *Education*, 5.11.1937, p. 476; 'Shiers v. Stevenson', *The Justice of the Peace*, 7.10.1911, pp. 441–2 — 'that Miss Duckworth had one assistant, a girl about fifteen years of age; that there were forty children attending [the] school, and that their ages ranged from three and a half to fourteen years of age. That Miss Duckworth had only one room in which to give instruction to her pupils; that the same was contiguous to a factory, and approached from the street through a covered passage and an open yard; that there was no playground . . . that the desks, teaching apparatus and general equipment of the school were not efficient . . . that the ventilation . . . was inadequate; and that noises from the machinery in the adjoining factory were audible in the room.' See also Miss Duckworth's letters of protest to the Board about her treatment at the hands of the Local Authority in P.R.O. Ed. 18/245.
27. P.R.O. Ed. 18/217. Letter to the Board, 11.6.1917, p. 2.
28. Ibid.
29. Ibid.
30. P.R.O. Ed. 18/217. Reports by Hibbett, 16.5.1917; 22.5.1917.
31. P.R.O. Ed. 18/217. Letter to the Board, 11.6.1917, p. 2.
32. In full, this section reads, 'If either —

(1) The parent of any child above the age of five years who is under this Act prohibited from being taken into full time employment, habitually and without reasonable excuse neglects to provide efficient elementary instruction for his child; or
(2) Any child is found habitually wandering or not under proper control, or in the company of rogues, vagabonds, disorderly persons, or reputed criminals;

it shall be the duty of the local authority, after due warning to the parent of such child to complain to a court of summary jurisdiction, and such court may, if satisfied of the truth of such complaint, order that the child do attend some certified efficient school willing to receive him and named in the order, being either such as the parent may select, or, if he do not select any, then such public elementary school as the court think expedient, and the child shall attend that school every time that the school is open, or in such other regular manner as is specified in the order.

Any order under this section is in this Act referred to as an attendance order.

Any of the following reasons shall be a reasonable excuse:

(1) That there is not within two miles, measured according to the nearest road, from the residence of such child any public elementary school open which the child can attend; or

(2) That the absence of the child from shool has been caused by sickness or any unavoidable cause.'

33. *Walsall Observer*, 19.5.1917, p. 5. Also see *Walsall Pioneer*, 19.5.1917, p.3.

34. P.R.O. Ed. 18/217. Board Minute, 13.6.1917.

35. *Walsall Observer*, 19.5.1917.

36. P.R.O. Ed. 18/217. Report of Visit . . . Hibbett, 22.5.1917. Also see *Walsall Education Committee Minutes*, 23.5.1917.

37. P.R.O. Ed. 18/217. Letter to the Board, 11.6.1917, p. 2.

38. Other defendants in court were Joseph Day, a window cleaner of Tantarra Street; Alfred Farr, a railway inspector of 57, West Bromwich Road; and Herbert Rosamond from Walhouse Street, a munitions worker. See *Walsall Pioneer*, 2.6.1917. Note the persistence of the conflation of 'school' with 'public elementary school' in the bye-laws as compared with legislation. The difference of meaning between the two probably explains why the Local Authority issued three summonses under Section 11 of the Act of 1876, and three under their own bye-laws.

39. *Walsall Pioneer*, 2.6.1917. It is perhaps worth noting that only a few weeks later, Dr Carroll was one of the authors of a report which was highly critical of the physical conditions of some of the Local Authority's own public elementary schools. See 'Walsall's Defective Schools', *Walsall Observer*, 21.7.1917.

40. *Walsall Observer*, 2.6.1917.

41. *Walsall Pioneer*, 2.6.1917.

42. Ibid.

43. *Walsall Observer*, 2.6.1917. A Board of Education Minute observes that 'the assistant Town Clerk . . . was more successful in irritating than in convincing the Bench . . .'. P.R.O. Ed. 18/217.

44. P.R.O. Ed. 18/217. Letter to the Board, 11.6.1917, p. 3.

45. *Walsall Observer*, 2.6.1917.

46. Ibid.

47. *Walsall Education Committee Minutes*, 4.6.1917, pp. 165–6. Two weeks later, Victor Crooke was the recipient of an increase of £50, bringing his salary to £350 per annum. This was in respect of the 'large amount of outside work done by Mr. Crooke — he was always willing to help anyone — which meant a great deal of labour for which he was not paid'. *Walsall Observer*, 16.6.1917.

48. *Walsall Pioneer*, 9.6.1917. Also P.R.O. Ed. 18/217. Letter to the Board, 11.6.1917, p. 3. Many of the papers relating to the appeal are in the Walsall Record Office, under Miss Beetlestone's name.

49. Walsall Record Office, Letter, Beetlestone File.

50. The Secretary of the Education Committee wrote to the Town Clerk on 3 July; 'Unless you think it necessary to do otherwise I shall not make any reference to the refusal of the Magistrates to state a Case, in the Public Report of the General Purpose Sub-Committee.' Walsall Record Office, Letter, Beetlestone File.

51. Following Leeder's death, the Education Committee could write in more conciliatory terms to Miss Beetlestone's solicitors; 'As you are probably aware, the Defendant in the recent School Attendance Case died a week or two ago and the proposed Appeal against the Magistrates' decision consequently falls to the ground.

The Education Committee have decided, in view of the Magistrates' strong expression of opinion that Miss Beetlestone should make such alterations as would bring her school up to modern requirements, to give her every opportunity of carrying out the Justices' recommendation, and, for this purpose, have decided to defer taking any further action until the end of the present year.' Walsall Record Office, Letter 19.7.1917, Beetlestone File. In reality, the appeal did not fall to the ground on Leeder's death — if had already been rejected two weeks earlier.

52. P.R.O. Ed. 18/217. Letter to Board, 11.6.1917, p. 3.
53. Ibid., p. 4.
54. P.R.O. Ed. 18/217. Board of Education Minute, 15.6.1917.
55. Ibid.
56. P.R.O. Ed. 18/217.
57. Ibid.
58. Ibid.
59. Ibid. Letter from Clerk to Walsall Education Authority to the Board, 19.7.1917. See also note 51 above.
60. Ibid. Board of Education Minute, 30.7.1917.
61. Ibid. Board of Education Minute, 25.7.1917.
62. Ibid., 26.7.1917.
63. P.R.O. Ed. 18/217. Letter from the Board, 1.8.1917.
64. Further descriptive detail of the school can be found both in the material at the P.R.O. and in that at the Walsall Record Office.
65. This lower fee was recalled only by Ada, who was at the school at an earlier period than the others.
66. *Education*, 3.9.1937, p. 240. The legal position of private schools — particularly as regards inspection — had altered materially following the Acts of 1918 and 1921. See letters in *Education*, 5.11.1937, p. 476; 12.11.1937, p. 510; 26.11.1937, p. 571. One of the correspondents here — John Stevenson — was the primary agent in disposing of Miss Duckworth's school in 1910. One of his Attendance Officers in Birmingham recalls him as 'a tyrant' who 'hounded this woman'. (Interview with Frank Houghton, b. 1896.)
67. *Education*, 8.10.1937, p. 372.
68. *Walsall Observer*, 2.10.1937.
69. Ibid.

APPENDIX A: Methods employed in identifying private schools from the Population Census

The central interest of the census for this work lies in the returns of declared occupations, and in particular in all those individuals returned as being in some way connected with teaching. From an analysis of such returns, it was hoped to move from a known number of teachers to an estimated number of schools. The difficulties involved in this work were considerable.

The first problem is presented by the sheer volume of the sources. In 1851, 137,328 people lived within the municipal boundaries of the City of Bristol; by 1861, this total had risen to 154,093; and in 1871, it stood at 182,552. Each individual census entry — a total of 473,973 — had to be scanned for occupational references to teaching. Allowing for a small margin of error — due for example, to the illegibility of an original entry or to a simple failure to spot a relevant entry — the total of such individuals in any census year should closely approximate to the printed abstracted totals. Having checked that this was indeed so, the real problems began.

There was no easy way of jumping from the number of declared teachers to the number of existing working-class private schools. Relatively few of the entries classified a respondent as unequivocally a private school-keeper; entries, for example, such as 'Keeps a small school', or 'Dame School'. The majority of the entries are not as self-explanatory as this. It is apparent that the enumerators made little effort to apply a consistent or unambiguous nomenclature. An important problem then, lay in distinguishing teachers who were working in schools which were, in one way or another, public; that is, in receipt of some form of public financial aid, or under some form of public control or supervision. Fortunately, large numbers of such teachers *are* distinguished in the returns. Thus Clarissa Little for example, is given in 1871 as 'National School Mistress', William Pryor in 1851 is 'Teacher in a Grammar School', Harriet Jones in 1871 is 'British School Mistress' and so on. Pupil teachers again were regularly returned as unequivocally such. It might well have been the case that most public teachers were at pains clearly to establish themselves as *not* to be confused with teachers of 'inferior private schools'. There is however another check to eliminate teachers of public schools, for the majority are listed in the relevant Directories as such. The names of teachers so listed have been deleted from the list of those who were likely keepers of private schools. It is possible that some error will remain, that some teachers who were in fact working in the public sector have been categorised as potential private school teachers. This scale of such error should not, considering the evidence positively identifying 'public' teachers, be great. Moreover, a useful check on possible inaccuracies would be provided by comparative analysis of the three lists (1851, 1861, 1871) of teachers classified as potential private school teachers. The problem of distinguishing 'private' from 'public' teachers, though difficult, is not then an insurmountable one.

But another problem of classification remains. Having attempted to establish the condition of privateness, the issue of social class remains. In the nineteenth century, private schools existed for all classes of society, but this study is centrally concerned with those schools with a distinctively working-class character. Thus, for example, the widow Rachel Hall who lived in a strong working-class district of the parish of Bedminster in 1851 and who was returned as 'School Mistress. Pauper' is as obviously a relevant case as that of Mrs Mary Light who, together with three daughters and two assistants, ran a Ladies' Boarding School in the exclusive residential suburb of Clifton, is not. (Households with more than one teacher were of course calculated as a single school.) In this case, the difference in the type of private school is apparent though Mary Light is returned, like her humble contemporary as 'School Mistress' and was classified alongside her in the Census Abstracts which list 372 school mistresses in the city for that year. Though accurate differentiation on the basis of social class was essential, it was not always as straightforward as in this example, and several methods were tried. Extreme care was exercised and each entry was checked at least twice on separate occasions. The most satisfactory method was that in which each relevant occupational entry (that is, each potential private school) was classified according to the apparent social composition of its immediate locality (which would constitute the likely catchment area). It was impossible to list the occupational and household details of each relevant locality — this would have meant reproducing practically the whole census, and a process by which each was represented by a written summary was found to be similarly unworkable. Some sort of quick but unacceptably accurate form of shorthand grading was therefore unavoidable.

In achieving each individual grading, four criteria were applied. First, what was the occupational and social profile of the household in which the teacher lived? Second, what was the occupational structure of the immediate neighbourhood? Third, how did the information from the first two sources measure against other sources of local information of the city in the period? Fourth, were there any other observable factors which made the entry particularly unusual or incongruous? After consideration of these four criteria in combination, a letter grade was assigned to each entry. Not infrequently, it seemed that a split grade was the fairest decision, though in final totalling, each split grading relating to a potential working-class private school was rounded downwards; all C/Ds for example, became straight Ds. Whilst occupational structure was not the only factor considered, it was, given the limitations of the census information, unquestionably the most significant. A rough indication can therefore be given of how the grades approximate to the occupational structure relating to each entry.

A = *Principally unskilled working class*, e.g. labourer, porter, charwoman, servant, pauper, washerwoman, etc.

Shading into —

B = *Mixed unskilled and skilled working class*, as above, but with numbers of carpenters, masons, shoemakers, blacksmiths, wheelwrights, decorators, etc.

Shading into —

C = *Principally skilled working class with occasional lower middle-class additions*; as B, but including skilled craftsmen of all kinds as well as a few clerks and small shopkeepers.

D = *Predominantly lower middle with some middle class*; small businessmen and masters, shopkeepers, clerks, accountants, etc. Households in this type of district frequently include a single live-in servant girl. This is a characteristic which is effectively non-existent in categories A–C.

E = *Mainly affluent professional and commercial middle class.*

F = *Wealthy merchants, senior clergy, landowners, aristocrats.*

The schools operated by the two teachers mentioned earlier are at opposite ends of this scale, Rachel Hall being rated 'A' and Mary Light 'F'. Substantial numbers of entries were similarly not excessively difficult to classify and dramatic amendments on re-checking were rare. The proportion of entries where classification was very troublesome was relatively small. It will be clear that those entries which could accurately be described as probably relating to working-class private schools were to be found in categories A, B and C. Very particular care was taken in classifying entries which seemed to lie on the edge of the distinction between C and D, or to put it more clearly, on entries which fell in a grey area between the strongly working-class or the strongly middle-class districts. This type of entry was relatively numerous and might be seen as relating essentially to the specifically lower middle-class form of private school, which considerably outlived the working-class variety. All C/D entries, having been rounded down to D, were excluded from the final totals. This will explain why the bulk of the entries which have been characterised as potential working-class private schools are graded A or B, and comparatively few have been included in category C. For each of the three censuses, 1851, 1861 and 1871, the percentage of potential working-class schools labelled C is 20.4 per cent, 18.2 per cent and 14.7 per cent respectively. The remainder are A or B.

Table A.1: Totals of Working-class Private Schools 1851–71 According to Classification

	1851	1861	1871
A	97	54	41
B	76	109	117
C	45	37	33

APPENDIX B: The working-class private schools of Bristol, 1851–71

As we have seen, sources of evidence relating to working-class private schools and which are untainted by middle-class bias, are few. Analysis of the Population Census has however provided one such source, and it has been utilised throughout this study. The purpose of this section is to draw together those findings of the analysis which have not been fully explored in earlier chapters. What more then can the Population Census tell us of the schools of this single city?

If we look at the birthplaces of the teachers of private schools, we find, as we have done in several other respects, a remarkably constant pattern emerging. In each case, about half of the teachers were natives of Bristol and half from elsewhere, though many of these were from north Somerset, Gloucestershire or South Wales. In 1851, 109 of the teachers (46.6 per cent) had been born in Bristol, 125 (53.4 per cent) had been born elsewhere. In 1861, the figures were 111 (51.6 per cent) and 104 (48.4 per cent) respectively, and in 1871, 100 (49.3 per cent) and 103 (50.7 per cent) respectively. In 1851, four teachers originated in Ireland, one from Calcutta and one from Canada. In 1861, there were also four from Ireland, one from South America and one from East India. Three came from Ireland in 1871, and one each from Bombay, Barbados, British Guinea and Madras.

The relative ages of the teachers fit once more into a markedly uniform pattern. In 1851, the youngest teacher was 13 and the oldest 77; in 1861, the comparative ages were 13 and 88; and in 1871, they were 16 and 78. The average of all the female teachers in 1851 was 40.3 years; in 1861 it was 43.5; and in 1871, 37.1. For male teachers, the average ages over the three censuses were 45.3 years; 42.4 years; and 40.4 years respectively.

The full breakdown of the marital status of the teachers does show some interesting variations, particularly in the relative decline in the number of widows and the increase in the number of unmarried daughters in the parental home. This variation is acccompanied, as might be expected, by a slight decline in the average age of female teachers.

Table A.2: Marital Status of Working-class Private School Teachers, 1851–71

Marital Status	1851	1861	1871
Widow	54	49	30
Married, female	51	33	37
Married – no husband	12	7	9
Unmarried	48	54	46
Unmarried daughter at home	43	48	64
Widower	3	2	1
Married, male	17	12	11
Unmarried, male	6	10	5

The nomenclature used to describe Bristol's working-class private teachers was very varied, though several designations were particularly widely used. Most popular was simply 'Schoolmistress'. This was used 130 times in 1851, 112 times in 1861, and 85 times in 1871, 13 of these relating to teachers known also through the 1870 Education Survey. Next came the synonymous 'Governess', employed 47 times, 38 times and 42 times respectively, with 7 of the latter also reported by the 1870 Survey. Beyond this, there were as many as 42 other designations used less regularly to indicate private teachers. Examples include, 'Keep a small school for children'; 'Keeps a school'; 'Governess private school'; 'A Day School'; 'Child's School Mistress'; 'Keeps a School'; and 'Cottage School'.

Male teachers were commonly returned as 'Schoolmaster', with 22 so described in 1851, 20 in 1861 and 13 in 1871 along with 8 further designations, usually employed on a single occasion.

Probably a large proportion of the designations were determined and entered on the Householder's Schedule by the teachers themselves. This makes them particularly valuable as the only existing personal statements known to us. However, we have already seen that enumerators and Registrars did modify some of the entries, whilst some of them appear to have been framed by enumerators in the first place. The description 'Dame School', for example, employed in both 1861 and 1871, seems unlikely to have stemmed from the teachers involved themselves.

There remain two further, more extensive ways in which the Population Census can illuminate our understanding of the working-class private school. In the first place, it can provide a detailed picture of the changing geographical distribution of the schools within the city. In the second, it can furnish us with a limited number of empirical features for each school. The first undertaking can be approached systematically, but the second leads, by the nature of the evidence, to brief and necessarily repetitive anecdote. All we have in each case is no more than the name, age, sex, birthplace and occupation of each teacher. There is no way at present of putting much more flesh on these dry bones. However, we will make the most of the available material if we combine an account of geographical distribution with a limited descriptive selection of a few of the hundreds of schools which the analysis discovered (see Figure A.1).

The picture that emerges from the distribution map (Figure A.1) is of slow change within a pattern marked by clear recurring

Figure A.1: Bristol; Numbers of Working-class Private Schools by Parish, 1851, 1861, 1871

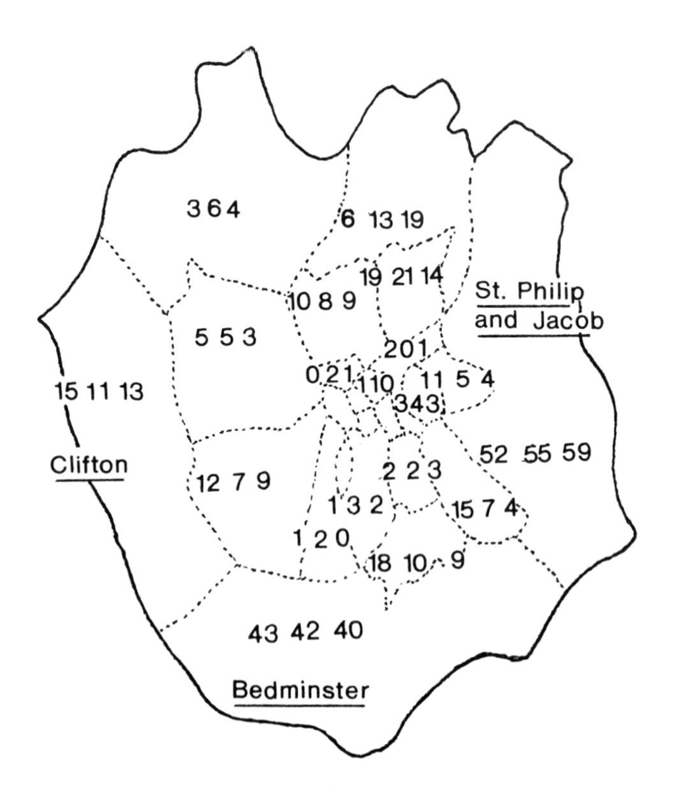

features.[1] Most obvious is the absence of working-class private schools in the western part of the city. This is not surprising. This area of high ground above the Avon Gorge comprises the exclusive Georgian development of Clifton. Characterised by its elegant crescents and squares, its lofty mansion houses and its airy and uncrowded open spaces, Clifton maintained its dignified cultural and social distance from the rest of the city even after its incorporation into Bristol in 1835.

The only noteworthy presence of working-class private schooling in the western part of the city was in the dockland enclaves along the Hotwells Road, which runs in the shadow of Clifton's heights, towards the city centre. In the old central parishes, many of the main thoroughfares were lined with high, tottering medieval houses. These supported large numbers of working-class families, though increasingly from mid-century onwards, the city centre was being drained as the population resettled in the expanding new suburbs. The construction of these, particularly in the predominantly working-class parishes of St Philip's and St Jacob's in the east, and Bedminster to the south, represented a major shift in the pattern of working-class housing. The new developments were characteristically of narrow-fronted through-terraced houses.[2] Sometimes these were occupied by a single working family, perhaps with one or two lodgers, but more frequently, the six rooms they commonly provided were shared between two or more families.

> Many of the very poor from the old [central] dwellings demolished . . . and those people perhaps who have emancipated themselves from the gloom of the courts, have found their abode in these new cheaply-built houses, in some of which there are families in almost every room; and in others the house is divided between two families, each paying about 2s. 6d. a week for three rooms — one of the best conditions under which the struggling poor seem able to live.[3]

As the distribution map reveals, homes of this type increasingly supported private schools in the 1860s and 1870s. Nevertheless, even in 1871, a large proportion of working-class schools continued to be held in the older types of inner-city dwelling — the tenement house and the court — which were the principal hosts for schools in 1851. Such habitations dominated the old city, stretching through much of the central area to the poorest district of St Jude's in the east, and south into the parishes of Redcliff, Temple, and Bedminster. The standard of such housing was notoriously bad, with scores of individuals crowded together and entire families sometimes confined to a single room. The Liberal weekly newspaper, the *Bristol Mercury*, proclaimed as late as 1884 that,

> In Bristol we have squalid homes, many blind courts, sadly wanting light and ventilation; large dilapidated tenement houses, where families of human beings are 'caged' almost as closely as the group of curious birds and quadrupeds in a travelling menagerie. And some of the latter, carefully nourished and cared for, would form a 'happy family' whose 'housing' would be pronounced cleanly and comfortable quarters compared with that of the human beings herding together in places we have seen in a day's visit to courts to be found between the centre of the city and St. Jude's.[4]

The school kept by Jane Porter in Temple Back in 1851, for example, operated in a building which housed 17 individuals — dressmakers, labourers, a sugar baker, a waiter, a cap maker, and children.[5] The old house in Church Lane, St Philip's where Elizabeth Cole managed her school was shared between five families — 22 individuals in all.[6] Elizabeth Cole's eldest son, at 13, had started his working life as an errand boy, whilst three of her remaining children, aged between 5 and 10, were 'scholars at home', being taught by their mother alongside other local children. Equally crowded were the dark and airless little courts which led off from the old city streets. One such was Pinnell Court in St Jude's. This was probably the court described by the *Mercury* with a characteristic mixture of reforming concern and cultural abhorrence.

> We climb [a] . . . rickety staircase, grimy, dirt-mantled, and dark, in a court off Pinnell Street, where room after room is occupied by families. No ray of light finds its way there, and as you touch the greasy, clammy walls to keep your footing on the crazy steps the coating of filth sticks to your fingers. A lady so devoted to this true 'mission work' that she has come from Clifton to live close to the scene of her labours amongst the outcast poor tells us as we ascend that she finds it necessary to wash her hands after one of these climbs, unless she takes a special pair of gloves for the occasion.[7]

One of the families dwelling here in 1861 was headed by Lydia Britton, who, at 72, made her living selling vegetables, while her daughter Ellen kept a school.[8] Sheat's Court, on the other side of Old Market Street, housed the school of Sarah Gallard, born in London in 1790.[9] Like many solitary teachers, she lived as a lodger in a single room. In this case she lodged with a butcher, his boot-binder wife and their three children. Returned as 'scholars', these might well have been receiving their education from Sarah Gallard; this would have meant simply moving from one room to another.

Sarah Gallard's life in her old age must have been a hard one. Some private teachers were in more fortunate circumstances, being able to take in lodgers rather than be so themselves. One such was Eliza Ashbury who lived in Nelson Place, one of the warren of courts and alleys running off Temple Street.[10] Though sharing a house here with two other families and having been widowed in her twenties, she was able to supplement her income by letting one of her rooms to two lodgers — a porter and a 'lunatic dependent on friends'.

Ann Shorland, who was 'Governess of School' at nearby Pimm's Entry, probably enjoyed as great a degree of financial security as a teacher of a working-class private school could hope for. Number Five, Pimm's Entry, was shared between two families, the larger being headed by Ann Shorland. In addition to the income from her school, there were three children in their twenties bringing in money — a mariner, a labourer and a dressmaker. Finally, one of the family's available rooms was let to two lodgers — a cooper's assistant and a shoe binder.[11]

Subletting was clearly a common method of boosting family income, where the room could be spared. It was not however always successful. Elizabeth Tanner, for example, rented rooms in Gough's Court, a few hundred yards behind Temple Church. In addition to the income from her school, there was the weekly rental from the family of basketmakers who lodged with her. Nevertheless, Elizabeth Tanner was one of the small number of school-keepers in the city in receipt of parochial relief.[12]

Wherever people lived in the old city, there were schools. There were schools in shops, in pubs and lodging houses, and in odd corners with designations such as 'Rooms above Timber Yard', 'Back of Pithay' and 'Behind No. 58 Redcliff Street'. Perhaps the most singular examples, however, are those to be found in the long-established squatters' encampment to the north of Newfoundland

Road. This was sited on an area of allotments bounded by Lower Ashley Road, Newfoundland Road and St Nicholas' Road. The latter was newly built in the 1870s at the start of the clearance and redevelopment of the site with new housing. By the early 1880s, there were

> . . . few of these crazy-looking, oddly-built, tumbledown cabins left to mark the place where the colony of 'Squatters' once held possession of the Newfoundland Gardens . . . they serve to show the wretched straits to which some of these poor people were driven in housing themselves in homes which look unfit for pigs to be littered in . . . All the squatters were their own architects, and these low-roofed cabins varied in size and form, but were always one-floor dwellings . . . in olden times [the land] was let in garden allotments, the holders of which first built tool houses and then summer houses there; gradually a fire grate and chimney were added and then squatter after squatter took possession. Upwards of a hundred cabins and cottages were thus erected and the colony gradually increased to 500 or 600 people who bred fowls and ducks and pigs, and were famous for monster vegetables. Lanes and avenues were formed through the squatters' land, and St. Nicholas road now stands on what was Beehive lane . . .
>
> The rage for speculative building a few years ago rapidly changed the appearance of the whole neighbourhood, the squatters after some resistance had to give up their cabins . . .[13]

Even here the people had their own schools. Jane Lacey kept a school in Beehive Lane in 1851.[14] Ten years later, there were two schools in Ware's Gardens running north from Beehive Lane. These were kept by Sarah Barrow and Jane Carey, both in their seventies.[15] Finally, Maria Gill ran a school in Beehive Lane in 1871.[16] In the three latter cases, not only were all the teachers solitary, but — very unusually — each was the sole inhabitant of the dwelling. However, this would have been unusual only in the context of a conventional court or tenement dwelling. We have seen how different the area around Beehive Lane was, and it is likely that in these cases, the teacher's habitations were little one-roomed cabins.

One further, parenthetical, point arises here, well illustrating the possible confusions which this type of research has to encounter, and which we have drawn attention to elsewhere. Up to now, the research has suggested a total of four different teachers working in this area over a 20-year period. This might well lead us to ask questions of the kind that were faced in Chapter 3 about the restricted longevity of working-class private schools. It is only now, at the point of writing, and not during research or collation, that a simple mistake — due principally to the poor legibility of an enumeration book — comes to light. Jane *Lacey* is recorded in 1851 as a 'Schoolmistress', as being 61 years old and as married to a coachmaker. Her birthplace was Plymouth. Jane *Carey*'s details are, 'Keeps an Infant School'; 71 years old; a widow; born in Plymouth. The two Janes are therefore the same person, and suddenly, we have another school with a longevity of at least 10 years to add to the list. And exposed once again is the fragility, the ease of misconception inherent in the documentary record.

By 1871, schools kept in locations like those off Beehive Lane were on the decrease, and being replaced by those kept in the new suburban terraces. The total number of working-class private schools in the old districts of Redcliff and Temple, for example, fell from 36 in 1851, to 31 in 1861, and to 20 in 1871.

The chief feature of the new developments was the relatively greater degree of comfort, space, and sometimes privacy which they afforded. For many dwellers from the old city, such homes — though at two or three times the rental — must have seemed a substantial improvement. Most prized of all was the luxury of a separate front door; a personal control over the chaotic comings and goings of the tenement and the court. Relatively few of the new houses were however occupied by a single family as we will see if we look at some cases in more detail.

A convenient and compact example is the little development of Summertown, on the eastern outskirts of the town, which was defined by the loops of the railway lines leading west to South Wales and north to the Midlands. The handful of streets here appeared in the 1860s. By 1871, the little community supported four private schools — two in Chancery Street, one in Richmond Street and one in Lincoln Street.

The first house in Chancery Street was shared between two families. Most of the dwelling was occupied by a coal haulier, his laundress wife and their four children. Probably restricted to a room or two were Peter Osborn who, as a mariner, was probably away for considerable periods, and his 46-year-old wife Jane, who kept a school.[17]

Further up the same street was a haberdasher's shop, kept by lone spinster Elizabeth Burt. She shared the accommodation here with a widower, John Reynolds, a bed sacking weaver and his young daughter, Emma, returned as 'Private School Mistress'. In this case it was certainly as well that the dwelling had only three permanent residents, for we know from the 1870 Education Enquiry that Emma Reynold's school had a remarkable total of 60 pupils in regular attendance.[18]

In the next street — Lincoln Street — number 52 was once more a shared house, though again with only three occupants. These were a young labourer and his wife and a widow, Mary Rickard, whose occupation is given with unusual specification as 'Governess over 30 children'.[19]

Finally, at number 29 Richmond Street, we find a single family of four — William Webb, a tailor, his wife and their two daughters, Emma, a dressmaker, and Georgina, who kept a school here.[20]

Unfortunately, all three of these streets have been redeveloped and the buildings which housed the schools have left as few traces as those who kept them. This disappearance is, incidentally, not surprising in view of the fact that, 'houses in Lincoln Street, Richmond Street and Morton Street . . . were erected with "Sun baked (as distinct from kiln baked) bricks" on slate and tar foundations'.[21]

Nevertheless, we can get some idea of what they were like by turning to a sounder, surviving development, south of the river, in Totterdown. There were no houses here in 1861, but ten years later, a busy community — made up mostly of railway workers — was established. There were at least eight private schools in this new neighbourhood, the best documented example being that of Paulene Dibble, held at number 143 Oxford Street.

The Dibble family in 1871 comprised six individuals; James, a blacksmith, his wife, his mother-in-law, and three children, aged from 11 to 16. The remarkable feature of the school carried on here is not only its size — 61 children in attendance — but that it was run not by the mother, but by her eldest daughter, Paulene. At 16, she was the youngest recorded private school keeper in the city.[22]

Notes

1. On the growth of Bristol in the nineteenth century, see H. Meller, *Leisure and the Changing City, 1870–1914* (1976), pp. 19–35.
2. See J. Burnett, *A Social History of Housing, 1815–1970* (1978), p. 77.
3. *Homes of the Bristol Poor*, reprinted from the *Bristol Mercury* (1884), p. 86; also p. 98.
4. Ibid., p. 10.
5. P.R.O. H.O.107/1947.
6. P.R.O. H.O.107/1949.
7. *Homes of the Bristol Poor*, p. 19.
8. P.R.O. R.G.9/1733.
9. P.R.O. H.O.107/1949.
10. P.R.O. R.G.9/1712.
11. P.R.O. H.O.107/1947.
12. P.R.O. H.O.107/1947.
13. *Homes of the Bristol Poor*, pp. 34–5.
14. P.R.O. H.O.107/1949.
15. P.R.O. R.G.9/1719.
16. P.R.O. R.G.10/2529.
17. P.R.O. R.G.10/2560.
18. *Bristol Times and Mirror*, 24.12.1870, p. 2.
19. P.R.O. R.G.10/2660.
20. P.R.O. R.G.10/2660.
21. M. Dresser, 'People's Housing in Bristol 1870–1939', Bristol's Other History, I. Bild (ed.), (Bristol 1983), p. 141.
22. P.R.O. R.G.10/2509.

APPENDIX C: Evidence of G. W. Procter, the Perpetual Curate of St Stephen's, Devonport

How do you account for the fact that in neighbourhoods where there are good infant schools under inspection, many parents still prefer to send their young children to a dame's school?

a. Some, because the dame's school is nearer their own home.
b. Some, because the dames receive the children without any remark at whatever hour the parent sends them and makes no remarks about irregularity of attendance, or upon curl-papers, or showy dress, or necklaces, and the like.
c. Some, because the dames will receive the children if a parent is busy, as on a washing day, or is out charing or the like, as early as eight o'clock, or sometimes seven o'clock in the morning, and take care of it until seven or eight in the evening for an extra penny and its food.
d. Some, because the dames do not require the payments to be made in advance every Monday morning, but will allow them to stand over for three or four weeks or more, which gives them, they think, a hold on the child.
e. Some, because the parents prefer their young children to be under the care of a motherly woman.
f. Some, because they prefer a school in which there are not more than twenty or thirty children. They say they receive more individual care, and that diseases are less likely to be propagated.
g. Some, because they prefer their children should not have any play during school hours, and especially should not be sent out into the playground.
h. Some, because they object to their children being drilled and exercised physically. They say it makes them eat too much and grow too fast, and so cost too much food and raiment.
i. Some, because they think that sufficient time is not given to reading and spelling or needlework.
k. Some, because they think that the infant school attempts to teach them too much, and requires too much mental exercise.

l. Some, because they would rather pay 2d. or 3d. a week, where they can dictate to the teacher what they would have done or have left undone.
m. Some, because they would not receive aid from anyone in the education of their children.
n. Some, because they do not understand Government inspection, and have been moved by political leaders or by dissenting ministers or other dissenting agents, as by interested parties, to regard it as a scheme for interfering, sooner or later, some way or other, with the liberty of the subject.
o. Some think pupil-teachers are too uppish and take too much upon themselves, and that the public infant schoolmistress does not sympathize with them, and is too independent of them.

(Extracted from Cumin, *Newcastle*, vol. I, pp. 144–5.)

APPENDIX D: A Private School Sketch

Mrs Luff's School

Extracts from 'The Village School' in *Somerset Folk* (1938), by E. Horne.

A Yew-Tree with a pond beneath it, and beyond the tree a low, straggling house with a thatched roof . . . Built for a farm, perhaps two centuries earlier, . . . the house — too big for a cottage, and too inconvenient for anything better — seventy years ago became the only school in the village.

The chief room during the days the place was a farm, was just as useful when the house was a school. The flag-stoned kitchen, with its great fire-place, not only held all the children, but enabled teaching to go on while the dinner was being cooked. The teaching in those days was scanty and expensive. Twopence for each subject was a price that sadly limited the learning, when wages were eight or ten shillings a week, and the children at home about as numerous as the shillings. Boys learnt 'summing' and reading, girls sewing and writing or reading, rarely the two latter together. When one of these arts was acquired, the other might be begun, but not till then, for the school-fees were generally limited to fourpence. It was only the better class, such as farmers' sons and daughters, who could indulge in the luxury of three subjects at once, and bring a silver sixpence Saturdays.

The children sat on forms or chairs according to their size in the kitchen. There were no classes with titles, and the word 'standard' was not born till years after the time of which I write. The teaching was of a domestic nature, being mixed up with the housework and cookery, and sometimes even with the baby, when the school-mistress happened to possess one. The idea that the teaching of cookery or washing, or housewifery in school, is a modern development, is a complete mistake, for these subjects were taught in a most practical, if not in a very scientific, manner seventy or eighty years ago.

. . . Before the final preparations were made for the day's dinner, the children were arriving for school. It is a damp morning perhaps — one of those days when, without exactly raining, a 'Mendip mist' wets everything through and through in the gentlest and most unsuspecting manner. The children, damp with the 'misk' as they call it, stand inside the old fireplace. Three or four make a group on either side, some of the bigger ones standing on the stone seats at the back, and the girls spreading out their 'pinneys' with both hands, hold them to the blazing wood to dry. When a sufficient number of children has arrived, Mrs Luff, with a great swinging motion of her arms, drives the children from the fireplace to their forms, much as if they were a flock of hens. The girls get their needlework, the boys their slates, and teaching begins. A certain amount of poetry has to be learnt by heart, but this is reserved till later in the morning. Many interruptions of the work take place, and they have the merit of preventing it from becoming monotonous. Mr Luff puts his head in at the door, and requires help with a new sack of meal for the pigs, and Charlie Moon, one of the biggest boys, is told off to give the necessary assistance. Ten minutes later a tramp knocks and asks for food. Mrs Luff hands him out the solid bottom crust of a home-baked loaf, and shuts the door with a suddenness which shows she is not pleased. Then the class goes on.

The teacher looks at the clock, and decides that it is time 'to put the fowl down', as the roasting operation is described. That being determined on, the children are set to learn poetry, which always means that for a while household cares were about to occupy the teacher's attention. Then the fowl, having been previously spitted, is set before the fire to roast, . . . As soon as it begins to turn in a satisfactory way, Mrs Luff comes back to hear the poetry. . . .

. . . 'Please, mum, he be stopped', calls out one of the boys, alluding to the fowl, which had ceased to revolve.

'Go and start 'un again, then, and watch what do make 'un drug (catch). Take thee slate over there the while', says Mrs Luff; and adds, addressing the poetry class: 'Now go on, Lizzie Stock'. . . .

. . . 'He be too heavy underside, mum', is the verdict of the boy who had been set to watch the failings of the chicken. 'Wants a bit t'other side'.

Mrs Luff appears not to hear. 'Now say the two new verses, and don't spile 'um. Next maid'. . . .

. . . It is not easy, after a lapse of sixty or seventy years, to find out exactly what the children, particularly the boys, really did learn. . . .

. . . Mrs. Luff's mathematical powers seem to have been limited, and as boys were apt to be unruly if over pressed, sums occupied but a small place in the educational system.

Mrs Luff had a husband who took a useful, if somewhat secondary part in the teaching work of the establishment. When some boy had become more than ordinarily out of hand, it was Mr Luff who was called in to meet the emergency. The correction took various forms, for it depended on what the old gentleman was doing at the time. If he was working in the garden — worst of all, if he was putting sticks to the peas or beans — he generally had something to hand that would meet the requirements of the situation. If he was sweeping the stable, he arrived with the broom or the whip at the school door, in response to Mrs Luff's call of 'Richard!' in a tone of voice that neither he nor the culprit ever misunderstood. Strangest of all was when he was in his little bakehouse across the yard at the back — he baked bread for others besides himself, for the neighbours thought no oven so good as the one in the old farmhouse — and was sent for suddenly to quell a riot that had taken place among these bigger boys. The heads of a couple of the most deserving — chosen more by reputation than for actual guilt — would show marks of floury fingers, and then the baking was resumed. Sometimes, when unforseen difficulties arose in the boys' sums, and Mrs Luff was not equal to them — she was not intended to be — the slate was ordered to the bakehouse for solution. If just out of the oven, there were steaming pieces of soft crust to be deftly picked off, while Mr Luff, slate in hand, was busy explaining the rules of subtraction.

Such was this old village school, and such its simple ways and teaching.

I am sorry the history of Mrs Luff's teaching establishment has to end in a cloud, but some fifty years ago, the disappearance of her husband was one of our village tragedies. . . . His wife tried to keep up the school, for she had nothing else for her support, but it slowly failed. The numbers grew less and less, as the teaching became poorer and poorer, and at last the four or five children that remained did not return when the school opened again after the following summer. Mrs Luff had never recovered the loss of her husband . . .

APPENDIX E: A Failed School

Christopher Thomson was born in Hull in 1799. Initially, he became a shipwright, like his father, but subsequently, he followed a variety of employments which at one point included school-keeping. Thomson's case is interesting for its implicit recognition that although, in the words of the author, '. . . anybody could make a schoolmaster', he himself failed. With the impatience of the autodidact — shared by another similar school-keeper in Thomas Cooper — Thomson blamed this upon the apparent narrowness of working-class educational demand. Unable to adjust his product to satisfy this demand, Thomson's income from the school dried up. The decision to open the school in the first place was prompted in part by the rejection of Thomson's application for a vacant post at a National School at Tickhill in Yorkshire in 1827.

As I could not get a school with a name, and rations 'to match', I set up on my own account. I took a room in an old projecting-storied building, called St Leonard's Hospital; yes, and also put a paper in my window, expressive of my business, with 'N.B. No connection' appended thereto. In the 'old hospital' I opened a school for boys and girls to learn plain work. There can be no surprise excited at my 'keeping a school', anybody could make a schoolmaster. People must live; and as well to keep a school as do anything else; every sixpence will buy a loaf; and to be a schoolmaster is one of the few comfortable trades which require no previous training. It has pleased the guardian spirit of England's mind and morals to furnish her with ready-made 'maisters and dames' fitted for school; and I was one of them. O privileged nation!

I was not quite so easy in my new stool as there are many of the rulers of the birch; I had scarcely time to 'Ahem!' and measure the distance from wall to wall, and tuck my hands under my coat tails, before I began to count over my qualifications for a teacher. *Imprimis*: I could read a little, write a decent hand, and figure simples and a few compounds; but the practice 'made me mad'. True I had a few boys to teach, and the sixpennies of those who did pay were useful; but others of them forgot to bring their pence on

Mondays. Some of their mothers promised to pay another time; perhaps they may, but as it is now beyond the 'limitations' they need not fear an arrest from me. Again, I had to counter direct opposition in my new line, from the Orthodox. It was charged against me, that I refused to *beat* the boys because they could not 'say their spellings', and that, with such mildness, the boys would be saucy, and over-bearing; and those who did read under me, read their books more like reading a play, than the Bible; that by teaching them to read 'poetry and stuff', the boys would, at some future time, all run away from their masters, or parents, and turn players. With such reports current, my school was soon at a discount; I struggled on for a time, but the school returns were insufficient for my family. By necessity I kept the school, until prejudice prevented it from keeping me. In vain I looked around for some means of support; I could discover none, except by a return to my former vocation in the Theatre. *The Autobiography of an Artisan* (1847), pp. 207–8.

APPENDIX F: A Private Schooling

John Harris was born at Camborne in 1820, the son of a copper miner. His recollections of schooling are worth recording in some detail.

Then came my first journey down the hill to Dame Trezona's school in the hamlet of Bolennowe under the trees, where I sat upon a low cricket to learn the ABC. She had some half-a-dozen boys and girls in all; and I was soon considered to be the best scholar in her establishment. I do not remember much about her at this far distance, only that she had reddish hair gathered under a high cap, that she wore spectacles and a cotton bedgown, and took snuff. I made fair proficiency in all the scholastic arts she could inculcate, and soon became very fond of books. My father presented me with a penny Robinson Crusoe with a rude frontispiece, which I carried to my bedchamber with me every night. This was my first book, except the school primer, which I could really call my own . . .

I did not continue very long under the tuition of Dame Trezona, but entered a similar institution kept by a woman named Penpraze, which was held in Troon Chapel . . . Leaving her and the old edifice, I was placed under the care of a harsh pedagogue, whose name, I believe, was Reed. He had a great number of boys under his charge, some of whom, I suppose, were unruly enough. But his discipline was singularly severe . . . I felt disheartened and begged to be sent to some other academy . . .

My next teacher was a miner, a mild pious man, of the name of Roberts. He had met with an accident in his work underground, depriving him of a leg, which was badly supplied with a wooden stump. In those days any shattered being wrecked in the mill or mine, if he could read John Bunyan, count fifty backwards, and scribble the squire's name, was considered good enough for a pedagogue; and when he could do nothing else, was established behind a low desk in a school. I do not think John Roberts' acquirements extended beyond reading, writing and arithmetic . . . His seminary was a thatched house by the road-side, in a poorly-cultivated district . . . Here I improved myself in reading, and learnt to write and spell, and to experience the puzzle of figures . . .

At nine years of age I was taken from school and put to work in the fields, to drive the horses in the plough . . . *My Autobiography* (1882), pp. 23–32.

APPENDIX G (i): Extracts from a letter from 'T.' to the School Board Chronicle

'SCHOOL' AS DEFINED BY THE LIVERPOOL BYE-LAWS

To the Editor of the *School Board Chronicle.*

Sir,

With a view to show, to some extent, the operation of these bye-laws, allow me to sketch a scene or two. The bye-laws of B ——. having been passed and approved by the Education Department, are put into force. An officer for this purpose has been appointed and duly instructed. Said officer, according to such instructions, is anxious to act with prompt energy and strict impartiality . . . We will take a case the like of which must occur in considerable numbers whenever compulsory bye-laws of the type given are attempted to be enforced. We vouch for the accuracy of the characters introduced as well as for the sentiments expressed by them.

In the court, a working shoemaker, whose earnings, with considerable fluctuations, average fifteen shillings weekly, has been summoned on account of his boy, aged six years, not attending a public elementary school. It is known to 'the officer' that the boy is attending a dame's school, and that he may possibly be well looked after and taught; but, as the man is recognised by his neighbours as a sensible and well-meaning man, they say that if he is to be allowed to act as he pleases in the matter of sending his boy where he likes, they shall do the same, and so send their children either anywhere or nowhere to school as they please. The officer, therefore, very rightly determines that, to settle the point of the parent's right to do as he thinks best, he must select some such case as the one now before us; we will call him Mr. C.:—

Mag.: Mr. C., you are summoned here, charged with a breach of the School Board bye-laws. What have you to say for yourself?

Mr. C.: Well, your worship, I do the best I can for our little Johnny. You see, he has taken that liking to Mrs. D., and she do make them so happy like, that there's no keeping the little chap from his school at all. It really do go agin me to think of taking our Johnny away to send him to one of them big schools. And there's our girl Mary, she were taught by Mrs. D., and though she is now not thirteen years old, yet her mistress says she's the best girl she ever had in her nursery yet.

Mag.: Then am I to understand that you do send your boy to school?

Mr. C.: Oh, yes. We ain't got any book larning ourselves, but we always said as Johnny should, as long as we could scrape together the few pence for his schooling. And Mrs. D. is not hard, I must say that for her; for when I was laid up and my missus wasn't strong, she wouldn't have the boy stay away, and said she know'd we'd pay her when we got round again.

Mag.: Yes, yes; that is all very well, but why get yourself into trouble by sending your boy to a place that is no school at all, when you might put him to a real school, approved by the Board, without any more expense?

Mr. C.: Why, as I said, the boy is that looked after, and he do go so pleasantly, and at night he reads that pretty, and cons over his lessons and puts down his figures, that I am sure he couldn't do no better if he was put to the Queen's own school, . . .

Mag.: You really do believe that he is learning as much with Mrs. D. as he would do if you sent him to a public school?

Mr. C. (brightening): Bless your heart. I really do believe he is learning More than he would anywhere else; for I know he would fret if he was took away; and that wouldn't help him in his learning anyway. Would it, now?

Mag.: Well, we must look into this. Policeman, go to Mrs. D.'s and ask her if she will be so good as to come here with you.

(Mrs. D., a plain and timid woman, dressed inexpensively, but in good taste, soon makes her appearance.)

Mag.: I hope I have not particularly troubled you by asking you to come here, but we want to know why this good man does not keep the School Board bye-laws.

Mrs. D.: Thank your worship. I was a little nervous when the policeman said that I was wanted here; but I shall be very glad if I can say anything for Mr. C., for he really does care for his children.

Mag.: Then you keep a school, Mrs. D., and this man's son attends your school?

Mrs. D.: Yes. I have kept a school for several years; and John C. is a good little boy, and comes very regularly.

Mag.: Do you hold a certificate? or has your school ever been inspected?

Mrs. D.: Oh, no! Mine is only a small private school; or, as some now call it, an adventure school.

Mag.: Then I do not see that I can admit it to be a school at all. It certainly is not according to these bye-laws.

Mrs. D. (a little excited): Not a school at all! Why, I teach them all myself. I do not set one to mind the rest. While I am hearing one class —

Mag. (interrupting): That is all right enough, Mrs. D., but were you ever trained in one of the colleges?

Mrs. D.: No, I never went to a training college . . . but I taught my brother and sisters; and when my husband died I thought I would rather teach than get my living in any other way.

Mag. (aside): I cannot convict this man; for to do so would be to force him to send his child to what may be a worse school. It would eventually shut up a good school that costs the public nothing, and deprive this good and brave woman of her living. The bye-laws may have been well intended, but they must have been hastily drawn. (In court, to Mr. C.): You have clearly infringed these School Board bye-laws, though without any intention to disobey the law of the land (in fact, I do not know that you have done that). The case stands over. I will consult some of my fellow-magistrates. (To Mrs. D.): I thank you for your attendance and evidence. You can go on with your school for the present. By-the-bye, would you object to any gentleman acquainted with school matters coming to your school, and then reporting what he thinks about it?

Mrs. D.: I am afraid I should be very nervous, and the children might be timid; but if the gentleman knew all about schools for little children, he would know how to deal with that. I should not object. And if he would be kind enough to point out anything that could be done better, I am sure I would try to carry it out.

Mag. (to School Board Clerk): Will you be so good as to represent to your Board the dilemma in which I am placed by the forced meaning they thrust upon the word 'school'? Either I must admit, with Mr. C., that your bye-laws go beyond the powers conferred, and are therefore waste paper; or, as in the last case, I must convict against my own conscience.

Clerk: I will do so. Can you suggest any modification that would meet the case?

Mag.: Officially I cannot. As one anxious to see the Act operative for good, I may say that the great difficulty would be removed, if you cancelled your present definition of school, and substituted for it a definition declaring that a school is any place of education that has been declared efficient by a person duly appointed, either by the Education Department or the School Board. The definition of the Act would then remain intact. I think that some such course has been recommended to the London Board by a committee appointed to consider the 74th Section of the Act.

Clerk: It is so. The difficulty was seen and pointed out by one of our own Board, but it was thought a frivolous objection.

Mag.: You know my opinion. The sooner you amend your bye-laws the sooner I shall be able to co-operate with you in putting the compulsory powers conferred by the Act into force.

Bristol, August 2nd., 1871. *T.*

(From the *School Board Chronicle*, 12 August 1871. pp. 407–8.)

APPENDIX G (ii): Memorial to the Education Department from the Hartlepool School Board

To

The Right Honourable the Lords
of the Committee of
Her Majesty's Most Honourable Privy Council on Education.

The Memorial of the School Board for the District of Hartlepool

Sheweth:—

First:— That difficulties are experienced by this Board in enforcing their Bye-Laws especially with reference to Dame or Adventure Schools.

Second:— That the experience of some School Boards proves that the efficiency of a School is a question left entirely to the discretion of the Magistrate, and this view is confirmed by the opinion of Counsel, which has been obtained by one of the large Boards.

Third:— That the Magistrates in some towns seldom, if ever, convict if the parent shews that the child is in attendance (even irregularly) at a Dame or Adventure School; and they appear to hold the opinion that the parent should have free choice of any school and that the Dames' Schools are efficient for the class of children attending them.

Fourth:— That the effect of such decisions in cases where pressure has been brought to bear upon irregular attendants at Public Elementary Schools, is that to evade the operation of the Bye-Laws the children are removed to Dames' Schools, in which they are practically getting no Education, and this Board have reason to believe that these inefficient schools, so far from decreasing, are actually increasing in number, and they are aware of their previously impeding the work of Education in Denominational, as well as in Board Schools.

Fifth:— That under the direction of the Government, the various Boards are building Schools for all the children now attending these inefficient Schools, consequently it must have

have been contemplated that these children would gradually be drafted into Public Elementary Schools.

Sixth:— That although it is possible that all Boards may not have experienced the difficulty to the same extent that we have, yet a more clearly stated law, as to what is 'an efficient School' will greatly facilitate their operations, as well as have the effect of causing the decisions of the Magistrates to be more uniform.

Seventh:— That the remedy this Board proposes is an annual inspection and registration of all Schools through the Education Department, so that the question of efficiency shall be decided by a competent Government Official, instead of being left, as at present, to the varying discretion of individual Magistrates: the admission or omission of the name of any particular School from such Register to be conclusive evidence of the efficiency or inefficiency of the School concerned.

Eighth:— That your Memorialists earnestly hope that now your Lordships have been made acquainted with the above facts you will cause such steps to be taken as will secure to your Memorialists the results desired in Clause seven hereof.

On behalf of the Hartlepool School Board this fourteenth day of January, 1875.

D. R. Falconer — Chairman of the said Board
Robert Edgar — Clerk of the said Board

N.B. This is the only such memorial preserved at the P.R.O.; other identical documents have been destroyed.

APPENDIX G (iii): Circular 103

1st September, 1875

Sir,

I am directed to request that your Board will have the goodness to furnish me, for the information of the Education Department, with certain particulars requesting the Private Adventure Schools (i.e. Schools carried on by Teachers at their own risk and for their own emolument) within the District of the Board.

The following are the points upon which detailed information is specially requested.

1. The number of Adventure Schools that were in existence when your Board submitted to the Education Department its First report on the School supply of their District.
2. The number of children that could be accommodated in such Schools, or who were, at that date, in attendance at them.
3. The number of Schools of this class (with the amount of accommodation) that were recognised by the Department as *efficient*, after the Reports of your Board and of the Inspectors of Returns had been received and dealt with.
4. The number of Adventure Schools existing now, (or at any recent date) and of Scholars attending them.
5. The efficiency of these Schools.

and 6. Their sanitary condition.

My Lords would also be glad to be favoured with the remarks of your Board as to the increase, or decrease, in the number of these Schools, during the last few years, and the reasons for it; as well with such suggestions as the Board may wish to submit to them, in reference to the best mode of dealing with any difficulties, in the enforcement of compulsory Bye-Laws, that may be caused by the existence of this class of Schools.

I have . . .

F. R. Sandford

APPENDIX H (i): Mr Bates' Report

COUNTY BOROUGH OF WALSALL.
REPORT OF MR S. BATES CHIEF ATTENDANCE OFFICER.
MISS BEETLESTONE'S SCHOOL

During the week ending Friday May 4th. 1917, I left this school under observation on the following days; Monday morning and afternoon, Tuesday morning and afternoon and Thursday morning and afternoon.

Monday morning 30th April.

Miss Beetlestone arrived at 9-57 together with two boys and two girls.

10-5 13 children entered school.

10-18 1 boy left school.

10-30 I met Winnie Mead aged 13, Leah Mead 11, Ethel Beetlestone 6 years, in Victoria Street. These three children would not arrive at school before 10-35 a.m.

12-0 Miss Beetlestone left school.

Monday afternoon 30th April.

2-55 Miss Beetlestone arrived. After some little delay she entered the schoolroom at the rear and then admitted three children by the front door.

3-1 A girl with a baby arrived.

3-3 Two boys arrived, one of whom immediately left and returned at 3-7.

3-10 Seven boys and three girls arrived.

3-50 Four girls left.

4-0 One girl and one boy left.

4-4 All the children left with Miss Beetlestone.

Note The maximum time spent in school by Miss Beetlestone was one hour six minutes.

Thursday morning 1st May.

10-18 Miss Beetlestone arrived and entered school accompanied by seven girls and four boys.

10-20 Two girls and two boys arrived.
10-25 One boy arrived.
10-45 One girl arrived.
11-0 Five boys and two girls left school.
11-10 One boy and one girl came out of school and played about the street until 11-38.
11-10 Two girls entered school for the first time that morning.
11-30 Remainder of children left school.
11-32 Miss Beetlestone left school.
11-35 Miss Beetlestone re-entered school, with three boys and two girls.
11-35 A boy left school and returned at 11-45 with two other boys who had left school at 11.
12-0 Scholars dismissed from school.
12-7 Miss Beetlestone left school.

Note Girl who came to school at 10-45 could not have received more than *one hour fifteen minutes* instruction. Three boys and two girls who left school at 11-0 and returned at 11-32 not more than *68 minutes*. Two girls who entered school at 11-10 not more than *50 minutes*.

Tuesday afternoon 1st May.
2-58 Miss Beetlestone arrived.
2-59 A girl left school and returned with two girls at 3–6.
3-5 Two girls entered school.
3-6 Four girls entered school.
3-7 Two girls entered school.
3-10 Three boys entered school.
3-37 Miss Beetlestone and twenty children left school. I followed them to Palfrey Park, where the boys sat down on the grass, while the girls played about in twos and threes. These children did not receive instruction of any kind.
3-55 Miss Beetlestone came from the bottom end of the park and on her way six children joined her. She went to the schoolroom and immediately left again, going up Dale Street to-wards home.

Note The maximum time any child was under instruction this afternoon was thirty-nine minutes. 11 of the children did not receive more than thirty-two minutes instruction.

Thursday morning 3rd May.

9-55	Miss Beetlestone arrived with one girl who immediately left and returned at 10-0 with 4 boys and 2 girls.
10-5	1 boy and 2 girls arrived.
10-15	2 girls and 2 boys arrived.
10-50	16 children left school.
10-54	Miss Beetlestone left school.
11-10	2 boys and 4 girls returned and played about until Miss Beetlestone returned at 11-28.
11-30	2 girls left school.
11-35	2 girls and 1 boy returned to school.
11-40	6 boys and 2 girls returned to school.
11-55	18 children left school.
11-59	Miss Beetlestone left school.

Thursday afternoon 3rd May.

2-55	Miss Beetlestone arrived accompanied by a boy.
3-2	2 girls arrived.
3-28	10 girls and 9 boys with Miss Beetlestone left school, some going to-wards Palfrey Park and 2 boys and three girls going towards Whitehall Road. These 2 boys asked others to go with them to New Mills, but on being refused promised to see them 'tomorrow'.
3-38	2 children left the park, passed the school and went off.
3-39	3 children returned from the park, passed the school and went off.

Note The maximum instruction given this afternoon was *33 minutes*, in the case of 10 girls and 9 boys.

APPENDIX H (ii): Mr Arnold's Report

The following is a fair account of the examination as undertaken by the presiding Magistrate on this occasion.

Calling the boy to his side the Magistrate asked him to spell the word 'Matthew'. The boy started, 'm a t' and hesitated, 'h' supplied the Magistrate, 'h' says the boy, 'e u', 'no' 'w' says the Magistrate, and the boy promptly spelt it 'M a t h e w'. The latter was next asked to spell the word 'George', which he did correctly. 'Spell Thomas' the Magistrate asked the boy, 'T o m a s' says the boy, and before the Magistrate could come to the assistance of the lad the prosecuting Solicitor asked him to note the omission. The Magistrate next asked the boy to spell 'Ironmonger' in two parts 'iron' and 'monger'. 'I o n' says the boy, repeated three times in spite of every encouragement and assistance given him. The boy then proceeded to spell the latter part of the word and started 'm o n' and hesitated, 'ger' says the Magistrate, 'g, e, r' says the boy and in this way spelt 'ironmonger' to the satisfaction of the Bench. The boy was then asked to name any large river and replied, 'The Severn'. When asked where the Severn flowed into he replied, 'The Irish Sea', which answer was accepted by the Magistrate. 'What river is the City of London built upon?' was the next question and the boy answered correctly 'The Thames'. This encouraged the Magistrate to go outside England and he asked what river the City of Paris was built upon, taking care to express himself that he did not expect the boy would be able to answer it. Following no attempt from the boy he promptly withdrew the question. The last question put was, 'Which is the nearest seaside place to Walsall?' and the boy replied 'Rhyl', not so much from his accurate knowledge of Geography as probably this was the only seaside place he had been to.

The Magistrates' Clerk examined the boy in reading, giving him some paper and doing his best to coax him to read from it. Between a series of sobs the boy eventually emitted a few sounds which appeared to satisfy the Magistrates' Clerk that nothing was lacking in reading.

The boy was finally asked to write his name on the paper supplied by the clerk, which was handed to the Magistrate, who was again apparently satisfied with his writing.

This is the examination upon which the Magistrates satisfied themselves that the boy was receiving an Education consistent with that received by the average school boy of Walsall.

J. Arnold, B.A.,
Member of Education Committee, Walsall.

BIBLIOGRAPHY

The following abbreviations are used in the bibliography:

B.J.E.S.	*British Journal of Educational Studies*
C.C.E.	*Minutes of the Committe of Council on Education*
C.E.C.	*Children's Employment Commission*
J.E.A.H.	*Journal of Educational Administration and History*
J.S.S.	*Journal of the Statistical Society*
M.S.S.	*Manchester Statistical Society*

Primary Sources

(a) *Public Record Office*

Population Census: Enumerators' Books
H.O. 107/1947 – H.O. 107/1955
R.G. 9/1712 – R.G. 9/1724
R.G. 9/1703 – R.G. 9/1706
R.G. 9/1725 – R.G. 9/1730
R.G. 9/1733 – R.G. 9/1739
R.G. 10/2519 – R.G. 10/2538
R.G. 10/2505 – R.G. 10/2510
R.G. 10/2539 – R.G. 10/2550
R.G. 10/2556 – R.G. 10/2560
R.G. 10/574
R.G. 10/580
R.G. 10/582 – R.G. 10/584

Education Series
Ed. 3 — Education Returns, London. 1871 to 1901.
Ed. 15 — Private Schools not recognised for Grant or Efficiency. 1914 to 1944.
Ed. 16 — L.E.A. Supply Files. 1870 to 1921.
Ed. 18 — L.E.A. Attendance Files. 1871 to 1927.
Ed. 10/11 — Memorials.
Ed. 12/378; Ed. 12/406–408 — Secondary Education. General Files.
Ed. 14/42 — General Files.

(b) *G.L.C. Record Office*

S.B.L. 1518. School Board for London. Tables of the Elementary Schools within the District of the Metropolis. August 1871.

(c) *Walsall Record Office*

Education Committee Minutes, 1916–17.
Beetlestone Papers.

(d) *Bristol Record Office*

Minute Books: Bedminster School Board, 1875–81.
Bristol School Board, 1871–6.
Admissions Registers: St Augustine's Holy School, 1873–88.
St Augustine's Girls' School, 1873–92.
North St Infants and Junior, 1858–63.
North St Infants and Junior, 1863–74.
North St Boys', 1867–84.
North St Girl's, 1859–68.
Barton Hill Boys', 1875–85.
Maze St Girls', 1874–98.
Log Books: St Augustine's Infants', 1863–93.
St Augustine's Boys', 1863–82.
St Augustine's Girls', 1863–80.

(e) *Greater Manchester Record Office*

Reports of Manchester Statistical Society, 1836–8.

(f) *Parliamentary Papers*

Minutes of the Committee of the Privy Council on Education, 1839–58.
Reports of the Committee of the Privy Council on Education, 1859–84.

1819 (224) ix, Pt. 1	Digest of Returns to . . . the Select Committee on the Education of the Poor.
1820 (151) xii	General Table showing the State of Education in England.
1833 (450) xx	First Report from Commissioners (Factories Inquiry Commission).
1835 (62) xli, xlii, xliii	Abstract of Answers and Returns relative to the state of Education . . .
1837–8 (589) vii	Report from Select Committee on the Education of the Poorer Classes.
1840 (639) xxiv	Copy of Report by Mr Hickson on the Condition of the Handloom Weavers.
1840 [217] xxiii	Handloom Weavers. Reports from Assistant Commissioners.
1840 [220] xxiv	Handloom Weavers. Reports from Assistant Commissioners.
1842 [381]xvi	C.E.C. Appendix to First Report (Mines), Pt I.
1842 [382] xvii	C.E.C. Appendix to First Report (Mines), Pt II.
1842 (31) [410] xxii	Reports from Inspectors of Factories.
1843 [430] xiii	C.E.C. Second Report of the Commissioners on Trades and Manufactures.
1843 [429] [523] xxvii	Reports from Inspectors of Factories.
1843 [431] xiv	C.E.C. Appendix to Second Report (Trades and Manufactures), Pt I.
1843 [432] xv	C.E.C. Appendix to Second Report (Trades and Manufactures), Pt II.
1844 [524] [583] xxviii	Reports from Inspectors of Factories.
1845 [639] xxv	Reports from Inspectors of Factories.
1846 [681] [721] xx	Reports from Inspectors of Factories.
1847 [779] [828] xv	Reports from Inspectors of Factories.

1847 [870] xxvii Pt I	Education in Wales. R. Comm. Reports.
1847–8 [900] [957] xxvi	Reports from Inspectors of Factories.
1849 [1017] [1084] xxii	Reports from Inspectors of Factories.
1850 [1141] [1239] xxiii	Reports from Inspectors of Factories.
1851 [1304] [1396] xxiii	Reports from Inspectors of Factories.
1852 [1439] [1500] xxi	Reports from Inspectors of Factories.
1852 (499) xi	Education in Manchester, Salford. Select Committee.
1852–3 (571) xxiv	Education in Manchester, Salford. Select Committee.
1861 [2794] xxi Pts 1–6	State of Popular Education in England. R. Comm. (Newcastle).
1863 [3170] xviii	C.E.C. Reports of Commissioners with Appendices. First Report.
1864 [3414] xxii	Second Report.
1864 [3414] xxix	Third Report.
1865 [3548] xx	Fourth Report.
1866 [3678] xxiv	Fifth Report.
1867–8 [3966] xxviii. Pt 1.	Schools Inquiry. R. Comm. Report.
1867–8 [3966–VIII] xxviii. Pt VIII.	R. Comm. General Reports. Midland Counties and Northumberland.
1870 (91) liv	Schools for the Poorer Classes in Birmingham, Leeds, Liverpool and Manchester. Special Reports.
1871 (201) lv	Return: Elementary Education (Civil Parishes).
1876 [1443] xxix	Report of Commissioners . . . Factory and Workshops Acts.
1876 [1443–I] xxx	Reports of Commissioners . . . Factory and Workshops Acts . . . Minutes of Evidence.
1897 [8447] xxv	Special Reports on Educational Subjects.
1898 [8943] xxiv	Special Reports on Educational Subjects.
1906 [2726] xc	Report on Children under Five . . . by Women Inspectors of the Board of Education.
1908 [3944] lxxxii	Regulations and Conditions affecting recognition . . . under Sec. 48 of the Elementary Education Act, 1876 . . .
1908 [4259] lxxxii	Report of Consultative Commission upon the School Attendance of Children below the age of five.

(g) *Newspapers and Periodicals*

Barnsley Chronicle
The Barrow Times
The Birmingham Daily Mail
Bristol Times and Mirror
Education
The Gloucestershire Chronicle
The Hull Packet and East Riding Times
School Board Chronicle
School Board Directory
School Government Chronicle
Sheffield and Rotherham Independent

The Times
The Times Educational Supplement
Walsall Observer
Walsall Pioneer
Western Daily Press

Nineteenth-century Books and Articles

Anon., 'A Condemned Institution', in *Good Words*, vol. 14 (1873), pp. 745–9.
'A Working Man', 'On the Education of the Working Classes' in *Cornhill Magazine*, vol. xlv (1866), pp. 283–98.
'An Assistant Master', *Private Schools and Schoolmasters* (1892).
Adams, Francis, *The History of the Elementary School Contest in England* (1882; rep. 1972).
Armstead, J., *On the Means possessed by the Church for the Education of the People* (1847).
Baines, Edward, *The Social, Educational and Religious State of the Manufacturing Districts* (1843).
———, 'On the Progress and Efficiency of Voluntary Education in England', in *Crosby-Hall Lectures on Education* (1848), pp. 3–50.
Barnard, Howard C., *On the Education of the Poor* (1809).
Bartley, George C. T., *The Schools for the People* (1871).
———, *One Square Mile in the East End of London*, 2nd edn (1870).
Blacket, Joseph, *Specimens of the Poetry of Joseph Blacket, with an account of his Life . . .* (1809).
Blatchford, Robert, *Dismal England* (1899).
Brierley, Benjamin, *Home Memories and Recollections of a Life* (1886).
———, *Job Thatcher's School* (1889).
Brougham, Henry, *Practical Observations on the Education of the People* (1825).
Bruce, Henry A., 'Address on National Education', *Transactions of the National Association for the Promotion of Social Science* (1867).
Carleton, William, *The Life of William Carleton* (1896).
Clare, John, *Sketches in the Life of John Clare* (1821).
Coleridge, Derwent, *The Education of the People* (1861).
Cooper, Thomas, *The Life of Thomas Cooper Written by Himself* (1872).
Couling, Samuel, *Our Labouring Classes: Their Intellectual, Moral and Social Condition Considered* (1851).
Craik, Henry, *The State in its Relation to Education* (1884).
Engels, Frederick, *The Condition of the Working Class in England* (1892; rep. 1969).
Fisher, Paul H., *Notes and Reminiscences of Stroud* (1871).
Fitch, Joshua G., 'Unsolved Problems in National Education', *Fortnightly Review* (1874), p. 754.
Gregory, Robert, *Elementary Education: Some Account of its Rise and Progress in England* (1895).
Hamilton, Henry P., *Practical Remarks on Popular Education* (1847).
Hamilton, W. R., 'Popular Education in England and Wales before and after the Elementary Education Act of 1870', *J.S.S.*, vol. 46 (1883), pp. 283–340.
Hampton, Richard, *Foolish Dick: An Autobiography of Richard Hampton, the Cornish Pilgrim Preacher*, ed. S. W. Christophers (1873).
Harris, John, *My Autobiography* (1882).
Hawkes, Henry, *Recollections of John Pounds* (1884).

Herbert, A., 'State Education: Help or Hindrance?', *Fortnightly Review* (1880), esp. pp. 50–7.
Hiley, Richard W., *Sundry Attacks on Private Schools* (1884).
Hill, Alfred (ed.), *Essays upon Educational Subjects* (1857; rep. 1971).
Hillocks, James I., *Life Story* (1860).
Hogg, James, *The Mountain Bard* (1807).
Holcroft, Thomas, *Memoirs of the Late Thomas Holcroft* (1816).
Hole, James, *Light, More Light!* (1861).
Holman, Henry, *English National Education* (1898).
Hook, Walter F., *On the Means of Rendering more Efficient the Education of the People* (1846).
Jones, John, *Attempts in verse . . . With some account of the Writer, Written by Himself . . .* (1831).
Kay-Shuttleworth, James, *The Moral and Physical Condition of the Working Classes Employed in the Cotton Manufacture in Manchester* (1832).
———, *The Education of the Poor in English and German Towns* (1853).
———, *Four Periods of Public Education* (1862).
———, 'Some Results of the 1870 Act and Code of 1870', *Fortnightly Review* (1876), pp. 685–705.
Kilgour, Agnes A., *Private Schools: Their Future Status* (1886).
Lackington, James, *Memoirs of the First 45 Years of the Life of J. Lackington* (1803).
Lee, John B., *Middle Class Education and the Endowed Schools Act* (1885).
Love, David, *The Life, Adventures and Experiences of David Love* (Nottingham, 1824).
Lovett, William, *The Life and Struggles of William Lovett* (1876).
Lovett, William and Collins, John, *Chartism: a New Organization of the People*, 2nd edn (1841).
Mackenzie, William W., *A Treatise on the Elementary Education Acts 1870–1891* (1892).
Morris, Master William, *Swindon Fifty Years Ago* (1885).
Peek, Francis, 'The Progress of Education in England', *Contemporary Review* (1879), pp. 862–74.
Pole, Thomas, *Observations Relative to Infant Schools* (Bristol, 1823).
Robertson, Mrs (Hannah), *The life of Mrs. Robertson . . .* (Derby, 1791).
Robertson, William A. S., *Middle Class Education* (1882).
Sadler, M. E. and Edwards, J. W., 'Some Statistics of Elementary Education in 1883', *Special Reports on Educational Subjects*, vol. 2 (1898), pp. 434–544.
———, 'Public Elementary Education in England and Wales 1870–1895', *Special Reports on Educational Subjects* (1896–7), pp. 1–71.
St John, James A., *The Education of the People* (1858).
Scott, W. A., *Middle Class Education* (1882).
Senior, Nassau, *Suggestions on Popular Education* (1861).
Somerville, Alexander, *The Autobiography of a Working Man* (1848).
Stow, David, *National Education: The Duty of England* (1847).
Surtees, Scott F., *Education for the People* (1846).
Symons, Jellinger C., *School Economy* (1858).
Thomson, Christopher, *The Autobiography of an Artisan* (1847).
Winks, W. E., *Lives of Illustrious Shoemakers* (1883).
Wolfram, H., *The Private Tutor's 'raison d'etre'* (1885).
Wyles, Thomas, *The Fitness of the Private School to British Wants and the British Character* (1886).
Wyse, Thomas, *Education in the United Kingdom — Progress and Prospects (1837).*

Twentieth-century Books and Articles

Adamson, John W., *A Short History of Education* (1919).
———, *English Education, 1789–1902* (1930).
Altick, Richard D., *The English Common Reader* (Chicago, 1957).
Archer, Richard L., *Secondary Education in the Nineteenth Century* (1921).
Atkinson, N., *Irish Education* (Dublin, 1969).
Avery, Gillian, *School Remembered — An Anthology* (1967).
Bagley, John J. and A. J., *The State and Education in England and Wales, 1833–1968* (1969).
Bailey, Peter, *Leisure and Class in Victorian England* (1978).
Balfour, Graham, *The Education Systems of Great Britain and Ireland* (1903).
Ball, Nancy, 'Elementary School Attendance and Voluntary Effort before 1870', *History of Education*, vol. 2 (1973), pp. 19–34.
Baron, Steve *et al. Unpopular Education* (1981).
Barnard, Howard C., *A Short History of English Elementary Education 1769–1944* (1947).
Barrell, G. R., *Teachers and the Law*, 4th edn (1975).
———, *Legal Cases for Teachers* (1970).
Bartle, G. F., *The History of Borough Road College* (1976).
Bernstein, Basil, *Class, Codes and Control* vol. 3, 2nd edn (1977).
Besant, Walter, *East London* (1903).
Bingham, John H., *The Period of the Sheffield School Board* (1949).
Binns, Henry B., *A Century of Education* (1908).
Birchenough, Charles, *History of Elementary Education in England and Wales*, 2nd edn (1925).
Bourne, Richard and MacArthur, Brian, *The Struggle for Education, 1870–1970* (1970).
Bradford Corporation, *Education in Bradford, 1870–1970* (1970).
Bryant, Margaret E., 'Topographical Resources: Private and Secondary Education in Middlesex from the Sixteenth Century to the Twentieth Century', in T. G. Cook, *Local Studies and the History of Education* (1972), pp. 99–122.
Burke, Peter, *Popular Culture in Early Modern Europe* (1978).
Burman, Sandra (ed.), *Fit Work for Women* (1979).
Burnett, J. (ed.), *Destiny Obscure* (1982).
Chancellor, Valerie (ed.), *Master and Artisan in Victorian England* (1969).
Clarke, John *et al.* (ed.), *Working Class Culture* (1979).
Clarke, Joseph N., *Education in Horncastle* (1970).
Colls, Robert, 'Oh Happy English Children!: Coal, Class and Education in the North-East', *Past and Present*, no. 73 (1976), pp. 75–99.
Corrigan, Paul and Frith, Simon, 'The Politics of Youth Culture', in, *Resistance Through Rituals*, T. Jefferson (ed.) (1975), pp. 231–9.
Corrigan, Philip (ed.), *Capitalism, State Formation and Marxist Theory*(1980).
Crossick, G. (ed.), *The Lower Middle Class in Britain 1870–1914* (1977).
Cullen, Michael, *The Statistical Movement in early Victorian Britain* (1975).
Curtis, Stanley J., *History of Education in Great Britain* (1948; 7th edn 1967).
Curtis, Stanley J. and Boultwood, Myrtle, *An Introductory History of English Education Since 1800* (1960).
Dale, Roger *et al., Schooling and Capitalism* (1976).
Dale, Roger, 'The Structural Context of Teaching', Unit 5, *Schooling and Society*, O.U. E202 (1977).
Dale, Roger and Esland, Geoff, 'Mass Schooling', Units 2–3, *Schooling and Society*, O.U. E202 (1977).
Davies, Brian, *Education and Social Control* (1976).

Davies, David, 'Popular Culture, Class and Schooling', Unit 9, *Society, Education and the State*, O.U. E353 (1981).
Davies, Maud F., *Life in an English Village*(1909).
Davies, Ross, *Women and Work* (1975).
Dent, Harold, C., *1870–1970. Century of Growth in English Education* (1970).
Dick, Malcolm, 'The Myth of the Working Class Sunday School', *History of Education*, vol. 9 (1980), pp. 27–41.
Digby, Ann and Searby, Peter, *Children, School and Society in Nineteenth Century England* (1981).
Dobbs, Archibald E., *Education and Social Movements, 1700–1850* (1919).
Donajgrodzki, Anthony (ed.), *Social Control in Nineteenth Century Britain* (1977).
Dowling, P. J., *The Hedge Schools of Ireland* (Dublin, n.d.).
———, *A History of Irish Education* (Cork, 1971).
Eaglesham, Eric, *From School Board to Local Authority* (1956).
———, *The Foundations of Twentieth Century Education* (1967).
Edwards, Bernard, *The Burston School Strike* (1974).
Elias, Eileen, *On Sundays We Wore White* (1978).
Entwistle, Harold, *Antonio Gramsci. Conservative Schooling for Radical Politics* (1979).
Esland, Geoff, 'Schooling and Pedagogy', Unit 6, *Schooling and Society*, O.U. E202 (1977).
Field, J. L., 'Private Schools in Portsmouth and Southampton, 1850–1870', *J.E.A.H.*, vol. X (1978), pp. 8–14.
Finn, Dan *et al.*, 'Social Democracy, Education and the Crisis', in *On Ideology*, D. Coffey *et al.* (ed.) (1978).
Fitz, John, 'Welfare, the Family and the Child', Unit 12, *Society, Education and the State*, O.U. E353 (1981).
Fletcher, Laadan, *The Teachers' Press in Britain, 1802–1888* (Leeds, 1978).
Foster, J., *Elementary Education in Nineteenth Century Skipton* (1974).
Frith, Simon, 'Socialisation and Rational Schooling: Elementary Education in Leeds before 1870', in P. McCann (ed.), *Popular Education*, pp. 67–92.
Frow, Edmund and Ruth, *A Survey of the Half-Time System in Education* (Manchester, 1970).
Garrett, John H., *Mass Education in England* (1928).
George, Dorothy, *London Life in the Eighteenth Century* (1925).
Giles, Ken and Woolfe, Ray, 'Deprivation, Disadvantage and Compensation', Units 25–6, *Schooling and Society*, O.U. E202 (1977).
Goldstrom, Joachim M., *The Social Content of Education, 1808–1870* (1972).
———, 'Education in England and Wales in 1851: the Education Census of 1851', in Richard Lawton (ed.), *The Census and Social Structure* (1978).
———, 'The Content of Education and the Socialization of the Working Class Child, 1830–1860', in P. McCann, *Popular Education* (1977), pp. 93–110.
Gordon, Peter, *The Victorian School Manager* (1974).
Gordon, Peter and Lawton, Denis, *Curriculum Change in the Nineteenth and Twentieth Centuries* (1978).
Gough, Ian, *Political Economy of the Welfare State* (1979).
Grace, Gerald, *Teachers, Ideology and Control* (1978).
Graves, John, *Policy and Progress in Secondary Education, 1902–42* (1943).
Hall, Stuart, 'Review of the Course', Unit 32, *Schooling and Society*, O.U. E202 (1977).
Hanbidge, William, *The Memories of William Hanbidge* (1939).
Harrison, John F. C., *Learning and Living* (1961).
———, *Robert Owen and the Owenites in Britain and America* (1969).
———, *Underground Education in the Nineteenth Century* (1971).

Haywood, W. A., 'M.P.s and the 1870 Education Act: A Study in Human Motivation', *J.E.A.H.*, vol. 4 (1971), pp. 20–30.
Henriques, U. R. Q., *Before the Welfare State* (1979).
Herbert, George, *Shoemaker's Window* (1949).
Hewett, S. (ed.), *The Training of Teachers* (1971).
Hewitt, Margaret, *Wives and Mothers in Victorian Industry* (1958).
Higginson, J. H., 'Dame Schools', *B.J.E.S.* (1974), pp. 166–81.
Holcombe, Lee, *Victorian Ladies at Work* (1973).
Hollis, Patricia, *The Pauper Press* (1970).
Holly, Douglas, *Society, Schools and Humanity* (1972).
Horne, Ethelbert, *Somerset Folk* (1938).
Horn, Pamela, *Education in Rural England, 1800–1914* (1978).
———, 'Victorian Villages from Census Returns', *The Local Historian*, vol. 15 (1982), pp. 25–32.
Humphries, Stephen, J., 'Schooling and the Working Class in Bristol, 1870–1914', *Southern History* (1979), pp. 171–207.
———, *Hooligans or Rebels*? (1981).
Hurt, John, 'Professor West on Education', *Economic History Review*, vol. xxiv (1971), pp. 624–32.
———, *Education in Evolution* (1971).
———, 'Drill, Discipline and the Elementary School Ethos', in P. McCann, *Popular Education* (1977), pp. 167–92.
———, *Elementary Schooling and the Working Classes, 1860–1918* (1979).
Hyndman, M., *Schools and Schooling in England and Wales* (1978).
Ingram, John H., *The True Chatterton* (1910).
Johnson, M., *Derbyshire Village Schools in the Nineteenth Century* (1970).
Johnson, Richard, 'Educational Policy and Social Control in Early Victorian England', *Past and Present*, no. 49 (1970), pp. 96–119.
———, 'Notes on the Schooling of the English Working Class', in R. Dale *et al.*, *Schooling and Capitalism* (1976), pp. 44–54.
Johnson, Richard, 'Elementary Education', in G. Sutherland *et al.* (ed.), *Education in Britain* (1977), pp. 5–37.
———, 'Educating the Educators: "Experts and the State, 1833–9"', in, A. P. Donajgrodzki (ed.), *Social Control in Nineteenth Century Britain* (1977), pp. 77–125.
———, 'Really Useful Knowledge: Radical Education and Working Class Culture', in, J. Clarke *et al.* (ed.), *Working Class Culture* (1979), pp. 75–102.
———, 'Education and Popular Politics', Unit 1, *Society, Education and the State*, O.U. E353 (1981).
Jones, Donald K., *The Making of the English Education System, 1851–81* (1977).
———, 'The Educational Legacy of the Anti-Corn Law League', *History of Education*, vol. 3, no. 1 (1974), pp. 18–34.
Katz, Michael, *Class, Bureaucracy and Schools* (1975).
Laquer, Thomas W., 'Working Class Demand and the Growth of English Elementary Education, 1750–1850', in L. Stone (ed.), *Schooling and Society* (1976), pp. 192–205.
———, *Religion and Respectability: Sunday Schools and Working Class Culture, 1780–1850* (1976).
Lawson, John and Silver, Harold, *A Social History of Education in England* (1973).
Lawton, Denis, *Class, Culture and the Curriculum* (1975).
Lawton, R. (ed.), *The Census and Social Structure* (1978).
Leinster-Mackay, D. P., 'A Question of Ephemerality: Indices for Longevity of 19th-Century Private Schools, *J.E.A.H.*, vol. X (1978), pp. 1–8.
———, 'Dame Schools: A Need for Review', *B.J.E.S.* (1976), pp. 33–48.

Levine, D., 'Illiteracy and Family Life during the First Industrial Revolution', *Journal of Social History*, vol. 4 (1980), pp. 25–44.
Lindsay, S. M., 'The State and Education', *Teachers' College Record* (September 1916), p. 311.
London Edinburgh Weekend Return Group, *In and Against the State* (1980).
Lowndes, George A. N., *The Silent Social Revolution* (1937).
Macdonald, Madeleine, 'The Curriculum and Cultural Reproduction', Units 18–19, *Schooling and Society*, O.U. E202 (1977).
Madoc-Jones, Beryl, 'Patterns of Attendance and their Social Significance: Mitcham National School, 1830–1839', in P. McCann, *Popular Education* (1977), pp. 41–66.
Magnus, Philip, *Educational Aims and Efforts, 1880–1910* (1910).
Marsden, W. E., 'Education and the Social Geography of Nineteenth Century Towns and Cities', in D. Reeder (ed.), *Urban Education* (1977), pp. 49–74.
———, 'Social Environment, School Attendance and Educational Achievement in a Merseyside Town, 1870–1900', in P. McCann, *Popular Education* (1977), pp. 193–230.
Marvin, Francis S., *The Nation at School* (1933).
Mathews, Horace F., *Methodism and the Education of the People 1791–1851* (1949).
McCann, W. P., 'Trade Unionists, Artisans and the 1870 Act', *B.J.E.S.* (1971), pp. 134–50.
———, 'Elementary Education in England and Wales on the Eve of the 1870 Education Act', *Journal of Educational Administration and History*, vol. II (1969), pp. 20–9.
———, (ed.) *Popular Education and Socialization in the Nineteenth Century* (1977).
———, 'Popular Education, Socialization and Social Control: Spitalfields 1812–1824', in P. McCann, *Popular Education*, pp. 1–140.
McLennan, Gregor *et al.* (ed.), *On Ideology* (1977).
Meacham, Standish, *A Life Apart: The English Working Class, 1890–1914* (1977).
Meller, Helen, *Leisure and the Changing City 1870–1914* (1976).
Middleton, Nigel and Weitzman, Sophia, *A Place for Everyone* (1976).
Midwinter, Eric, *Nineteenth Century Education* (1970).
Miliband, Ralph, *The State in Capitalist Society* (1973).
Monroe, Paul (ed.), *Cyclopedia of Education* (1912).
Montmorency, James E. G., *State Intervention in English Education down to 1833* (1902).
———, *The Progress of Education in England to 1904* (1904).
Morris, Margaret, *The People's Schools* (1939).
Murphy, James, *The Education Act, 1870* (1972).
Neave, G., 'The Free Schoolers', in D. Holly (ed.), *Education or Domination*? (1974).
Neff, Wanda F., *Victorian Working Women* (1929).
Neuburg, Victor, *Popular Education in Eighteenth Century England* (1971).
Newton, A. W., *The English Elementary School* (1919).
Newton, Judith L., *et al.* (eds.), *Sex and Class in Women's History* (1983).
Norton, J., *Guide to National and Provincial Directories of England and Wales* (1950).
Norwood, Cyril, *The English Tradition of Education* (1929).
Oakley, Ann, *Housewife* (1974).
Oakley, Ann and Mitchell, Juliet (eds.), *The Rights and Wrongs of Women* (1976).
Okey, Thomas, *Basketful of Memories* (1930).

Paz, D. G., 'Working Class Education and the State, 1839–49: The Sources of Government Policy', *Journal of British Studies*, vol. XVI (1976), pp. 129–52.
Pennethorne, R. A., 'The Private Venture', *Parents' Review* (August–September 1939), pp. 542–7.
Phillips, H. W., *Thornbury* (1977).
Philpott, Hugh B., *London at School* (1904).
Pinchbeck, Ivy, *Women Workers and the Industrial Revolution, 1750–1850* (1930).
Pollard, S. and Salt, J. (eds.), *Robert Owen: Prophet of the Poor* (1971).
Power, Edward, J., *Main Currents in the History of Education* (1962; 2nd edn, 1970).
Prideaux, Edmund B. R., *A Survey of English Elementary Education* (1914).
Pring, Beryl, *Education: Capitalist and Socialist* (1937).
Raymont, Thomas, *A History of the Education of Young Children* (1937).
Reeder, David (ed.), *Urban Education in the Nineteenth Century* (1977).
———, (ed.), *Educating Our Masters* (1980).
Rich, Eric, E., *The Education Act, 1870: a Study of Public Opinion* (1970).
Rich, R. W., *The Training of Teachers in the Nineteenth Century* (1933).
Rimmington, Gerald, *Education, Politics and Society in Leicestershire, 1833–1903* (1978).
Roberts, A. E. B., 'A New View of the Infant School Movement', *B.J.E.S.* (1972), pp. 154–64.
Roberts, Robert, *The Classic Slum* (1971).
Roberts, R. D. (ed.), *Education in the Nineteenth Century* (1901).
Robson, Adam H., *The Education of Children Engaged in Industry in England, 1833–1876* (1931).
Robson, D., *Some Aspects of Education in Cheshire in the Eighteenth Century* (1966).
Rock, Paul, 'Some Problems of Interpretative Historiography', *British Journal of Sociology*, vol. 27 (1976), pp. 353–69.
Rogers, Frederick, *Labour, Life and Leisure* (1913).
Ross, A. M., 'The Education of the Working Classes to 1870', *V.C.H. Middlesex*, vol.1 (1969), pp. 213–40.
Rubinstein, David, *School Attendance in East London, 1870–1904* (1969).
———, 'Socialization and the London School Board', in, P. McCann, *Popular Education* (1979), pp. 231–64.
Samuel, Raphael, *People's History and Socialist Theory* (1981).
Sanderson, Michael, 'Education and the Factory in Industrial Lancashire, 1780–1840', *Economic History Review*, vol. 20 (1967), pp. 266–79.
———, 'Literacy and Social Mobility in the Industrial Revolution in England', *Past and Present*, no. 56 (1972), pp. 75–104.
Sarup, Madan, *Marxism and Education* (1978).
Scarratt, William, *Old Times in the Potteries* (1906).
Schofield, R. S., 'The Measurement of Literacy in Pre-Industrial England', in Jack Goody (ed.), *Literacy in Traditional Societies* (1968), pp. 311–25.
Selleck, R. J. W., *English Primary Education and the Progressives, 1914–39* (1972).
Sellman, Roger R., *Devon Village Schools* (1967).
Sharp, Rachel and Green, Anthony, *Education and Social Control* (1975).
Shaw, Charles, *When I Was a Child* (1903).
Shaw, Jenny, 'Family, State and Compulsory Education', Unit 13, *Society, Education and the State*, O.U. E353 (1981).
Shaw, Sam, *Guttersnipe* (1946).
Silver, Harold, *The Concept of Popular Education* (1965).
———, (ed.), *Robert Owen on Education* (1969).
———, *English Education and the Radicals, 1780–1850* (1975).

———, *Nothing but the Present or Nothing but the Past?* (1977).
———, 'Ideology and the Factory Child: Attitudes to Half-time Education', in P. McCann, *Popular Education* (1977), pp. 141–66.
Simon, Brian, *Studies in the History of Education, 1780–1870* (1960).
———, *Education and the Labour Movement, 1870–1920* (1965).
———, *The Politics of Educational Reform, 1920–1940* (1974).
———, 'The 1902 Education Act — A Wrong Turning', *History of Education Society Bulletin*, no. 19 (1977), pp. 7–14.
———, 'Education and the Right Offensive', *Marxism Today* (February 1980), pp. 7–13.
Simon, Joan, 'Was there a Charity School Movement?' in B. Simon (ed.), *Education in Leicestershire* (1968), pp. 55–100.
Singleton, F., *The Industrial Revolution in Yorkshire* (1970).
Smith, Frank, *The Life and Works of Sir James Kay-Shuttleworth* (1923).
———, *A History of English Elementary Education* (1931).
Spalding, Thomas A., *The Work of the London School Board* (1900).
Spencer, Frederick H., *Education for the People* (1931).
Stedman-Jones, Gareth, 'From Historical Sociology to Theoretical History', *British Journal of Sociology*, vol. xxvii (1976), pp. 295–305.
———, 'Class Expression versus Social Control?', *History Workshop*, 4 (1977), pp. 162–70.
Stephens, W. B., 'Illiteracy and Schooling in the Provincial Towns, 1640–1870', in D. Reeder, *Urban Education in the Nineteenth Century* (1977), pp. 27–48.
———, *Regional Variations in Education during the Industrial Revolution* (1973).
———, (ed.), *Yorkshire Schools and Schooldays* (1976).
Stone, Lawrence, 'Literacy and Education in England, 1640–1900', *Past and Present* (1969), pp. 69–139.
———, (ed.), *Schooling and Society* (1976).
Sturt, Mary, *The Education of the People* (1967).
Sutherland, Gillian, *Elementary Education in the Nineteenth Century* (1971).
———, (ed.), *Education in Britain* (1971).
———, *Policy-Making in Elementary Education, 1870–1895* (1973).
Sylvester, D. W., 'Robert Lowe and the 1870 Education Act', *History of Education*, vol. 3, no. 2 (1974), pp. 16–26.
Tholfsen, Trygve, *James Kay-Shuttleworth on Popular Education* (1974).
———, *Working Class Radicalism in Mid-Victorian England* (1977).
Thompson, Edward, *The Making of the English Working Class* (1963).
———, 'Time, Work Discipline and Industrial Capitalism', *Past and Present*, no. 38 (1967), pp. 56–97.
———, *The Poverty of Theory* (1978).
Tizard, Jack *et al.*, *All Our Children. Pre-School Services in a Changing Society* (1976).
Tropp, Asher, *The Schoolteachers* (1957).
Vincent, David, *Bread, Knowledge and Freedom* (1981).
Wain, John, *Sprightly Running* (1965).
Waites, Bernard *et al.* (ed.), *Popular Culture: Past and Present* (1982).
Ward, Herbert, *Notes for the Study of English Education from 1860–1902* (1929).
———, *The Education Systems of England and Wales* (1935).
Wardle, David, *Education and Society in Nineteenth Century Nottingham* (1971).
Waugh, A., 'A Victorian Dame School', *Fortnightly Review* (January 1930), pp. 41–56.
Webb, Robert K., *The British Working Class Reader* (1955).
Webb, Sidney, *London Education* (1904).
West, E. G., *Education and the State* (1965).

———, *Education and the Industrial Revolution* (1975).
———, 'Resource Allocation and Growth in Early Nineteenth Century British Education', *Economic History Review* (1970), pp. 68–95.
———, 'The Interpretation of Early Nineteenth Century Statistics', *Economic History Review* (1971), pp. 633–42.
Whitbread, Nanette, *The Evolution of the Nursery-Infant School* (1972).
Whitty, Geoff, 'Ideology, Politics and Curriculum', Unit 8, *Society, Education and the State*, O.U. E353 (1981).
Widdowson, Frances, *Going up into the Next Class, Women and Elementary Teacher Training 1840–1914* (1983).
Williams, Raymond, *Culture and Society* (1958).
———, *The Long Revolution* (1961).
———, *Keywords* (1976).
———, *Marxism and Literature* (1977).
———, *Culture* (1981).
Willis, Paul, *Learning to Labour* (1978).
Wrigley, E. A. (ed.), *Nineteenth Century Society: Essays in the Use of Quantitative Methods for the Study of Social Data* (Cambridge, 1972).
Yeo, Stephen, *Religion and Voluntary Organizations in Crisis* (1976).
———, 'On the Uses of Apathy', *European Journal of Sociology*, vol. XV (1974), pp. 279–311.
Young, D. E. W., *Schools of Old Poole* (1981).

Theses

Board, M. J., 'A History of the Private Adventure School in Sheffield', Sheffield University, MA, 1959.
Davies, A. M., 'The Barnsley School Board, 1871–1903', Bristol University, Dip. Ed, 1964.
Evans, A. J., 'A History of Education in Bradford during the Period of the Bradford School Board', Leeds University, MA, 1947.
Leinster-Mackay, D. P., 'The English Private School, 1830–1914, with special reference to the private preparatory school', Durham University, PhD, 1972.
McCann, W. P., 'Trade Unionist, Co-operative and Socialist Organisations in relation to Popular Education, 1870–1902', Manchester University, PhD, 1960.
Nutter, R., 'A Study of the Implementation of the 1870 Education Act in Bristol with a special reference to the Newfoundland Road area', Bristol University, Dip. Ed, 1965.

INDEX